The Pictorial History of
AUSTRALIAN CRICKET

The Pictorial History of
AUSTRALIAN CRICKET

Revised Edition

Jack Pollard

J.M. DENT PTY. LIMITED
MELBOURNE   LONDON

in association with

AUSTRALIAN BROADCASTING CORPORATION

First published 1983 by J. M. Dent Pty. Limited
34-36 Wadhurst Drive, Boronia, Victoria, 3155 in
association with the Australian Broadcasting Corporation
145-153 Elizabeth Street, Sydney, New South Wales, 2000

Revised and enlarged edition published 1986

National Library of Australia
Cataloguing-in-Publication Entry

Pollard, Jack, 1926-
    The pictorial history of Australian cricket.
    Rev. ed.
    ISBN 0 86770 043 2.

1. Cricket — Australia — History. I. Title.

796.35'8'0994

Design: Roy Bisson
Production: Island Graphics
Typesetting: A. G. Markby – The Typesetting Studio Pty. Ltd.
Printed in Singapore by Kyodo-Shing Loong.

*Half-title page photo: Greg Matthews in a typically joyful mood
— News Limited*
Title page photo: 1975 Australian Cricket Team — Patrick Eagar
*Opp. contents page: Batsman's eyeview of Craig McDermott —
Patrick Eagar*

Contents

Acknowledgements   vi

Foreword: Alan McGilvray   vii

1. The Beginnings   1
2. Intercolonial Cricket   17
3. The First Tours   37
4. Test Matches Begin   55
5. A Famous Victory   73
6. The Legend of the Ashes   91
7. Lessons the Doctor Taught Us   105
8. Lord Sheffield's Shield   119
9. Australia in the Golden Age   137
10. The Players' Revolt   154
11. First World War Setbacks   177
12. The Services Lead a Comeback   197
13. The High-Scoring Twenties   217
14. Then Came Bodyline   237
15. The Bradman Era   258
16. The Challenges Multiply   273
17. The Biggest Throwing Row   287
18. Jumpsuits and Thongs   311
19. 'When Gimmickry Reigned Supreme'   345
20. A Game Without Loyalty   363

Acknowledgements

The author and publisher would like to thank sincerely, the following for their assistance in collecting photographs for this book:

Private Collectors
Ronald Cardwell, Geoffrey A. Copinger, Philip Derriman, Ric Finlay, Patrick J. Mullins, Swan Richards for access to his display in the Gray-Nicolls Mordialloc showrooms, Vic Shaw for permission to reproduce his paintings by d'Arcy Doyle, the late Albert Gregory whose 24-volume collection was invaluable, the late E.S. Marks, Professor D.J. Mulvaney and his *Cricket Walkabout*.

Photographers
Owen Stevens, Patrick Eagar, Barry Green, Ken Kelly, Martin King, Denis Wisken, Ern McQuillan, Richard Cashman, New South Wales Government Printer, Ric Smith and Vivian Jenkins, whose photographs came from the P.B.L. Marketing organisation.

Libraries & Galleries
Sylvia Redman for National Library of Australia photographs, Debbie Titheridge for photographs from Melbourne's Latrobe Library, the Fisher Library at Sydney University, Baiba Berzins and the staff of the Mitchell Library, Sydney, and the Dixson Gallery. Sport & General Press Agency, London, Warrnambool Art Gallery, gift of N.K. Morris 1968.

Cricket Magazines & Newspapers
David Frith of *Wisden Cricket Monthly*, London, Ken Piesse, of *Australian Cricketer*, Melbourne, Brad Boxall, of *Australian Cricket* newspaper, Sydney.

Cricket Clubs & Associations
Geoffrey Green, curator at Lord's for pictures from the M.C.C. Collection, Dr. John Lill, for permission to photograph many of the photographs and paintings in the museum at the Melbourne Cricket Ground, Roy Tanner, for photographs and paintings from the Queensland Cricketers' Club, the State secretaries of the Australian Cricket Society, Cliff Winning of the New South Wales Cricket Association, Ken Jacobs of the Victorian Cricket Association.

Newspapers
The Herald, Melbourne, the *Sun News-Pictorial*, Melbourne, the *Courier-Mail*, Brisbane, the *Daily Telegraph*, Sydney, the *Sydney Morning Herald*, *The Age*, Melbourne, *The Mercury*, Hobart, *The News*, Adelaide, the *Adelaide Advertiser*, the *West Australian*, the *Daily News*, Perth, and the *Sunday Mail*, Perth.

Special Thanks
Greg McKie for his reading of the text and his many valuable suggestions, the dozens of Test cricketers who offered photographs from their personal albums, Ian Fraser from Multi-Color for his assistance in colour photography, David Frith for the selection from his collection of cigarette cards, and the New South Wales Cricket Association secretary Bob Radford for permission to include the painting by Wesley Walters of Sir Donald Bradman scoring his 100th Test century, prints of which can be obtained from the New South Wales Cricket Association, 52 Clarence Street, Sydney 2000.

Foreword

Australian cricket has known many marvellous highlights since the first matches in Sydney at the turn of the 19th Century. For many years Jack Pollard, who is undoubtedly our outstanding sports historian, has been collecting illustrations of these big events, and here at last he presents that collection in this pictorial record of Australian cricket's colourful past.

For me, it is always inevitable when securing a new cricket book to flick through the pages looking for the photographs. This time we are offered a complete feast, with hundreds of black and white and full colour illustrations that offer a really satisfying portrayal of the game since its origins in Sydney's Hyde Park. Indeed I am sure many readers will find many of the illustrations quite breathtaking. But apart from the pleasure it provides the book offers an important historical record of our great game.

The text traces the origins of cricket in each State, the introduction of inter-Colonial and international cricket, the formation of the State associations and our national control body. The 70,000 words that support the illustrations and cover all the game's notorious incidents have all been painstakingly researched, as is the author's habit. How absorbing it is to read that the first Australian team to tour England was an Aboriginal side and simultaneously study the pictures of these men who played an amazing 47 matches while on tour.

The book traces the gradual improvements in Australian standards of play from the days when eighteen and fifteen players comprised the sides that met visiting English XIs to the first matches on level terms and the start of Test cricket. The first of all Test matches at Melbourne in 1877 is illustrated in words and pictures as colourful as the match itself.

The author stresses the influence England players and officials had on this development of Australian cricket and he underlines the big contributions of Lord Sheffield, W.G. Grace and the two Surrey players, Charles Lawrence and William Caffyn. The coaching these two began in Australia produced an amazing array of brilliant players who are each dealt with in turn . . . Joe Darling, Clem Hill, Syd Gregory, Victor Trumper, Monty Noble, Hugh Trumble and on right up to the Chappell brothers and the stars of today. I was particularly glad to see the First A.I.F. team and the Services side formed after World War II given glowing praise.

Bodyline, of course, receives close scrutiny, as do events like the throwing controversies, the players' revolt of 1912, the first tied Test at Brisbane 1960–61, and the remarkable Centenary Test which produced precisely the same result as the first England-Australia Test 100 years before. I was particularly keen to study the coverage of World Series Cricket, for I was at the ground in the south of England, where news of this great crisis first broke. The effect the breakaway had on the 28th Australian team's performance in England is accurately detailed, as are the court actions, and general acrimony that went on far too long.

Many cricket followers probably thought, as I did, that Jack Pollard had written the ultimate cricket book when he published his outstanding dictionary on the game *Australian Cricket — The Game and the Players* in 1982, for that remarkable book gave us coverage of every Australian Test cricketer, plus all the outstanding State players. But no, with his boundless energy he has produced a similarly impressive companion volume.

I am certain that it will fill many idle hours for thousands of cricket lovers all around the world, not just in Australia. I sincerely congratulate Jack on another magnificent contribution to cricket and thank him for the opportunity of writing this foreword. He has done me a great honour.

Alan McGilvray

1. The Beginnings

Australia's first recorded cricket match was played in Sydney in December 1803, fifteen years after European settlement began with the foundation of a penal colony under Captain Arthur Phillip. The *Sydney Gazette* 8 January 1804 reported:

> The late intense weather has been very favourable to the amateurs of cricket who have scarce lost a day for the past month. The frequent immoderate heat might have been considered inimical to the amusement, but was productive of very opposite consequences, as the state of the atmosphere might always regulate the portions of exercise necessary to the ends that this laborious diversion was originally intended to answer.

This report suggests that cricket was already well established in the colony but so far no written confirmation that the game was played before 1803 has been unearthed. The generally accepted view is that officers of the *Calcutta* were the first to play properly organised cricket in the days of 24-inch stumps and four-ball underarm overs. A government order of 6 October 1810, by which Governor Macquarie named Hyde Park in Sydney, referred to that area as having had a variety of names, including the 'Exercising Ground', the 'Cricket Ground', and the 'Racecourse'. In 1821 Macquarie ordered His Majesty's Lumber Yard in England to supply twelve cricket bats and six balls for the Reverend Thomas Reddall's school at Macquarie Fields, near the present site of Ingleburn Army Camp. Macquarie's son Lachlan was a student at Reddall's school.

Hyde Park was the venue for organised adult matches in which many players took the field barefoot or in stockinged feet with trousers rolled up. The popular spot for small boys, however, was a graveyard on the present site of St Andrew's Cathedral. The boys moved the gravestones about freely and were frequently chased away by police — harassment which they were prepared to put up with because the graveyard offered a good flat pitch of easy access.

An unsigned watercolour but probably by W.A. Cawthorne entitled "Picnic Cricket Match", showing the families of Sydney garrison troops watching play in 1830.
— Dixson Gallery, Sydney.
Inset
The Fourth King's own Regiment playing cricket at their military barracks in Sydney in 1845. A lithograph by C. Hutchins from a sketch by Captain Hext.
— Australian National Library.

An oil painting from the Pavilion at Lord's showing a cricket match in Melbourne in 1841. The artist is unknown but judging by the attitudes of the players he must have been a cricketer. — M.C.C. Collection, Lord's.

An 1830s illustration from the English Magazine The Tatler *of early settlers riding to an up-country match in Australia. The magazine said Australians would ride anywhere just to get a game. — Albert Gregory Collection.*

The first clubs in Sydney included the Currency Cricket Club, the Military Cricket Club and the Australian Cricket Club. The last-named club, which began in 1826, restricted its membership to Australian-born players. The Sydney Cricket Club was founded in 1829 but was disbanded when its players were ejected from 'a government paddock on the other side of the turnpike', apparently an area near the present Central Railway Station. Cricket clubs in Tasmania (then Van Diemen's Land) were not far behind those in Sydney and the game was well established on the island by the 1820s. Hobart Town Cricket Club was founded in 1832 and the Launceston Cricket Club, which still exists, was formed in 1843. Hobart newspapers reported a match between Hobart Town C.C. and a team comprising officers of H.M.S. *Hyacinth* and officers of the 21st Regiment in January 1835. Hobart Town made 83 and 84, the *Hyacinth* team 39 and 21.

Reports of Australian cricket matches became more frequent from about 1830, when the *Sydney Gazette* published this report:

> The cricket match on the Race Course yesterday, eleven aside, the competitors being equal numbers of military experts at the game and native-born youths, lasted from 11 o'clock in the forenoon till 5 o'clock in the evening. At 2 o'clock it was thought that the natives had no chance and that they must be beat. However, as the day's play advanced the Australians recovered all they had lost in the morning and at length won the game. A prettier day's play than this was certainly never witnessed in this colony. At 4 o'clock it was estimated that there were upwards of 100 spectators on the ground.

Stakes for this match were £20 a side, and the Civilians won by scoring 76 and 136 against 101 and 87 by the 57th Regiment, a 24-run victory. The *Sydney Monitor* recorded a further tense match for 10 guineas a side on 3 March 1830, when the 'Natives' scored 95 and 75 to defeat the 'Soldiers' (82 and 52) by 36 runs. The *Monitor* reported that this match produced heavy betting not only in money but also in pigs, sawn timber, boots, dripstones, maize, snakeskin shoes, fish, and butter. Victory was celebrated at Toby Green's Hotel in Pitt Street.

One of the best early teams in Western Australia was this Aboriginal side from New Norcia Mission, coached and captained by H.B. Lefroy (centre, with ball). They did so well in visits to Perth and Fremantle teams from these centres undertook the two-day coach journey involved in covering the 75 miles to New Norcia to play return matches.
— Albert Gregory Collection.

Cricket began in Australia in Sydney's Hyde Park but because of competition from horse racing and other sports soon moved to the Domain. This shot shows one of the early matches in the Domain.
— Mitchell Library, Sydney.

John Marshall, who between 1835 and 1855 established himself as the "champion cricketer of Hobart Town". He became Australia's oldest first-class cricketer when he played for Tasmania against Victoria at the age of 55.
— Newspaper Print, 1908.

A watercolour by J.B. Henderson of the match played at Richmond, Melbourne, between teams from Sydney and Melbourne in 1855. Notable families in the colony, including that of Commissary-General Cotsworthy, are shown in the foreground.
— Mitchell Library, Sydney.

Samuel Thomas Gill's well-known watercolour of the first cricket match between New South Wales and Victoria in the Sydney Domain in 1857.
— National Library of Australia.

An exciting watercolour by T.H. Lewis entitled "Cricket Match In Hyde Park", with the wicket-keeper standing a long way back.
—Dixson Gallery, Sydney.

Sam Cosstick, who played for Eighteen of Melbourne in the first-ever international match in Australia against Stephenson's England XI. Cosstick was the Melbourne Cricket Club professional for many years.
— Melbourne Cricket Ground Museum.

John Richard Hardy and his brother William — sons of the famous Rear-Admiral Hardy — arrived in Sydney in 1830 and introduced round-arm bowling to the colony. John had played for Cambridge in 1829. The Hardy boys taught the new bowling style to Australian-born Robert Still, who is believed to have been the first bowler to use the round-arm style in an Australian match. One problem was that wicket-keepers were so unaccustomed to round-arm bowling that they allowed a high numbers of byes when it was used. Still helped dismiss the opposition for scores of 49 and 73 in one game but there had been 18 byes in the first innings and 24 in the second.

The first Australian cricketers used rough, makeshift gear — stumps cut from saplings, bats cut from lumps of cedar or from the limbs of cherry trees — and played on unrolled pitches that had been crudely swept to remove pebbles. There were no boundaries and no limit on the runs that could be taken from a hit. Balls were cut from a fungus known as 'Blackfellow's Bread'. There were no pavilions and for important matches spectators formed a ring to mark the field. When heavy betting was expected, tents were erected to provide shade for punters. But with the introduction of round-arm bowling and the steady increase in crowds, more sophisticated equipment was called for. Rule books were sent from England and when copies of John Nyren's *The Young Cricketer's Tutor* went on sale in Hobart stocks lasted only a few hours.

Early publicans quickly recognised the value of cricket in promoting business, and decorations in the hotels by this time included scenes of Hyde Park cricket and panoramic views of Lord's. The Australian Cricket Club met at Flood's Inn in George Street, Sydney, which was the scene of great jubilation on 9 December 1833, when the club beat the Military Cricket Club by 8 wickets, thanks to a standard of fielding described as the best that had been seen in the colony. The Military immediately issued a challenge for a return match and their players trained hard for hours each day. The Australian Club batted first and scored 14 notches. The Military lost 6 wickets for 10 runs but hung on to win by 4 wickets.

The Currency Club was backed by William Tunks, whose hotel in Castlereagh Street became the regular meeting place for members. The Currency Club's star player was Harry Hilliard, who was apprenticed to a cabinet-maker in Pitt Street. Hilliard later wrote in the publication *Old Times* that players who dropped a catch were sometimes given a punching by team-mates. Hilliard wrote that windows were frequently broken by boys playing cricket in Hyde Park when they hit the ball into Elizabeth Street. Shopkeepers took to sitting on chairs in front of their windows, smartly fielding any hits likely to cause damage.

Edward Gregory arrived in Sydney in about 1813 and proceeded to sire seven sons, five of whom — David, Walter, Charles, Edward, and Arthur — played for the early New South Wales sides. The other two — Fred and Albert — were content just to play club cricket. The Gregorys were the first of a remarkable series of families who have helped give Australian cricket such a high international reputation. Dave and Edward played in the first of all Tests and Dave was Australia's first captain. It was during this time overarm bowling was introduced to the colony and 'Sydney grubbers', as they were known, began to disappear. Initially clubs banned overarm bowling by their members but were persuaded to permit it by cricketers newly arrived from England who brought word of its general acceptance.

Hyde Park, scene of the first cricket matches in Australia. This watercolour by John Rae shows play in progress during 1842.
— Dixson Gallery, Sydney.

An early sketch of Adelaide Oval viewed from Montefiore Hill showing the lush parkland setting for which the ground became famous.
— South Australian Archives.

Cricket grew with the settlements in Sydney, Van Diemen's Land, Port Phillip, Adelaide, Perth, and in Moreton Bay before it became part of Queensland. The first pitches in Victoria were laid on Batman's Hill where Spencer Street Station now stands and on 15 November 1838 Australia's most prestigious club, the Melbourne Cricket Club, was formed. A.M. Mundy, C.F. Mundy, F.A Powlett, Robert Russell, and G.B. Smyth were the first members. Powlett was a relative of the Reverend Charles Powlett, a leading member of England's Hambledon Club which fielded teams strong enough to challenge the best in the country. The *South Australian Gazette and Colonial Register* advertised for cricketers on 19 October 1839, urging those who wanted a game to meet at the London Tavern. In Perth, organised cricket began in April 1835 when labourers and mechanics working on the new Government House played a match against the builders working on the project.

Round-arm bowling was legalised at Lord's in 1835 and six years later the Duke of Wellington issued orders that cricket pitches were to be an adjunct to every military barracks. These orders were so strictly followed in Australia that garrison and barracks teams soon became the important sides to beat. In Sydney a pitch built by the soldiers behind their barracks at Moore Park became the best batting strip in the colony. Soldiers served out their fatigues for misdemeanours by working on the pitch. After 1840, however, when the transportation of convicts to Sydney was abolished, the dominance of soldier-cricketers gradually came to an end. Free settlers, many of them fresh from English cricket, became the stars, and the game spread to country centres.

Among the first country towns to organise a cricket club was Maitland, where cricket was first recorded in Feburary 1845. The *Maitland Mercury* reported that Holdstock's team defeated a side collected by a mill-owner named Honeysett by 10 runs, this win stemming from the skill of a fieldsman named Crumpton at long stop, where he conceded only 7 byes compared with the opposition's 21. Maitland Cricket Club had forty-four active members on its books when it travelled to Sydney to play the powerful Australian Club. In the words of the *Maitland Mercury:*

Top left
S.T. Gill's marvellous watercolour of an inter-Colonial match between New South Wales and Victoria in Sydney's Domain in 1859.
— Dixson Gallery, Sydney.

Bottom left
A drawing on stone by Henry S. Glover of the inter-Colonial match between Victoria and New South Wales in Melbourne between January 12 and 14, 1858.
— Melbourne Cricket Ground Museum.

Star New South Wales batsman Edwin Evans receiving an ovation from spectators at the Albert Ground after a fine innings against Lillywhite's England team in 1877.
— Sydney Mail.

The Australians for the past year or two have been so successful that they have had difficulty finding a match. Even when their challenges have been accepted, it has generally been on the condition that one or more of their best men should not play. On the present occasion, however, the challenge of the Maitland gentlemen was unconditional, which of itself spoke well for the spirit and confidence of the Maitland club.

The teams met on 19 May 1845, on a pitch saturated by overnight rain. The Australians batted first and scored 107. In their reply the Maitland batsmen found that the 'fine bowling of T. Rowley and Robert Still lowered their wickets for a short innings of only 44 runs'. Further rain prevented play for a day and when the match resumed the Australians reached 120. They then routed Maitland for only 19 runs. Rowley took 10 wickets in the match, Still took 9. Undaunted, the Maitland players challenged the Australian Club to play them at Maitland. When the visitors arrived, they were offered a choice of pitches.

From the Domain big cricket moved to the Albert Ground at Redfern, during the 1860s. The Albert Ground lost its place as Sydney's major venue following a dispute with the association and the ground's owners over match fees.
— Mitchell Library, Sydney.

Maitland batted first on a dry pitch and scored 34. The Australian Club responded with a score of 103. Here the *Mercury* was highly critical of the locals' fielding:

They appeared to us to be not only slower and less certain than their competitors but to be very confused and irregular, leaving openings for numerous runs of four, five and even a six by the Australians.

These long runs were partly aided by the ground, the Australians in changing from the ground usually used by the Maitland Club, having chosen a place on the verge of a declivity, down which the left-handed hits of Hatfield and Clarkson sent the ball at a fearful rate. It was Hatfield who made six runs off one ball down the hill.

Maitland needed to make 69 runs in their second innings to avoid an innings defeat but managed only 56. A week of intensive cricket continued with four-a-side and single-wicket challenges among the best players from each club,

but through deft use of a hill the honour of the Australian Club prevailed.

Tasmanian cricket meanwhile had developed an outstanding player in John Marshall, whose father was believed to have been connected with one of the early garrisons of Van Diemen's Land. Marshall, a splendid organiser, was involved with the creation of the Hobart Town Cricket Club in 1832. In 1835 he was responsible for the club's defeating a strong team drawn from officers of the 21st Regiment and H.M.S. *Hyacinth*: he remained at the crease for 105 minutes to score 13 in the club's first innings, and made 10 out of 84 in the second innings. As wicket-keeper and bowler he figured in eight dismissals in the Combined Services totals of 39 and 21.

Marshall left the Hobart Town C.C. soon after this notable victory and formed the Derwent Club. He was largely responsible for Derwent's impressive run of success over the next two decades. Marshall was born in England before registration of births was compulsory, but 1795 is generally accepted as his birthdate. This makes him Australia's oldest first-class cricketer, fifty-five when he first represented Tasmania against Victoria and fifty-eight when he retired after his third first-class match.

Tasmanian cricket followed the pattern on the mainland, with publicans helping to establish the game in places where there had been no planning for recreational facilities. Joseph Bowden, who built the Lamb Inn in Hobart soon after he arrived from Plymouth in 1824, put up a stake of 50 guineas for the winners of a match between civilians and garrison troops at Easter 1826. There were frequent matches each summer between clubs from Launceston and Hobart, despite the 150 miles of mountainous terrain which separated the cities, and the lack of a regular coach service. For unbroken activity, the Launceston Cricket Club, formed in 1843, ranks third behind the Melbourne and Brighton clubs in Victoria.

North versus South matches began on 20 April 1850, when teams from Hobart and Launceston met at Oatlands, about halfway between the two cities. North won by 12 runs but the South took the return match by 1 wicket at Campbell Town. These matches continued until 1977-78 when Tasmania was admitted to the Sheffield Shield competition and the North versus South matches were replaced by an intrastate competition, which was thought to be a more suitable preparation for Shield games.

Above
Colonel Richardson, last military commander of the ground pegged out by soldiers that became the Sydney Cricket Ground.
— Philip Derriman.

Below
In the days when long stops were a vital factor in any team's success this man, John Humphrey Morris, was a cricket hero. He was long-stop for the Albert Club, the Marylebone Club and for New South Wales against Victoria in 1859.
— Ronald Cardwell.

Queensland cricket began as a pastime for the tough pioneers who moved into unsettled country when Brisbane was established as a convict settlement in 1823. The *Moreton Bay Courier* published the first recorded reference to Queensland cricket on 27 June 1846, fourteen years before Queensland was separated from New South Wales and given its own identity:

As a finale to the amusement of Race Week, a challenge from the working men of Brisbane to play an equal number of gentlemen for five pounds ten shillings a side was accepted. The

match came off on the terrace leading to the government gardens. The gentlemen were successful, beating their opponents easily, and the stakes were generously handed over by the losing party. Arrangements were then made for another match to come off in next year's Race Week.

The same paper showed that there was keen interest in the game by publishing some basic laws under the heading 'Hints For Cricketers': 'The stumps must be three in number; twenty seven inches out of the ground; the bails eight inches in length; the stumps of equal and sufficient thickness to prevent the ball passing through.' The paper from then on published regular reports of matches on the Darling Downs and in other centres.

A club was formed at Ipswich during a meeting at the Old Court House and other clubs soon followed at Toowoomba, Dalby, and Maryborough. As the colony grew, the Moreton Bay Club changed its name to the Brisbane Cricket Club. As in other States, there were frequent matches between marrieds and singles and smokers and non-smokers.

The military rifle range next to the Association Ground in Sydney in 1877. The horse-drawn vehicles on the left are probably moving along what is now known as Moore Park Road. — Philip Derriman.

In South Australia cricket received its first boost when John Bristow, proprietor of the Great Tom of Lincoln Hotel in the Adelaide suburb of Thebarton, inserted the following advertisement in the *South Australian Gazette and Register* on 19 October 1839, three years after the colony was founded:

CRICKET

A grand match will be played on Monday, October 28, on the Thebarton Cricket Ground between Eleven Gentlemen of the Royal Victoria Independent Club and Eleven Gentlemen of Adelaide, for Twenty-two guineas a-side. Wickets to be pitched at 10 o'clock. Refreshments will be provided, and everything done that can add to the pleasure of the public,
By their obedient servant,
John Bristow.

Bristow showed plenty of enterprise by organising foot-races, juggling, and various sideshows to entertain spectators during breaks in the cricket. In October the same year a meeting was called at the London Tavern to which 'gentlemen cricket players and patrons of that old English and manly game were invited'. There was plenty of enthusiasm but little expertise until John Cocker arrived in the colony in 1846.

Cocker was a batsman of quality who had played in the Kent side against All England and taken the field alongside Alfred Mynn, Fuller Pilch, and F.W. Lillywhite. Like most other bowlers of the period, he bowled underarm but his batting had a really invigorating effect on local players. Cocker lived at the Kentish Arms Hotel in North Adelaide and formed a club called the Kent and Sussex, which soon proved strong enough to take on the Adelaide Club, whose headquarters were across the Torrens River.

Cocker included Tom Botten, the first South Australian round-arm bowler, in his team. Botten's bowling was regarded as unfair and there was great hostility towards him among spectators whenever he took the ball. Another colourful early cricketer in Adelaide was 'Pads and Gloves' Smith, a migrant who brought the colony's first pads and batting gloves with him from England.

Bottom left
A lithograph by H. Deutsch of play during a match between the United Victorian XI and Eighteen of Ballarat.
— La Trobe Library Melbourne.

The Melbourne Cricket Ground at Christmas, 1876, when New South Wales defeated Victoria by an innings and one run. Evans and Coates had Victoria out for 34 in their second innings.
— The Australasian Sketcher.

Clarence P. Moody, the diligent historian of South Australia's cricket past, wrote of a player named Colman who rode almost 50 miles from Strathalbyn to play an all-day game in Adelaide, then saddled his horse and rode the 50 miles home again after play had ended. Moody also described the sad fate of a sailor called Wilkins who arrived in Adelaide saying that he was related to Lillywhite and was ready to challenge anyone in the colony. Cocker took him on for ten pounds a side and selected his own pitch in Stanley Street, North Adelaide. He then hammered Wilkins' bowling all over the field until he reached 109 and let a ball from Wilkins hit his stumps. Wilkins replied with 7 runs in two innings and made no effort to invoke the agremeent giving the loser a return match.

In 1852 Mr Justice Bundey called a meeting to form the Union Cricket Club, which took its name from the Marryatville hotel where the meeting was held. As a schoolboy playing for Woodside in the Adelaide Hills, Justice Bundey had scored what is sometimes called the first century in the colony. On 11 Jaunary 1854 he signed an advertisement in the *South Australian Register* in which the Union Club challenged the rest of the 'Province of South Australia' to a friendly match. The challenge was accepted and the Union Club heavily defeated the Rest of South Australia by scoring 96 and 134, compared with 44 and 59. Cocker, with 20 not out and 10, was the only batsman for the Rest to reach double figures in either innings. Judge Bundey later claimed that this overwhelming win ruined the Union Club, for thereafter membership slumped through lack of opposition.

Score-sheets that have survived contain some curious entries, including run-outs credited to the bowlers and one batsman's dismissal given as 'kneed out'. Throughout the 1860s, clubs were formed in country areas, with matches held at Caltowie, Jamestown, Kadina, Kapunda, Mount Pleasant, Gawler, and Orroroo. But by the end of the 1860s the South Australian Club dominated cricket in the colony, thanks largely to their foresight in leasing six acres of the parklands where Adelaide Oval now stands. One of the club's first moves after securing the lease was to fence the area and start planning which grasses should be planted inside the fence.

Right from the start there were frequent controversies. In 1862 when a match was staged between British and colonial-born teams at Thebarton racecourse, the Colonials led by 22 runs on the first innings and set the British 146 runs to win. When the British reached 7 for 41, they claimed that stumps should be drawn and the match declared a draw because the light was too dim for play to continue. The umpires disagreed and when no further British batsmen went to the wicket they awarded the match to the Colonials, a result that created deep-seated anger.

Among South Australia's notable cricket pioneers were the Gooden family. They began playing with the Eastern Suburban Club — which had been founded by an ex-Kapunda player, J. Scandrett — but in 1865 moved to the newly formed East Torrens Club. Gooden, senior, had played a lot of cricket in England and he saw that his sons made good use of the vacant spaces near their Adelaide home. The Goodens figured in many of the single-wicket and 3-wicket matches that attracted keen betting in South Australia's foundation seasons.

In Western Australia a military base had been established at Albany in 1826 by a small contingent of soldiers and convicts sent from Sydney by the Governor of New South Wales, Sir Ralph Darling. Three years later Captain Charles Fremantle landed at the mouth of the Swan River to forestall further French attempts to claim the area. The first free settlers arrived from England soon afterwards and when Perth was founded cricket was not far behind. After the first match between tradesmen and builders of Government House, the *Perth Gazette and Western Australian Journal* commented that, 'the manly game of cricket has started with some spirit within the past fortnight, and we understand a club is likely to be formed at Guildford'. The paper said that the revival of the sports of England in a distant land formed a link which the population could be proud of.

The first major promotion in Perth was in the middle of May 1846, when the Perth Club played the Tradesmen of Perth. The Tradesmen made 38 and 26, the Perth Club 45 and 5 for 21, giving them a 5-wicket win. A batsman named Hall was given out 'touched the ball' in the Tradesmen's second innings. The score-book credited fieldsmen with dismissals when a batsman was caught and the bowlers received credit only if they hit the stumps. The game had spread into the country areas of Western Australia by the late 1840s and early 1850s, but the colony remained isolated from the rest of Australia. The best that Perth cricketers could hope for were matches at Fremantle, York, and Northam. Even a game at Bunbury involved a rugged sea trip and severe seasickness for the players. As standards improved, the strongest opposition for Western Australians came from teams from H.M.S. *Galatea*, H.M.S. *Barracouta*, H.M.S. *Sappho*, and H.M.S. *Sapphire*. Meanwhile, Australia's initial first-class matches had been organised in the eastern States and intercolonial cricket had begun.

The Tasmanian team that played Victoria in 1867 (L to R): Standing, T. Daley, W.A. Collins, W. Cowle (reserve), H.R.G. Dumaresq, J.L.A. Arthur; Seated, D. Burke (reserve), D. Barclay, T. Whitesides, W.H. Walker (captain).
— Ric Finlay.

The entire Melbourne Cricket Ground staff and all their equipment in 1877, just before the very first Test. The Members Pavilion is among the trees with a clock of its own, the public stand on the right.
— Melbourne Cricket Ground Museum.

MELBOURNE CRICKET GROUND
1877

Press and Scorers' Box

Members' Pavilion

Grandstand. "The Finest in the World"

This picture shows the entire Ground Staff and the Equipment.

2. Intercolonial Cricket

First-class cricket began in Australia in the summer of 1850–51, with the introduction of intercolonial matches. They began because players who had emerged as the best in the main cities wanted to test their skills against cricketers in other colonies and were ready to undertake uncomfortable voyages and spend their own money in order to do so. Intercolonial matches preceded interstate cricket by half a century, as it was not until 1901 that the States were officially designated. They produced much thrilling cricket, several acrimonious disputes, and quite a few brawls among spectators. Their success led to the formation of generally accepted control bodies in each colony and eventually to a national cricket control organisation.

On Monday 9 February 1851 a message was picked up at the telegraph station on Windmill Hill and relayed to Launceston. It read: 'The S.S. Shamrock two leagues off with Melbourne cricketers on board'. A few hours later the citizens of Launceston gave the Victorians a hearty welcome and a strenuous round of entertainments, interrupted only when the wickets were pitched at 10.30 a.m. on 10 February. The Tasmanian team for this initial intercolonial game comprised five from the Launceston Club, three from Hobart, and one each from Perth, Westbury, and Longford. John Marshall, the heavily bearded Tasmanian captain, won the toss and put Victoria in to bat.

The first ball in Australian first-class cricket was delivered by W. Henty, who shared the new red ball with a fellow Launceston player, R. McDowall. The Victorian captain W. Philpott held them up for a time with some stylish batting but the Victorians clearly had not recovered from a rough trip across Bass Strait and despite the occasional heavy blow were all out for 82. John Marshall and Du Croz opened the Tasmanian innings and took the score to 25 by lunch on the first morning. After the break Tasmania gained a first innings lead of 22 by scoring 104, Du Croz top-scoring with 27.

The Victorian team and officials in Adelaide for the inter-Colonial match against South Australia in 1889. Allrounder Jack Harry, wearing dark pads and with a bat is on the right. Team captain Harry Trott is in the centre in the striped blazer. — Victorian Cricket Association.

Henty's high-flighted slows puzzled batsmen throughout Victoria's second innings, and all the Tasmanians fielded gamely, sticking to their task on an uneven field through the constant encouragement of Marshall from behind the stumps. Victoria were dismissed for 57, Henty taking 6 wickets, to finish with 10 for the match. Victoria fought back doggedly in fading light and at stumps on the first day Tasmania were 6 for 15, chasing 36 to win. But next morning Tabart hit out boldly and his 15 not out gave Tasmania victory by 3 wickets. The Victorians refused to blame defeat on either the rough sea voyage to the game, or the boisterous home crowd which at times overflowed on to the field. They simply said that they had been 'well entertained and well beaten'.

The Victorians were keen to repay the unbounded hospitality of the Tasmanians when the return match was held at the South Yarra Ground on 29 March 1852. This time they found little difficulty with Henty's slow bowling and Hamilton in particular punished him severely, scoring 42 of the Victorians' first innings total of 80. Tasmania collapsed dramatically in their first innings, losing 5 wickets for 9 runs before Tabart and Maddox made a stand which ended when a hit on the shin forced Maddox to leave the field. Tasmania managed 65, to trail by 15 runs, but then Victoria consolidated with a workmanlike second innings of 127. Tasmania again failed in the second innings, losing 4 for 41 wickets by stumps, with 102 still needed for victory. The remaining 6 wickets fell cheaply on the second morning, for Victoria to win by 61 runs. The game had been watched by 'the elite of Melbourne' and attracted enough publicity to establish intercolonial cricket firmly.

George Moore, the Maitland cricketer who took 10 wickets in the first inter-Colonial match played in Sydney. Moore, a round-arm bowler born in Bedfordshire, England, was 52 when he first played for New South Wales. He lived until he was 96.
— Albert Gregory Collection.

The first inter-Colonial match was played in Launceston in 1851. This lithograph by S.T. Gill shows Sydney's first inter-Colonial match in January, 1857. New South Wales won by 65 runs in the Outer Domain.
— Mitchell Library, Sydney.

A third match was staged at Launceston in March 1854, but on this occasion the good fellowship apparent in the first two games disappeared. A string of Victoria's best players refused to make the trip, saying that as amateurs and businessmen they could not afford a fortnight away in Tasmania. A below-strength Victorian team included only three players who had appeared in the previous matches, Hall, Thomson and Powlett. Marshall won the toss for Tasmania and sent Victoria in. For 3 hours Victoria struggled against accurate bowling and enthusiastic fielding and were all out for 80. Tasmania responded with 97 but Victoria then were routed for 50, leaving Tasmania to score just 33 to win, a task they accomplished for the loss of only 2 wickets.

Despite their isolation the Tasmanians proved in these three matches that they could play efficient and attractive cricket, and they did this largely because of the influence of their captain, John Marshall, who was in his late fifties. He managed the team superbly and made major contributions to Tasmania's win in two of the three matches with personal skills of a high order and clever manipulation of his bowlers. The Melbourne papers acclaimed him as a cricketer 'seldom surpassed in England' and agreed that his wicket-keeping was 'almost perfect — as sharp as a needle'.

These three historic matches were watched by audiences that made each day's play a fashion parade, with the ladies in their finest dresses, sipping soft drinks under the shade of large tents, the men dressed as if for a christening. But Bass Strait and the seasickness its crossing invariably caused dissipated Victorians' enthusiasm and between 1854 and 1873 only six further Victoria-Tasmania games were played. Victorians looked instead to the neighbouring colony of New South Wales, and placed an advertisement in the Melbourne *Argus* challenging players in other colonies to play them for £500. A Sydney group, called together by William Tunks, who labelled themselves the 'Intercolonial Committee' accepted the challange but refused to play for money. They said that they preferred to play for the honour of the game.

Tunks collected donations, added a large sum of his own, and sent the best team Sydney could muster to play the Melbourne Cricket Club. Their encounter has become known as the first Victoria versus New South Wales match and it was also the first major match on the Melbourne Cricket Ground. Play began on 26 March 1856, on a pitch so rough that a batsman who made 10 was regarded as a hero. The toss was preceded by intense argument over such matters as whether the scorers for each colony should sit together, what the umpires should wear, and whether fresh pitches should be used for each innings. Commenting on the New South Wales team's refusal to play for money, the *Argus* said: 'The stake is now for the supremacy of local play respectively, and the broader grounds on which the contest is placed are decidedly more calculated to produce the better sport'. But the paper was not impressed by the New South Wales team's efforts in practice.

Thomas Wentworth Spencer Wills, who invented Australian Rules to prevent cricketers becoming soft in winter. He captained Rugby school in England and played for Kent, M.C.C. and Cambridge. He is regarded as the first outstanding Australian-born cricketer.
— Melbourne Cricket Ground Museum.

*The Jolimonters, a
popular East Melbourne
team, photographed in
their colourful striped
shirts during a visit to
Adelaide in the 1880s.
— South Australian
Archives.*

*Western Australia's first
Intercolonial team versus
Victoria, April 1st & 3rd,
1893.
— West Australian
Newspapers Limited.*

The witty old man known as "Garden Honey" who sold scorecards and pencils to spectators at inter-Colonial matches in Sydney in the years before big scoring boards were erected.
— Albert Gregory Collection.

By 1870 the inter-Colonial match between New South Wales and Victoria in Melbourne was a high fashion affair with vice-regal patronage. A clubhouse exclusively for Melbourne Cricket Club members was topped by the Club's flag.
— Town and Country Journal.

The *Argus* said that at 10.30 a.m. when the umpires tossed, the choice fell to the Victorians, but an argument ensued on the ground that the visiting team was always entitled to the choice of innings. The Victorians disagreed, claiming that the custom was obsolete. Finally all the arguments ended and Mather and Serjeant strode out to open for Victoria. Gilbert bowled the first ball for New South Wales and Serjeant drove it for 2, the first runs between New South Wales and Victoria. But Serjeant made only 5 more before an underarm 'trimmer' from McKone broke his stumps. Serjeant's 7, said the *Argus* had been obtained 'in the most gallant manner'.

With batsmen 'assuming the vacant timber', being compelled 'to lower their flag' and the bails rattling 'with a discordant note', the *Argus* reported the end of the Victorian first innings at 63, when Gilbert bowled the last man with a

shooter. New South Wales first innings opened with the dismissal of the left-hander Murray first ball. As wickets tumbled McKone began to play 'in a quiet and unobtrusive way'. At 8 for 19, Driver and McKone retrieved the New South Wales position with a stand of 36 runs, exclusive of wide balls. Morres replaced Goulstock in the Victorian attack but was 'especially prolific with wide balls'. The New South Wales tail wagged and took their team to a lead of 13 runs. Takings for the day were £60 5s.

Word of the dramatic events on the M.C.G. had spread beyond Melbourne and a big crowd was present for the start of the second day. Victoria made only 28 in their second innings and their failure drew the Melbourne *Herald* to strong criticism of the 'irregular bowling by the Sydney side'. The paper said the game proved that when 'irregular bowling [over-arm] is pitted against

An artist's impressions of the 1892 inter-Colonial match at Sydney, when South Australia achieved an upset win by an innings and 53 runs after two earlier heavy defeats. — Sydney Mail.

scientific batting, the display will be unfavourable to cricket', but allowed a little grudging praise for the visitors' splendid 'throwing in'.

The New South Wales batsmen had unexpected difficulty scoring the 16 runs needed for victory and lost 7 wickets in the chase. One of their players in the match was Dick Driver, who had gone to Melbourne expecting to umpire. When the New South Wales side was a player short, Driver substituted and made equal top score in their first innings, 18. He was one of four players who scored ducks in New South Wales' second innings, but this did not mark the end of his involvement with cricket as he later became the first president of the New South Wales Cricket Association. The road leading up to the main entrance of the Sydney Cricket Ground is named after him.

E.H. and C.W. Butler with W.H. Walker, right, in April, 1872 when they appeared for South against North, the annual Tasmanian match that produced so many internationals. All three played against England. — Ric Finlay.

This drawing of the teams that played in the 1866 inter-Colonial match between Victoria and New South Wales includes the All-England stars Charles Lawrence and William Caffyn, who both played for N.S.W. — Mitchell Library, Sydney.

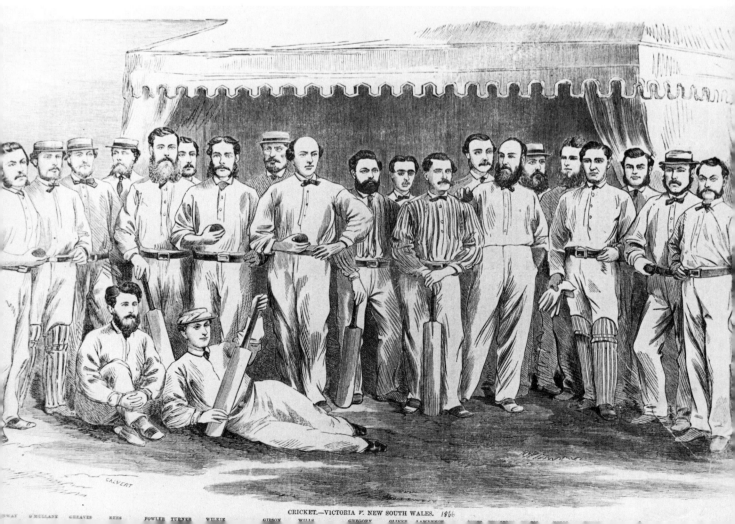

CRICKET.—VICTORIA v. NEW SOUTH WALES. 1866

Noted figures from inter-Colonial cricket in Sydney in 1903 (L to R): Standing, George Bonnor, Nat Thompson, C.W. Beal, Harry Boyle; Seated, Charles Lawrence, George Moore and Harry Hilliard. Beal managed the 1882 and 1888 Australian teams in England.
— Sydney Mail.

Top right
The Melbourne Cricket Ground during the match between Stephenson's first English touring team and Eighteen of Victoria, painted by Henry Burn.
— Australian National Library.

Bottom right
The 1878 Australian team — the first appearance in England — playing a match against Willsher's Gentlemen at Chilham Castle, Kent.
— Rex Nan Kivell Collection, Australian National Library

It was a notable match, and there were many memorable performances. Gideon Elliott took 7 for 24 or 7 for 28 (the scorecard is inconclusive) and 3 for 7 for Victoria. At the end of the 1982-83 Australian season he still held the record for the best figures by a Victorian bowler, having taken 9 for 2 in February 1858 against Tasmania. He was a master in bowling shooters with his fast right-hand round-arm action and produced many outstanding analyses in his career. McKone took 5 for 25 and 5 for 11 for New South Wales in this

first meeting between Australian cricket's arch-rivals. There were widespread celebrations when the *City of Sydney* arrived in Sydney some days after the match, bringing the news that the New South Wales team had won.

Victoria introduced a remarkable figure in Thomas Wentworth Spencer Wills for the return match in Sydney in January 1857. This was the man who, with his cousin Harrison, invented Australian Rules football; a former student of Rugby School who had played for M.C.C., for

More than a hundred years before Australia's major grounds offered sections of their grandstands to sponsors, Spiers & Pond did it at the Melbourne Cricket Ground for the first international match between the All England XI and Eighteen of Victoria in January, 1862. — Latrobe Library, Melbourne.

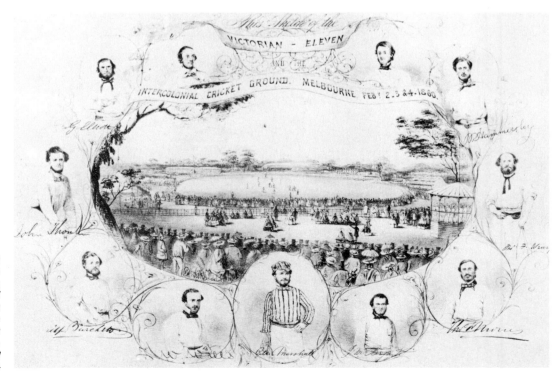

Inter-Colonial cricket quickly attracted wide coverage from newspapers and magazines. This elaborate layout was used to present the Victorian team to readers in 1860. — Latrobe Library Melbourne.

Kent and in one match for Cambridge. Wills can probably be regarded as the first great Australian-born cricketer. New South Wales also strengthened their team for the return match by bringing in Captain Ward, who ran the Sydney Mint and later became Major-General Sir Wolstonehome Ward. New South Wales won this second match between Australia's largest States mainly because of Ward's round-armers, but more significant than the result were the crowds. The second day's play attracted 15,000 spectators, an amazing crowd which comprised most of the population of Sydney.

After losing the first two matches against New South Wales, Victoria won five successive matches against that State, mainly because of the ability of Gideon Elliott, Tom Wills, and Sam Cosstick. Large crowds attended every match, increasing the tension among the players. Arguments flared up virtually every day. At Sydney in 1863, for example, the Victorian umpire ruled that the New South Wales batsman Jones had been run out. But the New South Wales umpire disagreed, saying that he had called 'Over' before the bails were dislodged. Amid boisterous debate, the Victorian players left the field and returned to their hotel. Overnight the Victorian captain agreed to drop the appeal for a run-out against Jones, but he lacked the support of his wicket-keeper

Marshall, who came from Nottingham, and of a player named Greaves. They refused to take any further part in the game and caught the next ship back to Melbourne. When he got home Marshall wrote to the Melbourne *Argus*:

The ball went through to the longstop and was returned to me. The batsman Jones, in attempting to regain his equilibrium, drew one foot over the crease and I put down the wicket, and threw up the ball. While the ball was in the air, the Sydney umpire called 'over', and on my appealing to our umpire, Jones was given out. The consequence was that a scene ensued which I am glad to say is never witnessed out of Sydney. The mob refused to let Jones retire or Thompson to come in, although the Sydney captain, Lawrence, ordered it, and we were all compelled to leave the ground.

Wills received a severe blow in the face by a stone thrown by a cowardly vagabond, and Huddlestone and Hope were both struck by heavy sticks from behind. I was bullied and threatened not only at the ground but even at my hotel, where deputations awaited on me with the avowed purpose of assaulting me.

FIRST · VICTORIAN · ELEVEN.

FIRST INTERCOLONIAL MATCH * PLAYED AT SYDNEY, 1859.
WON BY VICTORIA, BY 2 WICKETS.

By permission of
Messrs Rubira & Barbeta, hosie's Café, 307 Bourke St Melbourne

This is not the first Victorian Eleven as the heading indicates, but one of the best. With the help of bowler Sam Cosstick, missing from this photo, they had a run of five successive wins over N.S.W.
— Melbourne Cricket Ground Museum.

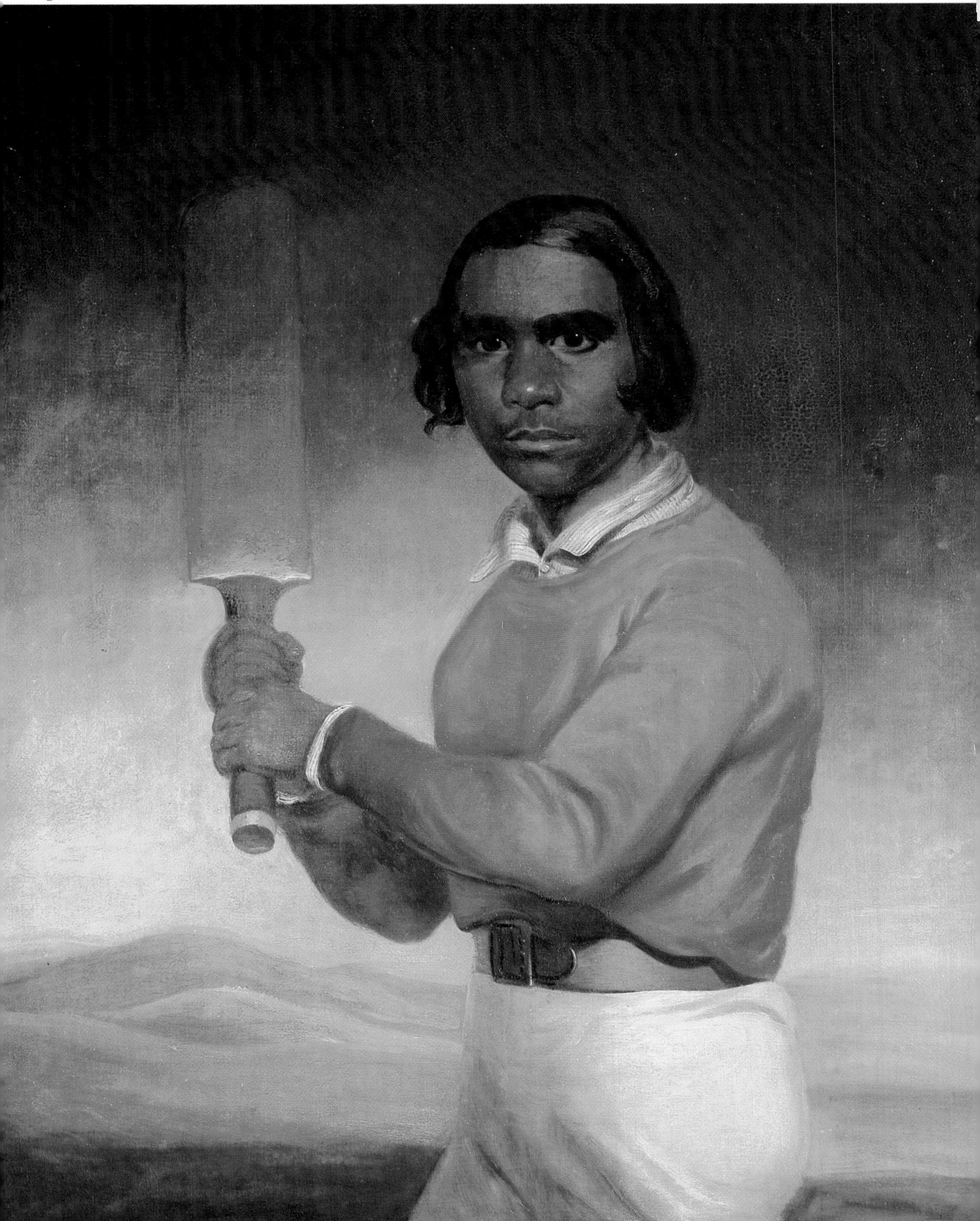

Marshall said he withdrew from the game in fairness to those in Melbourne who had subscribed money to send the team to Sydney. He strongly criticised the Sydney officials who had staged the game, and they in turn hotly denied his charges. A letter written by Wills to the *Sydney Morning Herald* in which he attempted to set the record straight, brought a quick response from Lawrence and Richard Driver. The result was that no match was played between the States in 1864. It was not until the M.C.C. at Lord's ruled that the Victorians were wrong and awarded the 1863 match to New South Wales that the series was resumed.

Perhaps the happiest result of the 1863 affair was that it convinced Victorian cricketers of the value of a bona fide control body. Previously the matches against Tasmania and New South Wales had been arranged by intercolonial match committees which disbanded after the matches were held. On 16 October 1864 the Victorian Cricketers' Association was formed, replacing a body known as the United Victorian Cricketers' Association, which had begun in 1860. The V.C.A. was dissolved before 1875, re-formed in that year, dissolved in 1879 and re-formed in the same year, dissolved in 1895 and re-formed in the same year in its present form as the Victorian Cricket Association. V.C.A. annual reports, however, list premiership winners from the 1860-61 season.

The Sydney committees that had arranged the initial intercolonial match against Victoria had quickly become aware of animosity towards their work. To forestall further dissension when the second match with Victoria was arranged, the New South Wales Cricket Association was formed in 1857 at a meeting at Cunningham's Hotel on the corner of King and Castlereagh Streets, Sydney. Officials from the Albert, Union, Royal Victoria, Australian, National, and Marylebone clubs attended and appointed the Governor, Sir William Denison, as the association's first president. The N.S.W.C.A. used the Domain for its early matches and secured permission to board up the ground and charge for admission when the State side met Victoria. Several of the early matches in the Domain were disrupted by hooligans and Sydney newspapers agreed with Victorians who claimed that Sydney cricket was 'degraded'.

South Australian cricket enthusiasts, aware that matches between colonies had begun in Launceston, Melbourne, Hobart, and Sydney, began moves in the 1860s for their own State control body. One cricket lover, H. Yorke Sparks, paid his own way to Melbourne just to inspect facilities at the Melbourne Cricket Ground and find out how the ground was administered. Back in Adelaide he discussed the prospect of establishing a main ground in the city with three clubs and finally persuaded the influential South Australian Club to back the project. In November 1869 Sparks sent a circular to all Adelaide clubs, part of which read:

I beg to inform you that an effort is now being made to form a Central Cricket Ground similar to those in the sister colonies, the lack of which has hitherto acted very prejudicially against the success of the game here, and as the Corporation has granted a suitable plot of ground, it is proposed to have it grassed, levelled, fenced, and surrounded by a belt of shrubs, trees etc., so as to render it both serviceable and ornamental and a place of pleasant resort.

Right: Aborigines playing cricket at Point Macleay. South Australia, probably in the early 1870s, when George Taplin, a missionary, was at Point Macleay. The bowler is using the round-arm style of delivery.
— *Prof. D. J. Mulvaney*

John Michael Crossland (1800-1858) painted this study of an Aboriginal pupil at the Poominindie Mission called "Boy Playing Cricket".
— *Rex Nan Kivell Collection, Australian National Library,*

The Victorian team that lost to New South Wales by 123 runs at Melbourne in December, 1895: Rear, E.D. Heather (scorer), A.E. Trott; Standing, P. Lewis, J. Taylor (scorer), S. Donahoo, W. Bruce, C. McLeod, M. Roche, R. McLeod; Seated, J. Harry, H. Trott (captain), H. Trumble; Front, F. Laver. Off-spinner Roche later distinguished himself with Middlesex. — Victorian Cricket Association.

Thus the establishment of Adelaide Oval preceded the formation of the State association. Sparks wrote to newspapers, advocating the need for an arena where all sports could be encouraged. His appeal raised £150 and with this the South Australian Cricket Club began to establish the oval in the north parklands, by planting couch grass in the centre for cricket pitches and fencing the playing area. This cost £50 more than Sparks had raised but the club met the additional expense. The Adelaide Corporation leased the ground to the South Australian Club for a peppercorn rental on condition that no charge was made for admission — a condition that created problems when the staging of intercolonial matches was discussed. Visiting teams' expenses were normally paid for in the eastern States from money raised in gate charges.

The Victorian team that lost by 10 wickets to South Australia in 1894 photographed in the Adelaide Botanic Gardens. Harry Trott is seated on the grass at right front, just in front of Frank Laver and Jack Blackham (with cane). — Gray Nicholls Collection.

On 31 May 1871 at a meeting attended by about sixty cricketers at the Prince Alfred Hotel in King William Street, Adelaide, the South Australian Cricketing Association was formed. The Norwood Club took the initiative in organising this meeting, which was supported by the North Adelaide, Kent, Gawler, and the South Australian clubs. The South Australian Club offered the association its new ground, now Adelaide Oval, on condition that the association paid the club's £50 costs for improving the ground.

John Darling, M.P. — father of Joe Darling who became one of Australia's greatest cricket captains — in September 1871, introduced a Bill into the South Australian Parliament empowering the Corporation of Adelaide to grant to the S.A.C.A. a lease on the ground. Formation of the S.A.C.A.

and the establishment of Adelaide Oval brought a rapid improvement in cricket standards throughout the colony. In 1873–74, Dr W.G. Grace's English team played a match in the South Australian country town of Kadina and were then persuaded to travel to Adelaide for a match against Twenty Two of South Australia, the first appearance by an English team in Adelaide. The following season, 1874–75, South Australia played their first game against another colony when a below-strength Victoria Eleven beat Eighteen of Adelaide by 15 runs. Takings for the three days' play amounted to £285. Victoria scored 92 and 98, with a bowler named Scott bowling unchanged through both innings for South Australia, finishing with 10 for 72.

A watercolour attributed to S.T. Gill entitled "The Grand Cricket Match," showing the All England XI led by H.H. Stephenson in action against New South Wales in the Outer Domain in January and February, 1862.
— Mitchell Library, Sydney.

In the 1876–77 season, a South Australian Eighteen defeated a Victorian Eleven on Adelaide Oval by an innings and 70 runs. South Australia finally graduated to eleven-a-side matches in November 1880 when they met Victoria on the East Melbourne Ground. In a curious match South Australia managed only 77 in their first innings but cast aside their nervousness to reach 314 in the second innings. Victoria scored 329 and 3 for 64 to win by 7 wickets. In April 1881 South Australia played their first intercolonial match on level terms against a full-strength Victorian side on Adelaide Oval. South Australia made 163 and 51, with Victoria scoring 191 and 174 to win by 151 runs.

South Australia had great difficulty persuading New South Wales officials to stage matches between the States until outstanding form by George Giffen, John Lyons, and the Jarvis brothers finally tipped the scale and a match was planned to be held in Sydney in February 1890. The N.S.W.C.A. agreed that they would send a team to Adelaide if the South Australians did well. Lyons had innings of 19 and 63 and Giffen 52 and 32 but the rest of the South Australian batsmen could not handle the bowling of Charlton, who capped a fine match with 7 for 44 in South Australia's second innings. South Australia dismissed New South Wales for 240 but managed only 158 and 148 on a strip that was far slower than Adelaide Oval, and lost by 9 wickets. But the N.S.W.C.A. kept their promise and in the following December New South Wales made their first appearance on Adelaide Oval against a steadily improving South Australian team.

This time the bowling of Sydney bank clerk John Ferris, one of the finest left-arm bowlers in history, was South Australia's undoing. Ferris relished the fast Adelaide pitch and took 14 for 192 in the match. South Australia scored 241 and 191; New South Wales, with 406 and 4 for 27, won by 6 wickets. Despite these decisive setbacks South Australia managed an astounding reversal in the third meeting with New South Wales at Sydney in January 1892. New South Wales were out for 215 on the first day. Rain fell at the start of the second day and with fieldsmen slithering about and bowlers unable to grip the ball properly Giffen and Lyons hammered all the New South Wales bowlers. Lyons lived up to his reputation as one of cricket's biggest hitters, with one of his blows for 4 smashing a paling in the fence. The New South Wales captain 'Alick' Bannerman persuaded the umpires to stop play but spectators kept up a barrage of noisy protest until the players returned. Lyons went on to 145 and Giffen was on

95 when the day ended. Next morning he moved to 120 and the South Australian total reached 330. South Australia then routed New South Wales for 62 to win by an innings and 53 runs.

Queensland began matches against New South Wales in April 1865, fielding teams of fifteen and eighteen players against New South Wales elevens until gradually Queensland's playing standards improved. In April 1893 the Q.C.A. (formed 1876) decided it was ready to play New South Wales on level terms. Several of their leading players could not make the long trip to Brisbane but it was still a strong New South Wales side that faced the Queenslanders, who — to the astonishment of the cricket world — won by 14 runs. New South Wales made 64 and 100, Hoare taking 6 for 12 in their first innings. Newell bowled splendidly for New South Wales, with match figures of 10 for 52, but Queensland still scored 100 and 78.

Meanwhile in Western Australia bold efforts were made to lift the standard of the game in the colony. By the late 1840s and early 1850s cricket had spread to the isolated country areas of the State and matches were reported at Derby, Bussel Town (now Busselton), and Northam. In 1862 a team from Fremantle undertook a two-and-a-half-day voyage to Bunbury where they beat an enthusiastic local side by an innings. In Perth, the strongest club in the State, the Perth C.C. made an important breakthrough when they secured government permission to use convict labour to clear a swamp and establish a cricket ground. The arrangement ended when two convicts attacked each other with pick handles. The swamp was left undrained.

In February 1879 an Aboriginal team coached and captained by a former Perth player, H.N. Lefroy, lost their first match to the Metropolitan Club in Perth but two days later defeated Fremantle by 8 runs. The Western Australian Cricket Association was formed at a meeting at the United Services Hotel in Perth on November 12 1885, with J.C.H. James the first president.

Western Australia were soundly beaten in their first venture against other colonies when they journeyed to Adelaide and Melbourne to play South Australia and Victoria in March 1893. Western Australia gained invaluable experience, scoring 111 and 131 against South Australia's 236 and 0 for 11 in the first match but failing badly against Victoria with scores of 38 and 130 compared with Victoria's 411.

All this activity in the fifty-one argumentative years of intercolonial matches brought forth many colourful personalities, most of them equipped with loud voices and pointed turns of phrase. Among the most memorable players were the near-sighted John Kinloch, a star New South Wales underarm bowler who wore a monocle, and Captain Ward, deputy-master of the Sydney Mint, whose posterior pointed at the bowler during his stance, with Ward peering at him over his left shoulder. Characters like these emerged as regularly as great players like Spofforth, Boyle, the Bannermans, the Gregorys, George Giffen, Hugh Massie, Billy Murdoch, and Ferris.

Just as fascinating in the first century of European settlement of Australia were the feats of Aboriginal cricketers. The first settlers who taught them cricket often included Aboriginals in teams that established the game's popularity in Australia. In 1835, when the Hobart and Carlton clubs met, an Aboriginal called 'Shiney' played for Carlton. When pastoral land in the Edenhope and Harrow regions of Victoria was taken up in about 1844–46 the Aboriginals Peter and Bullocky played regularly in teams raised on the properties. By 1865 there were records of fully Aboriginal teams defeating European teams in the Edenhope district. In 1869 an Aboriginal named Johnny Taylor scored 35 runs off a 4-ball over in a match in New South Wales where Canberra now stands. There were no boundaries and, as Taylor had to run out all his hits, he must have given each ball a mighty clump. In Western Australia an Aboriginal team from New Norcia to the north of Perth toured the colony regularly in the 1880s.

One of the greatest admirers of Aboriginal cricket was T.W.S. Wills, whose involvement as a keen coach of Aboriginal players had an ironic background. Wills' father, a Victorian M.L.A., had sold his properties around Geelong when Queensland was opened up. Believing there was a fortune to be made, the Wills family travelled north with their servants, ignoring all warnings. On 17 October 1861, they were resting from the heat when they were surprised by Aboriginals, who massacred nineteen men, women and children, including Tom's father. Tom only escaped this tragedy because his dray had broken down, and he did not reach the scene until the following day.

Tom Wills tried hard to fulfil his father's dream by working the Queensland property, but when George Parr brought the second English touring team to Australia in 1863–64, the prospect of playing big cricket again sent him south to Melbourne. Wills helped several Victorian teams against Parr's side and went to New Zealand to perform the same service for teams there. On his return to Victoria he began coaching Aboriginal teams again.

An artist's impression of play in the first inter-State cricket match between Victoria and Tasmania, with the Launceston Cricket Club's flag fluttering from the tiny grandstand.
— Jack Pollard Collection.

3. The First Tours

By the 1860s reports of the popularity of cricket in England regularly reached the Australian colonies. The most powerful English counties — Kent, Yorkshire, Lancashire, Sussex, Middlesex, Gloucestershire, Nottinghamshire, and Surrey — invariably attracted large, enthusiastic audiences to their matches. Eton, Harrow, and Winchester had firmly established amateur cricket and the game was booming at Oxford and Cambridge universities. In 1859 twelve English professionals had crossed the Atlantic to play in Canada and America, and for the opening day of their match against Twenty Two of New York attracted 25,000 spectators.

In Melbourne the restaurateurs and caterers Messrs Spiers and Pond saw that they could vastly improve their business by staging matches involving an English team. Early in 1861 they sent W.B. Mallam to England to arrange a visit. Mallam went straight to Birmingham to contact players involved in a match between the North and South of England. Mallam was aware that the players in the match represented the best talent in English cricket but when he invited a group of them to dinner they were not enthusiastic about touring Australia for £150 a man, plus first-class expenses. Indeed George Parr, the 'Lion of the North', scoffed at the idea of travelling all the way to Australia for such a paltry fee.

Mallam returned to London and explained his problems to the Surrey Club secretary William Burrup. This began the close association between Surrey and Australian cricket that still exists. Burrup helped Mallam organise a touring team that comprised Heathfield Harmon Stephenson, the Surrey captain who also skippered the South of England, William Caffyn, Charles Lawrence, W. Mortlock, W. Mudie, G. Griffith, and T. Sewell — all from Surrey — T. Hearne from Middlesex, R. Iddison and E. Stephenson from Yorkshire, G. Bennett from Kent, and G. ('Tiny') Wells from Sussex. They were a colourful, resourceful side, well led by H.H. Stephenson, an amiable figure who knew how to mix discipline with good fun.

International Cricket quickly built a vast public following in Australia. This is the scene at Melbourne Cricket Ground during the match between Dr. W.G. Grace's third English team and a Victorian Eighteen. — Melbourne Cricket Ground Museum.

The first English team to tour Australia — in 1861-62 — received a tumultuous welcome and covered tour expenses in the first match. Here the team is greeted outside their sponsors Cafe de Paris in Bourke Street, Melbourne, after driving triumphantly through crowded streets from the wharf.
— Melbourne Cricket Ground Museum.

The first English cricket team to visit Australia — in 1862 — was captained by Heathfield Harman Stephenson and managed by Spiers & Pond appointee M.W. Mallam. The team (L to R): W. Mortlock, W. Mudie, G. Bennett, C. Lawrence, H.H. Stephenson, M.W. Mallam, W. Caffyn, G. Griffith, T. Hearne, R. Iddison, T. Sewell, E. Stephenson.
— Melbourne Herald.

The match between Lord Harris' England team and Australia at Melbourne, later recognised as the Third Test between the two countries. Australia won by 10 wickets.
— Latrobe Library, Melbourne.

A lithograph by H. Deutsch of the match at Ballarat in March, 1862, between Twenty-two of Ballarat and the 1862 Eleven of All England. This was the ninth match of England's tour and was left drawn after Ballarat had made 122 and 107, England 155. Cosstick made 31 for Ballarat, Iddison took 13 wickets for England.
— Latrobe Library, Melbourne.

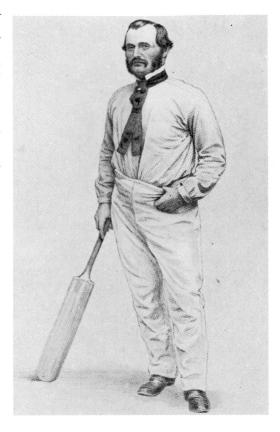

George Parr, captain of the second England team in Australia. He had refused an invitation to lead the first team to Australia saying the £150-a-man offered by Spiers & Pond was insufficient. His side was a powerful all-professional outfit apart from W.G.'s brother E.M. Grace.
— M.C.C. Collection at Lord's.

Stephenson's team left England in the schooner *Great Britain* on 18 October 1861, and arrived in Melbourne on Christmas Eve to a joyous welcome from more than 10,000 people crowding the wharf area to get a glimpse of them. Wild cheering greeted the players as they rode through the streets of Melbourne in a coach and four to an official welcome at the Cafe de Paris. Enthusiasm for their visit was so intense that when they practised they had to be driven several miles out into the bush to escape well-wishers. The professionals in the English team were pleasantly surprised that none of the social barriers which professionals experienced in England was present in Australia and that all team members were considered equal.

The first match had been set down between All-England and Twenty Two of Melbourne, but when Stephenson argued his players had not regained their land legs after the long voyage from England Spiers and Pond agreed to reduce the Melbourne team to eighteen. The Melbourne *Herald* condemned Stephenson's attitude but he remained firm, and the first match between an English and Australian team began on 1 January 1862 at the Melbourne Cricket Ground, which had been refurbished specially for the Englishmen's visit.

Below: Richard Driver, whose energy helped originate matches between New South Wales and Victoria. He was an original trustee of Sydney Cricket Ground.
— Philip Derriman.

William Caffyn, also known as "Terrible Billy," and "The Surrey Pet," who remained in Australia to coach after touring with the first and second England teams. He made an invaluable contribution to Australian cricket before returning to England to finish out his life.
— Albert Gregory Collection.

Understandably, the visiting team were astonished by facilities at the ground and by the lavish promotion of the entire match. Brightly coloured, flag-topped marquees circled the M.C.G. where a new stand was full to its capacity of 6,000 spectators. Beneath the stand Melbourne's leading publicans had leased space to sell cases of beer. As the All-England players entered the field to the strains of their national anthem, they were watched by more than 15,000 people, all in their Sunday best. Each player wore a light, helmet-shaped hat and a hat ribbon and sash of a colour specified in the score-sheets which were sold around the ground. Horse-drawn buggies and carriages blocked the streets around the M.C.G. throughout the game. A painter who took his high ladder did a big trade helping spectators climb to good positions in trees. Between innings fruit and sweet stalls and coconut shies did brisk business. There was a sweepstake with a first prize of £100 for drawing the batsman who made the highest score.

The Englishmen found the heat a bigger problem than the Melbourne batsmen and Caffyn had to stop bowling during the match because of mosquito bites on his arms. The captain of the Melbourne Eighteen was George Marshall (no relation to the Tasmanian cricket hero of the same name), who gave the match a bright start by scoring 27, and later kept wicket in fine style. But his team-mates could not cope with the accuracy of the English bowling and there were six ducks in the Melbourne first innings of 118. Bennett (7 for 53) and Griffith (7 for 30) took the bowling honours and there were three run-outs.

E. Stephenson and Bennett opened for All-England and, according to one account, ran up the 'snug little score' of 18 in an hour. The Englishmen made 305, Caffyn top-scoring with 79 and earning a gift of £10 from the man who won the sweepstake.

Left: Charles Lawrence, whose coaching dramatically lifted Australian cricket standards. He captained New South Wales from 1862 to 1870.
— Jack Pollard Collection.

Parr's second England touring team (L to R): G. Anderson, E.M. Grace, W. Caffyn, J. Jackson, R.C. Tinley, G. Parr, C. Lawrence (manager), T. Lockyer, J. Caesar, G. Tarrant, A. Clarke, T. Hayward, R. Carpenter. Carpenter topped the team's batting averages and at Ballarat made the first century (121) by an Englishman in Australia.
— Sydney Mail.

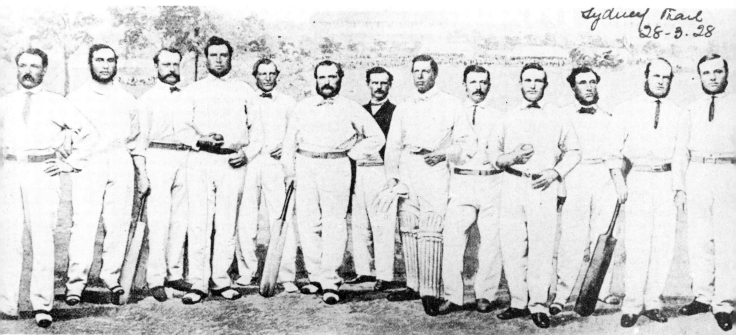

The Melbourne Eighteen managed only 92 in their second innings, this time with nine ducks. T. Sewell took 7 for 20. This gave England victory by an innings and 95, an impressive result but nowhere near as striking as the success of Spiers and Pond. The 45,000 people who saw the match at a minimum charge of 2s 6d enabled Spiers and Pond to meet expenses for the entire tour and emerge with a profit. Spiers and Pond further emphasised their enterprise when the match finished early and they organised the first balloon ascent seen in the colony. The balloon was called 'All-England' and had pictures painted on it of Queen Victoria and the English players. It drifted all over Melbourne for 45 minutes.

The English team played thirteen matches in all, plus two 'unscheduled' games. They were clearly too strong for Australian teams on level terms and their only losses occurred against Twenty Two of Castelmaine and against a combined Twenty Two of New South Wales and Victoria in Sydney. One of the highspots of the tour was the match billed as 'Surrey versus the World', in which the six Surrey players assisted by the best locals played the rest of their team-mates and five star locals. The team was welcomed just as enthusiastically in Sydney as in Melbourne and the Governor and his entourage watched all the play. Each evening there was a grand banquet.

The Melbourne Cricket Ground when Parr's team played Twenty-two of Victoria. The umpires lifted the stumps precisely at 6 p.m. when England needed only nine runs to win, declaring the match drawn.
— Melbourne Cricket Ground Museum.

The Melbourne Cricket Club's Eleven in February, 1865, in front of the club rooms at the M.C.G. Dick Wardill, the captain, has the bat tucked under his arm in the centre while Tom Wills is two to his right. Sam Costick is at the far right.
— Melbourne Cricket Ground Museum.

The Sydney Domain during the match between Parr's team and Twenty-two of New South Wales in March, 1864. The Englishmen won by four wickets.
-- Mtichell Library, Sydney.

William Caffyn, in his marvellous book *71 Not Out*, published some years later, wrote:

> Scarcely a day passed without our being entertained to champagne breakfasts, luncheons and dinners. A performance was given at the Victoria Theatre for our benefit and was packed out. Between the pieces, H.H. Stephenson read out a farewell address. After various speeches had been made we adjourned to Tattersall's where parting bumpers were drained. A large body of people escorted us to Circular Quay to see us start on our voyage to Tasmania. Rockets and blue lights were fired as we set out to sea.

The Englishmen were offered £1200 to stay in Australia an extra month but were not able to afford the time. Spiers and Pond, who made £11,000 on the tour, divided half the profits of the last match among the English players. The Melbourne Cricket Club showed their delight in the tour by donating a bonus of 100 sovereigns to the team, who agreed that the M.C.G. was a cricket ground of a standard unmatched in England.

At the end of the tour Charles Lawrence decided not to accompany his team-mates back to England. Instead he accepted an offer from the Albert Club in Sydney to remain and become Australia's first professional coach. Lawrence's appointment had a big influence on all the leading players in the colony, not just members of the Albert Club, for he improved the general standard of running between wickets, fielding where the captain wanted, and contributed to the important art of field placing. He was shrewd and knowledgeable, his pupils remarkably keen and observant.

Two years later George Parr, who had rejected the invitation to lead the first English team to Australia, captained a much stronger team. This team consisted entirely of professionals except for E.M. Grace, a brother of the legendary Dr W.G. Grace, one of the most influential players cricket has known. Caffyn was the only member of the original English team to tour again. Parr's formidable reputation as the fiercest legside hitter the game had produced, helped the tour sponsors, the Melbourne Cricket Club, in advertising the matches and once again large, enthusiastic crowds attended the games. They were not disappointed when Parr went to the crease, a powerfully framed figure with big blue eyes, thick auburn hair, generous whiskers and moustache.

Aboriginals practising for the tour of England in 1868, the first by an Australian team, 10 years ahead of the first white team to visit England. They showed remarkable stamina, playing 47 matches, winning 14, with 19 drawn. — Melbourne Cricket Ground Museum.

Parr's team included two fine fast bowlers, George Tarrant and John Jackson. Tarrant, nicknamed 'Tear 'em', made a deep impression on Australian spectators, one of whom was a tall, lean youngster born in the Sydney suburb of Balmain and named Frederick Spofforth. Years later, Spofforth wrote:

It was a perfect treat to me to see Tarrant bowl. His tremendous pace on hard pitches positively scared the batsmen. When he hit the wicket, time and time again the stumps were knocked completely out of the ground, and it was no uncommon thing for them to be split in pieces. I never failed in my allegiance to Tarrant and continued to bowl as fast as I knew how.

Tarrant's partner, Jackson — 6 feet 2 inches and 15 stone — kept a better length than Tarrant but was equally fast. He had a trick in bowling fast full tosses straight at the head of batsmen who were well set, and blew his nose loudly when he took a wicket, a habit that earned him the nickname 'Foghorn'.

Parr's team also included Tom Hayward, a gracious stroke-maker for Surrey and England, famous for his powerful driving all round the wicket; Julius Caesar, also of Surrey, a batsman of nervous temperament who had a strange fear of sleeping alone in hotel rooms but proved a 5 feet 7 inch powerhouse out on the field, where he showed a rare gift in timing his cover drives, pulls, and cuts; Tom Hearne, a tall lean figure who was a master of the 'draw' stroke played between his legs and the stumps; George Anderson, a Yorkshireman who could get runs on rough or wet pitches when team-mates were struggling; Tom Lockyer, a versatile wicket-keeper, the first not to leave balls wide of the leg stump for his longstops to field.

The Aboriginals after practising for their England tour (L to R): Rose, Bullocky, Cuzens, Mullagh, their Australian coach T.W. Wills, Peter, Tarpot, Paddy, Dick-a-Dick, and Mosquito. — State Library of Victoria.

The second English tour began on 1 January 1864, with a match against Twenty Two of Victoria who were considered to have done well in scoring 146 and 143. Parr's side replied with 176 and at 4 for 105 in the second innings were apparently coasting to an easy win when the umpires drew stumps. 'Though the general feeling was strongly in favour of the match being played out, the umpires were inexorable and promptly at six o'clock pulled the stumps', said a Melbourne *Herald* account of the game. Carpenter made 59 for England, Hayward 61, and Caffyn showed all the skill that had won him recognition as the finest player in England with a gem of an innings for 37.

Johnnie Moyes in his *History of Australian Cricket* recalled that in the third match on Parr's tour at Ballarat there was a notable spectator, a man of sixty who had travelled 300 miles to be present and had walked 100 miles of that distance. He explained that, 'forty years earlier he had played in some important matches at St. John's Wood (Lord's), and urged on by recollections of those games, was determined to see an English team in the field once again'. England kept winning and after defeating Twenty Two of Ararat — where their lob bowler, Tinley, dismissed batsmen as fast as they came in — made a short trip to New Zealand. On a visit to a Maori settlement, the Maori chief took a great liking to Parr, according to Caffyn and followed him wherever he went. 'Don't leave me, for goodness sake,' said Parr, 'I don't like this one bit.' Parr had then to go through the ceremony of kissing the Maori women, a ritual he was glad to get over quickly, said Caffyn, as he thought some of his team might 'turn awkward'.

Parr's team defeated Twenty Two of Otago in the first New Zealand match, thanks largely to Hayward, who took 15 wickets in Otago's first innings and 9 in the second. Otago made 71 and 83, England 99 and 1 for 58. Tinley's slow lobs troubled all the New Zealand batsmen. England drew with a combined Otago–Canterbury side, defeated Christchurch by an innings, and defeated Twenty Two of Otago by 198 runs in a return game. E.M. Grace and Tarrant then played eleven of the Otago players, whom Tarrant bowled out twice for 7 runs. He and Grace made 8 and 16. The English team then returned to Australia for matches in Melbourne, Sydney, Geelong and Ballarat. They left Sydney on the *Wonga Wonga* to sail south, but their ship had just cleared Sydney Heads when it ran into a small sailing ship, the *Viceroy*, which immediately sank.

Caffyn recorded that Parr was 'utterly dazed and paralysed with alarm', while Tarrant rushed below to collect all the gifts and curios they had been given during the tour. A boat was lowered to take the crew of the *Viceroy* and when Tarrant tried to get into it he was told by the sailors, 'in not very choice language', to keep out. By contrast Julius Caesar remained cool and did all he could to help the crew. The *Wonga Wonga* returned to Circular Quay for repairs and when it berthed the players discovered that Foghorn Jackson had slept through the whole affair.

Parr's team was unbeaten in its twelve matches in Australia. Bob Carpenter topped the batting averages with 299 runs at 22.11 on the tour, and Tinley took 171 wickets at only 3.65 with his lobs. Such big crowds attended all matches that the Melbourne Club was able to hand each player £250 after paying all expenses. Only a Twenty Two of New South Wales went close to spoiling the record of Parr's side, pushing them to a margin of 1 wicket amid intense excitement.

For Australian cricket, the big bonus from the tour came with the decision of Caffyn — variously described as the 'Surrey Pet' and 'Terrible Billy' — to accept an offer of £300 a year to remain in Australia to coach. At the time Caffyn was regarded as the finest player in the Surrey team, for whom he had first played in 1849. An impish free-scoring batsman, he was a top-class round-arm bowler, and the outstanding fieldsman of his time, brilliant at catching, throwing, and reading the batsman's intentions.

Caffyn found young Australians delightful pupils, always keen to learn a new stroke or correct mistakes, and exceptionally quick and confident in the field. Caffyn taught by demonstration rather than through laborious oral instruction and he was proud of the influence he and his former Surrey team-mate, Charles Lawrence, had on the early develoment of Australian cricket. After two years in Melbourne Caffyn moved to Sydney, where his wife set up a prosperous hairdressing business. Four of Caffyn's children, three boys and a girl, were born in Sydney, but two of the boys died there.

The photograph at Lord's of the 1868 Aboriginal team that toured England. Only the captain, Lawrence, and the managers, G. Smith and W.R. Hayman were white. Some of the players are shown with spears and boomerangs with which they gave exhibitions. — M.C.C. Collection at Lord's.

Johnny Mullagh, star of the Aboriginal team in England. He scored 1670 runs, topscore 94, and took 245 wickets at 10.16 on the tour. He later played one match for Victoria but until his death at 50 remained sensitive about racial issues.
— Mechanics Institute, Harrow.

'The best bat I ever saw or coached in Australia was undoubtedly Charles Bannerman,' Caffyn wrote in 1899, 'nor do I think his superior has yet appeared in that country. Spofforth and Murdoch, two mighty names, came to the front after my time.' Caffyn was also much impressed with Bransby Beauchamp Cooper, an Englishman who had learnt his cricket on the playing fields of Rugby and had played for M.C.C. and the Gentlemen and for Middlesex and Kent before he settled in the Geelong area south of Melbourne. Caffyn coached the Warwick Club in Sydney, Lawrence the Albert Club. The two clubs had many stirring matches. These two fine coaches advocated contrasting methods, however, and early Sydney cricket fans learnt to pick who had coached batsmen they watched. Caffyn favoured playing forward whenever possible to overcome the hazards of Australia's badly prepared pitches, while Lawrence stressed the value of playing back.

Between them Caffyn and Lawrence laid the foundation for a dramatic improvement in Australian cricket, but they were helped a great deal by Tom Wills, the Australian-born cricketer who had polished his skills at Rugby School and in the Kent and Cambridge elevens. Lawrence represented New South Wales from 1862 to 1870, Caffyn from 1865 to 1870 and Wills played for Victoria between 1856 and 1875. Wills not only strengthened the Victorian teams that played visiting English sides, but also travelled widely to help train country teams against whom England played. Caffyn and Lawrence instinctively cashed in on their skills and undoubtedly their professionalism rubbed off on their pupils. Wills may have been a true amateur while he was being educated in England but after the massacre of his family he began looking for appearance money and other side benefits.

Wills and Lawrence were both full of praise for the natural talents of the Aboriginals and when it was proposed that they should play a match on Melbourne Cricket Ground, Wills went to Edenhope, the strongest area of Aboriginal cricket in Victoria, to give them preliminary coaching. The idea for the match came from William Hayman, who had a holding in the Edenhope region and had been much impressed by the Aboriginals' cricket talents. He sent a photograph of Edenhope's Aboriginal players to William Rowley, proprietor of a refreshment pavilion at the M.C.G. suggesting that they play a match as a contribution to Aboriginal welfare.

The Melbourne newspapers announced the M.C.G. match for Boxing Day 1866 and the unusual names of the players likely to appear quickly captivated public interest. Just before the match attention was further stimulated when the *Argus* criticised the Melbourne Club for electing a noted bowler named James to playing membership two days before the game so that he could be included in the side to oppose the Aboriginals. The Aboriginal team for the match consisted of Wills (captain), Cuzens, Bullocky (wicket-keeper), Mullagh, Dick-a-Dick, Peter, Jellico, Officer, Tarpot, Paddy, and Sundown. Although several of the Melbourne Club's best players were away in Sydney, the match attracted 10,000 spectators and the size of their audience completely overwhelmed most of the Aboriginal team.

*The third England team, which toured Australia in 1873-74 under the captaincy of Dr. W.G. Grace (L to R): G.A. Bush, W. Oscroft, R. Humphreys, J. Southerton, M. McIntyre, F.H. Boult, A. Greenwood, W.R. Gilbert; Below: J. Lillywhite, W.G. Grace, H. Jupp, G.F. Grace.
— Melbourne Cricket Ground Museum.*

The Aboriginals batted first and were all out for 39, with Bullocky scoring 14 and Mullagh 16. The Aboriginals never recovered from the loss of Cuzens, one of their big hopes and their star opener, who was dismissed without scoring. The crowd was highly impressed by the fielding and throwing of the Aboriginals but their applause only made the visitors more ill at ease. Mullagh got both the M.C.C. openers cheaply but Dick Wardill made 45, lifting the club's first innings score to 100. Cuzens finished with 6 for 24.

Batting a second time the Aboriginals were all out for 87, Mullagh scoring 33 despite an injured hand and Wills contributing 25 not out. Melbourne C.C. won the match early on the second day by scoring the 27 runs required with the loss of only 1 wicket. The Melbourne *Herald* assessed the Aboriginals in these words:

That they have been thoroughly acquainted with various points of the game was manifestly evident by the manner in which they conducted themselves on the field. Mullagh and Bullocky showed themselves to be no mean batsmen. They not only stopped balls, but hit them, showing good direction and strong defence.

After the match, in an exhibition of their versatility, Mullagh cleared 5ft 3in in the high jump, Tarpot gave a display of running backwards at speed, and Mullagh threw a cricket ball 110 yards.

The following season, 1866–67, Mullagh and Cuzens were picked for Victoria against Sixteen of Tasmania, but on the day of the match Mullagh was ill and Bullocky took his place. Tasmania won by 5 wickets and the *Age* blamed Mullagh's absence as the chief cause of Victoria's defeat. At about this point a strange figure appeared — 'Captain' W. Edward Brougham Gurnett, who persuaded Hayman and Wills to sign a contract to manage and coach an Aboriginal team for a year-long tour of the colonies and England. Hayman recruited more players in Edenhope and the Aboriginal side played matches in Geelong, Bendigo, and Ballarat, returning to Melbourne for a game against a County of Bourke Eleven.

The public feared that the Aboriginals were being exploited and were unanimously sceptical about the proposed tour of England. These fears were justified when some of Gurnett's cheques were dishonoured and he had to make special arrangements with creditors before he could join the Aboriginal players in Sydney. The Albert Club defeated the Aboriginals on their ground at Redfern by 132 runs and plans for a Brisbane match were abandoned when Captain Gurnett's demands for financial guarantees were not met. The side returned to Melbourne destitute. The players were not paid and some of them became ill.

Despite these setbacks, Lawrence persisted with his efforts to get the Aboriginal team to England. His plan was opposed by the Aboriginal Protection Board and by doctors who claimed that the English climate would prove disastrous to the players' health. Lawrence and backers such as Alderman George Smith, a former lord mayor of Sydney, ignored all objections and the team sailed from Sydney in the *Parramatta* on 8 February 1868. They arrived in England ten years ahead of the first white Australian team.

The team gave an astounding show of stamina in England, where they played forty-seven matches between May and October, winning fourteen, losing fourteen, with nineteen left undecided. They were on the field for ninety-nine out of a possible 126 days and appeared in six different counties. They played seventeen of their matches in the bitterly cold weather of September and October, long after tours normally end. There were no tea breaks during their games and at the luncheon intervals they had to take their chances by lining up with spectators at refreshment tents. They were regarded as a novelty at first because of the displays of spear and boomerang throwing they gave at matches but these became burdensome as weariness overtook the players. Some English newspapers expressed surprise at their manly and dignified bearing. The *Rochdale Observer* called them 'stalwart men', a fitting label for a side that had lost three members — King Cole, who had died in London of tuberculosis, and Jim Crow and Sundown, who had been sent home because of illness.

Of the eleven team members left, Red Cap and Tiger played in all forty-seven matches, Twopenny and Cuzens in forty-six, Johnny Mullagh and Dick-a-Dick in forty-five. Three others and Charles Lawrence, the side's manager, played in forty matches. William Shepherd, a former professional player for Surrey, travelled with the team as umpire and played in seven matches, leading the side when Lawrence had to be rested. At York, the Aboriginals were banned from the lunch tent, but they were given a match at Lord's, where their opposition included a viscount, a lieutenant-colonel, an earl, and a captain.

The Victorian Eighteen which defeated Grace's 1873 side by an innings and 21 runs (L to R): Top, B.B. Cooper, S. Cosstick, G. Gibson, H.G. Wyndham; Second row, B. McGan, G. Hedley, G.P. Robertson (captain), J. Conway; Third row, L. Goldsmith, J. Coates, H.F. Boyle, C. Carr; Fourth row, W. Midwinter, F. Allan, T.J.D. Kelly, T. Horan; Bottom, W.W. Gaggin, Colonel Ward (umpire), H. Bishop. — State Library of Victoria.

A view of the Melbourne Cricket Ground during the match between Stephenson's 1862 team and Eighteen of Melbourne. The facilities and the big crowds for each day's play amazed the Englishmen. — Melbourne Cricket Ground Museum.

At Lord's, the M.C.C. scored 164 and 120, with Cuzens taking 10 wickets for 117 in the match. Mullagh top-scored with 75 in the Aboriginals' first innings of 185 but they collapsed for only 45 in their second innings, with Mullagh scoring 21. English cricket historian Arthur Haygarth described the Aboriginal tour as 'very lucrative', but according to other writers expenses were so high that there was little profit. The tour was completed without incident except at Bootle, where one of Mullagh's boomerangs veered off course and cut through a man's hat, inflicting a severe wound on his forehead. In one of their sports displays they competed at throwing a cricket ball with the legendary Dr W.G. Grace, who had throws of 116, 117 and 118 yards.

Far more was heard later of Dr Grace than of most of the Aboriginal cricketers, most of whom disappeared back to the bush when their ship, the *Dunbar Castle*, reached home. Cuzens played without success in one trial match for Victoria and Twopenny had one game for New South Wales. Johnny Mullagh played his only match for Victoria almost a decade later — against Lord Harris' 1879 English tourists. He died at the age of fifty, in 1891, but his story has remained part of the folklore of the Edenhope region.

Right: William Tunks, who put up £200 to enable the first New South Wales v. Victoria match to go ahead in Melbourne. — Philip Derriman.

4. Test Matches Begin

Nine years elapsed after the first two English tours of Australia before the redoubtable Dr W.G. Grace brought the third English team out for a fifteen-match tour that included four States. Grace's brother Fred was one of the four other amateurs in the English side. All the matches were against the odds and the English team won ten, lost three, and drew two. The tour attracted argument from the start, a common occurrence when the bulky doctor and his umbrageous beard were involved. Grace's team toured at the invitation of a group of Melbourne Cricket Club members who formed a syndicate to finance the tour and pay the guarantees sought by W.G. There is no record of what syndicate members thought of paying W.G. fees far in excess of expenses.

The voyage from England lasted fifty-two days, partly because Grace's team had to change ships at Colombo. They were taken straight from the ship in Melbourne to watch a match at the South Melbourne Ground, with their hosts boasting that Australian crowd control was superior to that in England. The Englishmen had barely taken their seats when a riot broke out over an umpire's decision, spectators rushed the pitch, and the game had to be abandoned. 'This, I am sorry to say, was a foretaste of some experiences which subsequently fell to our lot,' Grace wrote in his reminiscences. This was the book in which Grace described how one of his team hoodwinked an umpire after he had been bowled by replacing the bails and insisting that he always had a trial ball.

A rare photograph of four cricketers who boosted Australia's reputation when international cricket began (L to R): Fred Spofforth, Tom Horan, Jack Blackham and Harry Boyle.
— M.C.G. Museum Collection.

Tom ("Paddy") Horan, who played in the first of all Tests for Australia was born in County Cork. In 1885 he became the first Irishman to captain Australia, wearing brown pads 90 years before Packer's rebels played in coloured equipment. — Melbourne Cricket Ground Museum.

Before the first game against a Victorian Eighteen a story spread through Melbourne that Grace had backed himself for £50 to £500 that he would not be bowled throughout the Australian tour. There was unrestrained celebration when the then virtually unknown Harry Boyle knocked back Grace's leg stump with one of his right-arm medium-pacers, but Grace always denied that the bet had been made. The Victorians shocked the tourists by scoring 266. B. B. Cooper, who had once shared a stand of 283 with Grace for the Gentleman of the South against Players of the South, top-scored for the Victorians with 84. John Conway made 32 and Boyle 30. The Victorian bowlers, spearheaded by Allan and Boyle — later Test heroes — and the fine Victorian player Sam Costick, dismissed England for 110. England followed on with 132; Grace, who had taken 10 wickets for 49 runs, was undefeated on 51.

The *Australian Sketcher* in a review of the match hailed the left-arm fast medium Francis Erskine Allan as the best bowler in the colonies. The *Sketcher* praised all the Victorian Eighteen, but especially G.P. Robertson, of the Melbourne Club, a native of Tasmania and a former Oxford Eleven batsman of style, who captained the local side; Cosstick for his 'fast round-arm balls, executed from a low delivery and very true on the wicket', and Henry Bishop, of the Carlton Club, whom the paper acclaimed as 'a first-class longstop'.

Left: Frank Allan who dropped out of the First Test because he preferred to meet old friends at the Warrnambool Show. — Illustrated News.

The legendary W.G. Grace as he appeared to Australian opponents on his two pioneering tours of Australia. Right, the concentration that produced 54,896 first-class runs and 126 centuries. — George Beldam.

The shock of this first defeat can barely have passed when the inexperienced organisers of the tour sent Grace's side on a coach journey in intense heat over bumpy roads to Ballarat. Here in a temperature of 100 degrees W.G. made 126, his brother Fred 112, and England 440. Ballarat — whose players included Tom Wills, Allan, Costick and Gaggin, all of whom had played in the previous match at the M.C.G. — scored 276 in reply and the match was drawn. Worse was to follow as the tourists were moved 74 miles by Cobb & Co. coach from Ballarat to Stawell over a rough bush track 'quite undeserving the name of a road'. The local secretary and other enthusiasts greeted Grace's men 20 miles from town and from four miles out two brass bands played them into town. One of the horses took fright at the noise created by the bands and overturned a trap but nobody was injured.

Grace said the pitch at Stawell was 'execrable' and the match against Twenty Two of Stawell 'a ludicrous farce'. One ball from a Stawell slow bowler stuck in the pitch and never reached the batsman. Despite dropped catches Grace's team scored only 43, but the Stawell Twenty Two

'accustomed to such wickets kept us in the field for a couple of hours' and made 71. Stawell won by 10 wickets.

The next match was at Warrnambool, which they reached after changing coaches at 4.30 in the morning at Ararat. The tracks were muddy and wet and the coach wheels sank to their axles. All the Englishmen were soaked to their skins and after 5¼ hours they covered the 31 miles to Hexham, where B.B. Cooper, Jupp, Lillywhite, McIntyre, Southerton, and Humphrey remained behind to lighten the load. They reached Warrnambool at 11.30 p.m. after a coach ride of 19 hours. Cooper, Wills, Allan, Gaggin, and Conway were waiting at Warrnambool to play against them again. Southerton caught up with the main party before play began, however, and took a hat-trick that enabled the Englishmen to win by 9 wickets.

From Warrnambool Grace's team made a 'wretched trip' of 16 hours by sea to Melbourne, where they caught another ship to take them to Sydney to play Eighteen of New South Wales — a side that included F.R. Spofforth, who was just starting to gain prominence as a right-arm bowler. England were dismissed for 92 and 90. The New South Wales Eighteen made 127 and 9 for 57 to win by 8 wickets. One of the stars of the New South Wales team was a left-hand round-arm bowler named Joseph Coates, who had appeared for Victoria in the first match of Grace's tour. Coates took 6 for 29 in England's first innings in Sydney. Mercifully, the next match, against Maitland, was washed out and the Englishmen journeyed instead to Bathurst by coach for an 8-wickets win.

Back in Sydney after a tiring return coach ride Grace's men had a good win over a Combined Victoria and New South Wales Fifteen. During this match a dismissed New South Wales batsman left the field only to be persuaded by team-mates in the pavilion that he was not out. He returned to continue batting. Grace took his players off until sanity prevailed and one of the three New South Wales batsmen at the wicket left. The local team for this absorbing match included several fine young players who were just emerging as colonial stars, including Caffyn's protege Charles Bannerman, Dave Gregory, and Nat Thompson, who were supported by the Victorian heroes Cooper, Costick, and Conway. W.G. Grace made a stylish 73 in England's second innings of 236, twice hitting the ball over the fence.

Nottinghamshire round-arm bowler Alfred Shaw, who on March 15, 1878, in Melbourne bowled the first ball in Tests to Australia's English-born opener Charles Bannerman. He toured Australia four times.
— M.C.C. Collection at Lord's.

Alick and Charles Bannerman, first brothers to play Test cricket for Australia. Charles scored the first-ever Test century, retiring hurt with a match-winning 165. — Albert Gregory Collection.

Joe Clayton, first
secretary of the New
South Wales Cricket
Association. The
inaugural meeting was
held in the open in the
Sydney Domain.
— New South Wales
Cricket Assoc.

Billy Murdoch, Australia's
second cricket captain
and a man who played a
major role in winning
international recognition
for Australia. Here he
plays the draw shot,
glancing the ball between
his legs.
— Jack Pollard
Collection.

G.H. Bailey, a fascinating
figure in Australia's first
Test team and in the first
team to tour England. He
was born in Colombo,
then capital of Ceylon
(now Sri Lanka), educated
in England, and worked
all his life in Tasmania as
a banker.
— Ric Smith.

Apart from W.G. Grace, the most frequent recipient of invitations to tour Australia was this highly principled Yorkshireman, Lord Hawke. When he finally toured in 1887-88, his father died and he had to return home, handing the English team over to G.F. Vernon. — Ken Piesse, Australian Cricketer.

Another unpleasant voyage took them back to Melbourne for wins over Twenty Two of Sandhurst and Twenty Two of Castlemaine, where a local umpire disallowed an appeal for stumping by England's wicket-keeper G.A. Bush on the grounds that he had 'the tip of his nose in front of the wicket when he dislodged the bails'. By now the Englishmen had become accustomed to all the travelling and generous hospitality and, showing some of their best form of the tour, they beat Fifteen of Victoria by 7 wickets before sailing to Tasmania for two matches. They won the first against Twenty Two of Tasmania by an innngs and then defeated Twenty Two of southern Tasmania in a match made memorable by an innings of 154 from G.F. Grace, then far and away the highest score by an Englishman in Australia.

Further storms and seasickness overtook the Englishmen on the voyage to Adelaide for the next stage of the trip. They were the first English side to appear in South Australia but they had to travel from Adelaide for a further 100-odd miles to Kadina on Yorke Peninsula for their first match in that State. The South Australian Cricket Association had declined to put up the guarantee sought by Grace's side but the Kadina Club agreed to pay it. The Englishmen travelled from Adelaide to Kadina in a coach driven by Clem Hill's father. Grace wrote:

> When we reached Kadina we went out in search of the wicket. And a search it really proved. Finally when we came to an open space we asked to be directed to the cricket ground and were told this was it. There was scarcely a blade of grass to be seen and the whole area was covered by stones. On the morning of the match a bushel of pebbles was swept up.

Tom Wills had been coaching Kadina cricketers for weeks, and the side was reinforced by outstanding Adelaide players J.E. Gooden, S. Morcom and J. Chittleborough. Kadina batted first but the first 6 wickets fell for 2 runs. Gooden was wildly cheered when he hit a four to take the score to 11 for 8, but 19 Kadina wickets fell by the time the scored reached 25. Then Paqualin and Mottle staged a stand, scoring 7 each to take the innings total to 42. McIntyre took 9 for 4 and Southerton 11 for 29, with two run-outs. England were all out for 64 just before stumps on the first day, with W.G. Grace making 5.

The Twenty Two of Kadina were all out in their second innings for 13, of which only 8 runs came from the bat. The innings featured sixteen ducks and a top score of 2. McIntyre took 7 for 1 off 83 balls, Lillywhite 13 for 7 from 84 balls. Although they had won by an innings and 9 runs, England batted again to give the spectators some entertainment and W.G. Grace made 52 out of 102. As the day ended, word came from Adelaide that the S.A.C.A. had raised some money and still wanted Grace's team to appear at Adelaide Oval. Grace agreed to a three-day match for £110, plus half the takings. The Englishmen travelled through the night and when they arrived, at 3.30 p.m. they were taken straight on to the oval. The Twenty Two of Adelaide made 63 and 82, finding Lillywhite and Southerton far too clever for them. England made 108 in their first innings. W.G. Grace was out for 6 when Alexander Crooks took an historic catch.

Crooks bounced to overnight fame when he reached over the chains and caught a big hit from Grace in one hand. Grace objected vehemently, arguing that the ball had been caught beyond the boundary, but the umpire ignored his protests and insisted that he leave the crease. England had little trouble scoring the runs needed to win in their second innings for the loss of only 3 wickets, but they batted on for the benefit of a large crowd until they reached 73. This Adelaide match was such a financial success that the association made a grant of £150 to the Kadina Club, who claimed they had exclusive rights to Grace's team in South Australia and had threatened to sue the association. The Kadina Club had lost £700 in staging their match with the Englishmen, a poor reward for a bold promotion.

The Adelaide appearance of Grace's third English team, the last part of their pioneering romp through sparsely settled areas of Australia, brought wide notoriety to Crooks, the man who took the disputed boundary catch to dismiss W.G. The S.A.C.A. made him their treasurer and in 1882, when the Commercial Bank of South Australia needed a general manager to succeed a man who had been far too careless in lending the bank's money, they appointed Crooks. Unhappily, Crooks proved a better fieldsman than a banker, and over the next few years ran the bank into a debt of £1,162,679. Crooks went to gaol for eight years, the bank's accountant for six years, and the bank disappeared, paying creditors about three shillings in the pound.

Percy ("Greatheart") McDonnell, one of the first of Australia's big-hitting batsmen. He was run out when he appeared certain to become the first Australian to hit a century in each innings of a match. He made 124 and 83 at Adelaide in 1884-85.
— Jack Pollard Collection.

A charming portrait of the first great Australian bowler, Fred Spofforth. He was born in the Sydney suburb of Balmain but spent much of his childhood in New Zealand.
— Albert Gregory Collection.

Success of the English tour under W.G. Grace was in part the result of the great man's unfailing goodwill despite an absurd itinerary, combined with his instinctive flair for gamesmanship. In between jumping on and off ships and in and out of coaches, he headed his side's batting averages

William Henry Cooper, one of Australia's first leg-spinners. He was born at Maidstone, Kent, but did not take up cricket seriously until he was 27. In his Test debut he took 9 for 200, bowling 98.2 overs. Paul Sheahan, Australian player in the 1960s, was his great grandson.
– Albert Gregory Collection.

The first grandstand at Adelaide Oval, which was opened in 1882. Later a bicycle track was built inside the fence.
— South Australian Cricket Association.

with 711 runs at 35.55, including a masterly innings of 126. The next highest run-scorer was his brother, G.F. Grace, who made 398 runs at 25.22, top score 154. The team's bowling averages were headed by James Lillywhite, whose 172 wickets cost only 2.29 each. Southerton's 145 wickets were more expensive at 5.6 runs apiece, and W.G. chipped in with 65 wickets at 7.5 from his round-armers. The main lesson of the tour, however, was that Australian standards had improved dramatically in a remarkably short time. The colony was not far off playing England on level terms.

James Lillywhite captained the fourth English team to visit Australia in the summer of 1876–77, an all-professional outfit comprising players from Nottinghamshire, Surrey, Sussex, and Yorkshire, four of whom (Lillywhite, Jupp, Greenwood, and Southerton) had been in the previous English team led by W.G. Grace. The team played twenty-three matches, twenty against the odds and three on level terms. Of the matches on level terms, England won one, drew one, and lost one; of the matches against the odds, England won ten, lost three, and left seven unfinished. The tour was notable once again for many wild and adventurous trips by sea and land, heavy betting among spectators, and the primitive grounds on which the Englishmen were invited to play. On Sydney's

Moore Park that summer Marlborough were all out for 0 against Undaunted, the first instance of this in Australia.

Despite all the handicaps, the visit of Lillywhite's fourth English team was an historic event, for it marked the beginning of Test cricket. At Adelaide the tourists found that the groundsman was afraid to use the roller for fear of bruising the turf. At Ararat the only available roller was made of wood and only 10 inches in diameter. In New Zealand the tourists' coach stuck in the mud and they spent the night in inky darkness in a rising torrent in Otira Gorge. At Goulburn outfieldsmen were joined by young kangaroos. At Christchurch, England took the field after a road journey of 80 hours. Only tough, hardy men could have carried off such a tour without protest, even though they were deluged with wildly generous hospitality, banquets, special theatre performances, and boisterous dressing-room song fests by hosts ready to spend their last penny to ensure that they enjoyed themselves.

Lillywhite was a steady, shrewd leader, ever ready with advice to players, committees, or groundsmen. He magnanimously agreed to go ahead with what became known as the first of all Tests although England had arrived only the previous day, after a rough voyage from New Zealand with most of the players badly seasick. The match was variously advertised as 'All England versus All Australia' and 'United England versus United Australia', and Lillywhite was aware that weeks of preparation had gone into the staging of the match at the Melbourne Cricket Ground.

The Victorian Cricketers' Association apparently believed that a team comprising the best players from New South Wales and Victoria could fully extend Lillywhite's team. They had been encouraged by the victories of Fifteens of New South Wales and of Victoria in Sydney and Melbourne games against the tourists. The time appeared right for a full-scale test of the colony's standards on level terms. Lillywhite agreed, and so did his Australian adviser John Conway. No thought was given, however, to approaching New South Wales players through the New South Wales Cricket Associations and in staging the match the V.C.A. went straight to the players. They came across unexpected difficulties when Fred Spofforth refused to play unless he could have Billy Murdoch as his wicket-keeper, and Edwin Evans, probably Australia's finest all-rounder at the time, declined to play, for personal reasons.

The selectors stuck with John McCarthy Blackham as wicket-keeper, which meant that Spofforth would not play. Then the skilful Frank Allan broke his promise to play, withdrawing on the grounds that the Test was to be played at the same time as an agricultural show and he could not miss the chance of mixing with old friends. Allan, whom one critic had described as 'the bowler of the century', thus opened the way for the inclusion of one of the most fascinating of all Test cricketers, Billy Midwinter. The Melbourne *Argus* dismissed Allan with this comment: 'Great as is Allan's value on the field, his capriciousness is still greater, and we trust that for the future he will be studiously left in that retirement which he professes to be so loth to leave'.

Phil Sheridan, one of the first trustees (1875) of the Sydney Cricket Ground, running the ground with great skill for 35 years. The Sheridan stand is named after him.
— Philip Derriman.

John McCarthy Blackham, the prince of wicket-keepers. He kept for Australia in each of the first 17 Tests and dropped out in the 18th to support team-mates' demands for more pay. — Melbourne Cricket Ground Collection.

England were also below strength, as Edward Pooley, their No. 1 wicket-keeper, had been left in a New Zealand gaol to face a charge of malicious damage. This charge arose from a brawl in a hotel bar where Pooley had bet a Christchurch man he could forecast each of the local Eighteen's individual scores against England. Pooley wrote down 0 beside each player and when half of them made ducks offered a shilling for each wrong guess while claiming a pound for every correct forecast. Pooley was acquitted of the charge but fined for the damage done.

To captain the Australian team for the match, the players elected 6 feet 2 inch heavily bearded Dave Gregory, an intriguing choice by a predominantly Victorian team for a Melbourne match. Dave Gregory and his brothers Ned and Charlie had achieved distinction by defeating Victoria's finest — Tom Wills, John Conway, and Sam Costick — before 5000 Sydney spectators for a purse of £100. Of the eleven players led by Gregory in the first Test, five had been born in Britain and one in India. The team was: C. Bannerman, J.M. Blackham, B.B. Cooper, T.W. Garrett, D.W. Gregory (Captain), E.J. Gregory, J.H. Hodges, T.P. Horan, T. Kendall, W.E. Midwinter, N. Thompson.

Dave Gregory won the toss and at 1 p.m. on 15 March 1877, Charles Bannerman and Nat Thompson strode out on to the Melbourne Cricket Ground to open for Australia. In only his seventh first-class match, Bannerman, born at Woolwich, England, twenty-five years earlier, faced the first ball in Test cricket from the experienced Nottinghamshire round-arm bowler Alfred Shaw. Bannerman blocked the first ball and took a single, the first run in Tests, off the second ball, but in the second over Thompson, who had also had a single from Shaw, was bowled by Yorkshireman Allen Hill — the first wicket to fall in Tests. Play proceeded until 5 p.m., with a 50-minute spell for lunch and no tea break. At the end of the day Australia were 6 for 166, with Bannerman, hitting with great freedom and dramatic vigour, on 126. His partners, particularly Tom Horan and Bransby Cooper, sensed that Bannerman had the measure of the English bowling and played a big part by defending doggedly at the other end.

A crowd of 3000 watched the first day's play, well represented with what Melbourne newspapers called youth and beauty. 'Many of them took more than a passing interest in the game', one paper observed. Thomas Armitage, the Yorkshire lob bowler, amused the crowd with balls designed to pass over the batsmen's heads and hit the bails. His deliveries could only have been reached with a clothes prop, according to one paper. When his high lobs failed, Armitage resorted to grubbers, a style regarded by colonials as decadent and which they had long since discarded. The crowd's sympathy went to Ned Gregory who, in the midst of the stubborn Australian batting, made Test cricket's first duck.

On the second day Bannerman took his score to 165 before a ball from Ulyett — who at times bowled dangerously short as well as very fast — split Bannerman's finger and caused his retirement. Australia were then 240 and added only another 5 runs before the innings closed. The injury undoubtedly robbed Bannerman of the honour of batting right through the very first Test innings. Bannerman had not given a chance in 4 hours 45 minutes of batting and had hit eighteen fours. The next highest score in Australia's innings was Garrett's 18 not out and to get it Garrett had the benefit of being missed by substitute wicket-keeper John Selby.

One of the first Australian-born players to appear for an English County was Tasmanian Harold Hale, who was in the Gloucestershire side with W.G. Grace after playing for Cambridge University. This shot shows Gloucestershire's amateurs in 1886 (L to R): J.A. Bush, A.D. Greene, Hale, D.D. Radcliffe, G. Francis and W.G.
— Ric Finlay.

*Above: Charles, Dave and
Edward ("Ned") Gregory.
Charles, first batsman to
score a triple century in
Australia, died at 32.
Dave was Australia's first
cricket captain. Ned was
the first curator of Sydney
Cricket Ground and
helped make it a great
ground.
— Albert Gregory
Collection.*

*Right: Syd and Charles
Gregory with their father
Ned (seated). Ned made
the first duck by an
Australian Test cricketer
in 1877, when he played
for the Civil and Military
club in Sydney, where the
S.C.G. was their home
ground.
— Albert Gregory
Collection.*

England's first innings began at 3.30 p.m. on the second day, with the openers, Henry Jupp and Selby, giving the Australians a lesson in smart running between wickets. They moved to 23 with 'no false starts but each backing up the other and seizing every opportunity', before Selby was caught off Hodges. A fine stand then ensued in which Charlwood hit Hodges for several fours. Forced to make a double bowling change, Gregory brought on Midwinter and Garrett, and at 79 Charlwood was caught by wicket-keeper Blackham off Midwinter for 36. Jupp went on to top-score with 63 in England's total of 196, 49 runs in arrears. The Australians said that Jupp broke his wicket playing back early in his innings but the umpire missed it.

Only Paddy Horan (20) and Midwinter (17) offered any resistance in Australia's second innings of 104. Bannerman was clearly unhappy about batting with a bandaged hand and was clean bowled by a fast one from Ulyett. Shaw took 5 for 38 to go with his 3 for 51 in Australia's first innings. Needing 154 to win, England were hot favourites in the betting tents, but always struggled against Tom Kendall's fast left-armers. Selby and Ulyett added 40 in a plucky stand but England were all out for 108, giving Australia victory by 45 runs. Kendall's match-winning 7 for 55 was his best performance ever and he shared match honours with Bannerman. Midwinter was not far behind, with match figures of 6 for 101, including 5 for 78 in England's first innings when 21 of his 54 four-ball overs were maidens.

Author Ray Robinson, a painstaking researcher, calculated that during the match Dave Gregory gave Melbourne bowlers 159 overs compared with 42 by the Sydney men and that the Victorians took 17 of the 20 English wickets. The V.C.A. had gold medals specially minted for all the Australians but gave Dave Gregory a slightly larger one for captaining the side with a skill and authority respected by all. Dave Gregory and Conway — who, as selectors for the first Test, had refused to give in to Spofforth's demands — brought Spofforth in for the return match a fortnight later in Melbourne but insisted that Blackham remain as wicket-keeper. Murdoch was added to the side in place of Dave's brother Ned but was not given the gloves. Blackham justified the selectors' faith in him by brilliantly stumping Shaw in Spofforth's third over to break the English opening stand, standing right up on the stumps to take Spofforth's fastest balls in a manner previously considered impossible.

John Conway, the man who conceived the first tour of England by a white Australian team and carried it off despite opposition.

Below: A group of famous cricketers photographed at The Oval in 1880, with W.G. Grace standing in the middle of the front row in a striped blazer, holding a ball.
— Mitchell Library, Sydney.

England won the second Test by 4 wickets but there was clearly little between the teams. Like the first Test, the match went into the fourth day. Australia began with 122 in their first innings, Midwinter top-scoring with 31, and England took a lead of 139 with a solid team batting effort in which Ulyett top-scored with 52. Australia fought back impressively in the second innings, Nat Thompson and Gregory batting attractively in an opening stand of 88. England began badly, chasing 121 to win, but Ulyett produced another game knock to make 63 runs, which saw England safely home. One critic was unimpressed by the quality of the England side. 'We would counsel whoever may enter into future speculations for importing an England XI to bear in mind the great improvement in colonial cricket, and not to imagine that anything will do for Australia,' he wrote.

Lillywhite, whose international career ended with the two Melbourne Tests, ensured that all his players received £150, plus expenses. The colonials received only their expenses, but collections were taken for Bannerman, Kendall, and Blackham. By their efforts the colonials aroused an enthusiasm for big cricket that has never abated. Dave Gregory and Conway tried to interest the New South Wales and Victorian associations in an English tour to capitalise on the fine results in the first two Tests at Melbourne but officials considered such a tour presumptuous.

Organising the first tour of England by a non-Aboriginal Australian team was thus left to the players, who put up their own money to help finance the trip, on the proviso that each would share in any profits. In England James Lillywhite acted as the team's advance agent by setting up matches and arranging accommodation.

Conway picked the team in consultation with Dave Gregory and simply wrote privately to each player, inviting him to join the side. The ailing Tom Wills could not go, but he joined Conway in contributing to tour funds. There were several unfortunate withdrawals, including Nat Thompson and Edwin Evans, and when the team played a series of matches in Australia and New Zealand to boost tour funds there was little support from officials. The team left for England to a lukewarm farewell. Not long after the boat sailed the team had a meeting which elected Dave Gregory (at thirty-two their oldest member) tour captain. The eleven players had been promised Midwinter's help when they got to England. Ahead of them, in the English summer of 1878, lay a heavy programme of matches, fifteen of them first-class and one of which would produce a victory of such magnitude that it established the reputation of Australian cricket for ever more.

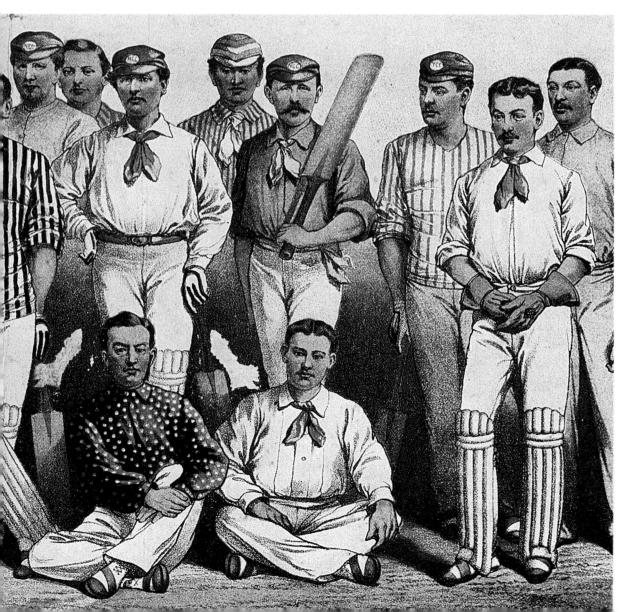

5. A Famous Victory

Before they left, the first Australian team to visit England bought an enormous canvas bag and had 'Australian Eleven' painted on it in bold letters. The players drew lots to decide who would carry the bag from match to match and as two men were needed to lift it the job came round about once a week. Only the very best cricketers owned bats or pads and the contents of the bag were much used. The players called the bag 'the caravan' and it went with them on 28 March 1878 when they sailed from Sydney in the *City of Sydney*, bound first for San Francisco. There they took a train to New York, and continued their trip aboard the *City of Berlin*, arriving in Liverpool on 13 May.

James Lillywhite had arranged a heavy programme of thirty-seven matches, twenty of them against the odds, and even with the assistance of Midwinter they knew that their stamina and health would be tested to the limit. Six of the team selected by Dave Gregory and John Conway were from New South Wales — Alex and Charles Bannerman, Tom Garrett, Billy Murdoch, Fred Spofforth, and Gregory; four from Victoria — Jack Blackham, Frank Allan, Harry Boyle, and Tom Horan; and one from Tasmania — George Bailey, the Colombo-born Tasmanian banker-batsman. The players wore blue-and-white sashes and blue-and-white stripes on their caps, which had no peaks. Most took the field wearing a tie or kerchief. Gregory was thirty-two, Allan twenty-eight, and all the others were under twenty-five. Garrett, who had not turned twenty when they arrived, was the team's baby. They each paid £50 towards tour expenses, three times the fare to England.

The historic first Australian team to tour England each contributed to tour costs. They were in action for 13 months, playing matches in Australia before and after the English visit. L to R: Back, J.M. Blackham, T. Horan, G.H. Bailey, D.W. Gregory (captain), J. Conway (manager), A.C. Bannerman, C. Bannerman, W.L. Murdoch; Front, F.R. Spofforth, F. Allan, W.E. Midwinter, T.W. Garrett, H.F. Boyle.
— M.C.C. Collection at Lord's.

*A.N. ("Monkey") Hornby, who opened for the M.C.C. with W.G. Grace on May 27, 1878, when Australia beat the cream of English cricket in an afternoon. M.C.C. made 33 and 19.
— Melbourne Cricket Ground Museum.*

*Harry Boyle, who hit the stumps five times to take 6 for 3 in Australia's dramatic win over M.C.C. in 1878. Boyle had 9 for 17 in a match that established Australia's reputation.
— Albert Gregory Collection.*

Midwinter, who had been born in Gloucestershire, joined them for the first match against Nottingham in appalling weather which made it impossible for the Australians to practise before play began. The Australians wore silk shirts and had to dive into their bags for their heaviest sweaters. Midwinter alone had experience of batting on saturated pitches and he alone reached double figures as the Australians were bundled out for 63. Dave Gregory and Billy Murdoch both made ducks. 'What on earth induced us to come all this way', Gregory moaned. 'I wish I was back in Sydney with the sun on my back.' Shaw who had done so well in Australia, took 5 for 20.

Nottinghamshire scored 153, with Selby batting splendidly for 66. Set to score 90 to avoid an innings defeat, the Australians were all out in their second innings for 76, Garrett top-scoring with 21. This time Shaw took 6 for 35. The only consolation for the Australians was Horan's 5 for 30 in the Nottinghamshire innings. For such a speculative tour, it is impossible to imagine a worse start than defeat by an innings inside a single day. It was a forlorn lot who left their London hotel for the next match at Lord's against the Marylebone Club and Ground.

The noted English cricket historian H.S. Altham reported the first day's play in these words:

> The Australians drove in their brake on to Lord's ground, practically unrecognised by the 500 or so spectators that had by then mustered. Twelve hours later England was ringing with the news that the flower of English cricket had been beaten in a single day, and the crowds came flocking to the Tavistock Hotel in Convent Garden to look at the men who had thus flung open a new era in the history of the game.

W.G. Grace and A.N. Hornby opened for the M.C.C. just after noon on 27 May 1878, and when Grace hit the first ball for four the crowd sat back to watch his customary display of hammering bowlers all over the paddock. 'These can't be Australians; they aren't black,' one M.C.C. member commented, apparently reflecting on the Aboriginal tour ten years earlier. It was a warm day and the Australians held every catch. With Spofforth and Boyle at their deadly best, they had M.C.C. out for 33. Midwinter started the rout by stealing round from his position at fine leg behind the doctor's vast back and catching him near square leg. With the score at 2 for 25, Spofforth took 6 wickets for 4 runs, including a hat-trick, off 23 balls. When Australia were out for 41, an 8-run lead, news of the sensational cricket spread around London and when the M.C.C. second innings began 5000 spectators were on hand, with others flooding in.

They were not disappointed. Spofforth had W.G. Grace missed off his first ball and bowled him with his second. But Boyle took the bowling honours for Australia, hitting the stumps five times to take 6 for 3. Spofforth had 4 for 16 and M.C.C. were all out for 19, with only W. Flowers reaching double figures. Spofforth's match figures were 10 for 20, Boyle's 9 for 17. Australia scored the 12 runs needed to win for the loss of Charles Bannerman's wicket and at 5.40 p.m. Paddy Horan made the winning hit. Altham said the scene as the Australians completed this famous victory 'beggared description' and the Australians could not have been more heartily cheered if the scene of their win had been Sydney or Melbourne. For the raw colonial boys to overwhelm the mighty M.C.C. was like a canoe sinking a gunboat, said Ray Robinson. All England took notice. In music halls and theatres, lines were changed to exploit the win. *Punch* printed this parody of one of Lord Byron's poems:

The Australians came down like a wolf from the fold,
The Marylebone cracks for a trifle were bowled,
Our Grace before dinner was very soon done
And Grace after dinner did not get a run.

Billy Midwinter, of Gloucestershire, Victoria, Australia and England. W.G. Grace's "kidnapping" of him badly weakened the first Australian team in England.
— Mitchell Library, Sydney.

The first Australian white touring team photographed at Niagara Falls on their way home (L to R): Back, Boyle, Murdoch, Gibbs (assistant manager), Garrett, Gregory, Horan, Allan; Front, Spofforth, Conway (manager), A.C. Bannerman, Blackham, Bailey. Absent: C. Bannerman.
— J.C. Davis Collection.

Tom Garrett, who was 18 years and 232 days old when he played in the first Test against England at Melbourne in 1877. He was one of the big successes of Australia's first tour of England the following year. — Jack Pollard Collection.

Alick Bannerman who made his Test debut against Lord Harris' side in 1878-79, played in 28 Tests altogether and made six trips to England. — Albert Gregory Collection.

A London paper called the *Globe* said that seldom in the annals of cricket had so small a score been made by the M.C.C. and never had so severe a humiliation been inflicted individually and collectively upon members of the club. 'The Eleven was as good a one as could be found to represent London and England, and probably the best the club has ever turned out,' said the *Globe*. 'Yet its best batsmen were bowled out one after another as if they were novices.' The London *Home News* said that although the Australians had some excellent bats and fielded brilliantly, bowling was their great strength. 'Left-handed Allan is known as 'Bowler of the Century'; 'Boyle is described as the "very devil", but Mr. Spofforth, the "Demon Bowler", carries off the palm,' said *Home News*. 'Spofforth's delivery is quite appalling; and balls thunder in like cannon shot.'

In just over 4 hours the international reputation of Australian cricket had been established. And the Australians showed it was no fluke by following with a striking 6-wicket win over the powerful Yorkshire Eleven. Spofforth took 4 for 30 and 5 for 31 in Yorkshire's innings of 72 and 73. Boyle had 5 for 32 in Yorkshire's first innings. The Australians batted soundly, with five men who had had very little practice reaching double figures. Murdoch finally got his chance to keep wicket in this match but showed that he was far inferior to Blackham.

Australia had its third handsome victory in a row by beating Surrey at The Oval, Spofforth taking 8 for 52 and 3 for 42. By now Midwinter's all-round ability had proved invaluable to the Australians for he always seemed able to take wickets or make runs when they were needed. He top-scored against Surrey with 32 out of 110 in the first innings. Surrey made 107 and 80 and Australia lost 5 wickets scoring the 78 runs required to win. Gregory's captaincy was also widely praised. The London *Standard* observed:

He changes the bowling with promptitude and excellent judgement and varies his field with quick appreciation of the peculiarities of different batsmen. He realises that his business is to get the other side out as soon as possible and not to prolong the innings by a series of useless maiden overs, which while they gratify the bowler's vanity, weary the field and the spectators.

The only criticism of Gregory's team was for the annoyance they showed when umpires ruled against them.

Midwinter had played ten innings for the Australians when he went to play for them against Middlesex at Lord's. He had padded up with Charles Bannerman to open the innings when W.G. Grace burst into the dressing-room and persuaded Midwinter that instead of playing for Australia he was duty-bound to appear across the Thames at The Oval for his native Gloucestershire against Surrey. W.G. bundled Midwinter into a carriage he had waiting and sped off for The Oval. The Australian manager, John Conway — Midwinter's schoolmate from their days on the Bendigo goldfields — and the Australian captain Dave Gregory, hired another carriage and chased the kidnappers.

W.G. Grace was waiting for them outside The Oval gates and a furious exchange occurred during which Grace called the Australians 'a nasty lot of sneaks'. Grace stood firm and the Australians returned to Lord's without Midwinter. Weeks of bitter letter-writing followed between the Australians and the Gloucstershire Club, who claimed that Midwinter was 'a Gloucestershire man who promised Dr. Grace he would play for the county in all matches'. The county said that it felt W.G. Grace's 'stormy language' was justified because the Australians had induced Midwinter to forget his bonds with the county by offering him more money than the county could afford. Eventually W.G. apologised and Gloucestershire agreed to play the Australians at Bristol. Midwinter dropped out through injury and in a real grudge match the Australians thrashed the county.

Badly weakened by the loss of Midwinter, the Australians had to call on a Victorian medical student, H.W. Tennant, to assist them. Manager Conway also chipped in with a useful 58 runs in two innings. After the victory over M.C.C. at Lord's everybody wanted to play the Australians. As a result, they took on extra matches which later caused disagreement among statisticians about the total number played. There seems no reason to doubt Conway's figure of forty-one matches — four more than in the original schedule — as he was closest to the arrangements. Conway said that when four of the agreed thirty-seven games finished inside two days the Australians agreed to play additional games so as not to disappoint spectators.

The England team that toured Australia in 1878-79 under Lord Harris. The team contained only two professionals Ulyett and Emmett and were billed as the "Gentlemen Of England."
— Mitchell Library, Sydney.

Billy Murdoch with W.G. Grace. Murdoch's dismissal at Sydney in 1878-79 caused the riot in which Lord Harris was attacked by larrikins.
— Albert Gregory Collection.

Sir Edmund Barton, one of the umpires in the Sydney riot, and the first Prime Minister of Australia. He said the run out decision against Murdoch that caused the Sydney riot was correct. — Mitchell Library, Sydney.

The second Australian team to tour England — in 1880 — which found matches hard to get because of the Sydney riot (L to R): Back G.E. Palmer, W.H. Moule, G.J. Bonnor, G. Alexander (manager), T.W. Groube; Centre, F.R. Spofforth, H.F. Boyle, W.L. Murdoch (captain), P.S. McDonnell, A.C. Bannerman; Front, A.H. Jarvis, J. Slight, J.M. Blackham.
— Public Library of Victoria.

*Above: William Caffyn,
on his return to England
after his seven years
coaching in Australia.
Charles Bannerman,
Australia's first great
batsman, was one of his
pupils.
— Jack Pollard Collection*

*Lord Harris, who had to
be persuaded to forget the
hooliganism in Sydney so
that Australia and
England could meet in the
1880 Test at the Oval, the
first on English soil.
— Melbourne Cricket
Ground Museum.*

Some of the matches against the odds produced astounding figures. Boyle had the amazing figures of 7 wickets with his last eight balls against Eighteen of Elland. At Longsight the locals included W.G. Grace in their Eighteen, but Spofforth (8 for 38 and 5 for 28) and Boyle (7 for 21 and 3 for 23) confounded hopes that this would bring a local victory. Grace got some prestige back when he led the Gentlemen to an innings win over the Australians. The Gentlemen scored 139 and then had Australia out for 75 and 63.

Australian P.E. Reynolds, in his book on the tour, said:

The Australians stood pluckily to their work in all their matches, notwithstanding that some of the crack players followed them from county to county, a by no means fair proceeding; and that the so-called Gentlemen cricketers team who beat them at Prince's was not really composed of Gentlemen cricketers. Messrs W.G. Grace and Gilbert received a sum of £60 for their services, and when Mr. Conway objected, it was asserted that W.G. Grace, G.F. Grace and Gilbert were invariably paid for playing. It is manifestly unfair that such men should be included in an Amateur and Gentlemen team.

The Australians had their setbacks on this historic tour but even when they lost played attractively. Perhaps their finest win apart from that over M.C.C. at Lord's was over Leicestershire. Trailing by 63 runs on the first innings, the Australians were set 210 runs to win and they did so for the loss of only 2 wickets. Charles Bannerman hit the first ball of the innngs for 4 blocked the next, and hit the last two balls of the four-ball over for 4. Bannerman went on to 133, the first century by an Australian in England, a masterly mixture of copybook strokes and powerful hitting. Charles Bannerman topped the English tour batting averages with 723 runs at 24.1 and was the sole century-maker. On the way home he also scored a century against Canada at Montreal. Clearly Caffyn was justified in acclaiming Bannerman as his outstanding pupil.

The strain of the long tour finally erupted when Gregory's side played in Philadelphia, where local sides had played touring international sides since 1859. Gregory led his players from the field when an umpire disallowed an appeal by Blackham. In the dressing-room Philadelphian officials quickly explained to the Australians that unless they returned to the field immediately, payment on a cheque the Australians had been given that morning to cover expenses would be stopped and they would not be given their agreed share of the takings. Gregory took his players back on to the field and the match ended in a tense draw after Australia had led on the first innings by 46 runs. The result in this match — the first between Philadephia and a national team on level terms — help build the international reputation of Philadelphian cricket.

The thirteen-month tour by Gregory's team ended with several matches in Australia after they arrived home. Each player received £750, a handsome dividend on the £50 invested, but they can be fairly said to have earned every penny. Spofforth, for example, took 281 wickets on the preliminary tour of Australia and New Zealand, 326 in England, 69 in Canada and the United States on the way home, and 88 on the final swing round Australia — a total of 764 wickets at a cost of 6.08 each. Among his best analyses were 19 for 108 against Fifteen of New South Wales, 17 for 125 against Eighteen of South Australia, 22 wickets in the match against Hawkes Bay, and 20 for 64 against Auckland. Boyle, Allan and Garrett also did an immense amount of bowling and all had days that produced spectacular figures.

George Bonnor, the giant (6ft 6in, 16st 7lb) from Bathurst in the mid-west of New South Wales, who in the 1880 Test at The Oval hit a ball so high the batsmen were on their third run when E.F. Grace caught it.
— Albert Gregory Collection.

The first South Australian team to play Victoria on level terms in November, 1880, L to R, Standing J. Chittleborough, J. Noel, H.A. Gooden, J. Hide; Centre, T.O. Richards, W. Bullough, J.E. Gooden (captain), A. Slight, A.M. Pettinger; Front, J.F. King, G. Giffen, W. Slight, J.E. Goodfellow.
— Victorian Cricket Association.

Although they did not play a Test, the first Australian team to tour England lost only four eleven-a-side matches — for an outfit that, following the loss of Midwinter, had only eleven players this was a prodigious result from such a long tour. Tactically, they were seldom defeated but one such notable occasion was when Edward Lyttelton led his famous Cambridge Eleven to victory over them. Lyttelton, one of the best cutters of all time, made 72 runs, without a third man to stop his flow of boundaries. They were punctual and smart in appearance, no matter who was bowling, and they fell quickly into their places. Only their sportsmanship disappointed enthusiasts in England and America, and this was to have unfortunate repercussions.

The Melbourne Cricket Club's efforts to sponsor a tour by an English amateur team finally proved successful when George Robert Canning, the fourth Lord Harris, brought a team to Australia in 1878–79. Lord Harris, after assessing his side, found that he had to include the professional bowlers, George Ulyett and Tom Emmett, because amateur bowlers of quality could not afford the trip. Lord Harris's team arrived in Adelaide on the day the Australian team led by Dave Gregory arrived home from England. The Englishmen began with an easy win over Eighteen of South Australia, Emmett taking 9 for 45 and 5 for 58. Fifteen of Victoria held England to a draw in the following match at Melbourne, with a second innings in which Donald Campbell, of the East Melbourne Club, scored a superb 128, which, of course, could not be counted in the first-class figures for his career.

On 2 January 1879 at the Melbourne Cricket Ground a match began between Lord Harris's side and an Australian team recently returned from England. This was billed at the time as 'Gentlemen of England versus the Australian XI', but it was later recognised as the third Test between the countries, which enabled three Australians (Allan, Alick Bannerman, and Boyle) and nine Englishmen (C.A. Absolom, the Fourth Lord Harris, L. Hone, A.N. Hornby, A.P. Lucas, F.A. Mackinnon [35th chief of the Clan Mackinnon], V.P.F.A. Boyle, S.S. Schultz, and A.J. Webbe) to make their Test debuts. With England at 4 for 46 in their first innings Spofforth performed the first Test hat-trick to take England to 7 for 46. Absolom then hit out valiantly for 52 and England reached 113.

When Australia batted, 'Monkey' Hornby bowled seven successive overs of grubbers — all maidens — and clean bowled Allan, but Australia still scored 256. Spofforth was at his best in England's second innings of 160 and Australia were left to score only 19 to win. They accomplished this without loss to win by 10 wickets. Spofforth's figures were 6 for 48 and 7 for 62 (13 for 110 in the match), and he had the satisfaction of knocking the Mackinnon-of-Mackinnon's stumps right out of the ground in each innings.

Lord Harris was so impressed with the young Victorian George Coulthard, a ground bowler with Melbourne Cricket Club, that he engaged him as an umpire to accompany his team. Coulthard travelled with Lord Harris's players to matches against New South Wales — which England lost by five wickets — and against Eighteen of Bathurst. He went with the team to Sydney's Victoria Barracks for a match against Twenty Two of New South Wales, before the return match on level terms with New South Wales. The match against New South Wales began well for England, who scored 267 on the first day, 7 February 1879, and on the second day (Saturday) New South Wales were dismissed for 177 by 3.30 p.m. Murdoch, who batted bravely for 82 after opening New South Wales' first innings, opened again with Charles Bannerman but with the score on 19, Murdoch was given out by Coulthard, who had been criticised by the *Sydney Morning Herald* for a blatant error on the first day.

Coulthard's decision against Murdoch created uproar. Shouts of derision came from the pavilion where a well-known bookmaker urged the demonstrators on. Murdoch was the crowd's hero and spectators first of all shouted for him to return to the crease and then rushed on to the field. The Englishmen refused to continue until they left. Dave Gregory went out to object to Lord Harris about Coulthard's umpiring but when his lordship defended Coulthard bedlam broke out as more spectators crowded towards the pitch. In trying to defend Coulthard Lord Harris was struck by a larrikin with a stick. As Hornby dragged the culprit from the field he took several heavy blows. After half an hour the ground was cleared but the Englishmen remained adamant that there was no reason to replace Coulthard. All efforts to resume play failed as spectators kept returning to the field, and finally play was abandoned for the day.

Next day's newspapers claimed that two English players had insulted the crowd by calling them 'nothing but the sons of convicts'. Undoubtedly the ill-feeling Gregory had caused on tour in England by complaining about umpiring influenced the Englishmen's stand in Sydney, but the gamblers who openly conducted operations at the ground clearly provoked the rioters. The English fieldsmen in the best position to assess Coulthard's decision — point and cover — both insisted that the decision was fair. Lord Harris's ire increased, however, when some Sydney newspapers referred to the English cricketers 'as if we were strolling actors rather than a party of gentlemen'.

The match was completed, with England winning comfortably, and two of the main offenders in the Sydney riot were convicted and fined. The Melbourne matches that followed wound up the tour in an affable atmosphere and the Melbourne Cricket Club gave Lord Harris and his side a dinner. They had won two eleven-a-side matches and lost three, including the Test. Of the matches against the odds, England won five, lost three, and played five draws, with the two professionals Hornby and Emmett finishing on top of the batting and bowling averages. But those who thought the tour discussions had ended at the Melbourne Club's dinner were in for a rude shock, for on 1 April 1879 the London *Daily Telegraph* published Lord Harris's letter to a friend in which his lordship alleged that his team had been 'insulted and subjected to indignities it distresses us to look back on'. The letter described the Murdoch run-out in detail and Dave Gregory's request for Coulthard to be replaced:

I asked Gregory on what grounds the objection was raised, and he said at first general incompetence, but afterwads admitted that the objection was raised on account of the decision against Murdoch. I implored Murdoch as a friend, and for the sake of the New South Wales Cricket Association, which I warned him would be the sufferer for it, not to raise the objection but he refused. I at once returned to the wickets, and in defending Coulthard from attack by the mob, was struck by a larrikin with a stick. Hornby immediately seized this fellow but in taking him to the pavilion was struck in the face by a would-be deliverer of the larrikin, and had his shirt nearly torn off his back.

Four of the heroes of Australia's 1880 tour of England (L to R): Billy Murdoch, Fred Spofforth, Harry Boyle and Alick Bannerman. Murdoch's 153 in the only Test eclipsed Grace's 152. — State Library of Victoria.

Lord Harris's letter went on to say that he stayed on the field at the centre of the howling mob for fear that if his side left the field New South Wales could claim the match. Lord Harris said that he in turn had asked the other umpire, Edmund Barton (later Prime Minister of Australia), if England could claim the match as no batsmen had appeared. Barton replied: 'I'll give it to you in 2 minutes if the batsmen don't come out'. Gregory agreed to send Thompson out with Bannerman and they did in fact appear between demonstrations, but the repeated invasions of the ground by the crowd made it impossible to bowl a further ball.

When Lord Harris's letter appeared in Australian newspapers, the N.S.W.C.A. called a special meeting at which its secretary J.M. Gibson was instructed to send a strong reply to the *Daily Telegraph*. Gibson's letter stressed that the New South Wales public had been loud in their protests against the demonstrators and that the association had expressed profound regret at what had happened. Gibson's letter also said:

Lord Harris has led the British public to suppose that in New South Wales 'a party of gentlemen travelling through these colonies for the purpose of playing a few friendly games of cricket should have been insulted and subjected to indignities,' while the Press and inhabitants of Sydney showed neither surprise nor regret. We cannot let a libel on the people of New South Wales so unfounded as this pass without challenge . . . The imputation is especially odious to Australians, who claim to have maintained the manly, generous, and hospitable characteristics of the British race.

The bitterness aroused by this needless exchange of letters lingered for a long time and in 1880 the second Australian team under Billy Murdoch — Dave Gregory having retired to his paymaster's desk at the New South Wales Treasury and to care for his sixteen children — found matches hard to arrange. County secretaries argued that this tour was too soon after the riot at Sydney and that an Australian team would not be welcomed by English crowds. The Australians were confined initially to matches against clubs in the Midlands and northern England and their match with Yorkshire was classified as 'non-official'. W.G. Grace tried to arrange a match for the Australians at Lord's but was rebuffed by M.C.C. committeemen who reminded him of the fracas in Sydney. Lord Harris offered to intercede provided that the Australians stipulated their tour was for pleasure and that they played only for pleasure and accepted expenses only. The Australians declined. In a letter to *Sporting Life*, manager G. Alexander challenged either the Players or the Gentlemen to a match, but without effect. Finally — after the Australians had defeated Yorkshire, Leicestershire, and Gloucestershire in fine style — Lord Harris agreed to forget the past and he helped arrange the first-ever Test in England.

The area set aside for smokes at the M.C.G. during the final Test between Australia and 'Plum' Warner's 1903-04 English team — with not a woman in sight.
— Charles Nuttall.

W. MURDOCK.

J. BLACKHAM.

G. H. BAILEY.

F. SPOFFORTH.

D. W. GREGORY.

T. HORAN.

A. BANNERMAN.

F. ALLAN.

H. BOYLE.

T. GARRETT.

C. BANNERMAN

J. CONWAY.

The match began on 6 September 1880 at The Oval, with three Graces in the England team. Australia was without Spofforth, whose finger had been broken at Scarborough by a bowler whom the Australians said threw every ball. England won the toss and opened with a stand of 91 by W.G. and E.M. Grace before 20,814 spectators. Then W.G. and Alfred Lucas added 120 for the second wicket. Lord Harris made 52 and the youngest Grace, G.F., a duck, and England scored 420. On the second day Australia were out for 149, with 19,863 people in attendance, and followed on 271 behind. They began badly, losing 3 for 14, but Murdoch, who had deposed Boyle as captain in a team election on the way to England, put on 83 for the fourth wicket with McDonnell. At 8 for 187, Alexander defended doggedly while Murdoch attacked, but when Alexander was out England still led by 32 runs. William Moule, Australia's last man, stayed with Murdoch in a gallant 10th wicket stand of 88 which ended when Barnes bowled Moule. Murdoch was left unbeaten on 153, 1 run more than W.G. Grace had made in England's first innings.

Chasing 57 to win, England lost 5 for 36, but then out of the gate came W.G. to guide England to victory. At that moment, how Australia must have wished they had Spofforth to bowl. The Australians received £1,110 as their share of the Test receipts, which enabled them to cover all the tour expenses. More importantly, Australia's fighting recovery had re-established their international reputation. W.G. gave Murdoch a golden guinea for scoring 153 and Billy wore it on his watch chain until he died.

An illustration from an unnamed American magazine recording Australia's first appearance in New York. The Australians also played in Canada, where Charles Bannerman made a century.
— Illustrated Sydney News.

HUGH HAMON MASSIE

GEORGE JOHN BONNER

WILLIAM LLOYD MURDOCH
(Captain)

FREDERICK ROBERT SPOFFORTH

SAMUEL PERCY JONES

JOHN M'CARTHY BLACKHAM

ALEXANDER CHAMBERS BANNERMAN

PERCY STANISLAUS M'DONNELL

THOMAS WILLIAM GARRETT

GEORGE EUGENE PALMER

GEORGE GIFFEN

HENRY FREDERICK BOYLE

CHARLES WILLIAM BEAL
(Secretary)

THOMAS HORAN

6. The Legend of the Ashes

Although defeated in the 1880 Test in England, Australia emerged from the difficult second tour there with a keen, colourful team, brimful of players whose talents could dramatically swing a match. Spofforth, the original demon bowler, had developed subtle changes of pace, swing, and cut almost to an art form. His machine-like accuracy and satanic appearance made him the most feared bowler in the world and he completed his second trip to England and the matches in Australia before and after the tour with 763 wickets at 5.49, 391 of his wickets in England. Joey Palmer took 266 wickets in all games at 7.84 and Boyle 280 at 7.4. Between them these three bowlers dismissed 909 of the 967 batsmen Australia accounted for in all games.

Behind the stumps Jack Blackham had revolutionised his job, fearlessly standing right up to the stumps and taking the fastest deliveries in gloves little better than today's garden mittens. In England clergymen complained that Blackham had eliminated the need for longstops, the positions they traditionally took in village games. Murdoch had become an inspiring leader and a great batsman, a highly intelligent and resourceful man with an impish sense of fun. The big hitting of 6 feet 6 inches George Bonnor had made him an immense crowd-pleaser, with spectators tense and expectant each time he went to the crease. In the only Test on the 1880 tour he hit a ball so high that the batsmen had turned for their third run before Fred Grace caught it. Alick Bannerman was on the way to becoming a legendary stonewaller, and Percy ('Greatheart') McDonnell had at the age of twenty-two shown exciting potential on the first of his four tours of England.

The third Australian team to England which in 1882 at The Oval won the most publicised Test in history by seven runs. They were one of Australia's great teams, cleverly captained and managed.
— Mitchell Library, Sydney.

The Ashes urn and velvet bag, a sporting legend that began with Australia's marvellous win at The Oval in 1882 and was carried on the following summer in Australia by women followers of Ivo Bligh's team.
— Melbourne Cricket Ground Museum.

An English artist captured the excitement of the dramatic match at The Oval in this way. Lord Harris, England's captain is running full pelt to try and prevent a four in the top sketch, and in the bottom sketch excited spectators jump the fence to cheer the Australians.
— Latrobe Library, Melbourne.

Famous Australian cricketers after they retired (L to R): Dave Gregory, Fred Spofforth, Hugh Massie, Alick Bannerman and Tom Garrett. All bar Gregory played in The Oval Test in 1882 that shocked English cricket.
— Albert Gregory Collection.

Small wonder that Australia faced the summer of 1881–82 and the tour of an all-professional English team, organised by Alfred Shaw, James Lillywhite, and Arthur Shrewsbury, with great confidence. Cricket in all States had made big advances. State control bodies now operated in New South Wales (formed in 1857), Victoria (1864), South Australia (1871), and Queensland (1876). Despite some fractional fighting, dissolutions, and re-formations of some associations they appeared to be progressing towards sound administration. In Western Australia moves that were to lead to the formation of the Western Australian Cricket Association in 1885 were afoot. In Tasmania cricketers based around Launceston were only a few years off the formation in 1886 of an association similar to that which had functioned as the Southern Tasmanian Cricket Association since 1858. Just as importantly, the number and standard of coaches had multiplied and at all the main centres big improvements had been made to grounds and pitches.

When the South Australian Cricket Association was formed, one of its first acts was to ask James Lillywhite and James Southerton to choose a competent coach for it. They selected Jesse Hide, of Sussex, who arrived in Adelaide in 1878 and stayed for three years on a salary of £200 a year. Hide laid the foundations for rapid advances by South Australian cricket, acting as the Adelaide Oval curator and adviser on turf pitches as well as coaching talented youngsters.

In Tasmania Tom Kendall had been signed to coach in Hobart when he was sent back to Melbourne 'for reasons other than cricket' after the first Australian team to visit England reached Perth. Kendall's appointment was combined with the fencing and re-laying of Hobart Oval. Sadly, the notable Melbourne coach Tom Wills had died by his own hand at the age of forty-four on 2 May 1880, while the second Australian team was in England. Wills had become increasingly depressed over the massacre of his family and had to be placed under restraint because of his drinking bouts. Finally he eluded his attendant, found a bayonet, and stabbed himself to death, a tragic end to the life of one of Australian cricket's most colourful personalities.

Jesse Hide, the Sussex cricketer who got the job as South Australia's first coach on the recommendation of James Lillywhite. He vastly improved playing standards and advised on Adelaide Oval preparation. — Ken Piesse, Australian Cricketer.

Shaw's sixth English team played five matches in America on their way to Australia. They began their Australian visit with matches against Twenty Twos in Maitland, Newcastle, Orange, and Bathurst, where a local lad named Charles Thomas Biass Turner took 17 English wickets in the match. More than 30,000 people watched England beat New South Wales by 68 runs at Sydney in the first of the main tour matches; 20,000 attended on the Saturday. The Sydney Cricket Ground was by then firmly established as the city's main cricket arena, big cricket having moved in turn from Hyde Park to the domain to the Albert Club's ground at Redfern, and finally to the ground developed by the Army at the back of Victoria Barracks, known originally as the Garrison Ground and then renamed the Association Ground. Intercolonial cricket was played on it in 1878 but by the time Shaw's side played there it was known as the Sydney Cricket Ground.

The Englishmen found that higher scores by Australian batsmen had come with improved pitches. Billy Murdoch scored 321 on the S.C.G. the season following the tour by Shaw's team. Massie also had brilliant knocks for New South Wales against Shaw's side, his powerful hitting demonstrating that he was a batsman to watch. In the second first-class match of the tour, the Englishmen trailed Victoria by 105 runs on the first innings and followed on. On a sticky wicket Shrewsbury made a masterly 80 not out and Victoria were set 94 to win. Betting was heavy all round the M.C.G. and odds up to thirty-to-one were laid against England by bookmakers eager

for trade. But Shaw was highly optimistic about his bowlers' skills on the sticky pitch and, in one of the few bets he ever had in his life, backed England. Peate and Bates justified his faith by dismissing the first six Victorian batsmen for 7 runs and although Harry Boyle hit out boldly, England won by 18 runs. There were persistent reports that two of the English players had agreed to 'sell' the match in the final innings. Shaw questioned some of his players about their fielding but found no confirmation of malpractice.

The first Test of England's 1881–82 tour ended at Melbourne in a draw, with Australia 156 runs short of victory and 7 wickets in hand. England included Midwinter in their team for this, the fifth of all Tests. He had played for Australia in the first two Tests. England opened with 294, Edwin Evans bowling with impressive accuracy to include 35 maidens in his 71 overs, finishing with 3 for 81. Hugh Massie was stumped for 2 off Midwinter when Australia batted, but a splendid 124 by Tom Horan took Australia to 320 and a lead of 26. England made 308 in their second innings, with W.H. Cooper taking 6 for 120 with 66 overs of leg-breaks. When Blackham was hurt, Murdoch replaced him behind the stumps. George Giffen in his Test debut added 107 with Horan in Australia's first innings but bowled only three overs.

Shaw then took his side to New Zealand for seven matches, returning after Christmas for three Tests against the team that Murdoch was to take to England in 1882. Australia was weakened by injuries but pulled off an outstanding win in Sydney by 5 wickets. Palmer had figures of 7 for 68 and 4 for 97 to set up victory. He and Evans (3 for 64) bowled unchanged throughout England's first innings of 133, made in more than 3 hours. England lost despite an opening stand of 122 in their second innings by Barlow and Ulyett, the first century opening partnership in Test cricket.

England were caught on a below-standard wicket for the next Test at Sydney, scoring 188. When Australia batted they were allowed to select and prepare a fresh pitch. Despite this advantage Australia were 3 for 24 at the end of the first day. Next day the not-out batsmen Bannerman and McDonnell took the score to 146 before rain ended play. On the third day McDonnell hit Bates over the pavilion at the northern end on his way to 147. His stand with Bannerman yielded 199.

After Midwinter bowled Bannerman, Peate found a nasty spot on the drying pitch and ran through the rest of the Australians. Australia led by 72 runs, a margin that should have been far bigger. Tom Garrett then took 6 for 78 to give Australia a total of 66 runs to win on the fourth day. Australia lost 4 wickets getting those 66 runs.

The fourth Test of the summer was played in stifling heat at Melbourne, and George Ulyett scored the first Test century by an Englishman in Australia. His 149 enabled England to reach 309, nobody else scoring 30. Australia replied with 300, Alick Bannerman helping Murdoch to put on 110 for the first wicket despite a bout of sunstroke. When Murdoch was out for 85, McDonnell delighted the crowd by hitting the unpopular Midwinter into the crowd. The match ended in a draw after four day's play because the English players had to catch a boat home. It was the second draw in the four-Test series caused by sailing dates, and the last drawn Test in Australia until 1946–47. Midwinter's four Tests in this season for England did not prevent him from playing for Australia again in 1882–83 and 1886–87.

A tumultuous welcome greeted Murdoch's team when they returned home to Sydney after beating the full strength of England for the first time in England.
— Jack Pollard Collection.

Arthur Shrewsbury, the best English professional batsman of the 1880s and 1890s, who toured Australia four times, three times as tour promoter in partnership with Alfred Shaw.
— Albert Gregory Collection.

The Hon. Ivo Bligh's team that defeated Australia 2-1 in 1882-83. Australia won an extra Test to square the series 2-2 but Bligh still took the Ashes home in his luggage. — State Library of Victoria.

After separation of the States under the Australian Colonies Bill in 1850, a "Public Rejoicings Committee" was formed in Melbourne. They gave priority to establishing a winning Victorian cricket team. At the M.C.G. this fine stand was built. — Albert Gregory Collection.

One of Australia's greatest teams toured England in 1882, an ideal blend of strong batting, penetrative bowling, superb wicket-keeping, shrewd captaincy (Murdoch), and athletic fielding in all bar the slips positions. Murdoch was close to being the best batsman in the world, Giffen a classical all rounder on the way up and with everything to prove on his first tour. Bannerman's relentless stonewalling provided a foil for the explosive hitting of Bonnor, McDonnell, and Massie. Horan was a superb player of fast bowling. Spofforth spearheaded a brilliant array of bowlers, supported by the steady, always reliable Harry Boyle, and the accurate, resourceful medium pace of Palmer and Garrett. Giffen bowled superbly at times — taking 8 for 49 against the Gentlemen at Lord's — but such was the team's bowling strength that he had fewer than 400 overs on the entire tour.

The tour opened sensationally when on the first morning against Oxford, Massie hit a century before lunch. Massie, undefeated on 100 out of 145 at lunch, made a further 106 in less than an hour after the break, tearing the Oxford attack apart with savage off-side hitting. Murdoch did even better in the second match, hitting 286 not out, Australia winning by an innings and 355 runs. The ominous strength of the Australians already had London critics calling for a more thorough preparation of England's Eleven, and for the staging of Tests trials to ensure that England's team included only the best players.

The Australians went ten weeks without defeat in spite of harsh wintry conditions. They were finally beaten by Cambridge University, who made 393 runs in the match, 297 of them from the bats of the three Studd brothers. C.T. Studd scored 118 in Cambridge's first innings and had 8 wickets in the match. The Australians considered, however, that the match turned on the bowling of the Queenslander R.C. Ramsay, who took 12 wickets for Cambridge, 7 in Australia's second innings.

Australia then won ten out of twelve games outright in a ten-week period which saw Spofforth at his peak, and the batting strength improving daily as some of England's finest sides were outplayed. Until then it had always been taken for granted that English cricket would triumph whenever her best players took the field together. Defeats in Australia and against the earlier Australian touring teams had been excused on the ground that England's best cricketers had not appeared. But now as Murdoch's Australians produced almost daily demonstrations of high class batting, bowling, and fielding it became obvious that England's cricket prestige would be

Spry's caricature in Vanity Fair of Fred Spofforth, the bowler whose 14 for 90 in the Ashes Test shattered English complacency about the superiority of their cricket.
— New South Wales Cricket Assoc.

at stake when the two countries met. Even when Australia lost to the Players and to Cambridge University Past and Present — despite 66 out of 76 in 30 minutes by Bonnor — it was clear to even the most ardent English fan that the lead England had held over the world for so many decades was in jeopardy.

Australia won the toss and batted first on a rain-soaked Oval pitch and were dismissed for 63 in 2 hours 15 minutes, Blackham top-scoring with a plucky 17. Refusing to blame the miserable conditions, Australia struck back with some superb bowling. Spofforth yorked W.G. Grace for 4 and had Barlow caught at 18. England lost 6 wickets before she passed Australia's score. Spofforth's 7 for 46 restricted England's first innings lead to 38, but with rain imminent England appeared in a sound position.

Next morning Massie attacked and in a masterly show of controlled hitting took care of the arrears while Bannerman defended as if life itself depended on it. Massie reached 50 out of 61 in 41 minutes, but when he was out for 55, only Murdoch (29) offered any resistance and England were left with only 85 to win. England took her score to 51 for the loss of only 2 wickets. With 34 needed, her batsmen dramatically lost their nerve. The most legendary collapse in cricket history followed, with England's batsmen unable to get the ball past fieldsmen, Spofforth bowling his break-backs at his spiteful best; Boyle at the other end sustaining an immaculate length; Blackham taking every ball that passed the batsmen only a yard or so behind them.

In the intensity of the struggle, one spectator dropped dead, another gnawed pieces from his umbrella handle with his teeth, and the English batsmen became so parched they could barely speak. The scorer's hand trembled so that when he tried to write Peate in his book he finished with something that read like 'Geese'. As maiden over followed maiden over, the nerves of fieldsmen and batsmen were strained to the utmost, and an oppressive silence fell on the crowd.

England's third wicket fell at 51 when Ulyett played for Spofforth's break-back and failed to detect the straight one, simply edging the ball to Blackham. Two runs later W.G. Grace miscued a drive and Bannerman took the catch at mid-off. The score edged to 60, with Lucas partnering Lyttelton. After twelve maidens were bowled in succession, Spofforth spoke to Bannerman who deliberately misfielded to give Lyttelton a single and bring him down to face Spofforth. Four further maidens followed before Spofforth scattered Lyttelton's stumps with a vicious break-back: 5 for 66, and 19 still needed.

Lucas lifted English hopes by hitting Boyle for 4 but immediately Spofforth struck back by dismissing Steel and Read in one over. Seven for 70, and 15 still required. Then came a two and 3 byes off Spofforth, before Lucas played Spofforth into his stumps. He was replaced by C.T. Studd, who had scored centuries against Australia in two earlier matches, but here Boyle's long stint of accuracy was rewarded. First Murdoch caught Barnes off his glove from a Boyle delivery that kicked. Then the last man in, Edmund Peate, swung the first ball for two, slashed wildly at and missed the next two, and had his stumps broken by the last ball of Boyle's over. Australia had won by 7 runs.

Spofforth, who had told team-mates as they went on the field for that dramatic final innings that the game could be won, bowled his last 11 overs for 2 runs and 4 wickets. This gave him 7 for 44 for the innings and 14 for 90 in the Test match, figures which were not bettered by an Australian in England until Bob Massie took 16 wickets at Lord's in 1972. When Peate was criticised for swinging at the last four balls and not giving his partner C.T. Studd a chance to score the required runs, Peate said: 'Mr. Studd was shaking with nerves and I did not think I could trust him to score a single run'.

George Giffen wrote that when Peate's stumps were knocked over to give Australia victory, the crowd sat for a moment voiceless and stunned. Then spectators broke over the ground in a wild rush to cheer the players who had produced the win. Spofforth was carried shoulder-high to the pavilion, his place in cricket history secure. 'Men who were noted for their coolness at moments of crisis trembled like a leaf, some were shivering as if from cold, and some even fainted,' said the Surrey secretary, C.W. Alcock.

The following day the London *Sporting Times* published this mock obituary written by Shirley Brooks, son of one of the editors of *Punch*.

A view of Adelaide Oval during the 1880s before the bike track was built. Non-paying spectators could still get a good view of the match.
— Corporation of Adelaide.

J. ATLEE   H. MUSGROVE   J. HEALEY

W. BROWN   V. TRAPP   W. MIDWINTER

W. PIDGEON   H. BOYLE   T. HORAN   E. P. HASTINGS

H. J. H. SCOTT   C. ATLEE   G. GORDON

McLEAN
CHALLENGE CUP
1882 3 - 4
WON BY EMCC WITHOUT A DEFEAT.

IN AFFECTIONATE REMEMBRANCE
OF
ENGLISH CRICKET

Which Died At The Oval On
29th August, 1882

Deeply lamented by a large circle
of sorrowing friends and acquaintances
R.I.P.

N.B. The Body Will Be Cremated, And
The Ashes Taken To Australia

The notice neglected to say that the Australians' resolve to win had been intensified by an incident in their second innings, when twenty-one-year-old S.P. Jones responded to a call for a run, completed a single, moved down the pitch to do some 'gardening', and was run out by W.G. Grace. After winning the only Test of their tour, the Australians found that the remaining matches lacked tension, but Bonnor, Massie, and McDonnell continued to provide entertainment for crowds with some memorable hitting. The team was managed by Charles Beal, who at twenty-seven was the youngest-ever Australian manager. Five players made tour centuries, Murdoch heading the batting averages with 1711 runs at 30.55. Spofforth took most first-class wickets, with 188 at 12.13, but Boyle headed him in the averages with 144 wickets at 11.68.

Apart from bowling so consistently Boyle played a vital role by fielding closer in at mid-on than fieldsmen from any country had done up to that time. He made such a specialty of the position that newspapers at first referred to it as "Boyle's mid-on" and later as "silly" mid-on, and his presence there undoubtedly added menace to Australia's bowling. He took his replacement as captain by Murdoch in commendable style and this contributed greatly to a happy tour.

Soon after the 'Ashes Test' at the Oval an English team captained by the Hon. Ivo Bligh, later Lord Darnley, left for Australia. Eight of Bligh's twelve players were amateurs. Near Colombo the English team's ship collided with a sailing vessel and fast bowler Fred Morley was knocked out and badly hurt. He could not play in half the team's matches and his left-arm pace bowling — a major feature of England's American tour in 1879 when he took 100 wickets at 3.54 — was sadly missed. It turned out that he had broken a rib and two years after Bligh's team ended their tour he died of 'congestion and dropsy'. Bligh himself sustained a hand injury in the collision and could not play in his team's first five matches.

Australian newspapers promoted the notion that Bligh's role was to recover the Ashes, and they devoted much space to his background as captain of Cambridge and captain of Kent. England had agreed to a schedule including three Tests and when they won the second and third Tests after Australia had won the first, Bligh was acclaimed for recovering the Ashes. Mrs Annie Fletcher, wife of J.W. Fletcher, secretary of Sydney's Paddington Cricket Club, suggested to Bligh when he visited the Fletchers' house in Woollahra that she should burn a pair of bails for him to take home as a memento of his team's victory in two out of three Tests. Bligh liked the idea and Mrs Fletcher, a gifted needle-worker, fashioned and sewed a velvet bag in which to keep the ashes. But when Bligh arrived in Melbourne later on the tour a group of ladies told him that the velvet bag was not as strong symbolically as an urn, which they promptly provided for Mrs Fletcher's ashes. One reason given for Bligh's preference for the urn was that the Melbourne ladies included the woman who became his wife.

Bligh's team played four Tests in Australia, with each side winning two. After the agreed three-Test rubber had been decided England agreed to play a fourth Test against 'United Australia'. Australia won this additional match but Bligh was allowed to keep his ashes. When he died in 1927 the urn containing the ashes was given to the M.C.C., as requested in his will. The urn has remained in a place of honour in the M.C.C. rooms ever since, although many small replicas have been made. In 1953 the urn was moved from the Long Room to the Imperial Cricket Museum near by, along with Mrs Fletcher's velvet bag, and a score-card of Australia's win at the Oval in 1882 which inspired the legend.

*Far Left
Since cricket began in Australia, it has always received a wide media coverage. This was how the* Australasian Sketcher *recorded the East Melbourne Cricket Club's third win in the McLean, one of many Melbourne Cup competitions, during the 1883-84 season. — Australasian Sketcher.*

A.G. Steel, who topped the tour averages for Ivo Bligh's side in 1882-83 for both batting and bowling. In the Fourth Test at Sydney, he scored a magnificent 135 not out but Australia won. — M.C.C. Collection at Lord's.

Sam Jones, whose unsportsmanlike run-out in the Ashes Test at The Oval in 1882 made the Australians more determined to win the match. Jones, then only 21, played in 11 other Tests.
— Jack Pollard Collection.

The Northern Stand at the M.C.G. in 1877. It was destroyed by fire in 1884 only eight years after it was built.
— New South Wales Cricket Association.

The Ashes had been a joke enjoyed briefly by Melbourne's society ladies and were virtually forgotten until 1894 when the erudite South Australian cricket writer Clarence P. Moody published *Australian Cricket and Cricketers*. In this book he set out to establish which matches between England and Australia were, and which were not, Tests. Moody did the job so well that his list of Tests was universally accepted. He also revived the Ashes story in his book. Ten years after the publication of Moody's book, England's cricket captain Pelham ('Plum') Warner was searching for a title for his book on the 1903–04 tour of Australia and settled on *How We Recovered the Ashes*. This gave the Ashes the symbolic status that they have enjoyed ever since, and what had started as a long-winded Victorian jest became part of cricket legend.

In 1970 Rowland Bowen, editor of the English magazine *Cricket Quarterly*, urged that the Ashes be abolished because of their frivolous origins: 'It all began as a joke, and then because of an historical mistake it became a fetish, and it is time it was abolished'. But Lord's remained unmoved. In 1982 Christopher Martin-Jenkins, editor of the influential English *Cricketer* magazine, discovered that servants at Lord Darnley's home had upset the urn and spilt the ashes all over the carpet. They had swept them up and then burnt some wood to provide a fresh set of ashes for the urn. Again Lord's remained silent. Over the years it has been suggested many times that the M.C.C. should send the original Ashes urn back to Australia for display (this happened again when Greg Chappell's side regained the Ashes in 1982–83) but the M.C.C. always takes the stance that the urn is too valuable to move from London.

The cricket matches that enabled the then Ivo Bligh to take the urn home, never to be returned, were played in a sportsmanlike spirit on uncovered pitches with rain unhappily influencing the outcome. Australia won the first Test at Melbourne by 9 wickets when rain fell after they had scored 291. The England attack included Read's underhand lobs and round-armers from Bates. Bonnor twice hit the ball into the crowd in top-scoring with 85. England struggled gamely on the wet pitch but found Palmer (7 for 65) too difficult as he seamed the ball about. Following on after scoring 177, England made 169 the second time, leaving Australia to score only 58 to win. They did this with the loss of only 1 wicket. England won the second Test at Melbourne just as handsomely, thanks to great bowling by Bates, the fifth bowler tried, who took 7 for 28 and 7 for 74.

Northern Grandstand M.C.G. 1877.
Robertson 1976
Built 1876 Destroyed by fire 1884

Australia appeared to have the advantage with England 5 for 75 in the third Test in Sydney but a fine stand by Tylecote and Read, who both made 66, took England to 247. Heavy rain fell during the night and again at lunch on the second day but Australia struggled to 1 for 133. Heavy rain fell on the Sunday rest day but the pitch did not misbehave until the fourth day when the faster bowlers bounced in all directions as Australia chased 153 to win. Australia slumped to 4 for 18 and despite a plucky 26 by Blackham never recovered and were out for 83, giving England victory by 69 runs. The series was notable for the first hat-trick in Tests by an England bowler, Billy Bates, who took the wickets of McDonnell, Giffen, and Bonnor in the first innings of the second Test in which he had 14 for 102. The crowd of more than 50,000 people who watched England win the third Test, generously applauded both sides.

The extra match between England and United Australia, later recognised as a Test, was another tense struggle. England reached 263 after A.G. Steel hit a magnificent 135 but Bonnor matched this for Australia with more spectacular hitting on his way to 87. Midwinter changed his allegiance again and turned out for Australia. Faced with a chase for 199 to win, Alick Bannerman surprised even his most ardent admirers by attacking from the start of Australia's final innings, unveiling strokes few believed he could play. When he was out, England had a chance at 4 for 107, but Blackham and Giffen added 55 before Blackham and Midwinter scored the necessary runs for Australia to win by 4 wickets. The match was unique because of the number of pitches used. The teams agreed before the start to experiment by using two separate tracks but in the event used four different strips, one for each innings, and the captains took a long time to pick out the pitches they preferred before the innings began. Experts have since argued that the Ashes should have remained in Australia as a result of the two-all result in the Tests, but Bligh took the Ashes home in his luggage, and the fourth match received Test status only when Moody made his ratings some twelve years later.

South Australian A.H. ("Affie") Jarvis, a fine wicket-keeper unlucky to be a contemporary of Blackham, who made four tours of England between 1880 and 1893. — M.C.C. Collection at Lord's.

John McCarthy Blackham, who revolutionised the art of wicket-keeping, standing up to the stumps for even the fastest bowling. In England clergymen complained that he eliminated the need for longstops, the place they occupied in village games.
— Melbourne Cricket Ground Museum.

7. Lessons The Doctor Taught Us

Costs of Australia's early tours of England were met by the players, who shared all profits when they returned home. They contributed fixed amounts each towards the cost of fares and hotel bills and raised extra money by playing matches around the colonies before they left. Murdoch's 1884 Australian team followed this system and quickly won a reputation for what English commentators called their 'commercial approach' to matches. In reply they simply pointed to the example set by Dr W.G. Grace, whose appearance fees th⍩ all envied.

Before the side left they scored 619 against the Rest, with Murdoch scoring 279 not out, McDonnell 111. At Sydney Harry Moses, who at twenty-six was just emerging as a top-class player, made a masterly 149 not out for Fifteen of New South Wales against the tourists. In the return match against The Rest, George Giffen became the first bowler to take all 10 wickets in an innings. He took 4 for 66 in a total of 113 and bowled 26 overs, 10 of them maidens.

On the voyage to England W.H. Cooper, who had done so well against Bligh's side in Australia, broke the third finger of his bowling hand — an accident that affected him for the entire tour.

The Australians won the first match of the tour against Lord Sheffield's team by an innings, with Palmer taking 10 for 72. It was in this match that W.G. Grace insisted on testing with a gauge the width of some of the Australian's bats, all of which had been made in England. One bat was slightly too wide a few inches from the bottom but this was attributed to the owner's good timing. The Australians then asked to test bats belonging to Grace. The first bat tested failed to pass the gauge.

The team Australia used in the 1884 Tests (L to R): Back, J.M. Blackham, H.J.H. Scott (umpire), W.E. Midwinter, P.S. McDonnell, W.H. Cooper; Centre, G. Giffen, H.F. Boyle, W.L. Murdoch (captain), G.J. Bonnor, G.E. Palmer; Front, A.C. Bannerman, F.R. Spofforth. There were the players who appeared in the first ever Test at Lord's.
— Jack Pollard Collection.

Key players struggled to reach form in cold weather. With three Tests scheduled for the first time on an English tour, the tourists lost three of their first six matches. An M.C.C. Eleven beat Australia after W.G. Grace, A.G. Steel, and William Barnes had scored centuries. At Birmingham the pitch for the match against an England Eleven was so bad that Australia won by 4 wickets in 6 hours. Spofforth had a spell in which he took 7 wickets for 3 runs in an England total of 26 and had match figures of 14 for 37. In the match against Lancashire Giffen had an outstanding double, scoring 113 and taking a hat-trick before play was washed out.

Throughout this tour the Australians had difficulty in coping with the bowling of Edmund Peate. First of a long line of great Yorkshire left-arm spinners, Peate took 10 for 51 for the North of England to pave the way to victory over Australia. It was after this display that Giffen found one of the Australian batting stars in his bedroom playing strokes in front of a mirror. Lunging

forward defensively, he called 'That's the way to play Peate', and 'How do you like that, Peate?'. As he swung into a hefty drive the bat struck a toilet set and smashed it to pieces. The next time that batsman faced Peate he was bowled first ball.

In the match against The Players, Australia wanted only 11 runs to win with 9 wickets in hand when play was adjourned for lunch. Spectators, believing the break had been taken simply to allow time for more fans to reach the ground, were incensed. They rushed the centre of the ground, where they pulled up the stumps and occupied the middle, refusing all requests to return to their seats. When they cheered Giffen, he was asked to speak to them and try and coax them off the pitch. He declined, and then Peate was asked if he would try: 'Naw, sir, ah didn't come here t' quell riot, ah cum t' play cricket.' The game was finished soon after lunch.

The first Test at Manchester was notable for the withdrawal from the England team of Lord Harris because of the selection of John Crossland, a notorious 'chucker'. A.N. Hornby took over the captaincy and Crossland was replaced by R.G. Barlow. The first day's play was washed out, confirming Old Trafford's reputation as the most rain-affected ground in England. England was out for 95 but the game ended in a draw after Australia led by 87 runs. England won the second

Test — in the first Test ever played at Lord's — by an innings and 5 runs, thanks to a score of 148 by the marvellous amateur batsman Allan Steel, who had played in the Cambridge side that defeated Australia in 1878. Australia made only 145 on a crumbling pitch in their second innings.

Australia dominated the third Test at the Oval but had to be content with a draw. Every member of the English team bowled as Australia scored 551 in the first innings, including Murdoch's 211, the first double century in Test cricket. England's wicket-keeper Alfred Lyttelton proved their best bowler by taking 4 for 19 with his slow lobs. W.G. Grace kept wicket while Lyttelton bowled. Australia was forced to bat out the innings because until 1889 declarations were not permitted. England was 8 for 181 when Walter Read, furious at Lord Harris for sending him in as the No. 10 batsman, hammered out 117 runs in about even time. This innings enabled England to reach a respectable 346 and was Read's sole century in eighteen Tests.

R. Ponsonby Staples' sketch of the Gentlemen versus Players match at Lord's, with the Players taking the field. Billy Murdoch is near the Gentlemen's gate in a striped coat, two to the left of W.G. Grace. A.E. Stoddart is the batsman at the gate waiting to go out.
— M.C.C. Collection at Lord's.

A portrait of George Giffen, first Australian to score more than 10,000 runs and take more than 1000 wickets in first-class cricket. On figures he ranks as Australia's greatest allrounder. — South Australian Cricket Association.

Below: The Melbourne Cricket Club's members' pavilion in 1877 was a modest structure, circled by elms planted by the first English team to Australia. — Jack Pollard Collection.

Giffen, in his book *With Bat and Ball*, rated Spofforth's feat in taking 216 wickets at 12.2 each on the 1884 tour superior to his previous tour triumphs because the opposing batsmen were better and the wickets firmer. Palmer ranked second to Spofforth in 1884 with 132 wickets at 16.14. Giffen too made a fine contribution with 82 wickets at 19.78 and 1052 runs at 21.04. Murdoch again topped the batting averages with 1378 runs at 30.62. Percy McDonnell also exceeded 1000 runs, with 1225 at 23.55. The tour ended with the marvellous match between Smokers and Non-Smokers in which the best players from England and Australia appeared in both teams. Bonnor hit 124 out of the 156 scored while he was at the crease. He hit sixteen boundaries and even clobbered Spofforth for 6.

When Murdoch's players arrived home, their discontent over pay for home matches produced one of the most unsavoury disputes in the history of Australian cricket. The all-professional English team, jointly promoted by James Lillywhite, Alfred Shaw, and Arthur Shrewsbury, encountered trouble almost from their first match, with Australian players pressing for a share of all gate receipts. The row over pay almost prevented the staging of the first Test ever held at Adelaide Oval from 12 to 16 December 1884. The Australians, demanding half the match proceeds, refused an offer of 30 per cent. Finally, the South Australian Cricket Association agreed to pay each team £450, much to the disgust of the Englishmen. Murdoch further annoyed the English party by insisting that Lillywhite, a highly experienced umpire noted for his fairness, could not umpire in the match, although there was not time to get an experienced replacement from the eastern States.

McDonnell, who had made 103 at the Oval in his previous Test innings against England, scored 124 in Australia's first innings. He was deprived of the honour of being the first to score a century in each innings of a Test when Giffen, troubled by lumbago, ran him out at 83 in Australia's second innings. England won by 8 wickets despite McDonnell's brilliance. Australia suffered a double disadvantage through the absence of Bannerman with a hand injury in the second innings combined with the fact that players who were demanding big pay rises had not kept themselves in practice since their return from England.

score freely off Spofforth. In 1877 in a preliminary match for the first Australian team that went to England he made 41 for a Combined Eleven against the Australians and in the process hit Spofforth out of the attack. Ned Gregory, as curator of the Sydney Cricket Ground, laid out and levelled the field that many regarded as the finest cricket ground in the world.

The organisers invited Ned Gregory to join the 1886 team to England but he declined for family reasons. This was the first Australian team to tour England under the sponsorship of a cricket club. The Melbourne Cricket Club organised the tour to return the visit by Lord Harris's side to Australia in 1878–79. The four Australian sides that preceded this team had been organised by private sponsors and the players themselves. After sounding out professionals like Ned Gregory, the club opted for an all-amateur touring party, which meant that Alick Bannerman could not be included. Murdoch preferred to concentrate on his law practice at Cootamundra, and Boyle and McDonnell were also unavailable. The M.C.C. appointed Henry ('Tup') Scott to captain the team, which included eight players who had previously toured England and four newcomers, William Bruce, Edwin Evans, John McIlwraith, and John Trumble. Major Ben Wardill, secretary of the Melbourne Club, managed the side.

Before a match had been played arguments developed among the players and Scott soon had his hands full adjudicating in disputes. Scott, educated at Wesley College, was a brilliant batsman in intercolonial matches and became the first Victorian to captain Australia. He was unable to stifle the rivalry between New South Wales and Victorian players. Spofforth, who was on his last tour of England, summed up this ill-feeling: 'The rivalry is not limited to the field. It extends from politics to society, to every side of life'. He then pointed out that ever since the selection of the first Australian teams the Press and public in both States had been widely at variance. One felt Victoria had been slighted, whereas the other championed New South Wales. On the tours overseas the players separated themselves as far as possible from compatriots of the other colony.

'There is no doubt that the cares of leadership affected Scott's run-getting,' wrote Arthur Haygarth in his *Scores & Biographies*, 'For quarrels among the players were many and he had not sufficient strength of character to cope with the situation.' *Wisden* in its review of the Australian tour regretted the lack of authority and experience in the captain. Scott still managed some splendid innings on the tour. At Lord's against Middlesex he made 123 in a marvellous

display of controlled hitting, scoring 155 for the first wicket with S.P. Jones. At Sheffield against Yorkshire he struck the last four balls of the match for 22 runs, with hits of 6,4,6,6. The umpire called 'over' after Scott had dispatched the first three balls and was corrected by scorers in the pavilion.

Scott's problems were aggravated by injuries to key players, which forced Major Wardill to play in one match. Dr Rowley Pope, who was not an official member of the team, played 8 innings for the Australians. The lack of discipline within the team culminated at the Oval, where W.G. Grace was dropped four times before he made 100. Grace went on to 170 in an innings in which he hit Spofforth into the crowd. Australia was then trapped on a glue-pot pitch and was beaten by an innings and 217 runs. The tour was a remarkable financial success, however. More than 33,000 people saw the three days of the Lord's Test. George Giffen was the only success among the Australian players, scoring 1453 runs at 26.9 and taking 159 wickets at 17.05 in a grand all-round effort. At one stage Giffen took 40 wickets in 5 successive innings.

C.W. Rock, the Tasmanian who played for Cambridge University and Warwickshire and took 5 for 51 for the Gentlemen against Scott's 1886 Australian team. — Ric Smith.

In the last of his 18 Tests Spofforth did not bowl at all in one innings because of the presence of these two young bowlers: Above, C.T.B. Turner, the former Cobb & Co. stable boy who became known as "The Terror", and Right, John Ferris, the left-armer who formed a formidable partnership with Turner. — M.C.C. Collection at Lord's.

Beaten three Tests to nil by an extremely powerful England side, the Australians returned home with commentators demanding changes. Percy McDonnell replaced Scott as captain for the two Tests against Shrewsbury's England side in 1886–87, and players who had missed the English tour by Scott's team returned. Three outstanding newcomers — J.J. Ferris, C.T.B. Turner, and H. Moses — made their debuts in the first Test at Sydney, ushering in a new era in Australian cricket. Ferris, a former Sydney bank clerk who was to win undying fame as a left-arm opening bowler, formed with Turner, the Bathurst right-hand medium pacer, one of cricket's greatest bowling partnerships. Moses proved to be one of the finest left-handed batsmen Australia has produced. Many believed he would have challenged Murdoch as the No. 1 Australian batsman of his time had he gone to England but he gave priority to his work with a Sydney wine merchant and to his role as president of the New South Wales Kennel Club.

The arrival in the Test arena of these gifted players coincided with the departure of one of Australia's master cricketers, the legendary Fred Spofforth, who did not even get a bowl in the first innings of his last Test. Turner and Ferris bowled unchanged and had England out for 45, with Turner taking 6 for 15, Ferris 4 for 27. Spofforth bowled 12 overs for 1 for 17 in the second innings but again Turner (2 for 53) and Ferris (5 for 76) had first use of the ball. Despite superb bowling by Turner and Ferris, England won the Test by 13 runs.

Spofforth retired from Test cricket at thirty-four. In eighteen Tests he had done more than anyone else for Australian cricket, taking 94 wickets at 18.41. He turned out occasionally for Derbyshire after he went to work in 1887 for the Star Tea Company and finished with 853 first-class wickets at 14.95. Giffen wrote of him:

What a sight it was to see Spofforth bowling when a game had to be pulled like a brand from the burning. He looked like a Demon every inch of him, and I really believe he frightened more batsmen out than many bowlers have fairly and squarely beaten. When the Demon meant business, the batsmen had to look out for squalls.

THE EARL OF SHEFFIELD.

8. Lord Sheffield's Shield

Above: The medals awarded to the winners of the first Sheffield Shield competition in 1892-93.

Left: One of the few known pictures of the Earl of Sheffield as portrayed by a Melbourne artist. Portly, unshaven, he wore scruffy clothes and hated speechmaking and photographers.
— Jack Pollard Collection.

The Australian summer of 1887–88 provided the remarkable spectacle of two English teams touring the sprawling, sparsely populated States seeking spectator support in opposition to each other. Lord Hawke organised and captained one team at the invitation of the Melbourne Cricket Club, but after the death of his father returned to England. George Vernon took over the captaincy. The other team toured as a promotional venture for Shaw, Lillywhite, and Shrewsbury and Charles Aubrey Smith (known as 'Round the Corner' Smith because of his strange bowling action), who later won fame in Hollywood playing British Army officers, and was knighted for his services to Anglo-American understanding. Umpires wore white coats in Australia for the first time when Vernon's XI played Victoria.

The financial results for the rival England teams in Australia were disastrous. They played attractive, enterprising cricket but easily defeated disgruntled, unrepresentative Australian teams worried more about their pay than their play. The English teams joined forces to field a combined team against Australia at Sydney under the captaincy of Walter Read, the only match granted Test status in that summer. Turner had match figures of 12 for 87 but Australia lost by 126 runs after being dismissed for the record-making low score of 42 in their first innings. This match was notable for the Test debut of Andrew Stoddart, who was to captain England at cricket and Rugby. The previous year Stoddart had made 485 for Hampstead against Stoics, but in Sydney he managed only 16 and 17. The match was a triumph for Bobby Peel who took 5 for 18 and 5 for 40. Postman George Giffen emerged that season as an all-rounder of the highest class.

Turner's technique captivated his English opponents for he completely ignored the advantages of body turn, preferring to deliver the ball facing square on to the batsman at right-arm medium-pace. Yet even on hard pitches like that of the Sydney ground he achieved exceptional 'nip' off the pitch and a hostile break-back. He was destined to form — with the left-armed John Ferris — the nucleus of Australia's Test attack for two complete tours of England.

Leslie Cobcroft, the Muswellbrook right-hand batsman who toured New Zealand with New South Wales teams in 1895-96 and 1898-99. He was in the State team for fifteen years.
— J.C. Davis Collection.

Andrew Newell, the Glebe club allrounder who made twenty-five appearances for New South Wales in the 1890s, and toured New Zealand with the State side in 1889-90.
— J.C. Davis Collection.

The noted English cricket historian Harry Altham calculated that on the 1888 English tour by the sixth Australian team Turner bowled 10,359 balls for 314 wickets at 11.38, Ferris 8890 balls for 220 wickets at 14.23. Altham wrote:

They knew that unless and until they got the enemy out, they and their fellows would continue to field. Bowl they had to and bowl they did. Together they took 534 wickets, or just 405 more than all the rest of their team put together, and this against the flower of English batting, with hardly a rest in 20 weeks of cricket.

The Australian team was weakened by the refusal of George Giffen to join in and by Sam Jones' collapse with smallpox soon after arrival. The manager, C.W. Beal, had a major financial stake in the tour and kept the nature of Jones' illness secret for fear that it would ruin the entire tour. Although only the captain Percy McDonnell, Bonnor, Alick Bannerman, and Jones had previous experience of batting conditions in England, the team won nineteen of their forty matches. Of the remaining matches they lost fourteen, and seven were drawn. They defeated England by 61 runs in the Lord's Test, with the strike bowlers Turner and Ferris dismissing a powerful side that included W.G. Grace, Abel, Barnes, Lohmann, Peel, and Gunn for 53 and 62. The Australians were able to win despite the fact that only Turner (12) and Ferris (20) made double figures in the second innings.

This 1888 Australian side was assisted by one of the most flamboyant characters in the history of Australian sport — Samuel Moses James Woods, the Sydney-born pace bowler whose batting flowered later in his career. Woods had begun his sporting education at Sydney Grammar School. Travelling to and from school every day he had sparred on the boat with the deckhand Peter Jackson, later world heavyweight boxing champion. He completed his education in England, where he captained Cambridge University at Rugby and cricket. He was regarded as one of the finest of all Rugby forwards, a man who revolutionised back-row play and kicked some amazing left-foot field goals. He captained Somerset and the Gentlemen at cricket and played Test cricket for both Australia and England. He was a superb marksman and runner and rode with the hounds, an enormously strong man at 6 feet 1 inch and 13 stone 6 pounds.

Sir Pelham Warner wrote that Sammy Woods was the most subtle and artistic fast bowler he ever saw, but he took only 11 wickets at 27.09 for the 1888 Australian team and in ten innings made just 54 runs. He left the team when Jones recovered. If only McDonnell had known that Woods had once taken 7 wickets in 7 balls in a Sydney match. As it was, the headlines were left to Ferris and Turner. At Old Trafford versus Lancashire Ferris took 8 for 41 in the first innings, at Stoke versus an English Eleven Turner had 9 for 15, and against an England Eleven at Hastings Turner took 17 for 50 in the match, clean-bowling fourteen of his victims. England won a low-scoring Test series two-to-one, with Abel's 70 in the second Test standing as the best score of the series.

By the time the seventh Australian team visited England in 1890, England had established definite supremacy. Australian hopes for the 1890 tour were boosted, however, when Murdoch returned to the captaincy after six years' absence. He had not played since the first Test against Shrewsbury's team at Adelaide in 1884 when he led the players' unsuccessful bid for half the gate receipts. The Australians included Hugh Trumble — making the first of his five tours of England — and former Test bowler Harry Boyle, an experienced manager. A curious aspect of the 1890 tour was that in the two Tests played the balls per over were increased from 4 to 5. A third Test was scheduled but was washed out.

Australia fielded five new players for the first Test at Lord's. Among them was Tasmanian Ken Burn, who had been selected as one of the team's wicket-keepers although he had never done the job in his life. J.E. Barrett, with 67 not out in Australia's second innings, became the first player in Tests to bat right through an innings unbeaten. Another highlight was J.J. Lyons's 50 in 36 minutes, but England still won by 7 wickets thanks to superb hands by Ulyett (74) and W.G. Grace (75 not out). Australia was on the point of winning a desperate struggle in the second test at The Oval when Barrett missed an easy run-out with both English batsmen stranded in mid-pitch, and an overthrow allowed England to make the necessary runs.

Murdoch headed the tour batting averages with 1459 runs at 23.35 but ended his career for Australia when he made an arrangement to finish his playing days with Sussex. He was a splendid captain — the first Australian batsman to rank with the best produced by England — whose wit and cheerfulness made him extremely popular. Like Ferris, who played for Gloucestershire after this tour, he subsequently played for England against South Africa.

By the 1890s strong women's teams such as the Snowflakes and Warrnambool Forget-Me-Nots were established in Victoria and the Seafoams in

Sydney. Women were advised to play with their hats securely strapped because catches were dropped through trying to take the catch with one hand and hold on to a hat with the other. Stopping the ball with their petticoats was banned. The first women's cricket match in Australia was played at Bendigo in 1874 when a report in the Melbourne *Argus* said the players wore calico skirts and red or blue tops, but no scores survive. The first match between organised women's clubs was played on Sydney Cricket Ground in 1896 between Siroccos and Fernleas. In 1890 Victoria played the first women's inter-State match against New South Wales and in 1891 Miss Rosalie Deane made 195 and 104 in a Sydney match. But the Australian Women's Cricket Council was not formed until 1931.

Above: The ladies cricket team 'Fernleas' who played in aid of charities in Sydney in 1886. Below the team 'Siroccos' who played against the 'Fernleas'.

Right: Zahn Rinaldo entertaining a large crowd at Melbourne Cricket Ground with acrobatics performed while hanging from a balloon. This was staged between innings in a Test match. — Michael Cannon.

The sixth Australian team which toured England — in 1888 — with only two strike bowlers, Ferris and Turner. (L to R): Back, J.J. Ferris, A.H. Jarvis, J. Worrall, C.W. Beal (top hatted manager), J.M. Blackham, H.F. Boyle, J.D. Edwards; Front, G.J. Bonnor, C.T.B. Turner, P.S. McDonnell (captain), G.H.S. Trott, A.C. Bannerman. Absent: S.M.J. Woods, J.J. Lyons and S.P. Jones (with smallpox). — Jack Pollard Collection.

Monty Noble, then vice-captain of the Australian team, with the world's smallest cricketer, Smaun Sing Hpoo, in England during Australia's 1905 tour.
— J.C. Davis Collection.

One of the most flamboyant characters in the whole history of sport, Samuel Moses James Woods, who assisted the 1888 Australian side. He played in three Tests for both Australia and England at cricket and for England at Rugby. Right, Woods' bowling was described by "Plum" Warner as the most subtle he ever saw. Left: Later in his career Woods blossomed as a hard-hitting batsman.
— Albert Gregory Collection.

The first New South Wales team that played in South Australia in 1890 (L to R): Back, A.P. Marr, H. Donnan, E.J. Briscoe, J. Portus (manager), J.J. Ferris, E. Moses; Centre, J.F. Wales, S. Callaway, F. Iredale, H. Moses (captain), P.C. Charlton, C.A. Richardson; Front, A.E. Clarke, S.E. Gregory, A.C. Bannerman. Only Briscoe, E. Moses, Wales, Richardson and Clarke missed Test selection. — New South Wales Cricket Association.

For Australia the most encouraging aspect of the 1890 tour was the improved form of Harry Trott and the big advances made by the gangling 6 feet 4 inch Hugh Trumble, an observant, reflective cricketer with exceptionally long arms and long sinewy fingers. Trumble became a slips fieldsman of the highest class, a medium-pace off-spinner who flighted the ball skilfully and turned it sharply enough to surprise the best batsmen of his time. He was a calm, resourceful batsman who made more than 5000 first-class runs, and was good enough to open for Australia.

Trumble leapt high in the delivery stride and let the ball go with his arm fully extended above his head, extracting bounce from even the most perfect pitches. His reach was legendary and he took dozens of catches off strokes batsmen thought were certain fours. 'The great camel, Hughie Trumble,' Sir Pelham Warner called him. Australia's Monty Noble was equally captivated by Trumble's prominent ears and big nose and the bowling approach run — 'sidelong and insinuating, with his neck craned like a gigantic bird'. He brought zest and colour to every game in

which he played, cagey but enthusiastic in all he did from the time he left Melbourne's Hawthorn Grammar School to pursue a career in banking and cricket.

The 1891–92 English team to Australia was financed by one of English cricket's great benefactors, Lord Sheffield — who accompanied the team — and captained by W.G. Grace. The visitors opened their tour in impressive style by beating South Australia, New South Wales, and Victoria. In the first Test at Melbourne, Grace's first in Australia, he encountered a formidable obstacle in Alick Bannerman. He batted for 435 minutes for 86 runs, scoring 45 and 41, establishing himself as one of the all-time masters of stonewalling. Grace made a stylish 50 in the first innings but Turner bowled Australia to victory by taking 5 for 51 off 33.2 overs in England's second innings.

In the second Test at Sydney, Abel became the first Englishman to bat through a Test innings with a score of 132 not out but Australia clinched the Ashes in winning by 72 runs. Bannerman, performing his 'barn door' act again, batted all the third day for only 67 runs. Briggs ended Australia's second innings with a hat-trick for England but South Australian John Lyons had already made the match safe for Australia with a blazing innings of 134, adding 174 for the second wicket with Bannerman. George Giffen (6 for 72) and Turner (4 for 46) were too much for England in the final innings, in which Giffen dismissed three Englishmen caught and bowled.

Stoddart made a dazzling 134 in the third Test at Adelaide, to set up an England victory by an innings and 230 runs. John Briggs, the cheerful Lancashire slow left-arm bowler who toured Australia six times, had match figures of 12 for 135. W.G. Grace captivated crowds in country centres, only occasionally challenging umpires' decisions in Camden, Bowral, Goulburn, and Ballarat. To express his gratitude for a happy tour, Lord Sheffield donated £150 for the advancement of Australian cricket. His team played twenty-seven matches, won six and lost two of the eleven-a-side games, and was unbeaten in the nineteen matches against the odds, winning seven and leaving twelve unfinished.

The States all had enthusiastic cricket control bodies and these became increasingly concerned about the profits made by the players and by private entrepreneurs. The leading players were extremely wary about supporting a national control authority, however, and strongly opposed suggestions that such a body should pick the teams for overseas tours and appoint the captains. In 1892 the Australasian Cricket Council was formed, with four representatives from South Australia, New South Wales, and Victoria. Its aims were to amend and interpret the laws of cricket, to settle disputes between State associations, to regulate intercolonial cricket, and to organise international tours. The founders hoped that New Zealand would join the Council but she failed to do so.

The Australasian Cricket Council lacked funds to finance overseas tours and the star players quickly made it clear to their State associations that a council that could not finance tours could not control them. Their objections were so vehement that the Council was exposed as a weak, ineffectual body. The Council held only a few meetings and was disbanded in 1898. Its main achievement had been to compile a list of twenty-two umpires whom member States agreed were efficient enough to stand in representative matches. The Council's major lasting contribution to Australian cricket was its decision to spend the £150 donated by Lord Sheffield on a shield for the winners of an annual interstate competition.

Ken Burn, the Tasmanian picked as wicket-keeper for the 1890 Australian team although he had never kept wicket in his life. He turned out a fine batsman, whose career produced 41 centuries and two scores above 350.
— Ric Smith.

The Council did the initial planning for the 1893 Australian tour of England but according to George Giffen offended the tour selectors by instructing them to include the flamboyant left-arm pace bowler Arthur Coningham, a former South Melbourne Club cricketer who had played for Queensland and New South Wales. The Council further annoyed the selectors — George Giffen, Blackham, Turner, Harry Trott, Alick Bannerman, and Lyons — by suggesting that it should name the team captain. Giffen wrote in his book, *With Bat and Ball*, that seven of the first eight Australian captains to tour England were elected by the players, usually after the teams sailed. The exception was H.J.H. ('Tup') Scott, whom the Melbourne Cricket Club appointed

captain when it organised and backed the 1886 tour of England.

The State associations remained unhappy that tour profits — which they believed should be spread through the clubs — went to members of the touring parties. They pointed to star players who had bought themselves fine homes on the profits received from English tours. But when the eighth Australian team went to England in 1893 to fulfil an itinerary organised by the Australasian Cricket Council, the team's composition and financial affairs were in the players' hands. They elected as captain, their most experienced member, Jack Blackham, who had been on every English tour to that time.

The Sheffield Shield, symbol of inter-State cricket supremacy, and the only noteworthy legacy of the Australasian Cricket Council, who bought it with Lord Sheffield's £150.
— Ken Piesse, *Australian Cricketer.*

The incomparable Hugh Trumble; a gawky, reflective giant with prominent nose, ears and long, bony fingers. He took 141 Test wickets including two hat-tricks. — Dave Gregory Collection.

Blackham's appointment, made without consulting the Australasian Cricket Council, was a highly contentious issue before a ball was bowled on the tour and by the end of it turned out to have been completely misguided. Billy Murdoch believed that he should have got the job despite his agreement with Sussex. The tour manager, V. Cohen, decided, however, to decline assistance from any of the Australian 'exiles' in England — Tom Garrett, Ferris, or Murdoch. The team included the best available talent, with the exception of Harry Moses who, sadly, had again declined to tour although he was still regarded as the finest left-hander in cricket.

Blackham's abject failure as a captain was no reflection on his wicket-keeping skill or his usefulness with the bat. He failed to lead Australia as impressively as Murdoch had done simply on the grounds of temperament. He was shrewd and popular but highly strung and his over-anxiousness gave his side the fidgets. He could not bear to watch close finishes. Instead he paced up and down in the dressing-room, hands and chin on his chest. Newspapers described him as 'a caged lion' when Australia was involved in tense finishes.

Blackham captained Australia eight times for three wins, three losses, and two draws. Behind the stumps he was still unsurpassed, but in two months lost 2 stone in weight as he mourned disasters and fretted over even minor failures. George Giffen wrote:

> One could not help but admire him as he stood behind the stumps at critical periods of a game. With dark eyes as keen as a hawk, and regardless of knocks, he would take the fastest bowling with marvellous dexterity, and woe betide the batsman who even so much as lifted his foot as he played forward and missed the ball.

Blackham, affectionately known to team-mates as 'old Jack' — the sobriquet also bestowed on the great racehorse Carbine — was a right-handed batsman who lacked style but whose brave slogging frequently saved Australia. He grew a beard at twenty-three and wore it all his life.

His team's major weakness on hard, fast wickets in a dry summer was that it lacked a fast bowler. When Trumble, Giffen, or Trott came on, they frequently faced batsmen who were well set. Harry Trott had some outstanding triumphs with his leg-breaks, particularly at Leicester where he had 5 for 29 and 6 for 58. Giffen and Trumble were superb off-spinners but Turner was nowhere near as deadly on true pitches as he had been on

turning strips. English critics were mystified that in the face of consistent failure to secure an early breakthrough the Australians did not give Coningham more chances with his left-arm fast-medium pacers.

Coningham appeared in only sixteen of the team's thirty-six matches and bowled only a fraction of the overs sent down by other bowlers. His career was sprinkled with batting, bowling, and fielding triumphs but he was such an eccentric that selectors could be forgiven for not entrusting Australia's international cricket reputation to him. He was a tall dark-haired man with striking pale blue eyes, immensely attractive to women. He had a habit of frequently absenting himself from the team without notice. In a match at Blackpool in cold weather he gathered some leaves and twigs and lit a fire in a far corner of the ground. He was also a brave man, and once dived into the Thames to save a boy in difficulties.

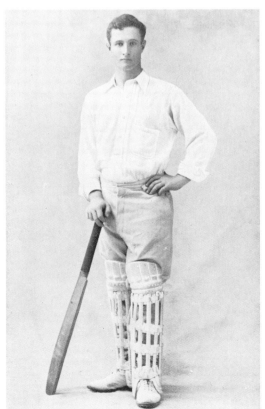

The ill-fated Australasian Cricket Council at a meeting in Adelaide on March 25, 1892 (L to R): Back, W. Bruce (Vic.), J.M. Gibson (N.S.W.), H.H. Budd (Vic.), R. Greig (Vic.), J.W. Coulton, J. Creswell (S.A.); Front, P. Sheridan (N.S.W.), H.Y. Sparks (S.A., chairman), G. Giffen, C. Beale (N.S.W.), G.M. Evans (S.A.), S. Rowe (Vic.), J. Portus (N.S.W.), V. Cohen (N.S.W.), W.O. Whitridge (S.A.).
— Dixson Gallery, Sydney.

Harry Graham, who in 1893 became the first Australian since Charles Bannerman in the first Test to score a century on debut for Australia. He did it at Lord's, the home of cricket.
— Melbourne Cricket Ground Museum.

A youthful Joe Darling as he appeared on his Test debut in 1894-95 in the first Test series to include five Tests.

The lanky Frank Iredale, who made his debut in the same Test. Both did well, but England won an exciting match by 10 runs.
— M.C.C. Collection at Lords.

Coningham scored only 249 runs at 13.10 in his sixteen tour matches but finished ahead of Harry Trott and George Giffen in the bowling averages, taking 31 wickets at 18.09. This was the man who scored the first-ever first-class century for Queensland when he made 151 against New South Wales. He was a champion clay target shooter, live bird shooter, bet-winning billiards and snooker player, a prominent runner, and a Rugby player and oarsman of repute.

Blackham's team played thirty-six matches in England on level terms. They won eighteen, lost ten, and eight were drawn. One of the three Tests was lost when F.S. Jackson made 103 for England at The Oval and the other two were saved as draws. Harry Graham became the first Australian since Charles Bannerman in the first of all Tests to score a century (107) on his Test debut in the Lord's Test and at the Oval Alick Bannerman became the first Australian to score 1000 Test runs. Perhaps the highlight of the tour was

Australia's score of 843 — then a record for a first-class innings — against Oxford and Cambridge Past and Present.

Blackham's poor record as a captain continued when he took the Australians to America on their way home. In the first match Philadelphia scored 525, the highest total by an American team in a first-class match. Australia scored 199 and 258 to lose by an innings and 68 runs. The Australians were rushed straight from their ship to the match but made no excuses for their defeat. Blackham's great career ended tragically in Sydney in December 1894 when he suffered a severe knock that prevented him from wicket-keeping again. He had made 74 — his highest Test score — in this remarkable match, adding 154 for the ninth wicket with Syd Gregory. The Australians were caught on a sticky wicket on the last day with only 64 runs wanted and 8 wickets left but lost by 10 runs.

The eighth Australian Cricket team, 1893: (L to R): Back, Carpenter (umpire), A.H. Jarvis, W.F. Giffen, W. Bruce, A.C. Bannerman, R. Thoms (umpire), G.H.S. Trott, H. Trumble, G. Giffen, J.M. Blackham, J.J. Lyons, R.W. McLeod, C.T.B. Turner; Front, H. Graham, A. Coningham, S.E. Gregory. Blackham proved a nervous, edgy captain.
— Jack Pollard Collection.

This was the first match in the first five-Test series ever played and ushered in a decade of tremendous Test struggles studded with brilliant cricket. It went to the sixth day, and resulted in England's winning after following on. Syd Gregory hit the second Test double century by scoring 201 in Australia's first innings of 586. George Giffen became the first player to score 200 runs (161 and 41) and take 8 wickets (4 for 75 and 4 for 164) in the same Test.* Joe Darling, Frank Iredale, Ernie Jones, Charlie McLeod, and John Reedman made their debuts for Australia in this epic affair — no cricketer could have had a more revealing introduction to the rigours of Test matches.

But for the injury to Blackham which disorganised Australia in the field in England's second innings England would never have been able to set Australia to score 177 to win the match. The Australians began their task so confidently that they reached 2 for 113 by the end of the fifth day. Victory appeared assured but during the night the rain poured down. George Giffen said that when he woke on the last morning with sun streaming in his window he was ecstatic. The first person he met at breakfast was Blackham 'with a face as long and dark as a coffee pot'. The wicket was now a vicious gluepot and with the sun on it England had just the bowlers to exploit it in left-handers Briggs and Peel. And exploit it they did, with Briggs taking 3 for 25 and Peel finishing with 6 for 67.

The second Test at Melbourne was just as dramatic. The eccentric left-hander Coningham took a wicket with the first ball of the match after new captain George Giffen became the first to give his opposition first innings on winning the toss. England were bundled out for 75, with Turner taking 5 for 32, but the great English fast bowler Tom Richardson responded with an equally impressive 5 for 57 to have Australia out for only 123. Andrew Stoddart then played one of Test cricket's immortal innings in scoring 173 out of England's second innings total of 475. Set to score 428 to win, Australia appeared well on the way at 1 for 190. Stoddart then brought on medium-pace Bill Brockwell who dismissed Trott, Giffen, and Darling and so swung the match, with Australia falling 94 short of her target.

*Giffen is still the only
player to have achieved
this feat.

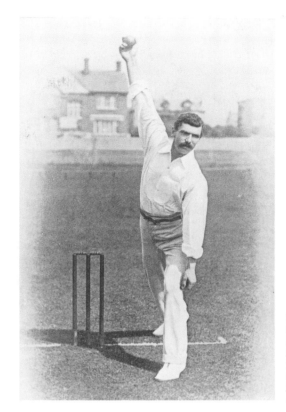

The indefatigable English fast bowler Tom Richardson. In 1894-95, he took 32 wickets in five Tests in Australia, best figures 5 for 57 at Melbourne.
— E.S. Marks Collection.

Melbourne fans were privileged to see one of Test cricket's great innings from this stocky little Yorkshireman, J.T. Brown, in March, 1895. He made 50 in 28 minutes, 100 in 95 minutes and finished with a match-winning 140, all this after England had lost 2 for 28.

Australia showed tremendous fighting spirit to recover from two-to-nil down to level the series at two Tests all, winning by handsome margins in Adelaide and Sydney. Iredale made 140 – the first of his two Test centuries — in a match played in intense heat at Adelaide, where big Albert Trott scored 110 runs (38 and 72) without being dismissed and bowled unchanged throughout England's second innings to take 8 for 43. Only two other bowlers have taken 8 wickets in an innings in their maiden Test — Alf Valentine for the West Indies in 1950 and Bob Massie for Australia in 1972. At Sydney, Stoddart won the toss and put Australia in. With Australia 6 for 51, his decision appeared justified. Then Harry Graham (105) and Albert Trott (85 not out) took Australia to 284 by the end of the second day. England were dismissed twice on the third day, for 65 and 72.

Turner took 8 wickets in both the second and fourth Tests to become the first Australian to capture 100 Test wickets but then was dropped from the side, a strange fate for a man who ranks among the greatest of all Australian bowlers. He was replaced for the fifth Test by Tom McKibbin, a controversial off-spinner from Turner's home town, Bathurst. Turner was incensed at being dropped and when he was invited to tour England with the Australian side two years later declined, saying that he was too busy. Thus one of Australia's finest all-rounders disappeared from big cricket. He had scored 3856 runs, with two centuries, and taken 993 wickets at 14.28, dismissing five batsmen in an innings 102 times. No other Australian has ever come near his feat in 1887–88 of taking 106 wickets in a season at 13.59.

With the teams level at two Tests apiece, **spectators travelled hundreds of miles to** Melbourne for the decisive fifth Test. Coastal steamers were booked out. Special trains were put on. For the first time in Test history, more than 100 000 spectators watched a match. They were not disappointed, for the cricket on both sides was of the highest quality — the fielding and 'keeping ('Affie' Jarvis was the new Australian wicket-keeper) were applause-winning stuff.

Australia began by scoring 414. England responded with 385, thanks to a superb 120 by Archie MacLaren. Tom Richardson then bowled like a man possessed to take 6 for 104 and restrict Australia to 267 in the second innings, knocking back the stumps four times. Faced with scoring 297 to win, England lost Stoddart and Brockwell for 28. Stocky little Yorkshireman John Brown came in and played one of Test cricket's greatest innings. He attacked the bowling from the first ball, made 50 in 28 minutes, and went on to 140, adding 210 with the Lancashire opening batsman Albert Ward (93). MacLaren and Peel then finished off the 40 required to give England victory in a memorable series.

Although beaten in this series by a great English side, Australia performed at a far higher and more consistent level than in any previous Test series, emphasising that standards in all States had improved as a result of the introduction of the Sheffield Shield competition in 1892–93. From its inception the Shield — 46 inches deep, 30 inches wide, and topped for some unexplained reason by a bosomy girl — has remained the symbol of interstate supremacy. The ideal training ground for Test players, the Shield competition repeatedly yielded brilliant cricket.

Until his death the donor of the Shield remained one of Australian cricket's most ardent supporters. Five Australian teams opened their English tours by playing on his private ground at Sheffield Park. Unfortunately he was not an outstanding player, but few have contributed as much to Australian cricket as Henry North Holroyd, 3rd Earl of Sheffield, Viscount Pevensey, Baron Sheffield of Dunsmore, Meath, Baron Sheffield of Roscommon, Ireland, and Baron Sheffield of Sheffield, Yorkshire. Fittingly, the Sheffield Shield bears the Australian and Sheffield coats of arms.

The South Australian team that defeated Victoria by an innings and 164 runs at Adelaide in November, 1981, thereby ensuring a place the next season in the Sheffield Shield competition (L to R): Back, J. Noel, W.F. Giffen, H.L. Haldane; Centre, I.A. Fisher (umpire), H. Moore, J.J. Lyons, J. Reedman, C.W. Hayward; Front, A.H. Jarvis, G. Giffen (captain), F. Jarvis, H. Blinman.
— Melbourne Cricket Ground Museum.

R. A. DUFF,
New South Wales.

M. A. NOBLE,
Paddington.

W. W. ARMSTRONG,
Victoria.

C. HILL

J. J. FERRIS.
GLOUCESTERSHIRE

E. G. MACARTNEY, N.S.W.

W. L. MURDOCH.
SUSSEX.

P. McALISTER, VIC.

H. CARTER,
Waverley.

V. TRUMPER

G. GIFFEN,
West Adelaide.

H. TRUMBLE

9. Australia in the Golden Age

The golden age of cricket has always been regarded as the period between 1890 and 1914. For in those years all the skills of the game flowered and an unprecedented array of great batsmen and bowlers delighted informed and appreciative galleries. More importantly, the players of that time set standards of sportsmanship and good behaviour that lifted cricket above other games and established it as a character-builder and an integral part of the social scene. The brilliance of the players was matched by their ethics: the friendliness between international teams made the achievement of Test status a goal for every youngster. Australia played a major role in these grand achievements in cricket.

The appearance of Ernie Jones and his steady development as a devastating strike bowler enabled selectors to dismiss the free-wheeling Coningham after one Test. Coningham returned from Queensland to play for New South Wales and in 1899 set up as a bookmaker on the flat at Randwick Racecourse in Sydney, with his money bag carrying the inscription 'Coningham the Cricketer' in large white letters. He ran a short-lived tobacco business and in 1899 sued his English wife, the former Alice Stamford, for divorce, alleging that Father D.F. O'Haran — administrator of Sydney's St Mary's Cathedral and private secretary to Cardinal Moran — was the father of one of the Coningham children. Coningham's barrister gave up early in the hearing and Coningham thereafter conducted his own case, alleging that he could not have been the father of his child because of an injury he received from a cricket ball. There were two trials, as the first jury could not reach an agreement. At one point Coningham had to be relieved of a pistol he wore at the waist in court.

Heroes of Australian cricket during the Golden Age as shown on cigarette cards popular at the time. Many of these cards are extremely valuable today.
— David Frith, Wisden *Cricket Monthly.*

Jones was more than an adequate substitute, a giant of a man whose handshake pulped other cricketers' hands, and who could bowl for hours at a furious pace. His strength came from his background as a miner. Australians saw in his vast shoulders and powerful chest the answer to England's master pace man Tom Richardson. First, however, he had to endure the process of transformation from a rough and awkward club pace bowler in Adelaide (where two longstops were set for him) to a Test bowler of well co-ordinated length and even a little guile. He was widely loved and even opposing players used his nickname 'Jonah' affectionately.

Jones remained the spearhead of Australia's attack from 1894 until 1902. He played in nineteen Tests and toured England three times. **On the first of these tours, in 1896, he improved** almost daily under the astute captaincy of Harry Trott, a postman whom English critics unanimously rated the best Australian captain since Murdoch. Trott, eldest son of an outstanding cricket family, was unruffled in any situation, master of himself and the team, skilled in changing his bowlers, and subtle in extracting superhuman efforts from tired players.

The 1890 Australians at Westbury-on-Trym during the match against W.H. Laverton's XI (L to R): K.E. Burn, H.F. Boyle, J.J. Lyons, W.L. Murdoch, and W.G. Grace. J.J. Ferris is on Grace's left holding the rifle and nuzzling the dog. C.T. Turner is two away from Ferris on the steps at the left. The ladies are unknown.
— Ric Smith.

Trott's team included some outstanding newcomers to England in Darling, Hill, Iredale, Kelly, Eady, and Johns. They were efficiently managed by Harry Musgrove, a gentlemanly figure with Test experience who was part of the famous Australian theatrical firm Williamson, Garner and Musgrove, later known as J.C. Williamson's. Jones' presence made a great difference to the performance of the Australian side as compared with that of previous teams. This was despite doubts over the fairness of his action when he really let one go, as on the occasion when he was reported to have bowled a ball right through W.G. Grace's beard. When the good doctor asked what he was up to Jones replied: 'Sorry, doctor, she slipped'. Trott and Musgrove had a more difficult problem with McKibbin, whose off-breaks turned so sharply that many observers thought he must **throw almost every ball. McKibbin was no-balled** for throwing three times in his career but never in a first-class match and he finished the 1896 tour without being called.

McKibbin's spin was pronounced enough to give him 101 wickets at 14.27 on the tour, including 11 wickets in the two Tests in which he appeared. Jones' pace produced 121 wickets at 16.4. But by general consent Trumble — who took 148 wickets at 15.12 — was the most dangerous of the Australian bowlers. The team would have improved on their record of nineteen wins in thirty-four matches, with nine draws and six losses, had they had a hitter or two of the calibre of Bonnor, McDonnell, or Lyons, who could produce runs in a hurry. Harry Donnan and Frank Iredale were reliable and resolute but too slow. The left-handers Hill and Darling both had exciting innings on their first trips to England: Darling finished with 1555 runs at 29.9 top score 194, and Hill with 1196 runs at 27.81, best score 130.

Darling's innate sense of fair play won him immediate respect among the great contemporary English players such as MacLaren, Hayward, Abel, Peel, Lilley, and Ranjitsinhji, and this was to have an important bearing on the spirit and conduct of many matches over the next decade. He was a tough competitor, a dashing or dour batsman as occasion demanded, and he learnt quickly under Harry Trott's leadership the tricks of field placement and lifting the morale of a side. When he first got into the Australian team, Ernie Jones had a habit of challenging newcomers to naked dressing-room wrestles after they showered. Darling won everyone's respect when he threw the immensely strong Jones — it was the first time anybody could recall Jones taking the brunt of the joke.

THE AUSTRALIAN CRICKETING TEAM, 1896.

Trott's team to England (L to R): Back, F. Lemmon (scorer), A.E. Johns, E.J. Eady, J. Darling, H. Donan, J. McKibbin, H. Graham, H. Musgrove (manager); Centre, H. Trumble, E. Jones, G.H.S. Trott, G. Giffen, F.A. Iredale; Front, J.J. Kelly, S.E. Gregory, C. Hill. — Jack Pollard Collection.

Trott captained Australia in the five Tests against England in Australia in 1897–98, helping to achieve a resounding four-to-one triumph. Darling became the first left-hander to score a Test century with an innings of 101 at Sydney in the first Test. But MacLaren made 109 and Ranjitsinhji 175 for England, who won by 9 wickets. Ernie Jones became the first bowler in Tests to be no-balled for throwing when Australian umpire Jim Phillips called him in the second Test at Melbourne. Undeterred, Jones shrugged and settled down to bowl more accurately off a short run and it became quite obvious that he threw only when he stretched for extra pace.

At Sydney in the third Test Joe Darling became the first batsman to score two centuries in the same series. He reached his second century in spectacular style, lifting the ball right out of Adelaide Oval for 6. In those days hits over the boundary counted 5; sixes came only from hits that cleared fences and stands. In Melbourne, Clem Hill, then only twenty, made 188, and at Sydney in the fifth Test, Darling scored his third century of the series (160), the first 100 in only 91 minutes. The series was also notable for the introduction of medium-pace bowler Bill ('Farmer') Howell and an all-rounder from the Paddington club, Monty Noble.

Harry Trott's feat in defeating Stoddart's strong 1897–98 side four-to-one in the Tests deservedly established him as one of Australia's greatest captains. His team were unanimous in finding him the finest tactician under whom they played, upsetting the English batsmen with rapid changes of bowlers, field settings that blocked favourite strokes, and inspired touches that revived tired players. When Ernie Jones' speed lagged, Trott got keeper 'Affie' Jarvis to stand right up on the stumps. Jones felt slighted and immediately resumed firing the ball down like cannon shot, quickly forcing Jarvis to retire. Ray Robinson called Trott a Will Rogers among cricketers, a man of personality and homespun humour. Hugh Trumble said Trott was the best captain Australia ever had and Clem Hill agreed. England's Archie MacLaren simply said: 'I would give anything to play the game as keenly and yet as light-heartedly as Trott's lads did'.

Not the least of Trott's achievements was to curb the devastating hitting of England's star, Ranjitsinhji. He had long discussions with Joe Darling about how to frustrate Ranji and their plans worked so well that England's captain Archie MacLaren said Ranji was 'in a blue funk'. The Australians exploited Ranji's habit of having a last look around the field before he settled down to take guard. They deliberately weakened the offside and stationed two men about 10 metres from Ranji, with one man deep to save four. The bowlers were instructed to peg away on the leg stump and pads. The Australians had noticed that all of Ranji's brilliant array of legside strokes travelled a few inches above the turf after they were hit and they set themselves to catch a percentage of these. As Darling wrote:

Ranji always used to have a look where we were fielding before the bowler started to deliver the ball. As soon as he had his last look and the bowler was on the point of delivering the ball, we shifted positions by a few yards, sometimes one way, sometimes the other. Occasionally only one would move and sometimes nobody moved at all. Ranji never knew where we were actually fielding when he was about to make his stroke and this eventually put him clean off his game. On one occasion he made a beautiful stroke on the legside, the ball travelling at great speed only inches off the ground and to all intents and purposes, right between the two 'silly' legs. But Syd Gregory, absolutely the finest fieldsman on our side, had shifted and he brought off a fine catch, much to Ranji's disgust. From that day Ranji was never the same batsman.

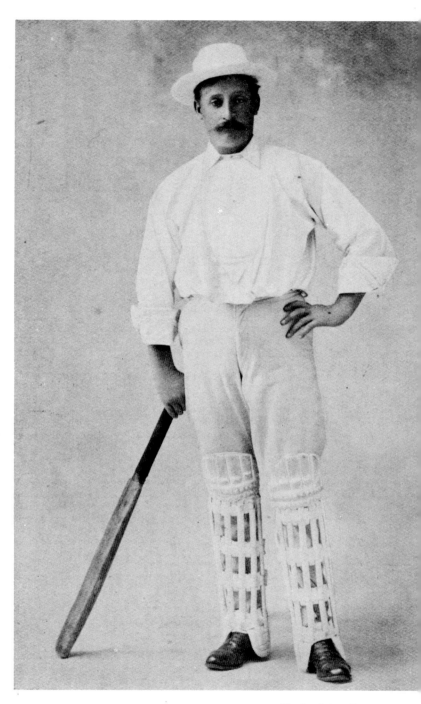

*The lugubrious Harry Trott, a dreamy-eyed postman, who always looked as if he was about to nod off to sleep. He proved a wide-awake Australian captain.
— Melbourne Cricket Ground Museum.*

Australian stalwarts of the Golden Age (L to R): George Giffen, Clem Hill, prolific Adelaide batsmen who could pulverise the best bowling; wicket-keeper James Joseph Kelly, one of a long line of skilful cricketers from the Paddington club; Tasmanian C.J. Eady, who once made 566 for Break-'-Day but turned out a better bowler than batsman in big cricket. — Rick Smith and Ric Finlay.

Harry Trott was such a popular Australian captain during the 1890s that people used to pause and pay homage outside his house in Melbourne's Albert Park. He was known to be a skipper who looked after his players and was at the head of discussions that led to the Australians receiving a pay rise of £10 to £25 a Test. The five South Australian Test players wanted £200 but Harry talked them into the smaller fee. As federation of the Australian States neared a Melbourne newspaper editorial commented: 'We believe that Harry Trott and his 10 good men have done more for the federation of Australian hearts than all the big delegates put together'.

Harry Trott was blamed for his brother Albert's departure to play county cricket for Middlesex. The truth was that the short-lived Australasian Cricket Council caused this sad loss to Australian cricket by insisting that the 1896 team to tour England be announced before the start of the 1894–95 Australian season. The Council was anxious to limit withdrawals by giving the tourists plenty of time to make arrangements for their

long absence. Albert produced his match-winning performances at Adelaide and Sydney in Tests played *after* the touring party had been announced. The Council was too absorbed in fighting for its own existence to bother with problems such as the injustice of leaving Albert Trott out of an English tour. He went off to England to prove himself one of the greatest all-rounders in history and Australia lost a crowd-pleaser of the highest calibre.

Victoria had won the first Sheffield Shield competition in 1892–93 by winning all four matches. The left-handers William Bruce, Bob McLeod, and Frank Laver all hit centuries for Victoria, but Harry Donnan was the first of all Shield century-makers with 120 against South Australia at Adelaide in December 1892. Frank Iredale made 101 for New South Wales at Melbourne in the same month. South Australia showed that misgivings about her inclusion in the Shield were ill-founded by winning the competition in its second season, 1893–94. But South Australia had to wait sixteen years before

she won the Shield again. In that period Victoria and New South Wales became fierce rivals, with all of their matches producing a tense 'needle-like' atmosphere. In all three States old heroes were being replaced as exciting youngsters appeared.

District cricket was introduced in Sydney in 1893–94, with East Sydney the first winners. Adelaide followed in 1897–98, first winners East Torrens, and Brisbane the same season, first winners Woolloongabba; Hobart in 1905–06, first winners North Hobart; Melbourne in 1906–07, first winners East Melbourne. District cricket was tried in North Tasmania in 1907–08 but was not a success. Oddly enough, district cricket did not begin in Perth until 1959–60 when South Perth were the first winners. In the summer which saw the introduction of district competition in Adelaide, Clem Hill made 360 not out for Prince Alfred College v. St. Peter's College.

The golden age of cricket found Australia bristling with talent. Clem Hill, Joe Darling, George Giffen, Affie Jarvis, Dinny Reedman, and John Lyons all performed with brilliance for South Australia. They did not, however, overshadow a New South Wales side that included Bill Howell, Harry Donnan, Syd Gregory, Frank Iredale, Monty Noble, and Jim Kelly. Victoria, too, had thrilling newcomers in Alf Johns, Jack Worrall, Warwick Armstrong, William Bruce, and John Harry, with the McLeod and Trumble brothers well established.

Harry Trott went back to his postman's duties and handed over the Australian captaincy to Joe ('Paddy') Darling after the four-to-one triumph over Stoddart's tourists in 1897–98. He had made four tours of England between 1888 and 1896, made more than 1000 runs on each visit, and taken 145 wickets. He scored six of his ten first-class centuries in England. His successor's nickname Paddy derived from his resemblance to boxing champion Paddy Slavin.

"Farmer Bill" Howell, who did not even see a first-class game until he was 25 but managed to play 25 Tests in his mature years. — New South Wales Cricket Assoc.

Tom McKibbin, Bathurst-born off-spinner whom many believed was a chucker. He was no-balled three times for throwing but never in a first-class match. His spin made some batsmen look foolish. — Albert Gregory Collection.

Expert opinion differs on whether Darling or Clem Hill was the finer left-handed batsman but Hugh Trumble had it right when he said that Hill was the more spectacular hitter who could destroy an attack, Darling the more dour fighter and superior on wet or damaged pitches. Darling's wealthy father at first thought Joe wasted his time playing cricket. When grain king John Darling, M.P., was finally persuaded to watch his son bat he was so thrilled by Joe's century against Stoddart's team on Adelaide Oval that he gave him a gold watch and a cheque representing £1 for every run he had scored. John Darling became a devotee and followed his son around Australia. But when Joe made 178 against England in Adelaide in 1897–98 he reduced his cheque to £78 — £1 for every run over 100.

Joe Darling always had a strong dislike for officials of the various State cricket associations, many of whom he considered were 'notoriety seekers and dead heads'. He wrote that in his first Test appearance at Sydney he was shocked to find when he went off for lunch that all seats in the dining-room were occupied by officials and their guests. He was one of the first to demand that a dining-room be set aside for players on both sides and this practice has continued ever since. Once during an interstate match in Sydney Darling got two South Australian players to confiscate the tea urn which had been so dominated by officials that players could not get a cup of tea at the tea interval.

Darling played a leading role in having the laws of cricket amended to award 6 for hits over the fence. When he came into cricket hits over the fence were worth 5 and the ball had to be struck clear out of the ground to score 6. Darling said:

I well remember the first ball I received in England in 1896 from W.G. Grace. I hit it right over the fence but scored only 4. Later when I hit a ball from Townsend over the pavilion at Crystal Palace, the umpire turned to Dr. Grace and said, 'Well, doctor, I suppose that's six', but W.G. said 'no, only four.' I asked W.G. how much further I would have had to hit the ball for six and he replied: 'Oh, about another 100 yards.'

On the 1899 tour the Surrey County Cricket Club gave Darling's Australians a dinner during which the Surrey president deplored slow and tedious cricket. Replying for the Australians, Darling suggested that batsmen would be more ready to take risks if they got 6 instead of 5 for blows over the fence. The idea was widely discussed and Darling was asked to write to the Marylebone Cricket Club advocating that 6 be awarded for all hits over the fence. When he returned home he moved at a South Australian Cricket Association meeting that the idea be universally adopted. The S.A.C.A. agreed to introduce the law for all its matches and the other States followed suit. England did so later. An interesting extension of the idea came in the 1929–30 Australian season when, in a bid to encourage brighter cricket, the N.S.W.C.A. introduced a law awarding eight runs for hits over the fence. The law lasted only one season.

Darling's 1899 team lost only three of their thirty-five matches, winning sixteen and playing sixteen draws. They won the Test rubber, the first in England to include five matches, by taking the second Test at Lord's by 10 wickets. All the other Tests were drawn in a long hot summer of high scoring. Victor Trumper, in only his second Test, paved the way to Australia's Lord's win with a chanceless 135 not out. Trumper had been a last-minute inclusion in the Australian team after failures in the first two of three selection matches. In the third he made a brilliant 56 and Darling and Hugh Trumble realised they had been wrong in not selecting him in their teams for England. They told the team organisers they had erred because they had not seen enough of Trumper, he was taken on as an extra player with an agreed bonus of £200 (for the rest of the team the bonus was £700), and he had to assist the manager, Major Ben Wardill, with letters, laundry, and team autographs.

Montague Alfred Noble variously known as "Alf" or "Monty" or "Mary Anne." He used a unique bowling grip modelled on American baseballers. Jack Worrall claimed he was a chucker.
— Sydney Mail.

Left: Harry Hilliard, who played in the first matches in the Domain and Hyde Park, photographed in Sydney in his 80th year.
— Jack Pollard Collection.

Prince Ranjitsinhji, Kumar Shri, later his Highness Jam Sahib of Nawanagar, who was known at Cambridge University as "Smith." Australians destroyed this legendary run-scorer's confidence with a magnificent tactical ploy based on magnificent fielding.
— Melbourne Cricket Ground Museum.

Albert Trott — a grievous loss to Australian cricket when he became upset at missing selection in his brother's team and joined the Middlesex County team.
— Albert Gregory Collection.

When Trumper made a brilliant 300 not out against Sussex at Brighton, the team management decided they could not pay him less than the other players and put him on the same terms. Darling made 60 not out in that match but — confronted by Trumper's brilliance — said he returned to the pavilion feeling he could not play the game at all. Trumper's health was so frail, however, that he did nothing for almost three weeks after the 300 not out against Sussex. In Darling's words:

> Trumper was a good fast bowler, but I could not bowl him as I had to nurse him for his batting. What a great allrounder he would have been had he been a stronger man. He was a fine slip field and one of the best outfields Australia ever had. Trumper had many bad days, but when fit and well there was only one cricketer in it as champion of the world.

Throughout the 1899 tour Darling carefully watched Trumper's health. When the team coach left hotels, he would never let the driver move until he had been told Trumper was aboard. Like all members of the team, Darling had two large cricket bags. After the Sussex match he did not open one of his bags for three weeks: when he did he found the bat with which Trumper had made his huge score, inscribed with the words, 'To Joe Darling, with Victor Trumper's compliments'. One of Darling's sons still has the bat.

This was the way players took the field in the days of the bike track. Opinions varied on whether the track or the fence should be the boundary but most captains preferred the fence.
— Albert Gregory Collection.

Syd Gregory, whose 57 Test appearances remained an Australian record until Neil Harvey beat it in the 1960s.
— Frank Laver Collection.

Alfred Johns, who toured England with two Australian teams but suffered from soft hands that were easily injured. Giffen said he had a genius for 'keeping, but Johns never played in a Test.
— Albert Gregory Collection.

The Tasmanian team that played Victoria in January, 1896, included players whose skill rates high even today (L to R): Back, J. Watt, E.A.C. Windsor, E. Maxwell, W.H. Savigny, C.W. Butler; Centre, E. Over (umpire), A.J. Douglas, C.J. Eady, J.H. Savigny, D. Roof (scorer); Front, W.P. Hood (manager), N. Westbrook, E.J.K. Burn, J. Bingham, C. Vautin.
— Ric Smith.

Charles McLeod, one of seven brothers who played for Melbourne Cricket Club, three of them for Victoria and two, Charles and Robert, for Australia. Charles acquired useful runs and wickets in most of his 15 Tests.
— Melbourne Cricket Ground Museum.

Brisbane Cricket Ground during the England v. Queensland match in 1897. Spectators raised umbrellas but the Englishmen made no complaints about the rain and remained on the field.
— Patrick Mullins.

Darling headed his team's batting averages with 1941 runs at 41.29; Noble scored 1608 at 37.39, Trumper 1556 at 34.57, Worrall 1202 at 35.35, Trumble 1183 at 27.51, Gregory 1181 at 27.46, and Iredale 1039 at 29.68. Hill made 879 at 39.95 but missed much of the tour because of a nose operation. This imposing display of batting strength was supported by equally impressive results from Australia's bowlers. Trumble, by now a master craftsman, took 142 wickets at 18.43, Jones 135 at 21.1, Howell 117 at 20.35, with splendid support from Noble (82 at 22.9) and Charlie McLeod (81 at 22.96). It was on this tour that Trumble curbed the prolific run-scoring of Gilbert ('The Croucher') Jessop, the spectacular England right-hand batsman, deceiving Jessop so often with subtle changes of pace that he lost confidence.

Another frequent Trumble victim was F.S. Jackson, who had trouble picking the slower ball. 'You old devil, Hughie,' he used to say. 'But I'll pick that slower one sooner or later.' To the Australian players, aware of Trumble's artistry, it was far more intriguing that professional cricketers who batted with a true-blue amateur like Jackson had to change in a different dressing-room and wait at the professionals' gate, allowing Jackson to take the field first. The amateur and professional members of the England team entered from gates 50 yards apart and only met in the middle. None of this sat easily with Australians who knew that W.G. Grace had been paid £3000 before he agreed to visit Australia with Lord Sheffield's team, and also had all expenses paid for himself and his wife.

For the Australians one of the remarkable events of their 1899 English tour occurred when a famous English amateur playing for Yorkshire called the masterful John Brown for a run and was refused. The amateur, who came from a wealthy family, told Brown he had to run when called. A little later Brown was called again and the wealthy amateur was run out, much to the Australians' joy. Darling considered that Australia had an advantage while they could field teams in which all players were equal. A special favourite of the Australians was the Notts right-hander William Barnes, whose committee had warned him not to arrive for matches the worse for liquor. The committee reprimanded him after he scored a match-saving century while he was drunk. 'How many of you could make a hundred, drunk or sober?' Barnes asked.

This great 1899 Australian side included yet another outstanding wicket-keeper in Jim Kelly, who matched the skills of Blackham and Jarvis on earlier tours. Indeed, Kelly was so good that he kept a most brilliant keeper — Alf Johns — out of the Test side. Johns had rare brilliance in stumping but had extremely fragile hands, which cut short his career although he twice toured England. George Giffen believed Johns was a genius but agreed when he was left out of Tests. Kelly came from the Paddington Club in Sydney, along with Noble, Trumper, and a long list of cricket's immortals. He hit three centuries in a first-class career that produced 4108 runs.

Left:
Victor Trumper's incomparable footwork as he boldly moved out to drive provided cameraman George Beldam with pictures renowned throughout the cricket world.
— Albert Gregory Collection.

Joe Darling's 1899 Australian team, which beat England in the Test rubber and lost only three of their 35 matches (L to R): Back, V. Trumper, H. Trumble, A.E. Johns, W.P. Howell, Major B. Wardill (manager), M.A. Noble, F. Laver, C.E. McLeod; Centre, J.J. Kelly, C. Hill, J. Worrall, J.J. Darling, F.A. Iredale, E. Jones; Front, S.E. Gregory.
— Melbourne Cricket Ground Museum.

Probably the most famous of all cricket photographs — Victor Trumper straight driving from a metre in front of his crease. Absence of fieldsmen suggests the shot was posed. — George Beldam.

By the turn of the century sixty-four Tests had been played, fifty-six of them between England and Australia, the rest between England and South Africa. England had won twenty-six Tests, Australia twenty, and ten had been drawn. But Australia's great effort to challenge the world's best had had its disappointments. The great Charles Bannerman had been forced to retire through ill health after only three Tests; Albert Trott, James Ferris, Billy Murdoch, and a marvellous Victorian bowler called Billy Roche had been lost to English counties. The players' antagonism towards administrators remained strong.

In 1899 Jack Worrall and Frank Iredale ended their Test careers, Iredale to become a commentator, and secretary of the New South Wales Cricket Association, Worrall because he was compelled to do so. Both Iredale, Worrall, and Paddy Horan before them made big contributions to Australian cricket in our newspapers. But their success as critics should never be regarded as proof that all retired Test players make worthy commentators.

Worrall left the game in unfortunate circumstances. He foolishly wrote a letter to a prominent English umpire advising him to no-ball both Noble and Jack Saunders on Australia's 1902 tour of England. The umpire showed the letter to Darling and Trumble, who naturally complained about Worrall's action. At a Victorian Cricket Association meeting the following motion was passed:

'That while admitting Mr. Worrall's great services to Victorian cricket, this association recognised that, as matters stand between him and members of the Australian team, it would be better for the interests of the game if Mr. Worrall voluntarily retired from the Victorian team.'

This ended the career of a plucky, gifted cricketer. Worrall's convictions about the alleged chuckers were only part of a world-wide feeling that something had to be done to define a legal delivery. English county teams bristled with chuckers — the great amateur C.B. Fry among them. Australia had bowlers like McKibbin, Saunders, and Jones with suspect actions. Although it was recognised that unfair overarm bowling styles persisted, however, nobody could define illegal bowling. To the average Australian cricket spectator it was puzzling that Jones' action could be challenged while that of the fast-rising New South Wales pace bowler 'Tibby' Cotter was rated perfectly fair. They had their answer when the Australian umpire James Phillips got to work in England.

Reviewing the 1898 season, *Wisden* said:

For the first time in our experience — with some trifling exceptions — bowlers were no-balled for throwing in England in first-class matches. C.B. Fry was no-balled by West at Trent Bridge, by Phillips at Brighton and by Sherwin at Lord's.

Wisden was particularly pleased over the no-balling of Fry, which it called a case of long-delayed justice. Phillips became the centre of a controversy which culminated when a conference of county cricket captains was held at Lord's. At that conference nine regular English county bowlers were labelled chuckers, Fry by eleven votes to one. Fry never bowled seriously again. Another casualty was Lancashire pace bowler Arthur Mold, whom Phillips had no-balled for throwing sixteen times in 10 overs against Somerset.

The England team that met Australia in the First Test at Nottingham in 1899 (L to R): Back, R.G. Barlow (umpire), T.W. Hayward, G.H. Hirst, W. Gunn, J.T. Hearne (12th man), W. Storer, W. Brockwell, V.A. Titchmarsh (umpire); Seated, C.B. Fry, K.S. Ranjitsinhji, W.G. Grace, F.S. Jackson; Front, W. Rhodes, J.T. Tyldesley. It was Grace's last Test at 50 years 320 days. — M.C.C. Collection at Lord's.

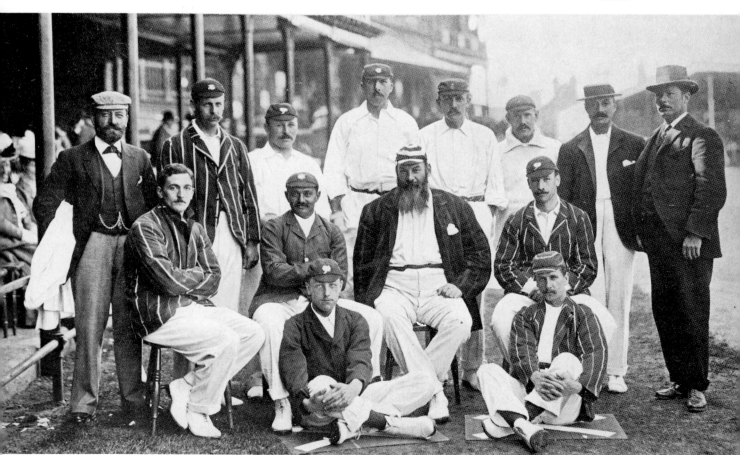

10. The Players' Revolt

The introduction of large comfortable steamships transformed the Australian cricketers' attitude towards overseas tours. The voyages to and from England were no longer wild, arduous journeys endured mainly in their bunks by some players, for the sake of the tour bonus that would buy a home or a business when the seasickness was over. Instead the tours themselves became as enjoyable and rewarding as the cricket. There was dancing on board, and fancy dress parties, card games, shooting . . . and ample scope for pranksters in the teams. Exchanges between Australian and New Zealand teams became more frequent. As their outlook became more international, Australians began to look away from the traditional rival, England, to other countries whom they could play.

Australian teams had played in New Zealand since 1878 when Dave Gregory's pioneering side played there before leaving for England. Most of the early matches were against the odds, as New Zealand faced a long struggle to lift her standards. When the 1880 Australian side played Fifteen of Canterbury, the Australian captain Billy Murdoch backed himself to score more runs than the Canterbury total. He won the bet, too, scoring 111 after Canterbury were out for 90. In 1883–84 when a Tasmanian team toured New Zealand a fire brigade had to be called to pump water from the ground in the visitors' first match against Otago. In 1890 the prominent Sydney player Joe Davis took a team to New Zealand and ran into problems with inexperienced umpires. In the Wellington match, Davis asked for the umpires to be changed and was told his team would not be paid their gate money if they persisted in the demand. The tourists finally gave up their gate money to get fresh umpires.

Below: A magnificent panoramic view of the Sydney Cricket Ground during the 1901-02 season matches against England. — New South Wales Government Printer.

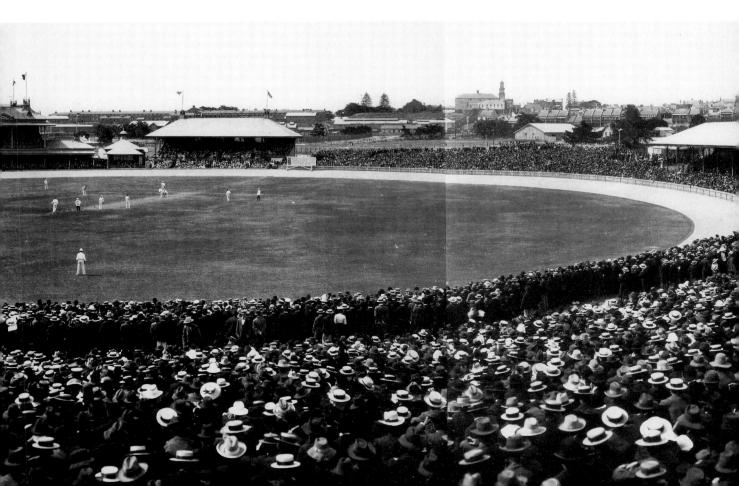

Archibald MacLaren, who succeeded Grace as England captain was dictatorial and aggressive, but he never won a series against Australia, although he won many championships as Lancashire's skipper.
— Albert Gregory Collection.

Opposite: William ("Micky") Roche was a freakish off-spinner with two fingers missing from his bowling hand and a stiff thumb. He bowled at medium pace for Victoria with such success visiting Englishmen suggested he try County cricket. He played for Middlesex in 1899 and 1900 and for the M.C.C. in 1897 and 1898. On his day he was deadly, a sad loss to Australian domestic cricket.
— David Frith, Wisden Cricket Monthly.

Despite these minor upheavals more and more good Australian players began to join New Zealand clubs as coaches — men like Walter McGlinchy who had played for both New South Wales and Queensland; Syd Callaway, the right-arm fast-medium bowler who played three Tests for Australia in the mid-1890s; the Sydney wicket-keeper Fred Burton, who had played for Australia while Blackham kept wicket; and the Sydney off-break bowler Les Cobcroft. The Melbourne Cricket Club periodically sent teams there but generally New Zealand was destined to remain a poor relation in the eyes of Australian cricket administrators for more than half a century.

The New Zealanders showed enterprise in 1899 by sending a team on tour for the first time. They began in Hobart with a fine score of 335 against southern Tasmania, but as their tour developed it became apparent that the New Zealanders' fielding was mediocre. At Melbourne when Peter McAlister made 224 for a Victorian Eleven, F.S. Frankish had five chances dropped from his bowling. In Sydney, Victor Trumper made the first of several huge scores against New Zealand sides with an innings of 253. The following season C.A. Richardson, a former New South Wales player, made 114 not out for a New Zealand representative side against a strong Melbourne Cricket Club Eleven — the first century ever scored for New Zealand.

The New Zealanders were surprised at the strength of Australian club cricket and envious over the practice of Melbourne, Sydney, and Brisbane clubs in hiring skilled coaches and ground bowlers of quality who bowled to members several afternoons a week. District or electorate cricket — which compelled cricketers to play for clubs in the areas where they lived — was established throughout Australia in the 1890s and has remained one of the strengths of the country's cricket ever since. Some famous old clubs were forced to close when this residential qualification was introduced but in the main the system has served the game splendidly. Club cricketers, graded according to their ability, develop great team spirit and camaraderie. They have the chance to win selection in the State teams, according to performance with Test selection then only a step away. Each of the district clubs has a voice in the State associations.

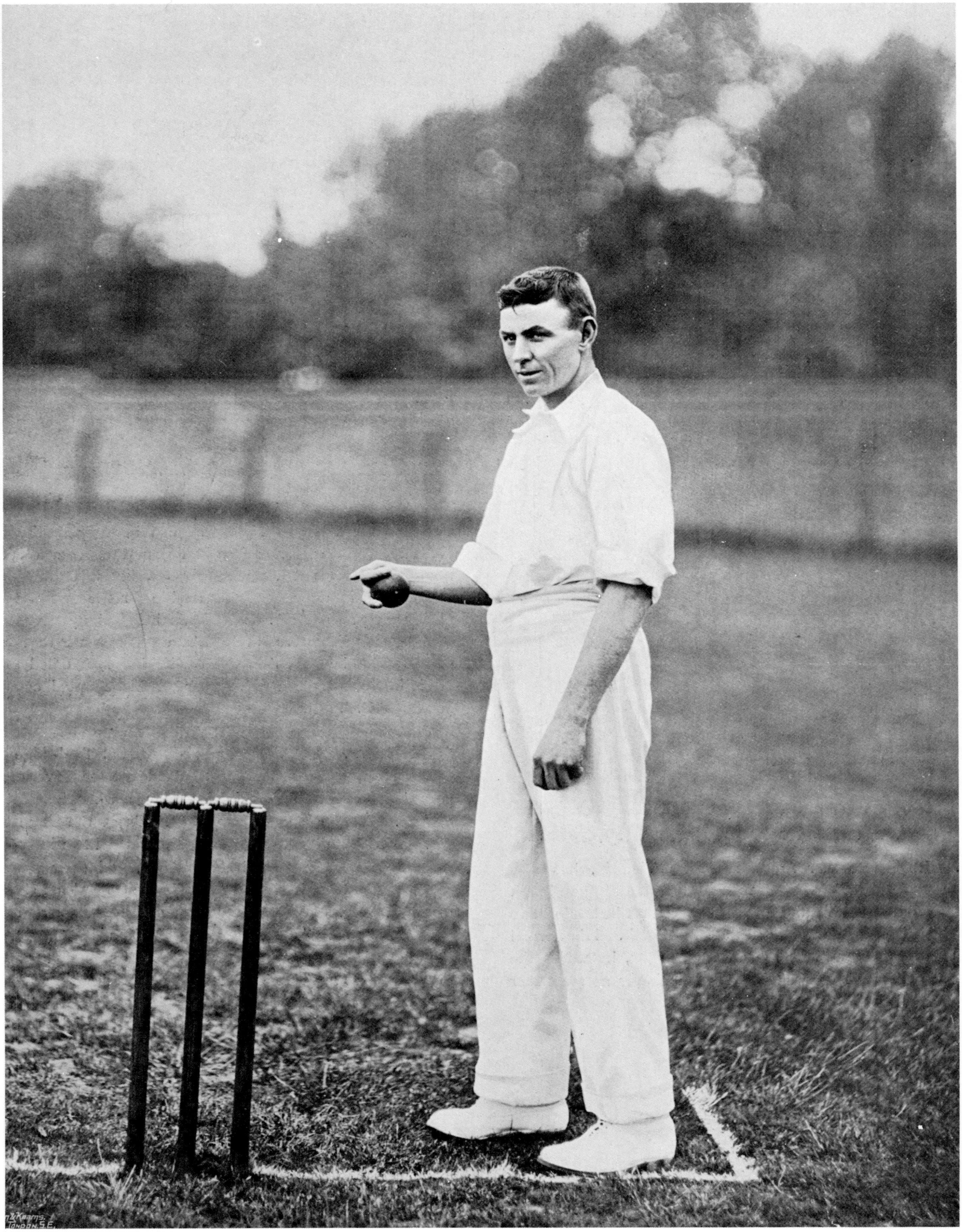
n & Kearns.
London. S.E.

The showpiece of each State association is its capital city ground. Even by the turn of the century these had all taken on a character of their own. The inside of the Sydney ground fence at that time was encircled by a concrete bicycle track, which caused many disputes over whether batsmen caught on the track were out. The world's leading cyclists raced on the track until it was torn up in 1920. The giant scoreboard at the back of the famous hill was a feature of the Sydney ground from January 1896. It was designed by the ground's curator, Ned Gregory, who built the board in a fortnight. Over the years modifications were made to it but the board constantly surprised overseas visitors because of the amount of information it displays. By contrast, Australians always find scoreboards in England singularly uninformative. Scoreboards like the one on the Sydney Hill had their disadvantages — it took six men, working on two floors, to operate the Sydney board. In the 1970s when poor attendances forced officials to make economies for Sheffield Shield matches, one of the first cuts was to close the Hill and with it, the scoreboard.

The Adelaide Oval is one of the world's most attractive cricket venues, with the Adelaide Hills stretching away to the north, lovely trees inside the ground, and the spire of St Peter's Cathedral rising above the scoreboard. But the boundaries are very short square of the wicket. Obviously the early designers could not cut or hook.

The ground that makes all the money for Australian cricket is the Melbourne Cricket Ground, which has long been an integral part of that city's life. It is the world's largest ground and attracted Test cricket's biggest crowd, 90 800, in 1961 for the second day of a West Indies versus Australia Test. Trees and flower beds that graced the ground at the turn of the century have since been replaced by massive concrete stands. The elms that were planted at the Melbourne ground when the first England team under H. H. Stephenson played there in 1862 grew into fine, mature specimens and became a feature of the ground. When Tom Horan was looking for a title for his column of cricket gossip 30 years later, he called it "Under The Elms". But, alas, even these historic trees have gone now and the public has to make do with an ugly electronic scoreboard.

The South Australian team photographed inside the Sydney Cricket Ground dressing-room in 1899 (L to R): Back A.H. Jarvis, A.E. Peters, E. Jones, F.T. Hack, G. Giffen, V. Hugo (12th), A.E. Green; Seated, J.J. Lyons, J. Darling (captain), F. Jarvis, C. Hill, J.C. Reedman; Front, P. Argall (umpire), H. Blinman (manager). — New South Wales Cricket Association.

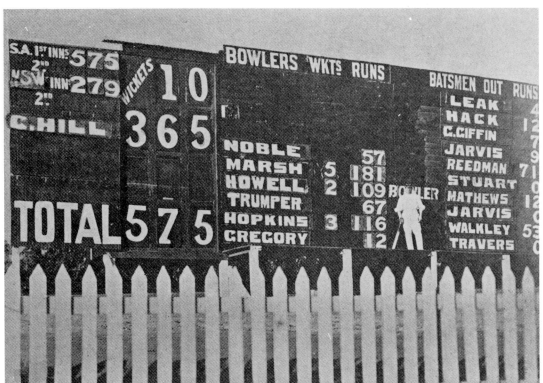

Clem Hill standing in front of the scoreboard showing his wonderful score of 365 not out against New South Wales in Adelaide in 1900-01. This remained the highest score by a South Australian until Bradman made 369 against Tasmania in 1935-36.
— Jack Pollard Collection.

The Australian team that played England in 1911-12: Back, H.V. Hordern, C. Kelleway, D.R.A. Gehrs, V.S. Ransford, T.J. Matthews; Centre, W.W. Armstrong, A. Cotter, C. Hill (captain), V.T. Trumper, W.J. Whitty; Front, H. Carter, W. Bardsley.
— New South Wales Cricket Association.

Four champion Australian left-handed batsmen just after the turn of the century (L to R): Harry Moses, Warren Bardsley, Vernon Ransford and Clem Hill. — Albert Gregory Collection.

Smallest of the Australian grounds is Brisbane Cricket Ground in the suburb of Woolloongabba, first dedicated as a cricket ground in 1895 but not given a Test until 1931. The only major ground owned by a State association is the Western Australian Cricket Association ground in Perth — the 'W.A.C.A.' — a former swampland over which the State Governor, Sir Frederick Broome, granted the association a 999-year lease in 1889. The W.A.C.A. was opened in 1893 and turf pitches were laid in the following year, but it was not until 1907–08 that an English team played in Perth — A.O. Jones' side, who defeated Western Australia by an innings and 134 runs.

The 1901 English team led by Archie MacLaren bypassed Perth. This tour was originally to have been conducted by the Marylebone Cricket Club but when four star players — Ranjitsinhji, Fry, Hirst, and Rhodes — declined to tour, the M.C.C. ended negotiations with the Melbourne Cricket

Club for the tour. The Melbourne Club then invited MacLaren to form a side. Keen followers of the game were stunned when MacLaren insisted on the inclusion of S.F. Barnes, a then little-known professional bowler. Barnes silenced the critics by taking 5 wickets in his first tour game against South Australia, followed by 12 for 99 versus Victoria, 6 for 65 in the first innings of the first Test, and 13 for 163 in the second Test.

MacLaren asked for the right to appoint one of the umpires in every tour match. South Australia and Victoria readily agreed in the first two matches but New South Wales objected, saying that the N.S.W.C.A. had appointed umpires for the England match in accordance with the Marylebone Club's rules for nominating umpires in Australia. MacLaren insisted on his rights but added that if his appointment of one umpire was granted the four county captains in his team would support Australia's right to appoint one umpire on the projected 1902 tour of England. The county captains were MacLaren (Lancashire), A.O. Jones (Nottinghamshire), G.L. Jessop (Gloucestershire), and C. Robson (Hampshire). Under pressure from all sides, New South Wales agreed that MacLaren should appoint one umpire for the New South Wales match.

George Giffen took 13 wickets for South Australia against MacLaren's team but when the Tests came round was, at forty-three, judged too old for the Australian side. George had always picked the tours and the games that suited him and sometimes refused to play unless his brother Walter, who was a class below his ability, was included. Giffen was the first Australian to take 100 wickets and score 1000 runs in Tests. The finest all-round performance in Australian first-class cricket came from Giffen in the summer of 1891–92 when he scored 271 for South Australia against Victoria and then took 16 wickets for 166. Only Monty Noble compared with Giffen among Australian all-rounders of that period.

MacLaren was justified in standing up for his players' rights, for the growing strength of Australian cricket presented them with a tremendously difficult itinerary. Playing Eighteen of Northern Districts at Maitland, for example, the England bowlers were given a merciless hammering. The Eighteen declared at 15 for 558 in a run riot started by R. Lindsay with 104. A batsman named Ernest Capp went in at No. 12 and scored 114 not out. England replied with 5 for 221 before the match was left drawn.

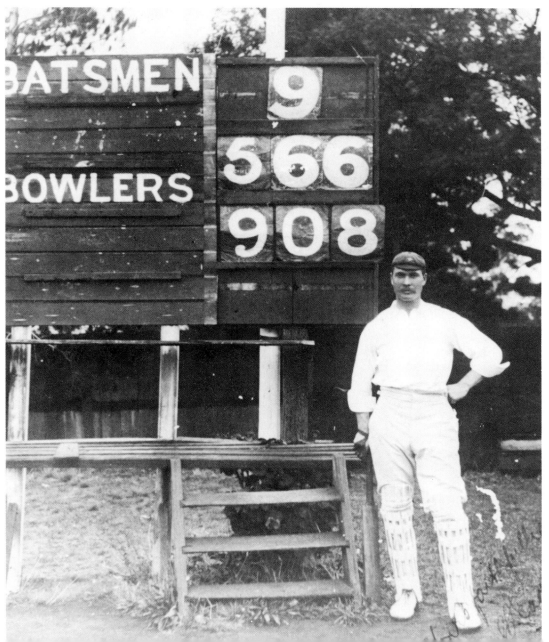

Tasmanian Charles John Eady in front of the scoreboard showing the 566 he made out of 911 for Break-O'-Day against Wellington. He batted on March 8 and part of March 15, 1902, reaching 419 not out. On April 2, he resumed his innings with only eight Wellington fieldsmen present, adding 147, before he was stumped. The 566 took 473 minutes, is in Wisden *but remains suspect among experts because of the missing fieldsmen on the third day of the innings. — Ric Smith.*

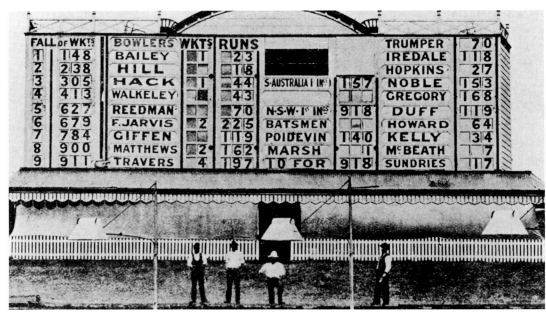

FALL of WKTS		BOWLERS	WKTS	RUNS				TRUMPER	70
1	148	BAILEY	1	23				IREDALE	118
2	238	HILL		18				HOPKINS	27
3	305	HACK	1	44	S·AUSTRALIA·I·IN	157		NOBLE	153
4	413	WALKELEY		43				GREGORY	168
5	627	REEDMAN		70	N·S·W·1ST·INGS	918		DUFF	119
6	679	F.JARVIS	2	225	BATSMEN			HOWARD	64
7	784	GIFFEN		119	POIDEVIN	140		KELLY	34
8	900	MATTHEWS	2	162	MARSH	1		McBEATH	7
9	911	TRAVERS	4	197	TO FOR	918		SUNDRIES	117

The Sydney Cricket Ground scoreboard showing the then record score for inter-State cricket of 910, made by New South Wales in January, 1901, against South Australia. Five N.S.W. batsmen made centuries.
— Albert Gregory Collection.

Dr. L.O.S. Poidevin, who played Davis Cup tennis for Australia but never for Australia's cricket team. He had to be content with scoring centuries for New South Wales and Lancashire.
— Ronald Cardwell.

At the centre of the umpiring argument was the Englishmen's determination to continue the campaign against chuckers. McKibbin had retired at the end of the 1899 season after bowling several batsmen with balls they considered were blatant throws and did not even attempt to play. But Ernie Jones was still in the Australian side and there were worrying reports about New South Wales country bowler Jack Marsh, an Aboriginal of fearsome pace, and of the Victorian left-arm slow-medium bowler Jack Saunders. The previous summer, umpire Bob Crockett (the Australian equivalent of England's Bob Thoms) had no-balled Marsh three times for throwing in the Victoria versus New South Wales game at Melbourne and nineteen times for throwing in the return match at Sydney.

When Marsh first appeared in grade cricket the secretary of the Sydney Club got a doctor to encase his bowling arm in splints and bandages after Marsh had been called for throwing. Marsh continued to bowl with the same hostility although it was obvious that he could not chuck the ball. MacLaren had not seen Marsh bowl but demanded his withdrawal when he was picked to play for Bathurst against England. 'I cannot allow my batsmen to risk injury against such a dangerous bowler,' MacLaren said. Under threat that England would not play, Bathurst officials omitted Marsh.

After losing to South Australia in Adelaide, England beat Victoria at Melbourne but was then defeated by 53 runs by New South Wales. Braund bowled his leg-breaks cleverly in New South Wales' first innings of 288 and England gained a 44-run lead. In their second innings, New South Wales reached 422, with Les Poidevin 151 not out. The England side fought gamely but were out for 325. Poidevin graduated in Arts at Sydney University and went to Edinburgh University to study medicine. He played first-class cricket and Davis Cup tennis in England, returning home occasionally to play again for New South Wales. He scored 5784 runs over seven seasons of English county cricket and made eleven of his fourteen first-class centuries in England. In 1905 he headed the Lancashire batting averages with 1376 runs at 44.38.

Australia flopped badly in the first Test against MacLaren's side at Sydney, where MacLaren made his fourth Test century. But thereafter Australia played outstanding cricket, with Hill scoring 99, 98, and 97 in successive innings. Warwick Armstrong and Reg Duff made their debuts in the second Test at Melbourne. Duff top-scored in both innings and became the third Australian to make a century on debut. Trumble completed Australia's win with a hat-trick dismissing Jones, Gunn, and Barnes. Australia won this match by 229 runs and the third Test at Adelaide by 4 wickets after Trumble took another 9 wickets (3 for 124 and 6 for 74). Australia brought in the controversial Saunders for the fourth Test but, although he took 9 wickets and spearheaded a win, dropped him for the fifth Test. His replacement, the South Australian Rhodes Scholar Joe Travers, had 1 for 14. Australia finished the series as four-to-one winners.

Despite the strong doubts over his action, Australia took Saunders to England in Joe Darling's 1902 team, one of the great Australian sides. This was the tour on which B.J.T. Bosanquet unveiled his invention, the googly — or, as some Australians call it, the 'bosie'. Bosanquet was well over 6 feet (183 centimetres) tall and brought the ball down from a great height, mystifying the Australians just as he had bewildered opposition batsmen while playing for Eton, Oxford, and Middlesex. At Lord's Australia's wicket-keeper Jim Kelly, after facing Bosanquet, went back to the dressing-room grumbling that 'there's a bloke out there bowling off-breaks with a leg-break action'.

IN MEMORY OF THE

AUSTRALIANS.

The Australians came like the wolves on the fold
And their faces looked tanned like the Australian gold
To the cricket field they all wended their way,
To see all England at cricket to play.

The Australia men, their players feel
The blighting, withering blast,
For full of hope, they thought to steal
The verdict at last :
Twas not to be, so let them lie
Deep in the silent grave,
And shed a tear, o,er their bier,
And the match they tried to save.

*When England were 4 for 92 chasing 124 to win the Test in Manchester in 1902, a local printer issued this "In Memorium" card expecting an English victory. The card was withdrawn from sale when Trumble and Saunders took the last six wickets for 28 runs and gave Australia a three runs win.
— Melbourne Cricket Ground Museum.*

*Right: One of Australia's unique cricket fields at Walhalla in south-east Gippsland, where miners used a huge amount of explosives to blow the top off a mountain and create space for the ground. Hits over the edge can travel miles.
— Walhalla Museum.*

*The dotted line traces the path of Victor Trumper's hit for "five" while batting for Paddington against Glebe at Redfern Oval in 1903. The ball travelled 150 yards to break a second storey window. Trumper made 335 in 165 minutes, his team 618 between 2.15 p.m. and 6 p.m. The broken window is preserved in South Sydney Leagues' Club.
— Sydney Sun.*

Brisbane Cricket Ground during the match between Queensland and Plum Warner's 1903-04 England team.
— Patrick J. Mullins.

Jim Kelly, Syd Gregory and Monty Noble after the match between MacLaren's team and New South Wales. All three were playing for the Paddington club but Gregory later moved to Waverley.
— Phillip Derriman.

After England had lost four successive rubbers, the M.C.C. stepped in and selected and sponsored a powerful side under Pelham Warner. To meet the challenge in Australia in 1903-04 Australia fielded this lineup with Monty Noble captain for the first time (L to R): Standing, A.C. Jones (umpire), J.V. Saunders, C.B. Jennings, W.P. Howell, F. Laver, J.J. Kelly, A.J. Hopkins, S.E. Gregory; Seated, V.T. Trumper, C. Hill, M.A. Noble, R.A. Duff, W. Armstrong.
— Albert Gregory Collection.

Warwick Armstrong in the years when he was trying to consolidate his place in the Australian team, tall, lean, no sign of excess weight.
— Public Library of Victoria.

Syd. Gregory was regarded as the finest fieldsman in the Australian team in the Golden Age of cricket, an unexcelled cover point who could gather and throw like this with dazzling speed.
— Melbourne Cricket Ground Museum.

Far Left: One of the forgotten members of the Gregory clan, Alban ('Doon') Gregory, a star batsman for Sydney Grammar who had some memorable partnerships with his brother Jack in Sydney's Manly club.
— Jack Pollard Collection.

Left: Happy tourists in England in 1909: Top, Bill Whitty and Jack O'Connor; Below, Hanson Carter and Roger Hartigan.
— J.C. Davis Collection.

Reg Duff who formed with Victor Trumper one of the best of all Australian opening pairs. Here he plays an authentic cover drive while practising in England. He kept the scorers busy.
— Jack Pollard Collection.

Kelly had his day of triumph at Manchester when Australia clinched the series by going to a two-to-nil lead in the fourth Test. On the first day Trumper scored his century in 108 minutes before lunch, a feat since equalled only by Charlie Macartney, Don Bradman, and Majid Khan. With Australia in desperate trouble in her second innings, Kelly and Hugh Trumble batted against Tom Richardson at his fastest to add 25 runs in an hour. Set to score 123 to win, England made 36 without loss but tumbled to 8 for 109. With 8 runs needed and the last pair in, heavy rain fell and the players left the field. When they returned, Fred Tate hit Saunders for 4 but was clean-bowled next ball when another four would have given England victory. Australia's 3-run margin remained the closest in Test cricket until England beat Australia by 3 runs at Melbourne in the fourth Test in 1982–83. Saunders, a heavily moustached figure noted for his sartorial elegance, always claimed it was his batting as much as his bowling that gave Australia victory, for he made 3, the margin of a famous victory.

After retaining the Ashes Darling's team called at South Africa on the way home for three Tests, the first between the two countries. They played the first Test on matting at an altitude of almost 6000 feet in Johannesburg, going straight to the ground when their ship berthed. South Africa was captained by H.M. Taberer in his only Test. Clem Hill made 142 in Australia's second innings but the three days scheduled for the match ran out with South Africa 114 short of victory with 6 wickets left.

Trumper hit a classic 218 against Fifteen of Transvaal but the effort flattened him for the second Test at Johannesburg in which he made only 18 and 13. Warwick Armstrong, who had made a solid, unspectacular tour of England, came to the rescue with 159 not out in Australia's second innings. The South Africans were unable to cope with Saunders' spin — he took 2 for 32 and 7 for 34 — and Australia won by 159 runs. J.H. Sinclair scored South Africa's first century (104) against Australia in the third Test at Cape Town but Howell (4 for 18 and 5 for 81) bowled Australia to a 10-wickets win. Hill made yet another Test 90 (91 not out) in this match.

At this time strong mid-week competitions flourished in the eastern States. The Wednesday Half-Holiday Cricket Association in Sydney attracted a large following. Spectators knew they could expect big hitting and thrilling finishes in the limited time available and some extraordinary big hits were made. Redfern had to overcome lively opposition from eight district clubs and a General Post Office team to win the 1902–03 mid-week premiership medals and the right to hold the Mitchell Shield for a year. In Brisbane the midweek competition was for the Aitchison Ale Trophy. One year in this competition Arthur Coningham performed the extraordinary feat of scoring all his team's runs. Coningham made 26 for Stanley against the Albert, and there were no extras, all his team-mates failing to score.

The 1903–04 England tour of Australia ended the tradition of privately sponsored tours. Pelham Warner led the first team selected and financed entirely by the M.C.C. at Lord's. The decision by M.C.C. to back the tour and ensure that the team was properly prepared was undoubtedly influenced by the supremacy Australia had established over England with the great teams led by Darling. Monty Noble, known affectionately as 'Mary Ann', took over the Australian captaincy for a series in which Australia introduced pace bowler 'Tibby' Cotter, batsman Peter McAlister, and the dashing South Australian batting star Algie Gehrs. England brought seven new men, including mysteryman B.J.T. Bosanquet. The good fellowship of the England players was immediately apparent, with amateurs and professional staying at the same hotels.

Batting first at Sydney in the first Test, Australia lost Duff, Trumper, and Hill for 12 runs, but Noble rescued the side with a gutsy 133, from a total score of 285. England lost her first wicket without scoring but at 4 for 117 Reg Foster (one of seven sons of a clergyman who played for Worcestershire) came in and batted for 7 hours in his Test debut. Foster hit thirty-eight fours in scoring 287, and in a memorable fifth-wicket stand with Braund, 102, added 192. England made 577, 292 ahead. Australia lost her third wicket at 191 and Trumper and Hill were really starting to hammer the bowling when Hill was given run out for 51. At the time the batsmen had run 4 and were trying for the fifth off an overthrow. Hill always said he had made good his ground and that the ball had passed behind him, but Victorian umpire Bob Crockett was just as certain that his run-out verdict was correct.

The crowd set up a chant of 'Crock, Crock, Crock', in among boos and shouts for Hill to be recalled. The noise was too deafening for play to continue. At the peak of the disturbance England's captain Warner went towards the members' stand to signal that he proposed to withdraw his players from the field unless the booing stopped but could not make himself heard by officials. He went on with the match out of appreciation for Australian captain Noble's attitude in coming down to the fence and expressing his regret at what had happened.

Trumper continued to 185 not out in Australia's total of 485, leaving England with 194 to win. Laver missed Hirst at short leg before he scored and went on to 60 not out. Tom Hayward was the match-winner for England after a magnificent struggle: he scored 91 before being stumped by Kelly off Saunders. At Melbourne in the second Test Wilfred Rhodes took 7 for 56 and 8 for 68, catching Australia on a vicious sticky wicket. Only Trumper mastered the pitch with a score of 74 in the first innings. He was first in and last out. Down two-nil Australia fought back superbly to win the third Test at Adelaide in which Trumper's 113 was his fourth successive top score and his fourth Test century. Australia won by 216 runs.

The New South Wales team that played Tasmania in Hobart in March, 1905 (L to R): Back, L.P. Dean (manager), A. Penman, J.R. Mackay, R. Hickson, J. O'Connor, E. Cresswick (manager); Centre, G. Garnsey, L. Redgrave, A. Diamond (captain), E. Waddy, H. Carter; Front, A. Johnston, F. Johnston. — Ric Smith.

A.J. Hopkins, a neglected Sydney allrounder of rare merit who played 20 Tests for Australia and for New South Wales for almost 20 years. He toured England three times in the first decade of this century.
— Mitchell Library, Sydney.

A women's cricket team from Launceston, Tasmania, in 1906 still wore full length dresses that restricted their movement. Hats had to be tied on in the field.
— State Library of Victoria.

J.A. Prout, who in
1908-09 made 459 for
Wesley College against
Geelong College. This
was then the fourth
highest score made
anywhere in the world
and an Australian Public
Schools record. Prout's
innings enabled Wesley to
score 710.
— Mitchell Library,
Sydney.

Two of Australia's
greatest batsmen enjoy an
evening at the piano in
their hotel room. Victor
Trumper is playing, Clem
Hill is watching.
— Jack Pollard
Collection.

One of the most entertaining batsmen in Australian cricket in the years leading up to the first world war was Englishman J.N. Crawford, a brilliant stroke player who appeared for South Australia while he worked as a teacher in Adelaide.
— Albert Gregory Collection.

England recovered the Ashes by winning the rain-affected fourth Test at Sydney but first was subjected to another demonstration. Angry over repeated interruptions, spectators threw bottles and rubbish on the bike track and hooted noisily in a display of hooliganism far worse than the earlier one on the same ground. Bosanquet took 6 for 51 in Australia's second innings and for most of the Australian players he was the difference between the two sides in a tense rubber. He had all the best Australians guessing from the time he bowled Trumper with the first googly he delivered in Australia. Hugh Trumble ended his own career and the fifth Test at Melbourne by taking a hat-trick, dismissing Bosanquet, Warner, and Lilley. Cotter bowled at an awesome speed to establish himself as a Test bowler of rich promise, taking 6 for 41 in England's first innings. England won the series four-to-one.

Cotter was the product of Great Public Schools' cricket, high-standard competitions in those days which produced many Test stars. At one stage the

King's School in Sydney was good enough to play in the first grade premiership. O.H. Dean made 412 in 210 minutes for Sydney Church of England Grammar School against Newington College in the 1904–05 Sydney G.P.S. competition. This stood as a world inter-schools record only until 1908–09 when J.A. Prout made 459 for Wesley College against Geelong College. Wesley's total of 710 remained a record for only a week when Cotter's old school, Sydney Grammar, made 916 against Sydney Church of England Grammar. J.C. Sharpe's 506 not out for Melbourne Grammar against Geelong College in 1914–15 remains the highest score in an Australian G.P.S. match.

At Sydney in January 1905 delegates from the Queensland, New South Wales, Victorian, and South Australian cricket associations drafted a constitution for a national control body. This authority aimed at replacing the defunct Australasian Cricket Council, and taking control of overseas tours. South Australia's delegates got no support for their proposal that players be represented on the new body. Meanwhile Australia's leading players, concerned that the projected English tour in 1906–07 was in jeopardy, sent a letter to the Melbourne Cricket Club agreeing to play against England if the club organised the tour as it had at times in the past. When the N.S.W.C.A. learnt that ten of New South Wales' best players had signed the letter, it held a special meeting at which the players who refused to retract were suspended. Only one — the Reverend E.F. Waddy — retracted. When Hill and Darling heard of the suspensions in Adelaide, they announced that they would not play in New South Wales until the Association reversed its decision. The N.S.W.C.A. promptly lifted the suspensions.

After an absence at his property in Tasmania Darling returned to lead Australia on tour in England in 1905. On the way they became the first Australian side to play in Fiji. The Australians encountered tough, well-organised opposition in England, with the M.C.C. now in firm control of all tours. The new English captain, F. S. Jackson, won seven tosses against Darling during the summer, five of them in Tests. Nine Australians hit centuries and they scored impressively against the counties. Armstrong made 303 not out versus Somerset and 248 against the Gentlemen. Noble made six centuries on the tour, top score 267. Hill, top score 181, was one of seven batsmen who made 1000 runs on the tour. But they could not win a Test and England held the Ashes by winning two Tests to nil.

This Queensland team defeated New South Wales by four wickets and Victoria by 66 runs on their southern tour in 1910 (L to R): Back, C.B. Barstow, W.J. Lewis, Alan Marshall, B.W. Cook, A.J. Jones, S. McCloy; Centre, W.T. Evans, S.J. Redgrave, S.C. Whittred (manager), J.S. Hutcheon (captain), S.J. Fennelly; Front, J. Bolton, H.G. Whittred (scorer), W. McLaren. Marshall's loss to Surrey was a sad blow.
— Patrick J. Mullins

The Fijian team that visited Australia in 1908. They appeared in native costumes, entering the field in single file wearing sulus or calf-length skirts, most of them barefooted. Their captain, Prince Ratu Kadavu Levu is in front in the centre, with the manager, Lieutenant Marsden on his right.
— Mitchell Library, Sydney

While the team was away the first meeting of the Australian Board of Control for International Cricket was held at Wesley College, Melbourne, on 6 May 1905. Only the South Australian delegates refused to join in approving the constitution drafted four months earlier, again arguing that the players should be represented on the new Board. Queensland joined the Board in September 1905 in return for a promise that Brisbane would get a Test — a promise the Board did not honour until 1928–29.

England's 1907–08 tour of Australia under A.O. Jones proceeded amid increasing bitterness between players and officials. Australia reversed the four-to-nil defeat by Warner's team four years earlier with a fighting all round display, and won all but the second Test, which England took by 1 wicket when Hazlitt threw wildly from cover with a run-out certain. England batsmen Barnes and Fielder scampered through for the winning run and Test cricket's first tie was postponed. This was the first England side to appear in Perth and the first visiting side to play under the law that no

longer made the follow-on compulsory. George Gunn, on holiday, in Australia was brought into the short-handed England side, made a century on debut, and proved a tour star.

Australia brought in new players Hanson Carter, Gervys Hazlitt, Charlie Macartney, Vernon Ransford, Roger Hartigan, and Jack O'Connor. Hartigan scored 48 and 116 in his first Test, going in at No. 8. He had leave from his Brisbane employer for only four days in Adelaide. When that time had expired, and Hartigan was still batting, his boss sent a telegram: 'Stay as long as you're scoring runs'. Despite this marvellous debut, Hartigan had trouble retaining his Test place in a period of outstanding Australian batsmanship.

The friction between the Board and star players increased when the Board organised a tour of England for the first time in 1909, and refused to make customary cash advances for pre-tour expenses to the selected players. Instead of the share of profits which they had previously enjoyed, the players were offered £400 each, plus all expenses. The players objected to the Board's appointing Peter McAlister as its own treasurer for the tour, but were allowed their own choice of manager, in Frank Laver. The side started miserably by losing three matches in the first month, including the first Test, but recovered to win the series two-to-one, suffering only their fourth defeat near the very end of the tour. Noble led the side superbly in their winning streak. Ransford and Bardsley proved left-handers of quality, and Macartney surprised with his left-arm bowling, winning the Lord's Test by taking 11 for 85. Manager Laver took 70 wickets on the tour at 14.97, but Armstrong was the all-round hero with 1480 runs at 43.52 and 126 wickets at 16.23.

Clem Hill took over the Australian captaincy from Noble for the following season in Australia when South Africa toured for the first time. On 3 February 1911 in the N.S.W.C.A.'s rooms in Sydney the power struggle between players and officials finally exploded. The Board's favoured son Peter McAlister became involved in a bitter argument with fellow selector Hill when they met to pick the team for the fourth Test versus South Africa at Melbourne. McAlister claimed that Hill was the worst captain he had ever seen. Hill reached across the table and slapped McAlister's face. McAlister then claimed he had been hit while his hands were down.

Hill lowered his arms and said: 'My hands are down now'. McAlister bounded to the other side of the table and grappled with Hill. Locked together they swayed around the room, fighting and wrestling, spattering the room with blood, which stained the clothes of witnesses Frank Iredale and Board secretary Sydney Smith. They fought for 20 minutes, until McAlister's nose and face were cut.

The Victorian team just before World War I included: (L to R): Wicket-keeper Jack Ellis, Len Mullett, the highly promising Johnnie Moyes, and pace bowler Ted McDonald.
— Victorian Cricket Association.

11. First World War Setbacks

Shortly after the Hill-McAlister brawl in Sydney, the *Australasian* published a blow-by-blow account of it that remains one of the curiosities of Australian cricket. This story made it clear that the fight was prolonged and spirited. In the words of Frank Iredale, one of the witnesses:

> They went at it hammer and tongs. Smith and I did our best to part them, but they were all over the place, and when the big table was upset I was pinned in a corner and strained my side. How long did it last? Well, I would say about twenty minutes. It all occurred as quick as lightning. They were both game and determined.

The fight ended when Smith and Iredale pushed McAlister out the door and prevented Hill from following.

Hill resigned as a selector but the Board took no further action after hearing secretary Smith's account of the affair. Hill completed the series against South Africa as Australia's captain, winning the series four-to-one. Bardsley (132), Hill (191 and 100), Trumper (159 and 214), Armstrong (132), and Macartney (137) all made Test centuries for Australia. Cotter took 22 wickets. For Australia, however, the big gains came from the bowling of left-arm fast-medium Bill Whitty, who took a remarkable total of 37 wickets in the series as Cotter's opening partner, and from the introduction to Test cricket of Dr H.V. ('Ranji') Hordern, perhaps our greatest exponent of the googly.

Whitty, who came from New South Wales, played almost all his first-class cricket in South Australia. He was 6 feet tall, had a high arm-action, and swung the ball appreciably at a brisk pace. He soon became known for his arguments with umpires. He had taken 77 wickets in England with the 1909 Australian side, but did not show his full potential until he took 6 for 17 versus South Africa at Melbourne in the second innings of the second Test. Hordern took 14 wickets in two Tests despite the fact that South Africa had in their team Reg Schwarz, an outstanding googly bowler and a former team-mate of Bosanquet.

Some of the Australians outside their London hotel before the first match of the 1912 triangular tournament (L to R): Back, W. Bardsley, E.R. Mayne, J.W. McLaren, D. Smith, E. Hume (scorer); Front, R.B. Minnett, G.R. Hazlitt, C.G. Macartney, S.E. Gregory, G.S. Crouch, W. Carkeek, W.J. Whitty.
— E.S. Marks Collection.

Queenslander G.S. Crouch, manager of the worst performed Australian side in 1912. He got the job when Victorian and New South Wales delegates quarrelled and refused to support each other's nominees.
— Ronald Cardwell.

Peter McAlister, a stalwart of the East Melbourne club who proved a plucky scrapper in the selection room but below Test class as a batsman.
— Ronald Cardwell.

Hordern was a fascinating bowler, a spinner who came in off a long run and seldom bowled loose balls like Mailey. He was a dentist and, as he could not afford to damage his fingers, played only thirty-three first-class matches, taking 217 wickets at 16.79. Hordern was born in North Sydney and played for the district club, before playing for New South Wales in 1905–06. He then spent several years in America studying dentistry and toured England in 1907 as a member of the Pennsylvania University team that played a series of matches against public schools. In 1908 he toured England with the Philadelphian team that played ten first-class matches in England. On these trips he had developed a googly of variable flight and exceptional accuracy.

By the time the eighteenth England team arrived in Australia for the 1911–12 season four strong-willed chairmen and a cagey secretary, W.P. McElhone, had won complete acceptance for the Australian Board of Control after its turbulent beginnings. But friction between leading players and officials continued. Joe Darling said he was disgusted at the manner in which the Board conducted its affairs when he attended as a South Australian delegate: 'Everything on the agenda was discussed privately before the meeting began by the delegates from Queensland, Victoria and NSW'. The Board had had a bad setback when their appointed treasurer, Peter McAlister, had failed to keep financial records of the 1909 tour of England. When they asked manager Frank Laver for his records of the tour, Laver said it had not been his job to keep records of costs but was ready to attend a Board meeting and answer all questions on finance.

Pelham Warner was captain of the English team when it arrived but after an innings of 151 against South Australia he became ill and did not play again on the tour. J.W.H.T. Douglas took over the captaincy. The Australian players were clearly dispirited but even in their happiest mood may not have been able to match this powerful England team. England's batting was immensely strong as they showed in compiling 563 in the first match against South Australia at Adelaide. In Jack Hobbs, Wilfred Rhodes, George Gunn, J.W. Hearne, and Frank Woolley they had an array of dazzling stroke-makers and in Foster, Barnes, Douglas, Hearne, Woolley, and Rhodes they had bowling talent to spare.

Australia's first outstanding googly bowler, Dr. Herbert Vivian ("Ranji") Hordern, who developed the art while studying dentistry in America. He took 46 wickets in seven Tests, retiring after two seasons because of fears of damaging his hands. — Albert Gregory Collection.

Ranji Hordern hoodwinked the English batsmen in the first Test, which produced Australia's sole win in the rubber. Hordern took 5 for 85 and 7 for 90. Five of his victims were bowled. But once the English batting stars worked out Hordern's googly technique they scored heavily. Barnes began the second Test dramatically by dismissing Kelleway, Bardsley, Hill, and Armstrong for 1 run in his first 5 overs. Australia never recovered. Jack Hearne sealed England's win by 8 wickets with a stylish 114. Australia brought in the tiny right-arm leg-spinner T.J. Matthews to partner Hordern in a spin attack for the third and fourth Tests but they could not stem the flow of runs. Hobbs made 187 in the third Test and 178 in the fourth, in which Rhodes (179) joined him in a massive opening stand of 323. England made it four-to-one in the fifth Test despite 10 wickets (5 for 95 and 5 for 66) from Hordern. Trade unions threatened industrial action against the fourth Test if J.N. ('Ginger')

McLaren (who had acted as a special constable in a strike earlier that year) played. The trouble was avoided when McLaren was made twelfth man, but he played in the fifth Test.

Australia had no answer to the bowling of Sydney Barnes and Frank Foster, one of the best bowling combinations England has ever had. Barnes took 34 wickets at 22.8, Foster 32 wickets at 21.6. Neither bowled faster than brisk medium-pace but they moved the ball sharply — Foster left-arm, Barnes right-arm. They were particularly adept at moving the ball across the Australians' bodies, pitching outside or on the leg stump and moving the ball towards the slips. Warren Bardsley, a great left-hander, was dropped after repeated failures against the English pair and it took him many hours of practice against left-handers to eliminate the weakness Foster exposed.

Syd Gregory in his New South Wales blazer as the Otway carrying his 1912 team neared the English coast. He proved too soft a captain, incapable of disciplining badly behaved team members, and the tour was a miserable end to a distinguished career.
— David Frith, Wisden Cricket Monthly.

The 1912 Australians by common consent the worst team Australia has sent to England (L to R): Back, G.S. Crouch (manager), R.B. Minnett, E. Hume (visitor), C. Kelleway, E.R. Mayne, S.H. Emery, D. Smith, W.J. Whitty, H. Webster, G.R. Hazlitt; Front, J.W. McLaren, T.J. Matthews, S.E. Gregory (captain), C.B. Jennings, C.G. Macartney, W. Carkeek.
— Ronald Cardwell.

Charlie Macartney
gossiping with 6ft 4in
Jack Massie, son of
pioneering Australian
opener Hugh Hammon
Massie. Big Jack was
considered the finest left-
arm fast bowler Australia
had seen but World War I
wounds ruined his career.
— David Frith, Wisden
Cricket Monthly.

Warren Bardsley, a
headmaster's son who
overcame through diligent
workouts in the nets
weaknesses exposed by
the brilliant Barnes and
Foster combination.
— Albert Gregory
Collection.

Henry Frederick Lorenze ("Bert") Kortlang, Melbourne-born right-hander, who played representative cricket in America and New Zealand, scoring heavily wherever he appeared. He scored six first-class centuries and once was known as "the champion cricketer of California". — Jack Pollard Collection.

Charles Kelleway, decorated for bravery in World War I but dismissed from the captaincy of the First A.I.F. team because a general assessed him as a disruptive influence. He was indeed a cold fish, but few cricketers have matched his dedication. — Mitchell Library, Sydney.

In this period — Australia sadly missed two gifted cricketers Albert Trott and Frank Tarrant, men right at their prime who would have been invaluable in the national team. Albert Trott — one of three Melbourne-born brothers who played first-class cricket — could bat, bowl, and field with match-winning brilliance. Piqued that he had missed selection in the 1896 team to England captained by his brother Harry, he preferred to play for Middlesex in the twelve seasons after 1898. He scored 10,696 runs and took 1674 wickets in first-class cricket and held 449 catches. At Lord's in 1907 in his benefit match against Somerset he ruined prospects of a big gate by taking 4 wickets in four balls and a hat-trick later in the same innings. For M.C.C. versus Sussex at Lord's in 1898, he hit Fred Tate to the top of the pavilion, striking the M.C.C. coat of arms. In 1899 at Lord's he struck a ball from Monty Noble right over the pavilion for M.C.C. versus Australia. Trott took 100 wickets in a season seven times and made eight centuries.

A third Trott brother, Fred, was also on the staff at Lord's for a spell, playing for Middlesex Second Eleven, but without achieving the fame of his brothers. Fred was a pro for eight years for Peebles Cricket Club in Scotland and for three years after the First World War at the Clydesdale Cricket Club.

Tarrant a right-hand bat and left-arm spinner of superlative skill, played ten seasons for Middlesex from 1905 and had a career total of 17,857 first-class runs and 1489 wickets. He had played only thirteen games for Victoria between 1898 and 1925. Tarrant took 10 wickets in a match thirty-six times and remains Australia's best exponent of the hat-trick with five in first-class matches.

Trott and Tarrant were probably glad they were absent when the showdown between the Board and the leading players finally came in the 1911–12 season. The South Australian delegate, G. Mostyn Evans, proposed at a Board meeting that the Australian team chosen for the Triangular Tournament in England in 1912 should elect their own manager on the same financial terms as their own. Treasurer Harry Rush then disclosed that the Board rule giving the players the right to appoint a manager had 'been swept away'. The Board then voted a longshot, Queenslander G.S. Crouch, to the manager's job.

Six famous players, realising that the assurances they had been given on the Board's formation had proved worthless, wrote to the Board saying that the appointment of Crouch was illegal. The letter said that if the players were not allowed to appoint their own manager as set out in the Board's original constitution none of the signatories would be available to tour England. The letter was signed by Clem Hill, Warwick Armstrong, Victor Trumper, Vernon Ransford, Albert Cotter, and Hanson Carter.

The Board said it would not allow cricketers to dictate to it and so the team that left for England for the Triangular Tournament was without Australia's six most famous players. It is generally regarded as the worst team Australia ever sent away. The team performed miserably and lost £1,268 on the tour. Manager Crouch strongly criticised the behaviour of some players in his tour report. The Board had recalled Syd Gregory at the age of forty-two to lead the team in England, an appointment that proved a complete failure for he lacked the strength of character to discipline players overfond of the bottle. Crouch's report said that some of the 1912 players conducted themselves so badly they were socially ostracised. He recommended that in selecting future teams the Board should consider factors other than cricketing skill.

Roy Baldwin Minnett, the most successful of three brothers who played cricket in Sydney with exceptional skill. He was the only one of the three to play for Australia, and had the misfortune to play with the miserable 1912 side.
— Ronald Cardwell.

Alby Wright, who holds the Australian first-class record for most ducks in succession (six) in 1905-06, in his job as curator of Adelaide Oval. He was pressed to play for a short-handed South Australia by players impressed by his bowling in the nets and had some big coups among his 110 first-class wickets.
— Adelaide Advertiser.

Bert Oldfield as a World War I corporal, badly wounded in France, sent this picture to his sister Maude in Sydney, in 1917. He became one of cricket's master wicket-keepers.
— Ronald Cardwell.

Captain Clarence Everard Pellew, perhaps the best outfielder Australia has produced, with a pick up and throw that ripped the heels off his cricket boots. Yet another St. Peter's College product.
— Ronald Cardwell.

Australian soldiers playing cricket on Shell Green, Gallipoli, on December 17, 1915. Major George MacArthur Onslow lost his wicket with this shot while shells passed overhead.
— Australian War Memorial, Canberra.

*William ("Barlow")
Carkeek, from the
Victorian mining town of
Walhalla, had vast hands
as befitted an ex-
blacksmith. He played in
six Tests but failed to
match the high standards
of his predecessors,
lacking speed in stumping
and manoeuvrability.
— Ronald Cardwell.*

*Syd Emery, who bowled
wrong-uns (googlies) off a
long run at a brisk pace.
On his day he was
unplayable but he
admitted those days were
few.
— Frank Laver.*

Left: Roger Hartigan, the fourth Australian to score a century in his Test debut and who did it going in at No. 8. He was an enterprising right-handed batsman born in Sydney but chosen for Australia while he played for Queensland.
— Patrick J. Mullins.

Corporal Herbie Collins, right, instructed by his commanding general to take over the captaincy of the First A.I.F. cricket team, won the respect of his team — with remarkable match results.
— Ronald Cardwell.

The Board invited four players — Syd Gregory, slow bowler T.J. Matthews, wicket-keeper Barlow Carkeek, and batsman Dave Smith — to a sub-committee meeting to inquire into the players' tour behaviour. Only Smith did not attend. The Board never disclosed the sub-committee's recommendations but adopted the proposal that it could exclude a player from any future touring side for reasons unconnected with cricket. The Board's silence left the field clear for the rumour-mongers . . . and there were plenty. Stories of fist fights in cabins were common. One reliable story was that the South Australian Edgar Mayne had refused to share a cabin on the voyage home with one of the malcontents. *Wisden* summed up the whole sorry affair: 'It may be added that some of the players were not at all satisfied with Mr. Crouch as manager'.

Deprived of her best players when they were all badly needed to overcome the supremacy established by Warner's 1911–12 side in Australia, Syd Gregory's team won only two of their six Tests. They defeated South Africa twice but were no match for England. Whitty bowled pluckily and Hazlitt joined him in taking more than 100 wickets on the trip but the attack sadly lacked a penetrative bowler like Cotter. Carkeek was far below Test standard as a wicket-keeper and as a result the fielding standard fell away. Even Syd Gregory, rated the finest cover-point cricket had known, could not inspire his team. Bardsley topped 2000 runs in an impressive recovery from his slump in form during the previous summer in Australia, and Macartney produced admirable all-round figures, but overall the side lacked the brilliance of a Trumper, Hill, or Ransford.

Highlight of the tour came in the first Test against South Africa at Manchester when tiny Jack Matthews performed the most extraordinary of all hat-tricks by an Australian. Matthews, a former groundsman from Williamstown, Victoria, took a hat-trick twice on the same day — his only wickets in the match — finishing with 3 for 16 and 3 for 38. The South African tail-ender T.A. Ward bagged a 'king pair', as the third victim in both Matthews' hat-tricks. Australia scored 448, South Africa 265 and 95.

England won four of her six matches to win the tournament comfortably, with two matches drawn. Australia finished second with two wins in six matches, one loss, and three draws, and South Africa lost five of her six matches, with one drawn. South Africa was far below Test standard and was dismissed four times in the series for less than 100 runs. English spectators stayed away and an ambitious promotion flopped badly, partly because of prolonged wet weather. In the decisive ninth match of the tournament Australia was dismissed for 65, chasing 310 to win in the last innings, Frank Woolley taking 5 for 20. Australia won only nine of her thirty-seven matches, with twenty draws and eight losses.

One of the disappointments in the Australian team was googly Sid Emery, known to cricket buffs as 'Mad Mick'. He could spin the ball prodigiously at medium pace rather than slow and had days when he was unplayable. Unhappily, his length was so uncertain that he sometimes took heavy punishment. For New South Wales against Victoria at Melbourne in 1909–10 he landed his googlies on a length often enough to take 7 for 28 in Victoria's first innings of 93 and 5 for 85 in the second innings of 185. This earned him the English tour when the six star players defected but he found English conditions too cool for him and seldom bowled in less than two sweaters. Emery's 67 wickets in England cost 23.89 apiece.

Norman Lindsay's skills began to emerge in World War I when he drew this cartoon for the Bulletin magazine.
— Mitchell Library, Sydney.

OUR OPENING MATCH.—" I say, Bill, you've got that pad on the wrong leg."
" Yus, I know.   I thought as I were goin' in t'other end !"

Emery was lucky enough to get two trips to America. He played in Philadelphia with the 1912 Australian team on the way home from England and was in the game Philadelphia won by only 2 runs. A year later he visited America again with an Australian team that included several veterans. Monty Noble told him he would be a great bowler if he could learn to control his googly. 'I'd be a great man, Monty, if I could learn to control myself,' said Mick. When the Australian manager, R.B. Benjamin, fined him $5 for being late for one match in Canada, Emery grabbed his bat, sold it to a spectator, and paid the fine on the spot. That tour proved the end of a career in which Emery took 5 wickets in an innings eleven times and three times took 10 wickets in a match.

Forced to retire prematurely from big cricket, Clem Hill looked around for enjoyment outside of cricket. He had been interested in horses since the days of his family's coaching business and he once recommended a horse called Queenie to Alby Wright, the Adelaide Oval groundsman. Queenie pulled the roller at Adelaide Oval for twenty years. Encouraged, Clem took a job as a stipendiary steward with the South Australian Jockey Club and Adelaide Racing Club, where he gained experience as a handicapper. The Victoria Amateur Turf Club appointed him handicapper in 1937 and for years he assessed the weights for one of Australia's biggest races, the Caulfield Cup. At sixty-six he took the less demanding job of handicapper to the Geelong Racing Club. He was killed in a traffic accident two years later when he was thrown from a tram in Collins Street, Melbourne.

Clem's close friend Alby Wright was one of the few leg-spinners to open the bowling for his State. Wright was a modest, sunburnt man who prepared the wickets at Adelaide Oval and bowled to the State side whenever they practised. He developed exceptional accuracy with his leg-breaks and when the State team was weak in bowling was pressed into service for South Australia in the 1910–11 season. He opened the bowling against New South Wales at Sydney, with medium-pacer Roy Hill, one of Clem's brothers, at the other end. Wright took 5 for 75 and 6 for 103. By the end of the 1911–12 season when he retired for good Wright had taken 110 first-class wickets at 30.81. He is best remembered, however, for his record run of six ducks in a row when he first played in the South Australian team in 1905–06.

South Australia always scored quickly in Clem Hill's time. One of his team-mates, Algie Gehrs, held the record for the fastest century in Australian first-class cricket for many years. Gehrs scored 119 in 50 minutes for South Australia against Western Australia in 1912–13. This remained unsurpassed until the 1982–83 summer when another South Australian, left-hander David Hookes, reached a century in 43 minutes and 107 in 55 minutes against Victoria on Adelaide Oval. Gehrs played many times before the first World War with the remarkable English all-rounder J.N. Crawford, who had joined the teaching staff at St Peter's College, Adelaide, after a dispute with the Surrey County Club in England.

Crawford, bespectacled son of a parson, was a batsman who could really hurry the score along. When Crawford, Gehrs, Darling, and Hill batted at Adelaide Oval spectators usually enjoyed a feast of runs. Playing for an Australian Eleven against the touring England team in 1911–12, Crawford made 110 in even time against the attack — Barnes, Foster, Rhodes, Woolley — that had Australia's best batsmen struggling. In 1914 Crawford and Victor Trumper put on 289 for an Australian touring team in only 69 minutes against Fifteen of Canterbury at Temuka. After Trumper was out, Crawford added 50 in 9 minutes with Monty Noble. He ended up with 354.

Not long before the first World War began a private sponsor offered to send a team on tour in England with the six rebels as the nucleus of the side, but the M.C.C. at Lord's refused to consider the idea. War began with Australian cricket in disarray. The sole consolation was that the Sheffield Shield continued to produce high-class performances. New South Wales had edged out South Australia for the Shield in 1913–14 when the left-arm pace bowling of Hugh Massie's giant son Jack showed unmistakable signs of greatness and in fifteen matches he took 99 wickets at 18.38. War began with Victoria holding the Shield thanks to outstanding bowling in 1914–15 by Queensland-born left-hander Bert Ironmonger, who took 32 wickets in a season of machine-like accuracy for only 17.15 each. Jack Ryder had given a hint of things to come with a blazing 151 for Victoria against South Australia.

Opposite: The companiable, much respected right hand batsman known to one and all as Ernie, otherwise, Edgar Richard Mayne. He played in only four Tests but toured England (twice), South Africa, New Zealand and North America (twice) with Australian teams. In his 40th year he made 209 out of a 456 partnership with Bill Ponsford.
— Ronald Cardwell.

— AUSTRALIAN ELEVEN 1897 —

Harry Trott's popular 1897 Australian team received a joyful welcome when they played a match against a Goldfields XI at Kalgoorlie in 1897. Here they are in the brake drawn by eight greys that took them from the station to their hotel in Hannan Street. Their opponents included miners from all States.
— *The West Australian.*

Victor Trumper cheered as he reached the crease during his benefit match in 1912-13. He received £2950 from the match.
— *Sydney Mail.*

Victor Trumper died in great pain from Bright's disease in 1915, aged thirty-seven. He was a teetotaller and non-smoker who never kept late hours and even at a crucial stage of the war his death made page-one headlines. For all who saw him he was the most brilliant of Australian batsmen who in the nineteen seasons between 1894–95 and 1913–14 scored forty-two centuries, including nine innings over 200 and a top score of 300 not out. Of his personality, his one-time team-mate Frank Iredale wrote: 'To be near him seemed to me to be a great honour. His was one of those natures that called to you, in whose presence you felt good to live. I never knew anybody who practised self-effacement as much as he did'. Trumper disliked self-promotion and once deliberately ran out Warren Bardsley. When Bardsley complained, Trumper said that having scored a century Bardsley should give his team-mates a turn to bat.

The great Dr W.G. Grace died in the same year as Trumper after a heart attack during a Zeppelin raid over London. He was sixty-seven and the best-known Englishman of his time. He was widely mourned by cricketers everywhere but especially in Australia, where his two tours as England's captain in 1873–74 and 1891–92, had proved invaluable in lifting playing standards. Many of the legendary tales about Grace's gamesmanship involve Australia. 'W.G. was a sneak,' said Sammy Woods, when told of Grace's death but there were tears in his eyes as he said it.

Grace took cricket to bush towns all over Australia, travelling over rough roads in gruelling conditions, frequently enduring uncomfortable interstate journeys that made his players ill and dispirited. He took the primitive nature of early Australian cricket in good part and contributed to its improvement, helped in getting maches for the first Australian teams to tour England, and without his intervention the first-ever Test in England would probably not have been played. The pioneer Australian captains Dave Gregory, Billy Murdoch, Tup Scott, Percy McDonnell, and Jack Blackham were among his closest friends.

With the Sheffield Shield suspended, the best cricket in Australia during the first World War was played in charity matches organised by the Melbourne Cricket Club and the Victorian Cricket Association. The N.S.W.C.A. refused to join in, claiming that the matches disrupted recruiting, but the V.C.A. selectors included noted New South Wales players like Monty Noble and Charlie Macartney. The first match, on Boxing Day 1915, was between Fifteen of Victoria and the Shield Eleven. The second match, on New Year's Day 1916, was between Warwick Armstrong's Eighteen and Victoria. Armstrong worked as a ground bowler with the Melbourne Cricket Club, wheeling down his leg-breaks and top-spinners to club members most afternoons for a few hours. He was exceptionally accurate but no more so than Bert Ironmonger who took 5 for 74 and 7 for 59 in one match.

Billy Bruce, first of a long line of outstanding Australian left-handed batsmen. He played in 14 Tests, twice toured England, scored 5,731 runs and took 143 wickets in first-class cricket, and could throw equally well with both hands.
— Melbourne Cricket Ground Museum.

Albert ("Tibby") Cotter, one of Australian cricket's major losses in World War I. He was a wild, hostile fast bowler of exceptional vitality who learned his cricket with Sydney Grammar School and the Glebe district club. He was killed by a sniper at Beersheba.
— Frank Laver's Collection.

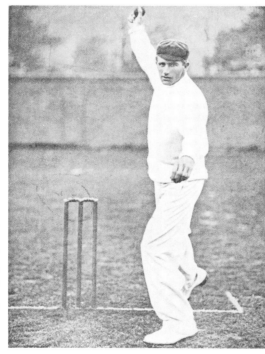

Monty Noble bowled like this with an American baseball grip, holding the ball between the thumb and forefinger and achieving pronounced swing. Jack Worrall, Melbourne critic, claimed Noble was a chucker.
— Albert Gregory Collection.

The Sydney undertaker Hanson ("Sep") Carter, who kept wicket for Australia in 28 Tests, was born in Halifax, Yorkshire. He returned to England three times in Australian teams, in 1902, 1909 and 1921 and would have gone in 1912 had he not joined those who challenged the Australian Board of Control's authority.
— Waverley Historical Society.

Ironmonger was a controversial cricketer all his career, largely because of accusations that he threw. He came from Ipswich in Queensland and had lost the tops of two fingers of his left hand while working as a youth in a timber mill. The story was that he lost part of one finger when he ventured too close to a circular saw. Some weeks later he was showing the foreman how the accident had happened when he again got too close to the saw and lost the second finger-tip. Opponents considered that he achieved extra spin by flicking the ball off the tops of the two short fingers but accuracy was the key to his success, not spin.

The Melbourne wartime matches were lavishly staged. Aeroplanes executed acrobatics over the M.C.G. and bands from three councils turned out. After play ended there was an auction on the ground to benefit the wounded. Billy Murdoch's bat brought 70 guineas, Clem Hill's 20 guineas, and a bat Victor Trumper had autographed just before his death fetched 55 guineas. Memorabilia on offer included photographs of players, commemorative plates, and even a letter home from Fred Spofforth on his first English trip. The main attraction was the ball used in the first Test at the Oval in 1882 when the Ashes legend was born, the day W.G. Grace said, 'I left six men to get 30 odd runs and they could not get them'. Amid all the excitement of that thrilling Australian win, Blackham had pocketed the ball. It was now offered to subscribers who, by paying £1 towards the war effort, had their names recorded in an album to be displayed with the ball at the M.C.G. The ball finally raised a total of £617, and the entire appeal £3,255.

This great South Australian quartette, Joe Darling, George Giffen, Clem Hill and Ernie Jones, were deeply involved in the players' fight to retain control of tours and team selections. All gave freely of their time at committee meetings.
— E.S. Marks Collection.

There was criticism from Sydney about the refusal of Victorian cricketers to join the services and this became a nasty issue that V.C.A. officials could not ignore. When the Sydney government official E.H. Oliphant gave a lecture at the Latrobe Gallery as a guest of the Victorian Public Library he chose as his theme 'Do We Deserve to Win the War?' and attacked sportsmen who had not joined up:

It is not only the footballers who are a disgrace to the community. While N.S.W. has sent nearly all her leading cricketers to the front Victoria has not provided one of her chief players. When one looks at young men disgracing themselves by devoting their days to cricket when their country needs them one might ask whether we deserve to win the war.

Ernie Bean of the V.C.A. replied that eleven Victorian Shield cricketers were serving overseas, but Oliphant was unmoved and said that not one of the victorious 1914–15 Sheffield Shield side had gone to the front. 'There was just one man whose name should be mentioned with honour, Dr. R.L. Park,' said Oliphant.

A few months later Bean was able to record in the V.C.A. annual report that Captain R. Grieve of the Brighton Cricket Club had won the Victoria Cross, the first Australian cricketer to do so. But the war years were sorry ones for cricketers. Albert Trott shot himself in his London boarding house in 1914, leaving his wardrobe and a few pounds to his landlady. His brother Harry died three years later at fifty-one, and Tom Horan — alias 'Felix', who reigned for years as Australia's best-informed and most readable cricket writer in the *Australasian* — died in 1916. In 1915 Gervys Hazlitt, who had been a Test player at nineteen and played cricket knowing he had a weak heart, died at twenty-seven. Then in 1917 word came that fast bowler Tibby Cotter, a trooper in the Australian Light Horse, had been killed in the charge on Beersheba. He had been ordered to report to headquarters for guard duty but instead rode with his mates from Khallassa in Southern Palestine in the attack that over-ran Beersheba. Had he obeyed orders he would have survived, but he rode with his friends and went down in a hail of machine gun fire. He was thirty-four.

Melbourne Cricket at the turn of the century. In the committee rooms discussions raged over players control and team selection.
— Victorian Cricket Association.

Frank Laver, star Victorian allrounder whom the rebels wanted to manage the 1912 Australian team to England. He had done the job splendidly in 1909.
— Albert Gregory Collection.

The Queensland team for the southern tour in 1913-14 (L to R): J.W. McLaren, L.P.D. O'Connor, H. Ironmonger, F.C. Thompson, visitor; Centre, R.K. Oxenham, S.W. Ayres, S.J. Fennelly, M.F. McCaffery (manager), S.J. Redgrave (captain), W. Rowe, R.J. Wilcocks; Front, J.F. Sheppard, J. Thomson, J. Downey. McLaren, Ironmonger and Oxenham won Test selection.
— Queensland Cricketers' Club.

PLAYER'S CIGARETTES

Mr. C. V. GRIMMETT,
SOUTH AUSTRALIA

PLAYER'S CIGARETTES

W. H. PONSFORD (VICTORIA)

PLAYER'S CIGARETTES

Mr. H. L. COLLINS
N S.W. AUSTRALIA

PLAYER'S CIGARETTES

L. O'B. FLEETWOOD-SMITH (VICTORIA)

PLAYER'S CIGARETTES

W. J. O'REILLY (N. S. WALES)

PLAYER'S CIGARETTES

A. JACKSON   NEW SOUTH WALES

PLAYER'S CIGARETTES

D. G. BRADMAN (N. S. WALES)

PLAYER'S CIGARETTES

W. A. OLDFIELD (NEW SOUTH WALES)

PLAYER'S CIGARETTES

W. M. WOODFULL
(VICTORIA)

PLAYER'S CIGARETTES

S. J. McCABE (N S WALES)

PLAYER'S CIGARETTES

Mr. A. A. MAILEY,
NEW SOUTH WALES

PLAYER'S CIGARETTES

A. F. KIPPAX (N S WALES)

12. The Services Lead A Comeback

At a meeting of the Australian Board of Control for International Cricket in Sydney on 6 December 1918 the following cable from the Marylebone Cricket Club at Lord's was read:

> Would you favour the idea of a tour of England in 1919 of an Australian team composed of those serving? If so would you nominate a representative here to negotiate with the M.C.C.

The Australian Board favoured the proposal and appointed Major Gordon Campbell, a former South Australian Shield player as its representative in negotiations with the M.C.C. The Board insisted that it should have complete control over the team, although it was prepared to accept M.C.C. selection procedures. The Board decided that the touring party should be limited to fifteen players, with Major Campbell as manager-treasurer at a fee of £200. W.H. Ferguson, known throughout the cricket world as 'Fergie', was appointed scorer-baggage master but had to pay his own fares. Each member of the side was to receive £150 and the team was to be known as 'The First A.I.F. Australian Eleven'. The Board also asked the M.C.C. to indemnify it against loss should the tour not take place and decided that £500 should be subscribed by its member associations to finance the tour.

However, when the selectors — E.P. Barbour, R.L. Park, and Gordon Campbell — began discussions they found that many of the best Australian players then in England were unavailable for the tour. Doctors Barbour, Park, and Tozer were anxious to return home and re-establish their medical practices as soon as possible. Lieutenant-Colonel R.J.A. Massie, the New South Wales left-arm pace bowler, had been wounded in the left shoulder at Gallipoli and in the right foot in France and could not play cricket again. As his father had recently died, Charlie Macartney felt he should be with his family back in Australia. A.G. ('Johnnie') Moyes was unavailable because of war injuries.

Opposite:
The outstanding players who upheld Australia's cricket prestige so well in the 1920s and 1930s, shown in another valuable set of cigarette cards.
— David Frith, Wisden Cricket Monthly.

The tremendous reach of legendary allrounder Jack Gregory. He still holds the record for the fastest Test century by an Australian – 70 minutes against South Africa at Johannesburg in 1921-22, when he finished with 119.
— Albert Gregory Collection.

When southern States questioned Queensland's ability to prepare first-class pitches, enthusiastic members of the Queensland team took no chances, and helped with the rolling.
— Patrick Mullins.

The M.C.C., was surprised by the large number of gaps in the team, withheld their financial support and cancelled the scheduled Test matches in the belief that the A.I.F. side could not aspire to first-class status. The A.I.F. Sports Control Board then took over the team and the arrangement of matches, although the itinerary remained the same as that worked out by the cricket authorities in England and Australia. On behalf of the A.I.F. Sports Control Board, Captain Cyril Docker circularised units throughout England and Europe, calling for players to try out for the team. Applications poured in from a surprising number of grade and first-class cricketers and for weeks trials went on while the available talent was assessed. The Australian Government, the Australian Comforts Fund, and Australians resident in London all collected funds for the A.I.F. Sports Board.

Eventually eighteen players were invited to tour with the A.I.F. team: E.A. Bull, H.L. Collins, C.T. Docker, J.M. Gregory, H.F.T. Heath, C. Kelleway, A.W. Lampard, E.J. Long, H.S.B. Love, J.T. Murray, C.C. O'Connor, W.A. Oldfield, C.E. Pellew, W.S. Stirling, J.M. Taylor, W.L. Trenerry, C.B. Willis, S.C. Winning. Most of the team were unknown to cricket fans but before their careers were over some of them were to earn revered reputations in the history of Australian cricket. And by their performance on tour in England, in South Africa on the way home, and against Australian States, the A.I.F. team played an important role in re-establishing big cricket after four years of war.

When the A.I.F. team was first formed only Collins and Kelleway had established themselves in Australian first-class cricket, but they quickly developed into a happy combination in which the players' military ranks were forgotten. The team played bright, enterprising cricket and quickly won a reputation among spectators for their willingness to press for a result. They became even more attractive to watch when Field-Marshal Birdwood, commander of the Australian forces in Europe, sacked Kelleway as captain after only six matches and asked Collins, a lance-corporal in the Australian Light Horse, to take over. Kelleway was a notorious stonewaller, a captain with decorations for bravery, but Birdwood considered he had an abrasive temperament and did not get on well with his players. Birdwood also knew that Collins was the captain the players wanted.

Gregory in action as a pace bowler leapt high in the delivery stride, covering around three metres before he grounded his foot.
— New South Wales Cricket Association.

E.A. ("Ted") McDonald, Gregory's legendary fast-bowling partner on the 1921 tour of England, when he took 150 wickets. His approach run was so superbly balanced he left no marks on the turf.
— Jack Pollard Collection.

WHEN J. M. GREGORY BOWLS.

This was how a South African newspaper cartoonist saw Gregory's thunderbolts during one spell in which he took 5 for 9.
— Melbourne Cricket Ground Museum.

Herbie Collins removing his pads after practice. He captained the A.I.F. team with consumate skill and led Australia on the 1926 tour of England after Warwick Armstrong's retirement.
— Albert Gregory Collection.

The first A.I.F. team lost only four of its twenty-eight first-class matches in England and defeated a full-strength M.C.C. side at Lord's. Under Herbie Collins' shrewd leadership they did much to restore prestige squandered by the bad behaviour of the 1912 team in England. The A.I.F. side produced in Jack Gregory a fast bowler of thrilling pace who was to be Australia's main strike bowler in twenty-four Tests, and in Bert Oldfield one of cricket's great wicket-keepers, a dapper little fellow whose work was all craftsmanship and polish. Oldfield, a corporal in the 15th Field Ambulance Brigade, had been buried for several hours during German bombardment of Polygon Wood in 1917 in France, and was close to death when they dug him out. When Gregory's bouncer gashed the face of the A.I.F. team's original wicket-keeper Ted Long in one of the trial games, Collins invited Oldfield to replace him. Oldfield protested that he lacked the class required but agreed to join the team that night on the train to Oxford. Collins knew after only one over next day that the reports he had heard about Oldfield were true. When he enlisted, Oldfield had played only two first-grade matches with Glebe in the same team as Tibby Cotter.

The A.I.F. team's success hung on Gregory's consistent ability to break through the opposition's early batting. He leapt high in the air with what commentators called 'a kangaroo hop' as he reached the bowling crease and let the ball go from a full extension of his 6-feet 3-inch frame. He swung the ball away or bounced it into the batsman's body at blistering speed from a fourteen-pace approach run. Nobody was surprised to learn that he was Dave Gregory's nephew and a cousin of Syd Gregory. As the A.I.F. tour continued, big Jack developed into a magnificent slips field and a spectacular left-handed batsman who could strike the best bowling into the crowd with effortless grace.

In the field the A.I.F. team were invariably spectacular. 'Nip' Pellew was hailed by Pelham Warner as the finest outfielder he ever saw, a fieldsman of dazzling speed with a pick-up and throw of such vigour that he ripped the heels of some of his boots as he stopped and turned. Johnny Taylor was an equally exciting fieldsman wherever he stood, a former schoolboy athletics champion, rifle-shooting star, and representative Rugby player. John Tinline Murray 6 feet 3 inches tall with very fast reflexes and a powerful arm, fielded and batted with equal gusto.

One of the A.I.F. teams that helped rebuild cricket's popularity after World War I (L. to R): Back, C.S. Winning, E.J. Long, C.T. Docker, J.M. Gregory, C.B. Willis; Front, J.M. Taylor, E. Bull, H.L. Collins (captain), E.J. Cameron, W.L. Trenerry, W.A. Oldfield. On the field all rank was forgotten. In all 19 players appeared for the A.I.F.
— Mitchell Library, Sydney.

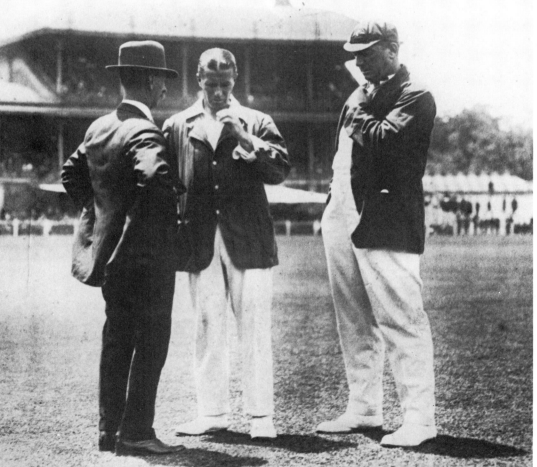

Rival captains, J.W.H.T. Douglas (England) and W.W. Armstrong (Australia) consult the curator, Bert Luttrell, before the start of the second Test at Melbourne in 1920. Australia won this, the first Test series for eight years, by 5-0, and stretched that to eight successive wins in England in 1921.
— Melbourne Cricket Ground Museum.

Gregory's pace bowling partner Ted McDonald. This shows his copybook high arm action just before delivery.
— M.C.C. Collection at Lord's.

Right: Dentist Johnny Taylor, one of the most entertaining batsmen in cricket immediately after World War I. His eight Tests yielded one century and eight scores over 50, plus a record last wicket stand of 127 with Arthur Mailey.
— Albert Gregory Collection.

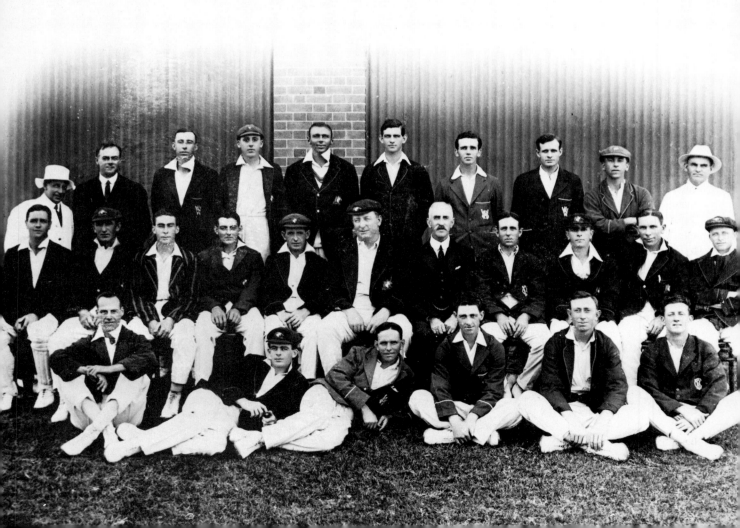

Among the highlights of the A.I.F. team's English tour were the defeats of the strong Yorkshire and Lancashire sides. Against Yorkshire Gregory took 3 wickets in 1 over to finish with 6 for 91 and have Yorkshire out for 224. The A.I.F. led by 41 runs and with Gregory bowling at his fastest Yorkshire was always struggling. Gregory dismissed Wilfred Rhodes, Roy Kilner, Robinson, and Sutcliffe, then hit the Yorkshire captain Burton in the face, ending his part in the match. Chasing 170 to win, the A.I.F. were 9 for 116, but Gregory and Long made 54 in 80 minutes to snatch a thrilling win. Lancashire had to follow on when they made only 125 in reply to the A.I.F.'s 418, but they managed only 148 in their second innings to give the A.I.F. victory by an innings and 157 runs.

The drawn match with Surrey was notable for the return to English first-class cricket of J.N. Crawford who had lived in Adelaide since 1909. He had patched up his quarrel with the Surrey committee and celebrated his return home with a superb innings of 144 not out after Surrey had lost 5 for 26 in chasing the A.I.F.'s 436. Johnny Taylor played one of the best innings of his career in scoring 146 in 150 minutes to set up the A.I.F. win over Essex. A feature of the A.I.F. displays was the slow left-arm bowling of Collins

who bowled more than 700 overs for the side, taking 106 first-class wickets, including 8 for 31 against Somerset. He never again bowled for prolonged spells once he had been discharged and his team disbanded.

Sir Abe Bailey, a vice-president of the South African Cricket Association, offered to guarantee the money required for the A.I.F. team to tour South Africa on the way home. The Australian Defence Minister, Senator Pearce, gave permission for a six-week tour. The team played ten matches, eight of them first class, and were far too strong for surprisingly weak South African opposition.

Gregory thrived on the hard, fast South African pitches, both with the bat and ball. At Durban against Natal he took 9 for 32 and ran out the other batsman. He failed to take a wicket against Transvaal at Johannesburg but made a quick 73. South African critics were unanimous, however, that Collins was the best player in the A.I.F. team. He took wickets regularly with his subtle slows and made 235 out of 441 against a South African Eleven at Johannesburg. Allie Lampard took 7 for 71 (12 for 100 in the match) against Western Province at Cape Town. The A.I.F. finished with eight wins and two draws and were never in danger of defeat.

The 1921 Australian team to England, ranked among the best three sides Australia has ever had (L to R): Back, W. Bardsley, J. Ryder, H.S.T. Hendry, J.M. Gregory, E.R. Mayne, T.J.E. Andrews, S. Smith (manager); Seated, A.A. Mailey, E.A. McDonald, H.L. Collins, W.W. Armstrong (captain), C.G. Macartney, H. Carter, J.M. Taylor; Front, C.E. Pellew, W.A. Oldfield. — Australian Cricket Board.

Opposite: Players who appeared in Frank Iredale Testimonial match in Sydney in 1921-22. Iredale, who served the game well as a player, writer, and administrator, received £1741, proceeds of the match between Australia v. The Rest. He is in the middle row to the left of the captains, Collins and Armstrong. — Ronald Cardwell.

Master Surrey opening batsman, Jack Hobbs, who had the daunting task of starting England's innings against Gregory and McDonald, partnered initially by Yorkshireman Wilfrid Rhodes.
— Albert Gregory Collection.

Far right: Armstrong on the boat going to England in 1921. His team travelled in the same ship as the England side they had just beaten 5-0. England used 30 players in the 1921 rubber, Australia winnng 3-0, with the last two Tests drawn.
— Melbourne Cricket Ground Museum.

The A.I.F. team played three first-class matches in Australia before the players took their discharges and split up. They received half the gate takings, plus expenses, from these games, which helped revive public interest in big cricket. They defeated Victoria at Melbourne by 6 wickets, with Gregory taking 7 for 22 and Lampard 7 for 99, Collins scoring 135 and Carl Willis 111. They had all the best of a drawn match against Queensland at Brisbane, where rain prevented a result. They then finished their campaign with a resounding victory over New South Wales. Gregory at his superb best scored centuries in each innings (122 and 102) and took 8 for 130 in the match, as well as holding three brilliant slips catches. Arthur Mailey, sometimes wrongly described as an A.I.F. team member, took 7 for 122 for the home side.

So long as cricket is played in Australia, the high reputation of the First A.I.F. team will endure. In three countries they played cricket that was unfailingly attractive, lost only four of their thirty-nine first-class matches, and won twenty. Big crowds watched wherever they took the field, and they provided ready-made Test players for the immediate post-war Australian side in Collins, Gregory, Oldfield, Taylor, and Pellew.

Of the six rebels who declined to tour England in 1912, Carter, Armstrong, and Ransford continued in first-class cricket after the war. None of them showed any misgivings about their challenge to the Board's authority. Armstrong, in fact, openly continued his feud with officials and conducted a bitter struggle with Victoria's Ernie Bean until the end of his career. Indeed, as he built up from the 10-stone (64 kilograms) stripling who at the age of twenty-three made his debut for Australia in 1902 to the 22-stone (140 kilograms) hulk known in 1921 as 'The Big Ship', his opinions became more forthright.

With the peace, the Australian district cricket system quickly provided a whole new set of candidates for representative honours. In Sydney a steady left-hander named James Bogle scored 1000 runs in a first-grade season for University, forcing his way into the New South Wales side in 1918–19 before the Sheffield Shield competition resumed. On his first appearance for New South Wales Bogle scored 145 in the second innings, adding 157 for the fourth wicket with the stonemason, Tommy Andrews, against a Victorian attack that included a newcomer from Tasmania, Ted McDonald. Andrews had been picked in the Australian team for the abandoned South African tour in 1914.

Jack Gregory and Tommy Andrews resume batting during their 286-run partnership for New South Wales in 1921-2. They were exciting craftsmen, differing in method, but able to swing matches.
— Albert Gregory Collection.

Australian 'keeper Bert ("Cracker") Oldfield follows the result of a deflection by English opening star Herbert Sutcliffe during the 1926 England-Australia series in England. Sutcliffe scored four centuries in the rubber.
— Sport & General, London.

Bogle scored 200 in his second season for New South Wales against South Australia at Adelaide Oval, batting faultlessly in stands of 203 for the second wicket with Bardsley, and 166 for the fourth wicket with Andrews. He made 103 in 1920-21 at Sydney against South Australia, starting a feast of runs that took New South Wales to 802. Despite his impressive form he was not among twenty-four players named for a Test trial in Sydney, where outraged newspapers called for the sacking of the selectors. There was only one New South Wales selector, cagey Herbie Collins, who was embarrassed by a surfeit of talent. Compensation for Bogle came in the form of a tour of New Zealand and a place in the Australian Eleven that defeated New Zealand in an unofficial Test by an innings and 227 runs. When Bogle graduated in medicine at Sydney University, he went off to practise in far north Queensland, his cricket career over.

Meanwhile Warwick Armstrong set himself to overcome on the field the opposition to his Test selection provided by Ernie Bean at committee meetings. Armstrong started the 1920–21 season with 157 and 245 not out for Victoria versus South Australia and followed with a masterly 158 in the first post-war Test against England at Sydney, where Australia fielded seven new players. Armstrong's driving in front of the wicket in that match was spectacular and he forced England's fieldsmen out on to the fence as he struck seventeen fours. He took 6 wickets in the second Test at Melbourne and made 121 in the third Test at Adelaide. The critics said Armstrong's captaincy in these matches assured him of the job in England in 1921, but Bean was still waiting his chance.

Armstrong did not practise on the day before the Victoria-NSW match at Sydney, but was seen at Randwick Racecourse. Just before play began next morning he withdrew. In Melbourne, the Victorian selectors took exception to this late withdrawal and dropped him from the State side to play England at the M.C.G. the following week. Armstrong's fans were so annoyed at this they organised a protest meeting outside the M.C.G. on the Saturday of the England match. Bean reacted by denying the protestors the normal pass-out tickets, which compelled them to pay when they re-entered the ground.

The turning point in the Second Test at Melbourne in 1924-25. Requiring 372 to win, England reached 200 with only three wickets down. Gregory then had Hearne lbw and clean bowled Hendren, shown here, to start an England slide that saw them end 81 runs short of their target.
— Sydney Morning Herald.

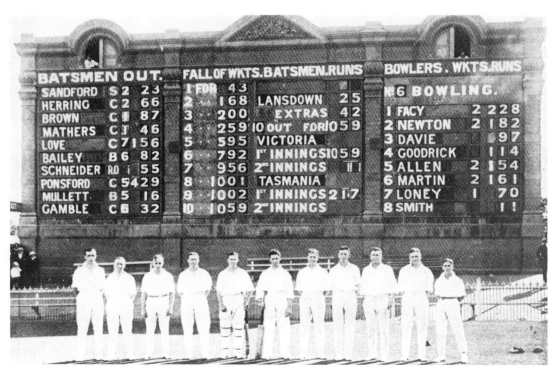

Two world records went in this 1923 match, which is generally considered to have begun the fashion of batsmen chasing quadruple hundreds. Victoria's total of 1059 was a new high for a first-class match. Ponsford, wearing pads with dark binding, achieved a score of 429. Neither record lasted long. The tiny figure on the right of this picture is the tragic Karl Schneider, a brilliant left-hander who died at 23.
— Melbourne Cricket Ground Museum.

The Sun
NEWS ~ PICTORIAL

DAILY AT DAWN

TRALIA'S BEST

341 Telephones: Cent. 9240, J3191.   MELBOURNE : WEDNESDAY, DECEMBER 29, 1926   (Registered at the G.P.O. Melbourne, for transmission by post as a newspaper) 1½

BATSMEN OUT.		FALL OF WKTS.	BATSMEN.	RUNS.	BOWLERS.	WKTS	RUNS
WOODFULL	C 7 133	1 FOR 375	ELLIS	63	5 BOWLING		
HENDRY	C 3 100	2 „ 594	BLACKIE	27			
PONSFORD	B 6 352	3 „ 614	EXTRAS	27	1 McNAMEE	1	124
LOVE	S 3 _ 6	4 „ 631	9 OUT 1107		2 McGUIRK	1	30
KING	S 3 7	5 „ 657	VICTORIA		3 MAILEY	4	362
HARTKOPF	C 3 61	6 „ 834	1ST INNINGS		4 CAMPBELL		89
LIDDICUT	B 2 36	7 „ 915	2ND INNINGS		5 PHILLIPS		64
RYDER	C 7 295	8 „ 1043	N.S.W.		6 MORGAN	1	137
MORTON	RO 0	9 „ 1046	1ST INNINGS	221	7 ANDREWS	2	148
		10 „	2ND INNINGS		8 KIPPAX		26

'Patsy' Hendren was in exhilarating form when the time for the protest arrived, but 8000 spectators still left the ground to hear the protest convenor, H.D. Westley. When Hendren passed 200 inside the ground, there were shouts of 'Give Ernie Bean a bowl'. England's score of 5 for 445 in the day was a striking demonstration of the folly of omitting Armstrong. At the next V.C.A. meeting Roy Park, doctor to the State team, explained that heavy bruising to Armstrong's legs had compelled his late withdrawal in Sydney. Shortly afterwards Armstrong's supporters staged a further noisy demonstration as he walked out to bat in the fourth Test on the M.C.G. with Australia 5 for 153. The story goes that Bean stood at the gate gloating as Armstrong went in, knowing that Armstrong had just downed several stiff whiskies. Armstrong made 123 not out in another inspired innings and when he returned, Bean, who normally did not drink, was drunk at the bar.

Despite Australia's five-to-nil defeat of Johnny Douglas' England team in that 1920–21 rubber in Australia, Bean still managed to raise enough votes to threaten Armstrong's appointment as captain for the tour of England in 1921. The late 'Johnnie' Moyes wrote that Armstrong was made captain only by 'the narrowest possible margin', indicating that there was only one vote in it when the Board made its captaincy selection.

Douglas' team undertook the Australian tour before English cricket was ready for it; the M.C.C. decided that the good of the game was more important than winning or losing the series. England's right-handed opening bat Harry Makepeace made 117 in the first match of the tour at Perth but thereafter England's bowlers struggled against a marvellous array of Australian batting talent. Arthur Richardson — a bespectacled figure with an enormously heavy bat which he wielded like a toy — made his first century for South Australia at Adelaide. Allie Lampard made a stylish 111 for Victoria in Melbourne and in Sydney Macartney and Collins had an opening stand of 244 in only 180 minutes.

England was defeated by 377 in the first Test, with Collins scoring a century in his Test debut. Australia won the second Test by an innings and 91 runs, with Pellew and Gregory each scoring maiden Test centuries. Hearne was unable to bat in either innings because of an illness that occurred after play began. Australia won the third Test at Adelaide by 119 runs, Kelleway batting 7 hours for 147. England's Cecil Parkin commented, 'He might be a good player in the next world, where time does not matter'. **Wisden** said of him: 'One Kelleway in a side is enough.

Two or three would be intolerable'. This Test produced 1,753 runs, a record aggregate for England-Australia Tests. Mailey took 4 for 115 and 9 for 121 in the fourth Test to give Australia victory by 8 wickets. In the fifth Test Macartney made his first century against England (170), contributing to Australia's 9-wickets win which brought the series result to an unprecedented five-to-nil. Mailey bowled in only four Tests but took 36 wickets, a record up to that time.

Armstrong took his great 1921 side on an arduous tour which included matches in Kalgoorlie and Perth, thirty-eight matches in England, and six in South Africa on the way home. At Perth he went out to toss with Western Australian captain Harold Evers, who also weighed more than 22 stone (140 kilograms). Their combined weight touched 45 stone (180 kilogams) but Evers belied his bulk by brilliantly stumping Jack Ryder, who had scored 102. Evers had previously captained New South Wales (in 1901–02). Every day on the voyage to England Armstrong joined Ted McDonald in the stokehold of their ship. Armstrong arrived with his weight unchanged but McDonald was stronger than at any time in his life.

Left: Victoria's 1059 against Tasmania lasted 3 years 1 month. In December, 1926, Victoria lifted their record to 1107 against New South Wales on Melbourne Cricket Ground. Mailey had 4 for 362.
— Sun News-Pictorial, Melbourne.

When Victoria went past 1000 runs against New South Wales the traditional enemy, this man, volatile wicket-keeper Jack Ellis, yelled: "Three to me and 1000 up. Long live, Victoria."
— Albert Gregory Collection.

Unsmilingly dedicated to bringing batsmen undone on the field, Clarrie Grimmett was a happy, laughing figure off it, often entertaining team-mates with dressing-room ditties. Here he arouses laughter in a radio interview.
— Bill O'Reilly.

Gregory and McDonald took sweet revenge on England's batsmen for the destruction of Australian batsmen in 1911–12 by Barnes and Foster. The Australian pacemen gave the Englishmen such a dusting that England fielded thirty players in the five Tests. They were a magnificent pair who, with their contrasting methods, gave batsmen no respite: Gregory leapt high in his delivery stride and hurled them down from the clouds with his long, sinewy arms; McDonald was so superbly balanced in his approach run that he left no marks on the turf. And for batsmen who survived the pace onslaught there was then the spin and guile of Mailey and Armstrong to face. These four were so successful that the left-arm spin of Macartney was not needed and he took only 8 wickets on the tour.

Armstrong's team won the first Test in two days, the second by lunchtime on the third day, and had taken the Ashes by 5 p.m. on the third day of the third Test. The Australians made thirty-seven centuries between them on the tour and had only eight scored against them. Of the fifteen players, eleven had captained their State or district teams and the side's overall knowledge of tactics enabled them to move automatically into position for a variety of opponents. In addition the side included the world's two best slips fieldsmen, Gregory and Hendry, the two best outfielders, Bardsley and Taylor, with Pellew used in the covers where he formed an unsurpassed pairing with Andrews. Wicket-keepers Carter and Oldfield were so good that it mattered little which one of them played for they went game after game without error.

Opinions differ about Armstrong's merit as a captain. Arthur Mailey used to say that Armstrong was a tenacious fighter, brimful of courage, who outbluffed many opponents. Other Test stars ranked Armstrong below Noble, Harry Trott, or Collins as a tactician. Armstrong never had to face moulding a winning team from nothing as Benaud and Ian Chappell did many years later. Armstrong himself perhaps made the most revealing comment when asked to compare his 1921 side with Joe Darling's 1902 team. 'The 1902 team would have beaten Twenty Two of my lot', he said. Even for a man given to grandiose views late in life it was a marvellous compliment to a 1902 side he considered without blemish.

Arthur Mailey was not a slum child — he came from the sandhills at the back of Waterloo, Sydney. He had an all too brief Test career of five years, taking 99 wickets. — Press Association .

Armstrong won his 1921 side's respect by arguing for more privileges for them. 'Stork' Hendry said in 1983 that many of the benefits players receive today are a direct result of Armstrong's efforts. When he asked for drinks to be served for his players in the Lord's dressing-room, the M.C.C. secretary F.E. Lacey replied that the bar was the proper place for drinking. But Armstrong won his point, arguing that weary cricketers were entitled to the privacy they could not get at members' bars. When Armstrong asked to change the team's schedule so that they had a rest day before Tests, most counties agreed.

Eight players scored more than 1000 runs in England, headed by Macartney with 2335 runs at 58.37 — including a majestic innings of 345 against Nottinghamshire in slightly less than 4 hours. Macartney, missed in the slips when he was 9, hit four sixes and forty-seven fours on a day when Australia scored 608 runs. 'No other batsman, not even Bradman, has approached Macartney for insolence of attack', wrote R.C. Robertson-Glasgow. 'Length could not curb him and his defence was included in his attack. He made slaves of bowlers.' When Macartney made 115 in the third Test at Leeds, it was his fourth century in successive first-class innings and Australia's sole century of the rubber.

All the Australians knew that Hanson Carter
had an unequalled knowledge of the laws of
cricket. When Lionel Tennyson attempted to close
the England innings at 5.50 p.m. on the second
day of the fourth Test at Old Trafford, Armstrong
consulted Carter who said the laws did not allow
such a closure. Armstrong backed Carter and told
Tennyson his declaration was illegal. The rule
book showed that the Australians were right as
there had been no play on the first day because of
rain. The players returned after 25 minutes'
absence from the field and Armstrong, who had
bowled the last over before the declaration,
inadvertently bowled the first over after the
resumption. This is the only instance in Test
history of the same bowler sending down two
successive overs.

Armstrong's last Test at The Oval in 1921 was
upset by rain. Armstrong showed his disapproval
of England's playing for a draw by resting his
regular strike bowlers and retiring to the outfield.
His vast foot trapped a piece of newspaper and he
startled both spectators and players by reading the
paper. When Arthur Mailey asked him why he was
reading the paper, the big man said, 'To see who
we are playing'.

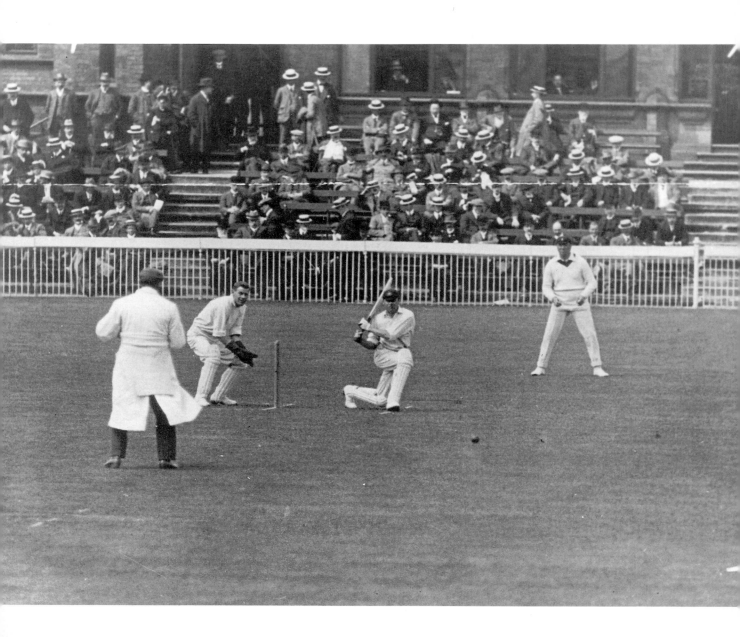

The only defeats suffered by the 1921 team
came right at the end of the tour at Eastbourne
and Scarborough. Mailey, who took 146 wickets
on the tour, captured all 10 wickets for 66 runs in
the second innings against Gloucestershire. Team-
mates kidded Mailey that he could have had 10 for
54 and Mailey smiled: 'I wanted a good title for
my book'. Three decades later he published **Ten
for 66 — And All That**. McDonald edged out
Mailey as Australia's leading wicket-taker, however,
with 150 wickets at 15.95 — the best result by an
Australian bowler in England since the days of
Turner and Ferris in 1888 and 1890. Bardsley just
shaded Macartney for the honour of scoring most
tour centuries, with nine against Macartney's eight.

Armstrong established links with a Glasglow
whisky firm during that tour of Britain — an
association that helped make him rich when he
returned to Australia. He was the perfect whisky
salesman, a connoisseur with a vast capacity for
the stuff. He gave up his job as pavilion clerk and
ground bowler for the Melbourne Cricket Club
and became Victorian manager for Peter Dawson
distillery. 'Stork' Hendry moved from Sydney to

take over as pavilion clerk in 1922. Armstrong was
appointed Australian general manager for James
Buchanan whisky in 1935 and moved to
fashionable Darling Point in Sydney. He was
highly paid for Test commentaries in which he
showed little compassion. During the Bodyline
series in 1932–33 he said, 'There was no doubt in
my mind that Bradman was scared of Larwood',
and called Bradman a 'cricket cocktail'. After
England had won the series, he wrote: 'Had
Bradman been built with more backbone, it is
possible the whole story might have been
different'. Armstrong died at sixty-eight in 1947,
leaving £90,000. His first-class career from 1898
to 1921 had included fifty Tests, ten of them as
unbeaten Australian captain.

At the Imperial Cricket Conference in 1921 at
Lord's Armstrong advocated the announcement of
Test umpires on the morning of the match. He
said there was so much betting on the matches
that it would be wise to remove umpires from
temptation. Lord Harris told the conference he
had no evidence of betting on Test cricket, to
which Armstrong replied: 'Well, if you would like

£500 on the next Test I'll get it on for you'.

Armstrong handed over the Australian captaincy to Herbie Collins on the way home from England for three Tests against South Africa, thus transferring Australia's cricket fortunes to a wan, poker-faced gambler who had played two-up in Flanders trenches and won all the money in shipboard poker schools. But although Collins often took risks at the racetrack or in the gaming clubs, he never made a careless move while entrusted with Australia's cricket prestige. Two of his first three Tests on matting in South Africa were drawn. Macartney starred in the first at Durban with a polished 116. In the second at Johannesburg Jack Gregory followed 203 by Collins with a century in 70 minutes on his way to 119. Gregory's century, the fastest in Test history, still did not prevent a draw. Australia won the rubber by taking the last Test at Cape Town by 10 wickets. Ryder made 142, and Macartney took 5 for 44 with his left-arm spinners. It was a fitting end to a memorable tour, with the spite of the 1912 revolt forgotten.

Six legendary Australian cricketers at the Adelaide Test between England and Australia in 1924-25 (L to R): Back, Clem Hill, Warwick Armstrong and "Nip" Pellew; Front, Ernie Jones, George Giffen and Jack Lyons.
— Jack Pollard Collection.

R.H. Bettington returned from a successful stint with Oxford University to captain New South Wales. Later he won an Australian amateur golf championship.
— Jack Pollard Collection.

13. The High-Scoring Twenties

There was no time-limit on Sheffield Shield matches throughout the 1920s; all matches were played to a finish. This produced some enormous individual and team scores. Victoria made 1059 against Tasmania in 1922–23, and in 1925–26 New South Wales won the Shield with totals of 708, 705, 642, 593, and 554. In 1926–27 at Melbourne, Victoria scored 1107, the highest-ever Shield total, against New South Wales, who were beaten by an innings and 665 runs. There were some outstanding bowlers in action around the States but the depth of batting talent was so great that the bowlers were unable to curb batsmen who could take their time. Victorian batsmen were adept at wearing down bowlers and many Victorian partnership records were set in Shield matches of unlimited duration.

Retribution came infrequently for bowlers but when it did it was usually in the form of a sticky wicket. This type of wicket was unique to Australia, with batsmen who looked masterly on hard pitches suddenly reduced to impotence. Hot sun on a pitch left uncovered through nights of heavy rain produced an amalgam of gluey mud held together by grasses of various origin. Star batsmen feared the sticky strips so much that many of them became nervous, testy weather-watchers when a few drops of rain fell in the night. When team-mates of the prolific Bill Ponsford went to breakfast, they would ask simply, 'How did Ponny sleep?' for it was well known that the merest trickle was enough to rouse Ponsford and make him toss uneasily at the thought of a sticky next day.

More than any batsman cricket had known up to his time, Ponsford ignored the satisfaction of a double century. This was merely a starting point, a time to take a fresh guard and begin again. Trumper had shown a legendary mercy to bowlers, looking about after he had made 100 for a deserving bowler to whom he could give his wicket. Ponsford began the trend towards accumulating mammoth scores, driving, pulling, cutting, and glancing for hours on end with machine-like precision.

Left:
Since cricket began in Australia it has inspired a long list of splendid artists, not the least of them d'Arcy W. Doyle, who executed this fine painting of a children's match in front of the legendary Birdsville Hotel, North Queensland. — Queensland Cricketers' Club.

Above: Brisbane solicitor Vic Shaw commissioned this painting of kids playing in an outback Queensland street by d'Arcy W. Doyle. It now hangs in the Queensland Cricketers' Club at the 'Gabba. — Vic Shaw.

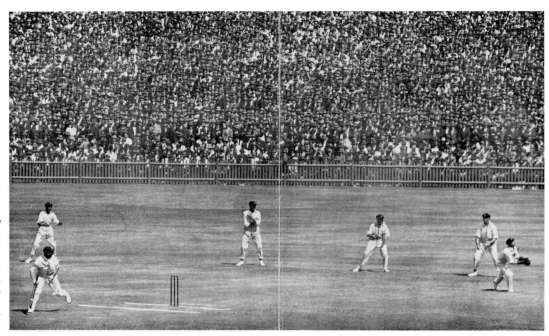

One of the most famous catches in Australian cricket history: Wicketkeeper Bert Oldfield moves several metres to his left to catch a firmly struck leg glance from Jack Hobbs at Sydney in the Fifth Test of the 1924-25 series against England.
— Sydney Morning Herald

A charming study showing some of the 1921 Australians in England (L to R): Standing, T.J.E. Andrews, E.A. McDonald, J.M. Gregory, their host (name unknown), J. Ryder, E.R. Mayne, H.S.T.L. Hendry; Seated, W. Ferguson (scorer), W.A. Oldfield, W. Bardsley, Syd. Smith (manager), A.A. Mailey, C.G. Macartney, C.E. Pellew. Identity of the ladies and little boy is not known, but the bearded man in front is Dr. Rowley Pope.
– Albert Gregory Collection.

He came into first-grade cricket for St Kilda Club in Melbourne at sixteen. However, after making his debut for Victoria in 1920–21 in his twenty-first year, he found it difficult to hold a place until he made 429 — at that time a world-record score — against Tasmania in 1922–23. He scored centuries in his first matches against four Australian States, and in 1927–28 lifted his world-record score to 437 against Queensland. When he made 352 to set up Victoria's record 1107 total against New South Wales, he played a ball from outside the off on to his stumps. He turned as if his ears had deceived him, surveyed the broken wicket, and said dolefully: 'Cripes, I am unlucky'.

Ponsford was a reserved, camera-wary cricketer, relieved when he got past photographers just inside the gate. His bat looked twice as broad as other batsmen's, and his backside assuredly was — a handy appurtenance for presenting to bowlers of bouncers. He made forty-seven first-class centuries and retired at thirty-four, satiated by run-scoring. He formed Australia's most successful opening partnership with Bill Woodfull, his Victorian team-mate. They had twenty-two century partnerships and five over 200, with Ponsford invariably the dominant scorer. Woodfull also scored more first-class centuries — forty-nine — with a top score of 284.

Both players had marked physical defects: Ponsford was colour blind; Woodfull suffered from troubles that prevented his enlistment in the first A.I.F. and stopped him playing regularly in a team until he was twenty-two. But they were remarkably similar in disposition, equally shy and suspicious of the Press and so withdrawn that team-mates who spent months on tour with them barely got to know them. But together they made the bulky green Australian cap world famous, for both had a characteristic way of tugging on their caps when a crisis loomed. The peak of Ponsford's cap moved around his head towards his ear as an innings progressed. 'When you saw the peak of Ponsford's cap disappear close to his left ear you knew he was heading for his second century,' wrote Ray Robinson.

Despite the mauling their bowlers received from noted southern batsmen like Ponsford, Woodfull, Bardsley, Andrews, and the fast-rising Alan Kippax, Queensland continued to press for a place in the Sheffield Shield competition. Delegates from New South Wales, Victoria, and South Australia kept arguing that the cost of sending teams to Queensland by train was too high and pointed to the lack of first-class pitches in Queensland, where sticky wickets were the most notorious in the nation. Indeed the tropical sun on a pitch saturated by a Brisbane thunderstorm

Keen pipe smokers Lionel Tennyson and Warwick Armstrong await the outcome as Douglas tosses before the Fifth Test at the Oval in 1921. — Mitchell Library, Sydney.

fully tested the skills of the world's best wet-wicket players. Undismayed, Queensland officials kept working on improving facilities and whenever funds permitted brought star-studded private teams to Queensland to help lift playing standards.

Ted McDonald had deserted Australian cricket after his triumphant tour of England in 1921, leaving Gregory without an outstanding pace-bowling partner. McDonald joined Nelson in the Lancashire League, one of the first Australians to appear regularly in that competition. Later he qualified for Lancashire and played an important role in the county's championship wins in 1926, 1928, and 1930. He took three hat-tricks in his career and seven times took more than 100 wickets in a season. A surly, introverted character, he was content simply to go through the motions against unskilled opposition. But when he faced world-renowned batsmen he bowled with fire and rare hostility, determined to dent their reputations. McDonald had a facility for attracting unsavoury friends, following a life-style that foreshadowed tragedy, but even his critics mourned when he was killed in a freak accident in 1937 in Lancashire. His car collided with another speeding car at Bolton and he climbed out of the wreck to help the other driver, only to be killed by a passing car.

Elegant Frank Woolley, who made 95 and 93 in the Second Test in 1921, innings studded with superb drives and cuts like this. His courage was memorable in another heavy England defeat.
— Sport & General.

New South Wales was lucky to have a player of the calibre of Yorkshireman Austin Diamond to captain the State side while the Test stars were away. He led the State fourteen times.
— Jack Pollard Collection.

Some of the triumphant 1921 Australian side at a Stamford Bridge, London, soccer match (L to R): E.A. McDonald, J.M. Gregory, H.S.T.L. Hendry, T.J.E. Andrews, A.A. Mailey, J.M. Taylor, H.L. Collins.
— Mitchell Library, Sydney.

Kelleway, who was little more than medium pace, opened the Australian bowling with Gregory against Arthur Gilligan's M.C.C. team in 1924–25. This tour marked the beginning of the memorable opening partnership of Hobbs and Sutcliffe, but even some of their best stands were not enough to prevent a four-to-one Australian win in the series, in which eight-ball overs were introduced to Test cricket. The rubber was played in a wonderful spirit, with both sides adhering to the highest standards of sportsmanship and sharing their pleasure in it with big crowds.

Arthur Mailey bowled without the assistance of the leg-before-wicket law that permitted appeals for balls pitched outside the off-stump. Dozens of times Sutcliffe and Hobbs pushed their pads out to his googlies spinning towards the middle stump. The ball was larger than it is today and harder to grip and the stumps were smaller. To overcome these gross disadvantages, he used resin to allow a better grip. Collins positioned Mailey in the slips briefed to keep lifting the seam to help his pace bowlers. When Douglas, the England captain, examined Mailey's hand and accused him of using resin, Mailey replied by lifting Douglas' bowling hand and pointing to the outside edge of the thumb nail where it was worn to the flesh. 'You've been lifting the seam,' said Mailey. They never raised the subject again.

At Sydney in the first Test, Johnny Taylor and Arthur Mailey put on a record 127 for the last wicket. Taylor finished with 108, Mailey was 46 not out. Maurice Tate had 11 wickets in the match but could not prevent an Australian win by 193 runs. Hobbs and Sutcliffe, who had had a stand of 157 in the first Test, added 283 before they were separated in the second Test. Sutcliffe made a century in each innings (176 and 127) to bring up his third successive century. Ponsford got his second century in two Tests (110 and 128) and Vic Richardson made 138 in only his second Test for Australia to win by 81 runs. Mailey's 5 for 92 in England's second innings at Melbourne proved the match-winner. The third Test at Adelaide was a thriller: Australia won by only 11 runs after Jack Ryder had made 201 not out and 88. Sutcliffe became the first batsman to score four centuries in a Test series with an innings of 143 in the fourth Test in Melbourne, in which England's victory by an innings and 29 runs ended a long losing run. Clarrie Grimmett joined Mailey in a brilliant Australian spin attack in the fifth Test at Sydney. In his Test debut at thirty-four, Grimmett took 5 for 45 and 6 for 37, routing England for 167 and 146. Kippax made a slightly less impressive debut with a stylish 73.

Kelleway withdrew from Australia's 1926 tour of England, although he was in peak form and an invaluable all-rounder. Mailey said his withdrawal was a form of idealism and that Kelleway was piqued because he was not among the first group of players named for the tour. This left Australia with a threadbare pace attack, a situation that worsened when Gregory broke down in England. He took only 36 wickets on the tour and although he hobbled through the five Tests he took a mere 3 wickets in the rubber. The bulk of the bowling fell to the bespectacled South Australian Arthur Richardson and the master spinners Mailey and Grimmett.

Arthur Gilligan watches a coin tossed high by noted two-up exponent Herbie ("Lucky") Collins during the 1924-25 series.
— Adelaide Advertiser.

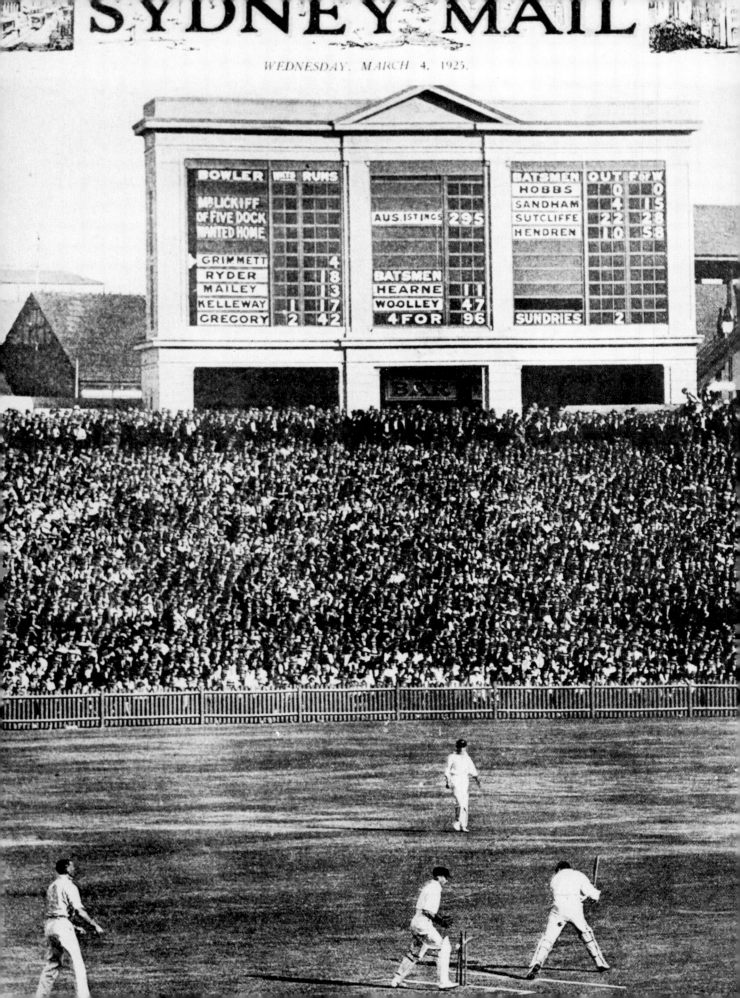

Two much discussed stumpings in the Fifth Test in 1924-25: Top, Jack Hobbs appears to have his foot in when Grimmett beat him in the Fifth Test and Oldfield whipped off the bails. Hobbs had made 13. Left, Herbert Strudwick brilliantly stumps Johnny Taylor off Tate after Taylor had scored 25. Both batsman accepted their dismissal without argument.
— Sydney Morning Herald.

Opposite: Clarrie Grimmett's first wicket in Tests came before 40,000 spectators in the final Test of the 1924-25 rubber when he clean bowled Woolley for 47. In a sensational debut, he took 11 wickets in the match, sealing Australia's 4-1 series win.
— Sydney Mail.

Collins and Bardsley, right, who proved a successful opening pair for Australia before Collins' illness in England in 1926 gave Bill Woodfull his chance in the job. Woodfull retained the spot until the end of his 35-Test career. — Sydney Mail.

Herbie Collins leads the Australians on to the field at Lord's in 1926 (L to R): W.A. Oldfield, A.A. Mailey, W.M. Woodfull, H. L. Collins, J. Ryder, J.M. Gregory, C.G. Macartney, T.J.E. Andrews and A.J. Richardson. Only J.M. Taylor missed the picture. — Sport & General.

For connoisseurs the spectacle of Mailey and Grimmett bowling together was one of the wonders of cricket, the sole blessing in the damp English summer of 1926. Mailey bowled like a millionaire, Grimmett like a miser, said Cardus. They were both short men and both based their attack on flight and turn but there the similarity ended. Mailey, the wise-cracking cartoonist and journalist, began with a shuffle, then jogged five easy steps to the stumps, weaving from side to side, and transferred the ball to his right hand only at the last moment. His right arm was hidden behind him as he looked over his right shoulder at the target, and his arm came directly over the top in classical style, his fingers working their magic on the ball. Grimmett moved up with a brisk, skipping approach run, shoulders hunched, and whipped his bowling arm around his body. His googly turned more than his leg-break but he bowled a lot of top-spinners that went straight on. Mailey deliberately bowled full tosses and gave away fours to make batsmen careless: Grimmett liked to save every run.

Mailey took 141 wickets at 18.7 on the tour (13 in the four Tests in which he bowled), Grimmett took 116 at 17.2 (8 in three Tests in which he played). None of the Test pitches was at all helpful to spin. The first four Tests were drawn and England regained the Ashes by winning the fifth Test at The Oval by 289 runs. This match turned on a second innings opening stand of 170 by Hobbs (100) and Sutcliffe. England appointed Percy Chapman to replace A.W. Carr (who had tonsilitis) as captain in the fifth Test and brought Wilfred Rhodes back to Tests at the age of forty-eight. Rhodes scored handy runs and took 6 valuable wickets (2 for 35 and 4 for 44). The match ended Frank Woolley's remarkable succession of fifty-two Test appearances for England since 1909. Warren Bardsley captained Australia in the third and fourth Tests while Collins was in hospital with neuritis.

Typical of the spirit of sportsmanship in big cricket at the time was the incident involving J.S. Stephenson in the match against Oxford. Ponsford threw the stumps down with Stephenson out of his ground and the umpire gave Stephenson out. Bardsley, leading Australia, informed the umpire that the bowler in following through had inadvertently obstructed Stephenson and the Australians withdrew the appeal. Spectators applauded the Australians as Stephenson returned and resumed his innings.

Bardsley was then in his forty-fourth year, the oldest player Australia ever sent to England and the oldest of all Australian Test captains. He scored 7886 runs on his four tours of England at an average of 49, and made an impressive twenty-seven centuries for Australia in England, on eighteen different grounds. Small wonder that English critics rate him among the finest left-handed batsmen cricket has known. In all first-class matches in a career that lasted for a quarter of a century (1903–28), he made 17,025 runs at 49.92, with fifty-three centuries. In between he gave marvellous service as a player and a selector to New South Wales and Australia and to Sydney's Glebe and Western Suburbs clubs. He never bowled an over in his life.

The remarkable Arthur Richardson, who made his maiden Test century at Leeds in 1926 at the age of 37 years 351 days. He remains the oldest Australian to do so, a bespectacled nomad who used a bat others found too heavy to handle.
— Melbourne Age.

Taciturn and shrewd, Bardsley was one of ten century-makers in the disappointing 1926 side's English tour. He had a top score of 193 not out, whereas Bill Woodfull (on his first tour) and Johnny Taylor both scored 201. Woodfull did a great job for a newcomer in scoring 1809 runs at 58.35, thus topping the Australian batting averages. On a tour that produced memorable googly bowling, the wicket-keeping of Herbert Strudwick for England and Bert Oldfield for Australia was memorable. The Australians played forty matches, won twelve, drew twenty-seven, and lost only the fifth Test, a record that would have been much improved if Sam Everett had been able to reproduce a semblance of his Australian bowling form. Everett, who bowled brisk right-arm seamers, had his only success of the tour when he hit a whirlwind 77 (twelve fours, two sixes) against Tasmania at Hobart on the way to England.

The 1926 side had more than its share of characters. Laughter was never far away, although Collins set a tone of quiet dignity for the team at important functions. There was Tommy Andrews the stonemason (the man who made Victor Trumper's gravestone) caught three times off no-balls on his way to 164 against Middlesex. And Jack Ellis, the building contractor from Victoria, who kept up a running commentary about the batsmen and bowlers from behind the stumps as he filled in for Oldfield. Ellis was notorious in Victoria for comments that upset batsmen but behaved himself in England. In the Australian summer after the team returned home it was Ellis who brought up Victoria's thousandth run on the

way to that record 1107. He pulled a ball from Andrews and shouted: 'Come on, there's three in it. Three to me and 1000 up. Long live Victoria!'

The 1926–27 season marked the end of the incomparable Arthur Mailey's career in big cricket. To many of those with whom he played Mailey was one of cricket's greatest brains, a bowler who studied every mannerism, every stroke and recurring habit of his opposing batsmen and exploited their weaknesses. He summed up his bowling whimsically: 'Sometimes I am attacked by waves of accuracy, but I don't trust them'. But behind the whimsy there was always subtle planning and a sharp eye for the unexpected. When he clean bowled Jack Hobbs in Melbourne in 1924–25 it was his second full toss in a row and the last ball Hobbs expected. Hobbs barely played a shot at it. The Australian Board of Control objected to Mailey's commenting on matches in which he played and, forced to make a choice, Mailey retired to concentrate on journalism — driven out of the game, according to his friends, after only five years of Test cricket.

This left Grimmett free to practise his tricks in Australia without a rival and he made a thorough job of hoodwinking batsmen, even those of the highest class. For fifteen seasons he was regularly written off as a has-been. Yet from 1924–25 to 1940–41 he was only twice headed as South Australia's leading wicket-taker — by Frank Ward in 1935–36 and in 1937–38. He took 668 wickets in all matches for South Australia, compared with 350 by the next best South Australian bowler, Ashley Mallett.

Queensland's first
Sheffield Shield team that
played New South Wales
at the Brisbane Exhibition
Ground in 1926 (L to R):
Back, H.D. Noyes,
E. Bensted, N. Beetson;
Centre, F.J. Gough,
F.M. Brew, R. Higgins,
R.K. Oxenham; Front,
W. Rowe, F.C. Thompson,
L. O'Connor (captain),
A.D.A. Mayes,
L.E. Oxenham.
N.S.W. won by 8 runs.
– Queensland Cricketers'
Club.

Left: When selectors
rebuilt the New South
Wales team in 1927-28
after the retirement of
several stars, they
gambled on this gifted
stroke-maker, Archie
Jackson. At 17, in his
initial season in first-class
cricket he made 500 runs
at 50.00, including two
centuries.
— Jack Pollard
Collection.

Far Left: Lisle Nagel, the
6ft 6ins Melbourne swing
bowler who once took
8 for 32 against England.
A ricked neck forced him
out of big cricket in
his prime.
— J.C. Davis Collection.

Grimmett was born on Christmas Day 1891 at Dunedin, New Zealand, but grew up in a house near the Basin Reserve in Wellington. He learnt to bowl spinners at Mount Cook Boys' School and played for Wellington in Plunket Shield matches and against visiting Australian teams. When he finished his apprenticeship as a signwriter at the age of twenty-three, he migrated to Australia, where he turned out for the Sydney District Club in 1914. In 1917 he transferred to Melbourne and played for South Melbourne and Prahran. He took a lot of wickets in district cricket but his opportunities in the State team were limited to five matches by selectors who had little use for spin. At the end of the 1924 season he moved to South Australia, just after taking 8 for 86 for Victoria against South Australia in a Shield match. Prematurely bald, he bowled in a cap, taking 216 Test wickets at 24.21 each in thirty-seven Tests spread over the next eleven seasons. He was lured to Adelaide by a deal that gave him an extra £10 a week for his signwriting.

Throughout the 1930s many splendid cricketers performed well in Sheffield Shield matches without winning Test selection. On hard, fast pitches Australia had an outstanding batting, fielding, and bowling side that restricted opportunities for newcomers, though the search for a top-class pace bowler continued. In his first match for New South Wales Dr Harry Owen Rock scored 127 and 27 not out in a style reminiscent of that of his father, the noted Cambridge Blue and Warwickshire county player, C.W. Rock. In his second match the younger Rock made 235 and 51 for New South Wales. Despite these fine performances he was dropped from the State side when Collins, Bardsley, Taylor, Andrews, and Kelleway returned from Test duty. Harry Rock played two other shield games and in a match against Western Australia he made 151. He retired to concentrate on his medical practice, leaving behind him an average of 118.5 for New South Wales and three centuries.

The Brisbane Exhibition Ground during Queensland's First Test in 1928.

ABORIGINAL BOWLER.

E. Gilbert, the Queensland fast bowler, about to deliver the ball. He took four N.S.W. wickets for 44 in the Sheffield Shield match yesterday.

Jack Ryder, the hard-hitting Victorian who captained Australia in 1928-29, the season of Bradman's big cricket debut. Ryder's pleas for a fast bowler in his attack went unanswered and England won an eventful rubber 4-1. — Melbourne Cricket Ground Museum.

Mayne was a lovable character, one of the first comperes when radio descriptions of cricket were introduced in November 1922 for the Bannerman testimonial match between teams captained by Collins and Macartney. Bannerman received £490 from the match and cricket a powerful new outlet for promoting the game. In 1924–25 Mayne provided the expert commentary as Victoria's captain when the Australia versus England Test at the M.C.G. was broadcast. Radio station 3AR paid the Melbourne Cricket Club £75 for exclusive rights to matches on the M.C.G. for the whole season.

The 1925–26 Australian domestic season was played to a background of arguments over the value of covering pitches. The undercurrent of ill-feeling provoked by the issue surfaced in the Victoria-South Australia match at Melbourne after Victoria had scored 604 in their second innings on a firm wicket. There was no play on the sixth and seventh days and when play got under way on the eighth day sticky patches were found on the pitch. The South Australian side continued under protest and was all out for 87, with Hendry taking 6 for 30.

Clem Hill, a South Australian delegate to the Board of Control said, 'Victoria is defying the Board and the Law by covering the wicket in Shield games if rain falls after a match has begun'. Because of the delayed play in Melbourne, the South Australians had to start the match against New South Wales on the following day in Sydney. Grimmett, who had bowled 416 balls in Victoria's innings of 604 in Melbourne, bowled 848 balls in the match with New South Wales, taking 10 for 394 in New South Wales totals of 642 and 593. This remains one of the great feats of endurance by a bowler in Australian first-class cricket. South Australia was set to score 761 to beat New South Wales but made 291. The match yielded 1929 runs.

In South Australia a dashing left-handed batsman named David Pritchard made 2958 runs in thrilling style at 34 an innings, hitting the ball exceptionally hard. He made six Shield centuries in three years but never looked close to Test selection. The quest for Test places was so intense that some players changed States, uprooting their homes and families in the hope of improving their prospects. E.R. ('Ernie') Mayne moved from South Australia to Victoria after eight summers in the South Australian side, so as to be nearer selection discussions. Mayne was at his prime when Australian batsmanship was immensely strong but he won selection in four Tests. Mayne's biggest triumph came in his fortieth year when he scored 209 in a partnership of 456 with Ponsford for Victoria versus Queensland in 1923–24.

Australia's team for the Second Test in 1928-29 (L to R): Back, W.M. Woodfull, W.H. Ponsford, H. Ironmonger, D.D.J. Blackie, O.E. Nothling, H.S.T.L. Hendry; Front, V.Y. Richardson, C.V. Grimmett, J. Ryder (captain), D.G. Bradman, W.A. Oldfield, A.F. Kippax. Bradman was made 12th man following his failures in his Brisbane debut. Blackie at 46 years 253 days remains the oldest Australian to make his Test debut.
— Mitchell Library, Sydney.

The most famous of all Australian barrackers, Yabba, with his cartload of rabbits. His voice from the Sydney Hill could be heard right across the ground.
— Richard Cashman Collection.

Bert Ironmonger, left, and Don Blackie during their days with the St. Kilda club. They were the oldest Australians to break into Tests, Ironmonger at 46 years 237 days, Blackie at 46 years 253 days. Blackie continued in first-class cricket until he was 51 years 231 days old, Ironmonger until he was 51 years 298 days.
— Ken Piesse, Australian Cricketer.

In the years that they were rebuilding the N.S.W. team by experimenting with youngsters like Jackson and Bradman, the selectors temporarily gave the captaincy to this burly eye specialist, Dr. Reginald Henshall Brindley Bettington, who had captained Oxford and played for the Gentleman.
— Jack Pollard Collection.

Hobbs bends low to execute a cut backward of point during one of his big innings against Australia. Wicket-keeper Bert Oldfield matches the great batsman's concentration.
— Sport & General, London.

Queensland entered the Shield competition in 1926–27 and against all the odds almost won the very first game against New South Wales. Only a fighting 127 by Alan Kippax enabled New South Wales to score 280 in the first innings. Queensland established a handy lead by scoring 356. New South Wales made 475 in their second innings, which left Queensland to score 400 to win. Queensland began disastrously, losing three cheap wickets, including the first innings century-maker Frank Thompson, for sixteen seasons a Queensland team stalwart. Brave, sensible knocks by Leo O'Connor and Ron Oxenham gave spectators at Brisbane's Exhibition Ground hope of victory, but with 8 runs to go Gordon Amos ran out O'Connor with a marvellous throw to thwart Queensland.

New South Wales had to rebuild their team that summer because Collins and Bardsley had retired, a knee injury kept Gregory out of the game, and business commitments prevented Taylor and Kelleway from playing. Selectors brought in a stylish seventeen-year-old Balmain player, Archie Jackson, and got Don Bradman up from Bowral for a trial at the S.C.G. nets. They gave Bradman a place in the State Second Eleven, where one of his team-mates was Bill O'Reilly, a tall, strapping youngster from Wingello, a country town 100 miles south of Sydney, where his father was the local schoolmaster. O'Reilly and Bradman had often played against each other in country matches. Bradman at the time thought he might become a house decorator. O'Reilly was training to follow his father into teaching. O'Reilly had learnt to bowl with a ball fashioned (with the help of his brothers) from a banksia tree root. He had an awkward delivery stride caused by bending his right knee and was kept busy declining suggestions from experts that he change the grip he used for medium-paced leg-breaks, googlies, and occasional off-breaks.

Kippax — an unfair and illogical omission from the 1926 tour of England — did a splendid job remodelling his New South Wales side, but he had to do a lot of the run-getting himself. He made 127, 131, 187 and 217 not out in compiling 1035 runs in the 1926–27 summer, scoring 884 at 88 in the Shield. He made 131 in the Macartney benefit match between Australia and the Rest. The match brought Macartney £2,598. Of the twelve benefit matches staged for first-class cricketers before then, only Victor Trumper's benefit in 1912–13 had raised more money, £2,950. But the undoubted highlight of the 1926–27 season was Queensland's victory over New South Wales in Sydney. After getting so close in Brisbane, they made no mistake in the return match, with O'Connor scoring a century in each innings (103 and 143 not out) as well as keeping splendidly. New South Wales fought back dramatically after being 290 behind on the first innings. Kippax and Jackson made stylish centuries and Queensland had to score 299 in the final innings to win. They did it for the loss of 5 wickets; O'Connor remained unconquered.

This incident in the Third Test of the 1928-29 series led to an official enquiry. Kippax was apparently bowled off his pads attempting a leg glance. Nobody noticed the dislodged bail and players changed ends for the next over. Sighting the bail on the turf, the square leg umpire asked the players what had occurred. 'Keeper Duckworth was adamant that he had not touched the ball. So Kippax walked.
— Sydney Mail.

*Chapman caught and
stumped by Oldfield in
the First Test of the
1928-29 series. He had
made 27 and was one of
Grimmett's nine victims in
the match.
— Mitchell Library,
Sydney.*

O'Connor's all-round skill and his fighting qualities as a captain largely justified Queensland's inclusion in the Shield competition and this had a more important long-term benefit for Australian cricket than Victoria's 1107. Newspapers called O'Connor an inspiring captain. He was rewarded for his great efforts with a place in the Macartney benefit match and scored a fine 101. He was one of four Queenslanders who played in a Melbourne Test trial in 1928–29, but he was not selected. He was thirty-eight and missed out on the Test place that he probably would have earned had Queensland been brought into the Shield competition earlier. O'Connor played forty-three matches in all for Queensland, between 1912–13 and 1928–29, and captained his State thirty-one times.

The 1927–28 season produced several memorable events. O'Connor sent Victoria in to bat at Brisbane after winning the toss and Victoria made 793, of which Ponsford, batting for almost two days, scored a world record 437. Hendry made 129 and Ryder 70. Then two of the oldest players to appear in first-class cricket — Don Blackie (6 for 46) and Bert Ironmonger (5 for 88) — bowled Victoria to victory. Blackie was then approaching his forty-sixth birthday and admitted it. Ironmonger was a year younger (44) but claimed he was forty-one.

While the two veterans were bowling Victoria to an innings win in Brisbane, New South Wales and South Australia were playing a historic match at

Adelaide, where Don Bradman scored 118 in his first appearance in first-class cricket. New South Wales reached 519 in the first innings, in which Phillips and Kippax also contributed centuries. South Australia replied with 481, with Karl Schneider hitting 108. Grimmett then produced one of his magical spells to take 8 for 57 and rout New South Wales for 150. South Australia, left to score 189 to win, got the necessary runs amid intense excitement with their last batsmen at the crease.

Bradman's prolific scoring in bush cricket had won him a place in the New South Wales side after impressive net trials. In his first season of Sydney club cricket he travelled up on the train from Bowral for his appearances with the St George Club. For the second season, 1928–29, he moved to Sydney to stay with St George secretary Frank Cush. He made his bid for Test selection with innings of 131 and 133 not out for New South Wales versus Queensland. That display earned him a place in the New South Wales team to play the England team captained by Percy Chapman. Bradman made 87 in the first innings after England had made 7 for 734. When New South Wales followed on, he saved the match with an unbroken stand of 249 with Kippax, finishing with 132 not out. He was twenty and was included in Australia's team for the first Test ever played at Brisbane, making his debut with Bert Ironmonger, who at 46 became our oldest Test player.

The Victorian women XI assembled in Sydney in 1931 for their match against New South Wales. Four years later Australia's women players entertained the first touring team of English women cricketers. — Sydney Mail.

14. Then Came Bodyline

Donald George Bradman was not born at Bowral, as legend has it, but at 89 Adam Street, Cootamundra, in the house of the local midwife Mrs Eliza Ellen Scholtz. His father, George Bradman, was the hardworking son of English migrants attracted to New South Wales by gold strikes near Bathurst. Don's mother was a member of the Whatman family which had a long history in the Bowral-Mittagong district; when her health caused concern the family moved from a tiny cottage at Yeo Yeo to Bowral in the southern highlands, where it was felt the climate would be better for her. Don was two when the move to Bowral was made and he quickly developed into an energetic little boy who relished all games. After school he amused himself hitting a golf ball against the brick base of an 800-gallon (3640 litres) water tank with a cricket stump.

Don's father George never made a century in his life and his brother Victor was only an average cricketer. Flair for the game came from his mother's side of the family. His uncles, George and Dick Whatman, were intensely keen members of the Bowral Cricket Club, and George Whatman was the power behind Bowral cricket for many years with his splendid wicket-keeping and opening batting. Bradman used to score for the Bowral Club as a boy, travelling to matches sitting on a wooden box in the back of a lorry that ran on solid rubber tyres. He played only if the team was short.

In 1921 George Bradman took his son to Sydney for two days of the England–Australia Test, during which Don watched every ball of Macartney's brilliant 170. Travelling back to Bowral in the train Don realised that what he wanted to be most was a Test cricketer. In his first encounter with O'Reilly, he made 234 for Bowral versus Wingello, and he followed this with a score of 300 spread over three Saturdays against Moss Vale. These big scores started the 'Boy from Bowral' legend and won him an invitation to attend the N.S.W.C.A. nets in Sydney in October 1926.

The lowpoint of the Bodyline series, when popular Bert Oldfield was struck on the head by a ball from Larwood. To Australians this represented shameful, unsportsmanlike tactics. Oldfield's skull was fractured but not seriously.
— South Australian Cricket Association.

Bill Ponsford, the man who took a fresh guard after scoring 300. He made two scores in excess of 400. O'Reilly found him harder to bowl to than Bradman.
— John Fairfax & Sons.

One of those impressed by Bradman's batting at the Sydney nets was State selector 'Mudgee' Cranney, who tried to persuade the committee of his club, Cumberland, to pay Bradman's expenses to and from Bowral by train each Saturday so that he could play for the club in the district competition. Cumberland decided they could not raise the money, a sad decision in the light of the fortune Bradman later attracted in gate money all around the world. Another State selector, Dick Jones, took the opportunity to persuade the St George Club to pay Bradman's train fares. The St George Club did not see much of Bradman, however, once his first-class career got under way.

After his century on debut for New South Wales at Adelaide, Bradman made 33 in the second innings and scored 31 and 5 against Victoria in Melbourne. Back in Sydney he was bowled, for a duck, by Queenslander Frank Gough off the first ball he received on Sydney Cricket Ground. But in the last match of the season he made 134 not out, the first of many big scores at the S.C.G. He had played in only five first-class matches, and had scored four centuries when he appeared in his first Test at Brisbane. He made 18 and 1, batting on a sticky wicket — which he had never seen before — in Australia's second innings of 66. England won by a massive 675 runs. When cagey 'Farmer' White had caught Bradman in the second innings, Maurice Tate called, 'What do you mean by stealing my rabbit?'

It was a tough initiation into Test cricket, but it only sharpened Bradman's resolve to make sure that the 'rabbit' was a major headache for England bowlers in the future. When he was dropped for the second Test at Sydney, Don Blackie went into the side to form an amazing spin attack with his friend, Bert Ironmonger, and Otto Nothling was given a place in the hope that he would stiffen the batting. England won by 8 wickets after Hammond had made 251 of a record total of 636. Bradman fielded for 11 hours in this game because of an injury to Ponsford. Recalled for the third Test at Melbourne, Bradman made 79 and 112 against the bowling of Tate, Larwood, Geary, and White at their best. Hammond won the match for England by 3 wickets, with another double century.

Bradman's feat in scoring the first of his twenty-nine Test centuries at the age of twenty undoubtedly influenced the selectors for the fourth Test at Adelaide in choosing Archie Jackson, nineteen years and 152 days old. Jackson's 164 in Australia's first innings is regarded as one of Test cricket's classic scores. He opened the batting with Woodfull and remained unruffled as Australian wickets fell at 1, 6, and 19.

Right: Jack Fingleton and Vic Richardson going out to bat at the Melbourne Cricket Ground during the Bodyline series. Both were known for their courage, a quality that was needed when the bouncers flew.
— *The Age, Melbourne.*

Selectors who watched Bradman and Archie Jackson bat in the nets could not separate them for brilliance. Seldom did a ball get past them. In the field, they chased the ball gleefully. Jackson played the first brilliant Test knock, shown here on the Adelaide scoreboard in February, 1929, 164 runs that thrilled the world.
— *Jack Pollard Collection.*

*Squeezed between Australia's triumphant 1930 tour of England and the acrimonious Bodyline tour, came the second Australian visit by a South African team, captained by H.B. Cameron. The scoreboard shows the sorry tale of the South Africans' Fifth Test effort. They were dismissed for 45 and 36 on a wicket that mesmerised them.
— Melbourne Cricket Ground Museum.*

One of the finest of Tasmanian teams, which in 1932 played Victoria. (L to R): Back, R.O.G. Morrisby, S. Putnam, W. Cahill, Col Mullins, D. Jones, L. Richardson, A.C. Burrows; Front, C. Parry, D.C. Green, J.A. Atkinson (captain), P. Driscoll, A.C. Newton, L.J. Nash, C.L. Badcock. Parry was Australia's smallest ever first-class wicket-keeper, a jockey type of less than 8 stone.

William Maldon Woodfull was known as "The Unbowlable", and "The Rock", because he seldom used a backlift or raised his bat. Here we have him in an uncharacteristic attitude, bat above his head.
— Sydney Morning Herald.

Woodfull's 1930 Australian team, which was pilloried by critics but came home with the Ashes (L to R): Standing, S.J. McCabe, A. Hurwood, T.W Wall, P.M. Hornibrook, A.E. a'Beckett, C.V. Grimmett, W.A. Oldfield; Seated, D.G. Bradman, W.H. Ponsford, V.Y. Richardson, W.M. Woodfull, C.W. Walker. A. Jackson, A. Fairfax. — Sport & General, London.

Australian singer Harold Williams, who played Hiawatha, shakes hands with Don Bradman during the Australians' visit to the Royal Albert Hall, London, in 1930. — London Daily Mail.

Clarrie Grimmett, left, and the Duke of Portland, with team captain Bill Woodfull, during the triumphant 1930 Australian tour of England. Lord Chelmsford, a onetime governor of N.S.W. and Queensland was then president of M.C.C. — Patrick J. Mullins.

Test heroes Hugh Trumble, left, and Jack Blackham together at the Melbourne Cricket Ground during the 1930-31 rubber against South Africa. Blackham died in 1932. — Jack Pollard Collection.

Bodyline depended on field placements. Batsmen were left unable to defend themselves without the near certainty of edging a catch to a cluster of close-in legside fieldsmen, as shown here with Larwood bowling at Sydney.
— Sydney Morning Herald.

The kind of field setting that aroused Australian's anger, with Woodfull forced to duck under or be hit or put the bat to a catch for this cluster of leg-side fieldsmen.
— Sydney Morning Herald.

His footwork was light, his cuts and glances elegant and cleverly placed. Holding the bat high on the handle, he displayed a mastery of timing and ability to find gaps in the field that was remarkable for his age. Hammond had another superb match, with scores of 119 not out and 177, clinching an England win and the Ashes. Bradman made 40 in the first innings and appeared set for a century in the second innings when he was run out for 58.

The fifth Test at Melbourne was the first to be played over eight days. Hobbs, at forty-six years eighty-three days, became the oldest batsman to make a century in England versus Australia matches by scoring 142 in England's first innings. Leyland also made a century for England but Australia was equal to the challenge. Woodfull (102) and Bradman (123) scored centuries for Australia to trail by only 27 runs. Throughout the series Australian captain Jack Ryder had been pleading with selectors to give him a pace bowler following the unhappy breakdown and departure from cricket of Jack Gregory in the first Test. Now Ryder was given South Australian paceman Tim Wall. He did not disappoint, taking 5 for 66 in England's second innings of 257. Australia needed to score 287 to win. They got the runs with Ryder and Bradman featuring in a breezy, unbroken sixth-wicket stand of 83. Wall — tall, dark, and durable — became the first bowler to take all 10 wickets in a first-class match when in 1932–33 he took 10 for 36, 6 of them bowled, against New South Wales.

For the rest of his career Bradman dominated international cricket as no batsman had ever done, scoring a century at a rate better than every third time he batted. Crowds quickly realised there was a very good chance of seeing him make a century and they flocked to watch him, bringing an undreamt of prosperity to Australian cricket. He turned batting into a precise art as he punished all bowlers with an almost arrogant confidence. He made it his job to score from the first ball he received and once this had been done and his authority asserted he found the gaps for hour after hour. No batsman has hit the ball along the ground as consistently as Bradman and there have been few better runners between wickets. He was run out only once in fifty-two Tests and only four times in 338 first-class innings. Two-thirds of his first-class centuries were chanceless and he seldom lofted the ball until his team was dominating a match. Only W.G. Grace is comparable with him as cricket's most influential player.

Ron Morrisby, who in the late 1930s proved himself a batsman of the highest quality, elegant, purposeful and full of strokes. By living in Tasmania he denied himself Test selection. — Ric Finlay.

Among Australian batsmen, probably only Ponsford could bat with Bradman without being overshadowed. Their partnerships were duets of impregnable batsmanship in which their enjoyment of hammering good bowlers conveyed itself to spectators. Bradman made 117 first-class centuries, played thirty-seven innings over 200, six over 300, and had one of 452 not out, which is still the highest score in Australian first-class cricket. The only bigger scores were made on matting pitches in Pakistan, so Bradman's innings stands as the highest ever on turf. He was also a brilliant fieldsman, gathering and throwing in dashing style. He took 36 wickets with right-arm leg-spinners. His batting was so consistent that posters of disbelief appeared around Australian news-stands when he made a duck.

Bradman's 452, a milestone in Australian cricket, was achieved in the 1929–30 Australian season against Queensland at Sydney and took 415 minutes. He was 205 not out on Saturday night and had the benefit of a rest all day Sunday at the Cushs' home. He went on to the fastest quadruple century — 377 minutes — ever scored by tea on Monday. He hit forty-nine fours in scoring at 65.34 runs an hour without a single wild stroke. Despite his amazing success, however, doubts were expressed about his batting and he set off for his first tour of England in 1930 knowing that Percy Fender, an England test star and captain of Surrey, claimed he hit across the ball too much to succeed in England.

Amid the newspaper discussions on whether Bradman would succeed, cricket followers tended to forget the sad omission of Bill O'Reilly from the team. O'Reilly was then twenty-five and had been written off by Bradman as a medium-pace bowler who could turn the ball both ways in country matches but who would never achieve outstanding success on turf wickets. This remains one of Bradman's few errors of judgment in a career noted for wise assessments of his fellow players.

Only four of the 1930 team captained by Woodfull had been to England before and those who believed Fender's prophecy were numerous enough for the Australians to be regarded as rank outsiders to regain the Ashes. None of the four previous tourists — Woodfull, Grimmett, Ponsford, and Oldfield — was a communicator and, as they preferred to keep their secrets to themselves, it was left to the fledglings to prove themselves on the field. In his first innings in England, Bradman astonished critics of his technique by flogging the bowling to every point of the field to score 236 in 280 minutes against Worcestershire. Vic Richardson's fielding and Grimmett's cleverness won praise but Australia's victory by an innings and 165 runs was mainly Bradman's. He followed this with 185 against Leicestershire, 78 versus Yorkshire, 40 and 48 not out versus Lancashire, 66 and 4 versus M.C.C., 44 versus Derbyshire, and 252 not out versus Surrey.

The England team that toured Australia in 1932-33, bringing into question the game's highest ethics (L to R): Back, G. Duckworth, T.B. Mitchell, Nawab of Pataudi, M. Leyland, H. Larwood, E. Paynter, W. Ferguson (scorer); Centre, P.F. Warner, L.E.G. Ames, H. Verity, W. Voce, W.E. Bowes, F.R. Brown, M.W. Tate, R.C.N. Palairet; Front, H. Sutcliffe, R.E.S. Wyatt, D.R. Jardine, G.O. Allen, W.R. Hammond. — Melbourne Cricket Ground Museum.

The bowler on whom the whole Bodyline tactics depended — Harold Larwood — a bowler of rare pace, stamina, accuracy and power. — Press Association, London.

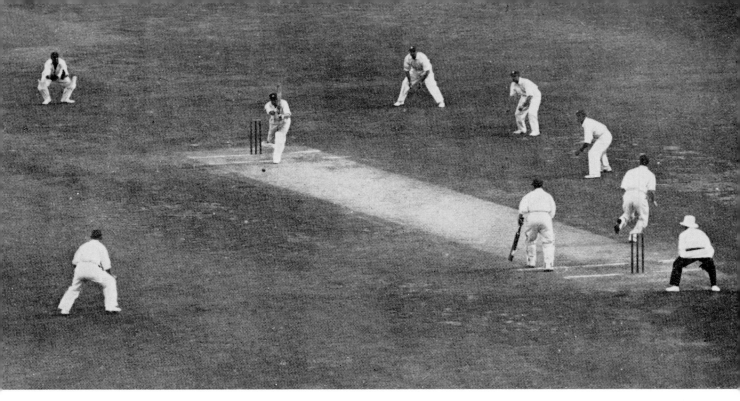

Bill Voce bowling his fast
left-armers to Woodfull,
with Ponsford at the
bowler's end. Australians
have always argued that
this field is fair unless
bouncers are bowled at
the batsman at speed.
— Sydney Morning
Herald.

Stan McCabe, whose
three innings of grandeur
each ended in Australian
losses, during his
memorable 187 not out
against England in the
First Test of the Bodyline
series.
— Sydney Sun.

His innings against Surrey was a masterpiece for
he thwarted all efforts by Fender to restrict his
scoring. Fender carefully positioned fieldsmen
before each over but Bradman played magnificent
cricket, driving the bowling to a standstill. He
made 200 in 225 minutes, extended to 252 not
out in 290 minutes, in which he offered only one
chance — a sharp one at 207; 156 of his runs
came in fours. It was the perfect response to
Fender for his comment that Bradman was, 'one
of the most curious mixtures of good and bad
batting I have ever seen, a batsman who does not

correct mistakes or look as if he was trying to
do so'.

Bradman became the first Australian to score
1000 runs before the end of May, joining four
Englishmen who had accomplished the feat. He
made 8 and 131 at Nottingham in the first Test, a
thriller which England won by 93 runs. Bradman
appeared to have set Australia on the path to
victory until he did not play at Robins' googly and
was bowled. Australia still managed a record 335
in the final innings, however. He made amends for
this lapse in the second Test at Lord's, batting 339
minutes for 254 in Australia's total of 6 for 729
declared. Woodfull made 155, and Australia won
by 7 wickets despite scores of 173 by Duleepsinhji
and 121 by Percy Chapman.

At Leeds in the drawn third Test Bradman
scored 309 not out on the first day — still a
record for all Test cricket — 105 before lunch,
115 between lunch and tea, and 89 in the final
session. When his score was 138, he passed 1000
runs in only seven Tests. Next day he took his
score to 334 before he was caught behind by
Duckworth off Tate. Larwood bowled 33 overs,
taking 1 for 139. After the third and fourth Tests
had been drawn, England dropped a bombshell by
sacking their captain Percy Chapman and
replacing him with Bob Wyatt. England got away
to a fine start in the decisive fifth Test but after
Sutcliffe's dismissal for 161 only Wyatt (64) gave
support. All out for 405 England then took an
awesome hammering from the Australian batting.
Woodfull and Ponsford began with a stand of 159,
with Ponsford going on to 110. Bradman then
played one of his greatest innings for 232,

contributing to Australia's score of 695 and eventual win by an innings and 39 runs. Australia regained the Ashes on their captain's birthday, a fitting tribute to Woodfull's restrained but firm leadership.

Bradman's aggregate of 974 runs in five Tests, average 139.14, remains a record for a Test rubber and was achieved with Larwood, Tate, and Allen bowling to orthodox fields. His only misjudgments were against the spinners Robins and Peebles who both deceived him with their googlies. Grimmett bowled cleverly to take 29 wickets at 31.89 in a high-scoring series. The deposed England captain, Chapman, praised the batting of Ponsford, Woodfull, and Kippax, paid tribute to the spin of Queenslander Percy Hornibrook, and said it was a rare pleasure to play against a wicket-keeper as good as Oldfield: 'He is so neat, so exceptionally efficient, and so unscrupulously fair that, if he appeals, one need not look at the umpire, but can go straight home'.

Woodfull's 1930 team — the seventeenth Australia had sent to England — included six century-makers, but youthful Stan McCabe was not among them. He made 96 against Cambridge and 91 against Oxford but had a top score in the five Tests of only 54. Grimmett took 142 wickets at only 16.79 on the tour. Hornibrook was next best bowler with 93 wickets at 18.5 and looked a bowler of real quality when he slowed down his pace and allowed the spin to take. Most of the Australians fielded brilliantly. Fairfax and Vic Richardson were outstanding but Bradman was not far behind them. Ponsford and Woodfull repeatedly gave the team good starts but in the Tests Tim Wall could not prevent Hobbs and Sutcliffe from occupying the crease for long, sometimes dull, periods. The headlines all went to Bradman for his record 2960 runs at 98.66 on the tour, but the players' praise all went to Woodfull for winning the Ashes by two Tests to one. J.E.C. Moore also won his share of publicity when in a minor match at Griffith he hit a ball a measured 170-yards 17 inches, the longest authenticated hit in Australian cricket.

Jardine's legside cordon of fieldsmen while Voce was bowling to Oldfield during the Third Test at Adelaide, a field bastman regarded as a "hit out or be hit" proposition. Here Oldfield edged a ball over Hammond's head. Shortly after he was knocked-out. — Adelaide Advertiser.

Three batsmen on whom Australia's fortunes depended in the Bodyline Tests (L to R): Len Darling, Leo O'Brien and Don Bradman, emerging happily from a session in the nets.
— The Herald, Melbourne.

The West Indies toured Australia for the first time in 1930–31, two years after they had entered Test cricket by playing England at Lord's. They had only seven Tests behind them when they arrived in Australia under the captaincy of George Grant, a former Cambridge cricket and soccer Blue. The team was badly chosen for Australian conditions at the time. The attack was based on pace and bowlers who could have been invaluable with their spin were left at home. The team had a disappointing record but gained a hefty reputation as entertainers. Learie Constantine hit some prodigious sixes and his acrobatic bowling and fielding sent a buzz round every ground he played on. George Headley showed why his batting had earned him the tag, 'the black Bradman'. The pace bowlers H.C. Griffiths and G.N. Francis bowled with character but not much luck.

The West Indians were immediately exposed to high-class spin bowling and found wanting. In the first match against New South Wales Hughie Chilvers took 4 for 84 and 5 for 73 to clinch victory with his leg-spinners. At Melbourne against Victoria, Ironmonger's left-arm spinners accounted for thirteen victims, 5 for 87 and 8 for 31, the West Indies scoring only 212 and 128 in reply to Victoria's 594. At Adelaide in the third match Grimmett took 4 for 71 and 5 for 43 to set up a 10-wicket win for South Australia.

Despite all the controversies of the Bodyline series, the touring Englishmen had a good time, even if they did not get their trousers pressed often enough. L to R: P.F. Warner. Maurice Leyland, T.B. Mitchell, Maurice Tate and Bill Ferguson (scorer).

Stan McCabe and Vic Richardson going out to bat. Selectors believed Richardson's hooking possibly provided the answer to Bodyline but he lacked the technique that would have set up chances to hook.
— Jack Pollard Collection.

When Bradman returned after missing the first Test of the Bodyline series, all Australians hoped he had an answer to England's unscrupulous tactics. In the event he danced about, slashing at the ball, reasoning that he must not be hit. A miscalculation such as this when he was bowled by Bill Bowes was almost a national disaster.
— The Argus, Melbourne.

Ernie Bromley, rated the longest and most accurate thrower in Australian cricket. He had to quit cricket in Perth to earn a Test place in Melbourne. — Jack Pollard Collection.

The Australian team for the Fourth Test at Brisbane in the 1932-33 Bodyline series, included "Hammy Love", and the South Australian B.J. Tobin, a truly amazing selection. The team (L to R): B.J. Tobin, T. Wall, W.J. O'Reilly, H. Ironmonger, E.A. Bromley; Front, H.E. Love, W.H. Ponsford, V.Y. Richardson, W.M. Woodfull, S.J. McCabe, D.G. Bradman, L.R. Darling. — Courier Mail, Brisbane

Australia led four-to-nil in the Tests after resounding wins based on a spin attack and efficient, stylish batting. The tour looked a complete disaster for the West Indies when against all odds they staged a dramatic recovery, defeating the powerful New South Wales side at Sydney by 86 runs. They then went on to produce one of cricket's major upsets by beating Australia by 30 runs in the fifth Test at Sydney. This win stemmed from first innings' centuries by F.R. Martin (123 not out) and their best batsman, George Headley (105). Australia made 224 and 250, failing to overcome pace men Griffith, Martin, and Constantine on a sticky wicket. Griffith set up the win when he bowled Bradman for a duck in Australia's second innings, a feat that earned him a standing ovation. Grimmett had a further 33 Test wickets at 17.96 and Bert Ironmonger 22 at 14.68.

South Africa, who had lost the rubber four-to-one in their first visit to Australia in 1910–11, returned for a second visit in 1931–32 under the captaincy of wicket-keeper–batsman H.B. ('Jock') Cameron. Their fielding was poor, a weakness they paid dearly for against superb Australian batting. Bradman had Test scores of 226, 127, 2,

167, 299 not out, and did not bat in the final Test because of injury. McCabe (112), Keith Rigg (127), and Woodfull (161) also made Test centuries. The biggest problem for the South Africans, however, lay in Australia's spin attack. Grimmett took 33 wickets at 16.87 in the five Tests, although he did not get a bowl in the fifth Test when South Africa, caught on a sticky wicket, was out for 36 and 45. Australia won the series five-to-nil by scoring 153 in their only innings on the sticky. Ironmonger, who took 5 for 6 and 6 for 18, ended the rubber with 31 wickets at an amazing cost of only 9.67 apiece. The series introduced some notable players to Test cricket: H.C. ('Slinger') Nitschke the noted racehorse breeder, left-arm spinner Bill Hunt, big Bill O'Reilly, H.M. ('Pud') Thurlow, the Queensland pace bowler, Jack Fingleton, the stylish and plucky New South Wales opening batsman, and Laurie Nash, the Tasmanian fast bowler.

An important change to Sheffield Shield conditions occurred in 1930–31 when all matches were limited to four days. Almost overnight the capital city scoreboards started to show more realistic totals; the days of regular totals of more than 500 runs were gone. At the conference tables Western Australia started to press for inclusion in the Shield competition but met stiff opposition from States concerned about the high cost of sending teams by rail to Perth. The result was that promising players from Western Australia migrated east to push claims for representative teams. The best of them was probably Ernie ('Slogger') Bromley, a tall, loose-limbed left-handed batsman with a fabulous throwing arm. Bromley made his debut for Western Australia in 1929–30, moved to Victoria in 1932–33 when he appeared against England, and in 1934 toured England in the Australian team.

At the end of the 1932 English season the M.C.C. appointed Douglas Jardine to captain the team to visit Australia in 1932–33. Jardine was an ardent admirer of the tactical acumen of Percy Fender, under whose captaincy he played at Surrey after coming down from Oxford. Jardine, who had been vice-captain of the English team that toured Australia in 1928–29 under Percy Chapman's captaincy, had his candidature heavily supported by Pelham Warner, who was to manage the M.C.C. team in Australia and who regarded Jardine as an exceptional cricket brain. Warner's influence at Lord's won the appointment for Jardine against opposition from committeemen who considered Jardine a cold, cantankerous character with few friends and a minimum of personal warmth.

*The prize wicket of Bert Sutcliffe was missed when he played on without breaking the wicket in this incident from the First Test in the 1932-33 rubber. McCabe has his hands up in despair. Richardson is the close-in fieldsman.
— Sydney Morning Herald.*

*Douglas Jardine, the man whose tactics threatened the entire future of international cricket, going out to bat. His unfriendly, imperious bearing did not help when he incurred the wrath of barrackers.
— Sydney Sun.*

Craftsman Bert Oldfield stumps Joe Hardstaff to break the world wicket-keeping record in the First Test at Brisbane, against England, 1936. Hardstaff was Oldfield's 85th victim in Tests against England. — Courier Mail, Brisbane.

Jardine knew that to regain the Ashes he had to curb Bradman, who since his astonishing English tour in 1930 had continued to score centuries and double centuries with machine-like efficiency. Even before the England team was finalised Jardine began to consult old Test players about tactics and methods of destroying Bradman. According to an unfounded story that had been circulated in the English counties, Bradman had flinched when Larwood bowled bouncers at him off a responsive damp pitch when he and Jackson returned to bat for 5 minutes in The Oval Test in 1930. So Jardine began to plan a form of leg theory liberally sprinkled with bouncers and balls directed at the batsman's body.

Just before Christmas 1931 Queensland Aboriginal fast bowler Eddie Gilbert bowled Bradman for a duck in Brisbane, producing blistering pace that had a star-studded New South Wales lineup back-pedalling. Gilbert was only slightly built as was Alec Henry, the Aboriginal who had bowled fast for Queensland between 1901 and 1905. Like Henry and the New South Wales Aboriginal speedster Jack Marsh, Gilbert was accused of throwing. Aboriginals had taken

readily to cricket in the first years of white settlement and the 1868 Aboriginal team had done well on tour in England. Since then a certain moodiness of character has limited the Aboriginal first-class cricketers to Henry, Marsh, Gilbert and more recently Graham Thomas (New South Wales) and Ian King (Queensland).

Bradman married Jessie Menzies, daughter of a Mittagong farmer, in April 1932 and shortly afterwards they left on a whirlwind fifty-one match tour of America, organised by Arthur Mailey. The Board of Control gave permission for the American tour on condition that none of the players received more than £100 from tour profits, but lifted its ban on wives accompanying touring teams to allow Jessie Bradman to go on what was virtually a honeymoon trip. Three of the team paid their own expenses but all the leading players, including the Bradmans, had their expenses paid. None of the team's matches was first class and half of them were against the odds.

The oldest member of the team was wicket-keeper Hanson Carter, the colourful undertaker from the Sydney suburb of Waverley who occasionally turned up for grade cricket matches

in a hearse, having come straight from the cemetery. Carter was then fifty-four. The team was: A.A. Mailey (player-manager), V.Y. Richardson (captain), D.G. Bradman, P.H. Carney, H. Carter, L.O'B. Fleetwood-Smith, W.F. Ives, A.F. Kippax, S.J. McCabe, R.M. Nutt, E.F. Rofe, E.K. Tolhurst, with the inimitable Dr Rowley Pope as baggage-master, able to substitute for injured players. Grimmett was originally asked to go but had to withdraw and Fleetwood-Smith, the handsome Victorian left-arm spinner replaced him. When Vic Richardson asked Fleetwood-Smith if he would like to go to America, he said: 'My oath I would'. Carter lost the sight of an eye as a result of a blow on the eye by a ball from McCabe (on a coir matting pitch) during the tour.

The Americans lionised Bradman as another Babe Ruth and he had to play in forty-nine of the fifty-one tour games for he was the player spectators wanted to watch. In fifty-one innings on the tour Bradman made eighteen centuries, including 260 versus Eighteen of Western Ontario, 159 not out against Eighteen of Edmonton (which included 50 in 7 minutes), and a stand of 168 runs in 34 minutes in San Francisco with Tolhurst. Pitches, outfields, umpires' decisions were often ludicrous but no more so than the antics of American batsmen against the spinners. Fleetwood-Smith, then twenty-two, took 249 wickets at 8 runs each, Mailey 240 wickets at 6 each. With this light-hearted preparation behind them, they returned home to face bodyline and the most acrimonious season in Australia's cricket history.

The Australians realised immediately they encountered it that the success of bodyline depended on the threat of injury to batsmen. By intensifying legside field placings and positioning only two men on the offside, Jardine made it risky for the Australians to protect themselves. If they pulled or hooked, fieldsmen on the fence waited for the catch. If they defended, it was only a question of time before England's fast battery, Larwood, Bowes, Allen, or Voce, forced a close-in catch from an edged shot. Bradman was unfit for the first Test but when he returned tried to play bodyline by ducking away towards the leg and flogging the ball through the unguarded offside. He was only partially successful and finished the rubber with an average of 56.57, top score 103 not out in the second Test.

Left-hander Maurice Leyland caught at midoff by substitute fieldsman Ben Barnett off Bill O'Reilly for 153 in the Third Test at Manchester in 1934. England made 627 but the match was drawn.
— Sport & General, London.

The Australians took some fearful blows to the body as cricket's high standards of fair play were forgotten. Ponsford and Woodfull ached from bruises and in Adelaide — where England's shameful tactics culminated with mounted police circling the ground to prevent irate spectators from rushing the players — Oldfield received a fractured skull. The Board of Control sent an injudicious cable of protest to the M.C.C. at Lord's, who promptly offered to call the tour off. Gentleman Bill Woodfull snubbed Pelham Warner when he came to the Australian dressing-room to sympathise with Woodfull over his injuries.

Feeling became so intense that England players agreed not to play in the fourth Test unless attacks on their sportsmanship by the Board of Control were withdrawn. Recently it has been disclosed that Prime Minister Joe Lyons, worried that Britain might not renew loans vital to his Depression economy, pressured the Board to withdraw their criticism of England's sportsmanship. The Board did this in the last of their series of cables to the M.C.C. An incredibly grim series ended with England four-to-one victors and Australians convinced that they had been the victims of sharp practice.

The only humour in the bodyline series came from spectators who by then had won a frequently publicised place in Australian cricket. On the Sydney Hill a coarse-voiced rabbit hawker, Stephen Harold Gasgoigne, popularly known as "Yabba", had become a legend. The barrackers had ideal material when a faulty ball had to be replaced after two overs in the second Test at Melbourne. A new ball was produced and amid hilarity Jardine threw the ball and Woodfull hit it about until it complied with the regulation that was "as like as possible to the one discarded". Spectators had fun, too, at Adelaide when flies pestered Jardine. "Here, Jardine, leave our flies alone," cried one voice, and another hollered: "They's the only friends you've got in Australia."

Archie Jackson died in Brisbane on the last day of the fourth Test, aged twenty-three, after having dropped out of Test cricket two years earlier with tuberculosis. His former schoolmate Bill Hunt flew to Brisbane at 'Doc' Evatt's expense to bring Jackson's body back to Sydney for burial. The players went straight to the funeral from the train that brought them all back from Brisbane. Pallbearers Bill Woodfull, Vic Richardson, Don Bradman, Bert Oldfield, and Alan Kippax at the Field of Mars Cemetery had to negotiate huge crowds mindful of the touch of genius in Jackson's batting.

Arguments over bodyline and the harm Jardine did to cricket are as heated today as in 1932–33, but they should never erase the grandeur of McCabe's 187 not out in the Sydney Test. It was one of cricket's masterpieces. For 242 minutes he drove, hooked, cut, and pulled, striking twenty-five authentic fours. He scored his last 51 runs in a tenth-wicket stand of 55 in 33 minutes. As he went in to bat McCabe asked his father to stop his mother from jumping the fence when he was hit by bouncers. In the midst of McCabe's bold attack on England's pace bowlers, Jardine demanded that 'Gubby' Allen let McCabe have a few bouncers. 'You can take me off if you want, but I won't bowl that way," said Allen.

Cricket was lucky that Woodfull was Australia's captain in the bodyline series, for his tact and good sense helped prevent the disintegration of international cricket. He went to England in 1934 in the role of peacemaker and nobody could have been better equipped for the task. His team produced further marvellous batting and the spinners compensated for the lack of penetrative pace bowlers with remarkable figures. O'Reilly, Grimmett, and Fleetwood-Smith all took more than 100 wickets on the tour.

Australia won a splendid rubber two-to-one to regain the Ashes by winning the fifth Test by 562 runs. Bradman, who had made 304 in the fourth Test, had a second-wicket partnership of 451 in 316 minutes with Ponsford, playing in his last Test. This stand was Australian batting at its best, with lovely strokes flowing from the two masters of the high-scoring art. Ponsford made 266, Bradman 244, and Australia 701. Woolley, recalled to the England team at forty-seven, had to deputise as wicket-keeper when Ames was hurt in Australia's second innings and, sadly, allowed 37 byes. Woodfull, one of the five Australians to score a double century during the tour, had the great satisfaction of leading Australia to fifteen wins in thirty-four matches, with only one loss — a notable effort for a side demoralised only fourteen months earlier by bodyline.

15. The Bradman Era

By the time Don Bradman took over the Australian captaincy from Bill Woodfull, the job was the most prestigious and glamorous in Australian sport. Australia's cricket captain was as frequently discussed as the Prime Minister — indeed thousands of Australians knew the line of succession of Test captains but could not list the Prime Ministers. The twenty men who had held the job had built up this special aura through their dignity and depth of character and the wisdom of their decision-making and team control.

Bradman's transition from innocent son of country-town carpenter to prosperous businessman was not only a remarkable personal achievement; it was a windfall for Australian cricket. He made the turnstiles click as never before, attracting spectators who knew they had better than a one-in-three chance of seeing him make a century. Many women were among this new cricket audience, for it had become socially advantageous to have watched the great man. When he was not out by the luncheon interval, word spread like magic, and people kept arriving all through the break, pressing through to vantage points.

Bradman was the Australian embodiment of the American democratic romance — from log cabin to the White House — a country lad who seized his chances. But he was not the only bush cricketer who made the Test team. Stan McCabe first played in the New South Wales country town of Grenfell, Bill O'Reilly was from Wingello, Arthur Chipperfield from Maitland, Leslie Fleetwood-Smith from Stawell. The formidable list of country cricketers who, right from the days of C.T.B. Turner, have overcome obvious disadvantages to play Test cricket for Australia is nothing short of phenomenal.

This painting by Wesley Walters was commissioned by the New South Wales Cricketers' Club to commemorate Don Bradman's 100th first-class century and shows Bradman scoring the magic run that gave him this wonderful record. The original of the painting was presented to Sir Donald by the association but prints can still be obtained from the NSWCA, 52 Clarence Street, Sydney, for $144 each.

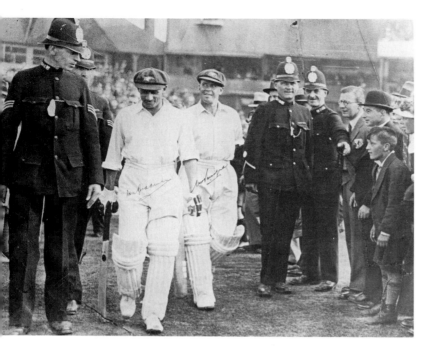

The little boy on the right looks with awe as Bradman and Ponsford are escorted on to the field by police at The Oval in 1934. They put on 451 in 316 minutes, the highest stand for any wicket in Test cricket. Ponsford made 266, Bradman 244, and Australia 701. — Press Association.

Don Bradman at the start of his first series in England as Australia's captain looks fit and relaxed as Cyril Badcock puts his movie camera to work. — Ric Smith.

Leslie O'Brien Fleetwood-Smith, one of many Australian Test players from country centres. He came from Stawell and learned left-arm spinners after breaking his right arm. — Melbourne Herald.

Poor crowds attended the first international cricket for women in 1934–35, when an English team captained by Betty Archdale was unbeaten in 21 matches in Australia, with 15 wins and six draws. By contrast Bradman's initial series as captain in 1936–37 — the first to make covering of pitches obligatory — attracted 943,513 spectators to the five Tests, which remains a record for any Australian series. Bradman reigned as Australian captain from 1936 to 1948 and did not lose a series, but his players were far from unanimous that he was the best captain they had known. Stan McCabe gave that honour to Woodfull.

Before Bradman was appointed captain Australia had been to South Africa and enjoyed a wonderful tour under the captaincy of Vic Richardson. Bradman was unavailable for this tour, having come close to death with a gangrenous appendicitis which caused his collapse at the end of the 1934 England tour. Only emergency surgery by the brilliant Australian specialist, Sir Douglas Shields, saved him. For days he was critically ill. Only the Australian manager, Harold Bushby, was permitted to see him. Jessie Bradman rushed to his London bedside and they went to Switzerland and then to the Riviera for Bradman to recuperate. While Richardson's side were in South Africa, Bradman was resting at his father-in-law's farm at Mittagong.

Victor York Richardson was a public idol when Bradman moved from Sydney to Adelaide, an astounding all-rounder who represented South Australia at golf and tennis, starred for Sturt in three premiership Australian Rules teams, played first-grade hockey and basketball, and represented Australia at baseball as well as cricket. His fielding was so fearless that newspapers like the *Sydney Morning Herald* wrote editorials about it. Richardson's team in South Africa won four of the five Tests, with one draw. The players agreed it was the most enjoyable trip in their lives. Not the least of the highlights was a baseball match against South Africa, won by Australia when 'Grum' Grimmett, running backwards, took a magnificent catch in the wrong hand (the ungloved one).

Stan McCabe played the second of his three immortal innings for Richardson's team in South Africa by scoring 189 not out in the second Test at Johannesburg. He hit the ball with such fearsome power that when a heavy cloud-cover restricted visibility, the South African captain appealed against the light on the grounds that his fieldsmen were in danger. Grimmett had another picnic in South Africa, where he became the first Test bowler to take 200 wickets, and Fingleton scored three successive Test centuries.

Top Left:
Eddie Gilbert, the Queensland Aboriginal fast bowler who had Bradman out for a duck in 1931 after five balls of what Bradman called the fastest over he ever faced. Gilbert was no-balled for throwing but his arm often moved so fast nobody could truthfully say if he chucked or not.
— Melbourne Herald.

Top Right:
Cyril ("Jack") Badcock, rated the finest batsman produced in Tasmania, had a confident, almost cocky air as he went out to bat. He was a prodigious run-scorer in Shield cricket but not in Tests.
— The Mercury, Hobart.

Vic Richardson, right, broadcasting for the A.B.C. with Monty Noble after his retirement. Some thought Richardson badly treated when Bradman replaced him as South Australia's captain.
— Daily Telegraph, Sydney.

Australian troops at Pakchon in the Korean War Zone in 1950 playing cricket during a lull in the fighting.
— Herald & Weekly Times.

Harold Cotton, no-balled for throwing in the 1936-37 match between South Australia and Victoria. He was a bowler of exceptional pace who scared the wits out of club cricketers with his bowling for the Prospect Club.
— *Adelaide Advertiser.*

Don Tallon, whose omission from the 1938 team to England created a furore in his native Queensland. His subsequent form certainly proved he should have been picked.
— *Courier-Mail, Brisbane.*

Wally Hammond batting on a sticky wicket in the Third Test of the 1936-37 series. Many considered England would have won this match and taken the Ashes had Allen declared before England reached 9 for 76.
— *Melbourne Herald.*

The 1938 Australian team to England (L to R); Back E.L. McCormick, M.G. Waite, L.O. Fleetwood-Smith, W.J. O'Reilly, E.S. White, F.A. Ward, W.A. Brown, J.H. Fingleton; Seated, S.G. Barnes, S.J. McCabe, D.G. Bradman (captain), B.A. Barnett, C.W. Walker; Front, A.L. Hassett, C.L. Badcock. The selectors preference for Ward ahead of Grimmett proved very costly.
— Melbourne Cricket Ground Museum.

The Australian Services team with their Tasmanian opponents during their final match at Hobart. Keith Miller is second from the end of the middle row on the left, next to Keith Carmody. Services captain Lindsay Hassett is fourth from the right in the front row. The side disbanded after this match.
— Ric Finlay.

Bradman fractured a shin bone while bowling in the Fifth Test at The Oval in 1938 and had to be carried off. O'Reilly waves wearily to Bradman from the ground after bowling for much of England's mammoth innings, which reached 7 for 903.
— Sport & General, London.

Bradman moved to South Australia to take up the offer of a splendid job in a stockbroker's office. He had been a salesman for the sports department of a retailer who required him to run clinics for aspiring youngsters and the new job gave him a chance to work outside cricket. Supporters of Victor Richardson disagreed with the immediate appointment of Bradman as State captain. To regain peak fitness after his year out of cricket following the critical operation in London, Bradman took up squash and at his first attempt won the South Australian amateur championship, defeating Davis Cup tennis player Don Turnbull in the final. In his first three innings for South Australia, Bradman scored 117, 233, and 357, when he made 109 before lunch on the second day. Then in March 1936 he and Ron Hamence put on 356 runs in 181 minutes in a record third-wicket stand against Tasmania, Bradman finishing with 369.

The 1936–37 Test series against England turned on Allen's timing in the third Test of his

declaration in England's first innings. England was caught on a sticky wicket after Bradman declared at 9 for 200. Allen batted until his side had reached 9 for 76, when many thought he should have declared much earlier to give excellent damp-pitch bowlers like Verity and Voce an opportunity against the Australians. The pitch had dried out by the time Allen declared and Australia scored 564 in their second innings, Bradman finding form for the first time in the series with 270. Bradman shrewdly started that match-winning second innings with his tail-enders to give the pitch further time to dry. O'Reilly, who opened the batting with Fleetwood-Smith, was the only casualty before bad light ended play for the day. Fleetwood-Smith was out third ball next morning but Frank Ward and Keith Rigg then defended stubbornly while the wicket dried. At 5 for 97, with the pitch fully recovered, Bradman joined Fingleton and they put on 346 runs, the highest partnership in Australia until then for the sixth wicket.

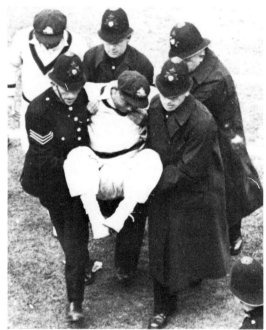

Tiger Bill O'Reilly bowling against New Zealand in his last international match. He ranks with Spofforth, Hugh Trumble, Grimmett, C.T.B. Turner and Benaud as the best Australian exponent of spin.
— Sydney Sun.

Sid Barnes being carried from the field after being hit in the kidneys while fielding a few yards from the bat in the 1948 Test at Manchester.

Barnes assisted from the field when he attempted to bat two days later.
— Sport & General, London.

The three Harvey brothers who played in the same side for Victoria in 1947-48. Ray, Mervyn and Neil. The six sons of Horace Harvey all played for Fitzroy, four of them in interstate cricket and two of them, Merv and Neil, in Tests.
— Victorian Cricket Association.

Ray Lindwall, match-winning fast bowler for Bradman's 1948 team and Australia's No. 1 strike bowler in 61 Tests. He bowled in the period before the front foot rule was introduced.
— Australian Cricket Newspaper.

Batting, bowling or fielding, Keith Miller could swing a match in a few minutes. Here he takes a hot slips catch to dismiss England's Norman Yardley in Sydney in the 1946-47 series.
— Melbourne Herald.

Bradman batted throughout despite a severe chill and when England began batting on the fifth afternoon with 689 to score for a win, McCabe took over the Australian captaincy. Leyland made 111 but England was dismissed for 323. A crowd of 87,798, a then world-record for a Test, attended the M.C.G. on the holiday Monday during this match, which drew an aggregate attendance of 350,534, the highest number of people ever to watch a cricket match. Bradman's 270, Fingleton's 136, and the last innings bowling of Fleetwood-Smith (5 for 124) had enabled Australia to take the chance offered by Allen's delayed declaration and get back into a series that appeared lost. Bradman then made his second successive double century (212) to set up victory and level the series at Adelaide in the fourth Test. England had to score 392 to win in the final innings and reached 3 for 148. Fleetwood-Smith ended the match when he clean bowled Hammond, a match-winning delivery and one of his 10 wickets (4 for 129 and 6 for 110) in the match.

For the first time since 1894–95 the teams went into the fifth Test at Melbourne with two wins each. Bradman (169), McCabe (112), and Badcock (118) all made centuries in Australia's first innings but Ross Gregory's brilliant 80 pleased the crowd most. In two Tests Gregory's artistic stroke-play had established him as a batsman with a rich future. Australia made 604, enough for the pace and spin attack to win the match and the series, against weary, spiritless batting. Tasmanian footballer-speedster Laurie Nash (4 for 70) and O'Reilly (5 for 51) had England out for 239, and in the second innings McCormick (2 for 33), O'Reilly (3 for 58), and Fleetwood-Smith (3 for 36) had them out for 165. Bradman's first rubber as captain had attracted 960,794 paying spectators, plus ground members, and gate takings of £90,909 for twenty-five days plus two balls.

Selection of Australia's team for the 1938 tour of England under Bradman aroused widespread debate and, in Queensland, quite a lot of anger. On form shown in the Sheffield Shield competition, Grimmett remained a powerful strike bowler and should have gone instead of Frank Ward who was known to be suspect under punishment. 'Ginty' Lush, the fiery New South Wales fast bowler, looked a far better partner for McCormick than Merv Waite or Ted White. Lush had topped the Australian first-class bowling averages in 1936–37 when he took 6 for 43 and 7 for 72 for New South Wales against England, and had a spell of 3 wickets in four balls. But the decision not to take Don Tallon, the brilliant youngster from Bundaberg, as one of the team's wicket-keepers upset enthusiasts most, particularly as Australia's prospects obviously hung on the spinners O'Reilly and Fleetwood-Smith and Tallon was known to be brilliant when spinners operated.

The selectors preferred Victorian Ben Barnett and South Australian Charlie Walker to Tallon whose claims should have been strengthened by his splendid batting skill. In 1935–36 he had made 193 against Victoria at the age of nineteen and followed it with innings of 56 and 86 against South Australia and the wily Grimmett. Understandably, Queenslanders claimed Tallon was the victim of a southern States prejudice against Queenslanders. At the time only ten Queenslanders had played for Australia, beginnng with the eccentric Arthur Coningham in 1893. Less vitriolic fans in New South Wales believed that a place should have been found in the Australian team for Hughie Chilvers, an outstanding leg-spinner and probably the best of his type never given the chance to play for Australia.

Chilvers, born at Sawbridgeworth in England, came to Australia at an early age, and in a decade of outstanding Australian batsmanship repeatedly outwitted the best in the land. He was harshly treated in 1935 when the Board of Control refused to let him join Frank Tarrant's team on tour in India. Tarrant wanted to include Chilvers but the Board refused to let him go on the grounds that he might be needed by his State. This turned out to be the only chance of an overseas trip Chilvers ever had, as the selectors preferred Frank Ward for the 1938 tour of England. Ward won Australian team selection by a most circuitous route. He played in Melbourne when he could not win a regular place in the New South Wales team but did no better with Victorian team selectors. Finally he moved to South Australia where he won selection as Grimmett's bowling partner.

Nevertheless, Bradman's 1938 team managed to share the Test series with England: each side won a match, two others were drawn, and the third Test — scheduled for Old Trafford, Manchester — was abandoned without a ball being bowled. Australia owed everything to Bradman, Brown, and O'Reilly and to a wonderful innings of 232 by Stan McCabe at Trent Bridge. Australia saved the Ashes at Headingley, winning a marvellous match only minutes before rain deluged the ground. It was a series full of incident and drama, Test cricket at its best, with a wonderful resurgence in England's playing strength.

Keith Miller, debonair as ever.

A dramatic moment in the Fourth Test at Sydney in 1946-47 with Bradman bowled for a duck by Bedser, who was using a packed legside field. The bails are circled.
— Melbourne Herald.

*The Australians strolling across the lawns of Balmoral Castle during a visit on the 1948 English tour. Bradman is in discussion with King George VI on the right, hands in pockets.
— Daily Express, London.*

*The trio who enjoyed wide popularity through their postwar broadcasts of big cricket: Arthur Gilligan, Alan McGilvray and Vic Richardson. They were heard by millions across the world, with McGilvray's "and what do you think, Arthur?" the subject of many cartoons.
— Australian Broadcasting Commission.*

In the first Test at Trent Bridge Charlie Barnett opened the England innings with Len Hutton and hit with such power that he seemed certain to reach his century before lunch. But the Australians were jealous of their record of having supplied the only batsmen to make centuries before lunch in Tests (Trumper, Macartney, and Bradman) and as the interval neared fielded like men inspired to prevent Barnett from scoring the runs he needed. Barnett was 98 at lunch and completed his century off the first ball after lunch, going on to a stand of 219 with Hutton. Barnett (126), Hutton (100), Eddie Paynter (216), and Denis Compton (102) were the century-makers in England's total of 658.

McCabe played one of cricket's legendary innings when Australia reached 6 for 194 in reply. In a series of magnificent partnerships in which he shielded the tail-enders and outwitted all Wally Hammond's manoeuvres to stop him from getting the strike, McCabe scored 232 of the 300 added while he was at the crease. He added 69 for the seventh wicket with Ben Barnett and, by dazzling stroke-play, 127 out of the 148 scored in 80 minutes after the seventh wicket fell. He made 44 off 3 overs from Doug Wright and climaxed a wonderful effort by adding 72 out of 77 runs in 28 minutes with Fleetwood-Smith for the last wicket. Bradman went round the Australian dressing-room calling his players to watch it, for he realised that this was one of the greatest hands cricket had known. He described his feelings in the book *Farewell to Cricket*:

When Stan returned to the dressing-room at the conclusion of this epic performance, I was so moved by the majesty of his performance I could hardly speak. I gripped his hand, wet with perspiration. He was trembling like a thoroughbred racehorse. I recall expressing my congratulations and saying that 'I would give a great deal to play an innings like that.'

McCabe's innings, as with his two other masterpieces — the 187 not out at Sydney in the bodyline series and the 189 not out against South Africa in 1935–36 — did not bring an Australian victory. But it enabled Australia to save the game. In the follow on after McCabe had taken the first innings to 411, Australia held out against the England bowlers for more than 8 hours to reach 6 for 427. Billy Brown played a wonderful hand by batting for 5 hours 20 minutes and Bradman stayed 6 hours 5 minutes, his 144 not out including fifty-six singles and only two fours. England suffered badly from the lack of a second pace bowler to support Ken Farnes.

On his first appearance at Lord's in 1934 Brown had scored a century, defying Hedley Verity on a rain-affected pitch tailor-made for Verity's left-arm skills. Now on his second Test appearance at this most famous of all cricket grounds, Brown made 206 not out, thus enabling Australia to score 422 in reply to England's 494 (Hammond 240, Paynter 99, Ames 83). Hammond declared England's second innings closed at 8 for 242, leaving Australia to bat out the remaining 170 minutes. Bradman was never fearful of an Australian defeat although wickets fell around him, and batted almost light-heartedly to make another Test 100 (102 not out).

After the wash-out at Manchester the fourth Test at Leeds proved the showdown in a tense rubber, highlighted by the arrival of a splendid array of brilliant English youngsters. All the players who appeared in this Test consider it one of cricket's greatest games with Hammond and Bradman matching wits as captains and batsmen at times appearing certain to triumph, only to be cut down by fine bowling. Strangely, the Australian players involved believed the result was probably determined by an umpire's call.

Bill O'Reilly, always at his best when angry, was bowling to Hardstaff when the umpire had the temerity to no-ball him. Livid with rage but forced to accept this outrage like a gentleman, O'Reilly thundered up to the wicket with that awkward but somehow beautifully rhythmical action and let loose with a vicious fast leg-break that bounced high and removed Hardstaff's off bail. Next ball O'Reilly had Hammond caught by Brown for a duck. Those two balls in England's second innings virtually gave Australia the Ashes. Bradman's 103 in the first innings when he batted on despite atrocious light had given Australia a 19-run lead. Now when O'Reilly went to work England could only set Australia a target of 107, and he matched his first innings of 5 for 66 with 5 for 56.

Realising that this was their chance, the Australians batted on beneath a dark and ominous cloud-cover. Rain seemed to be only moments away as the Australians pushed the score along. England had a chance when Australia was 4 for 61, but Hassett, who had an otherwise quiet tour, produced an attacking gem that took the score to 91, 14 away from victory. Badcock and Barnett made the extra runs just before rain flooded the ground. Hassett's 33 was worth more to his side than most centuries, but it might have been different if the call of no-ball had not aroused the Irish passions in 'Tiger' O'Reilly. With his first and second fingers wrapped round the ball and the others folded on to the palm of his

vast hand, O'Reilly had produced two balls that decided a series.

The excitement of retaining the Ashes in the Leeds showdown had barely subsided, however, before Australia suffered one of her most humiliating defeats. For the fifth Test at The Oval England packed her side with batsmen (and after Leeds nobody could blame the selectors) and went into the game with only three front-line bowlers — Bowes, Farnes, and Verity — and five Yorkshiremen. In a Test played without a time-limit, the toss was vital: after winning it and batting on a pitch made to last, England was never headed.

Four outstanding bowlers of the 1948 side at a reunion 32 years later: Bill Johnston, Ernie Toshack, Keith Miller and Ray Lindwall.
— Jack Pollard Collection.

Bradman clean bowled for a duck in his last Test at the Oval in 1948. He only needed four runs to finish with a Test average of 100. The bowler was Eric Hollies.
— Sport & General, London.

Hutton, who at the time was probably surpassed in skill only by Hammond and Bradman, opened with Bill Edrich to the far from hostile bowling of Merv Waite and Stan McCabe. Australia's sole paceman, Ernie McCormick, had had a frustrating tour from the time he was no-balled for overstepping eight times in his first over in England (leading to a total of thirty-five times in the match). By his tenth appearance he had passed a century of no-balls. Even so, he was fast enough to make the best batsmen flinch when he got his action working. He would approach the crease without swinging his arms, letting the ball go from high up with his stiff-armed approach. Before the Lord's Test, however, he had decided to forsake the stiff-armed approach and pump his arms as he ran in, and this had helped him take seven wickets in the match. Now, as he was all set to redeem an unhappy tour, injury forced him out of the fifth Test.

England's first innings total of 7 for 903 declared and the margin of her victory — an innings and 579 runs — are still Test records. The pitch was a horror for the spinners, prepared to last indefinitely, and O'Reilly shared the elation of Fleetwood-Smith who hooted for joy towards the end of the second afternoon, having finally got a ball to turn. Hutton batted almost entirely from within the confines of the crease, collecting runs ponderously with deflections and cuts into the spaces. After losing Bill Edrich at 29 he took the score to 411 with Maurice Leyland before the second wicket fell. Hutton was 300 not out after batting for two days and next day the Australians fielded brilliantly as they defended Bradman's record Test score of 334. Burly 'Chuck' Fleetwood-Smith bowled superbly in this period but after 12 hours 19 minutes of batting, Hutton reached 335. Hardstaff completed his century after Hutton's dismissal for 364 as injuries deprived Australia first of Fingleton, and then of Bradman, who damaged his ankle when bowling his third over. When England declared, Fleetwood-Smith had bowled a massive 87 eight-ball overs, followed by O'Reilly with 85 overs, Waite with 72, Barnes and McCabe with 38 each.

Facing an impossible task without Fingleton and Bradman, the Australian batsmen were told not to make their bowlers bowl again and Australia surrendered for scores of 201 and 123. There were still six matches of the tour to play and Australia had only a skeleton crew available. Six batsmen topped 1000 runs for the tour — led again by Bradman with 2429 runs at 115.66 — but only O'Reilly took 100 wickets (114 at 15.98) in a woefully short-handed attack. Australia was left with five players unavailable when Fingleton and Bradman were hurt, joining the injured

Barnes, Chipperfield, and McCormick. For the remainder of the tour Australia had to borrow a twelfth man.

The 1938–39 Australian summer produced record-smashing feats by Bradman and Tallon, who proved the validity of critisicm of his omission from the 1938 side in England. He dismissed twelve New South Wales batsmen, six in each innings — nine caught, three stumped — and a few weeks later became the first of four Australian keepers to dismiss seven batsmen in an innings (four stumped, three caught). He did not allow a bye in this innings. Bradman scored six centuries in successive innings, starting with one in the Melbourne Cricket Club's centenary match at the M.C.G. This equalled the record set by C.B. Fry in 1901. Thousands of people who flocked to the Adelaide Oval for the last match of the season were able to witness Bradman's attempt to surpass Fry's sequence, but he was out for 5. By then his influence on cricket finances was enormous, and even in club games for Kensington Park in Adelaide big crowds turned up to watch him hammer bowlers of all types and sizes for an unending stream of fours and sixes. Grimmett showed up the error of leaving him at home in taking 27 wickets at 20.85 apiece to top the South Australian bowling averages yet again.

The 1939–40 season produced a further surfeit of runs from Bradman who scored 1475 at 122.91, making 251 and 90 not out versus New South Wales, 158 versus Queensland, 267 versus Victoria. In the midst of all this, he was out for a duck against Queensland in Brisbane, an event that won more headlines than some of his hundreds. One of the features of this last season before the second World War was the big hitting of a burly New South Welshman, Cecil Pepper, who in an innings of 81 against Queensland hit seven sixes, including six off Don Tallon's whimsical brother Bill. Three landed outside the ground — one in Vulture Street and two in Stanley Street — the first time this had happened since Victor Trumper and J.N. Crawford were in action before the first World War.

When peace came after four years without big cricket, Pepper starred in the Australian Services team, captained by Lindsay Hassett, which played five Victory Tests in England, and toured India and all the Australian states. The Board of Control had suspended the Sheffield Shield competition after the 1939–40 season, but at the request of the Federal Government organised several matches to assist wartime charities. In one of these a youngster named Keith Miller, who had played a couple of seasons for Victoria, was forced to open the bowling when Stan McCabe and

Morris Sievers were injured. He let go two or three loose balls and then settled down to bowl high-kicking deliveries at a pace that had all batsmen ducking for cover. Pepper, Miller, Keith Carmody, Stan Sismey, and Bob Cristofani were among the Australians who, throughout the war, managed to play in regular games of a high standard in the Middle East and England. They formed the nucleus of Hassett's Services side.

Just as the First A.I.F. team had done after the First World War, so the Services Eleven played a major role in reviving big cricket after the Second World War. The Services Eleven won the first Victory Test at Lord's by 6 wickets against a strong England side, with Pepper scoring the winning runs in a blazing innings of 54 not out. England won the second Test at a bomb-scarred Bramall Lane, Sheffield, by 41 runs, but Australia recovered to win the fourth Test at Lord's and draw the fifth, again at Lord's, where Miller's big-hitting entertained large crowds as he landed the ball high up in the stands. Despite a remarkable 101 by Cristofani, England won the final Test at Old Trafford by 6 wickets, to end the series with two wins apiece. More importantly, big cricket had re-established its high appeal with a war-weary public.

Within a few months of their discharge from the services, Miller and Hassett were in action for Australia. They were in the side captained by Bill Brown which in March 1946 defeated New Zealand at Wellington by an innings and 103 runs, in the first official Test between the countries. This was Bill O'Reilly's farewell to international cricket after taking 744 first-class wickets at 16.6. Rated by Bradman as the greatest bowler he ever faced, O'Reilly ranks with Fred Spofforth, Hugh Trumble, C.T. Turner, Grimmett, and Benaud as one of the best-ever Australian exponents of spin. He took 5 for 14 and 3 for 19 as Australia dismissed New Zealand for 42 and 54. Always an outspoken supporter of country cricketers, O'Reilly could take comfort from Ernie Toshack's 4 for 12 and 2 for 6 in that match — as Toshack had learnt to bowl his left-arm medium pacers and slows at Cobar, a small mining town in western New South Wales.

The following November Miller, Toshack, and Hassett were in the Australian team captained by Bradman which defeated Wally Hammond's England team three-to-nil in the first post-war Test rubber in Australia. Bradman had been invalided out of the Australian Army with fibrositis and he was unsure if he could get through the early matches. Ross Gregory and Charlie Walker had been killed in the war, as had the highly promising Ken Ridings, member of an outstanding Adelaide cricket family. Bradman went to Brisbane for the first Test with a rebuilt team that included the classy left-handed opening bat Arthur Morris from Sydney, the ex-Air Force spinners Colin McCool and Ian Johnson, the left-arm spinner George Tribe, and — at long last — keeper Don Tallon. Bradman made 187 in Brisbane, figuring in a 276-run third-wicket stand with Hassett (128) that did him more good than any of the treatment he had been given for his fibrositis.

At Sydney in the second Test Bradman and Sid Barnes both made 234 to set up Australia's second successive win by an innings. In the drawn third Test at Melbourne, McCool (104 not out) and Australia's impressive new pace bowler, Ray Lindwall (100) both made maiden Test centuries. The fourth Test at Adelaide provided another draw despite a century in each innings by Morris (122 and 124 not out) and a magnificent hand of 141 not out from Miller. Australia rounded off an outstanding series by winning the fifth Test at Sydney by 5 wickets, with Lindwall taking 7 for 63 in England's first innings, McCool 5 for 44 in the second innings. The next summer in Australia, 1947–48, Bradman scored his historic hundredth first-class century against India at Sydney. In the Tests that season he had scores of 185, 13, 132, 127 not out, 201, and 57 retired hurt. Australia won the rubber four-to-nil. The series was memorable for Mankad's run-out of non-striker Bill Brown when he backed up too far at the bowler's end.

Bradman's fourth tour of England as captain of the great 1948 team brought him eleven more centuries, including 138 in the Nottingham Test and 173 not out at Leeds, where Australia became the first side to score 400 runs to win in the last innings of a Test. This was the most notable achievement of a team that had no weaknesses, an ideally balanced selection of powerful batsmen, first-rate bowlers of varying styles, and brilliant fieldsmen, supported behind the stumps by Tallon. Bradman's century at Leeds was the last of his twenty-nine in Tests, nineteen of them against England. When he walked to the wicket for his final Test innings at the Oval, the capacity crowd stood and applauded him all the way to the crease. The England players gave him three rousing cheers. He took guard and faced leg-spinner Eric Hollies in a highly emotional moment, needing just 4 runs to average 100 in his fifty-two tests. Even Hollies was disappointed when with his second ball he clean bowled Bradman for a duck.

One of the major shocks of early postwar cricket was Western Australia's win in the Sheffield Shield the first season they competed. Here team captain Keith Carmody and Dick Bryant (both wearing dinner suits) hold the Shield for team-mates. — West Australian, Perth.

16. The Challenges Multiply

Understandably, the marvellous entertainment provided by Bradman's players in 1948 earned the team comparisons with the finest Australian touring sides of the past. They were the first Australian team to remain unbeaten after an English tour and probably only Joe Darling's team in 1902 and Warwick Armstrong's 1921 side — each of which lost two matches — bear comparison with Bradman's last team. Between them the 1948 side made fifty-four centuries in thirty-four matches and surpassed all records by winning four of the five Tests. Seven of the seventeen players made more than 1000 runs,

with Sam Loxton only 27 runs short when he broke his nose in the final match. They scored more than 300 in twenty-seven matches and apart from the Tests no team made 300 against them. They dismissed their opponents for under 200 no less than thirty-four times and eight times had them out for less than 100. At Southend against Essex they scored 721, still the record total for one day's first-class cricket.

Darling's 1902 team had also produced seven players who scored more than 1000 runs, headed by the majestic Trumper who made 2570 runs despite throwing his innings away several times when he reached 100. They had two masterly left-handers in Hill and Darling, a top-flight fast bowler in Ernie Jones, two exceptionally reliable keepers in Carter and Kelly, gifted all-rounders in Noble, Armstrong, and Trumble, and the whole side fielded superbly. England had offered far stronger opposition than the 1948 side encountered but the Australians had kept their nerve, winning the decisive fourth Test by 3 runs. It had been no disgrace to lose the final Test when England, needing 15 to win with 9 wickets down, got them in singles.

Darling, Armstrong and Bradman, captains of Australia's three best teams. Conditions varied so much it is impossible to select the best team, but Bradman's 1948 team was the only one unbeaten.
— Jack Pollard Collection.

The 1921 team had had similar all-round strength — eight players who scored more than 1000 runs, a marvellous pair of spinners in Armstrong and Mailey to support the blistering pace of Gregory and McDonald, and a glittering array of fieldsmen in all positions. They had met England teams appreciably below their own standard in batting, bowling, and fielding and had not been forced to bat on wet pitches as had frequently been demanded of the 1902 side. But in Macartney they had a genius just as capable of audaciously demoralising opposing bowlers as Trumper had been. Of the two matches they lost, the first had been against an England Eleven whom they had dismissed in the first innings at Eastbourne for only 43. The Australians had taken the match too lightly from then on and been beaten by 28 runs. The second defeat had come in the last match of the tour when C.I. Thornton's Eleven had beaten them by 43 runs in a festival match at Scarborough.

These were unquestionably the three best national teams Australia has produced, but who could say which was the best? I am inclined to think that on rain-affected pitches the 1902 side deserved the honour but that under the conditions in which they played in 1948 Bradman's team were the best. Pitches were covered against rain in 1948 and Bradman was allowed a new ball every 55 overs, which meant that he had little difficulty resting his pace bowlers, Lindwall, Miller, and Johnston. His spinners seldom got a bowl and Bradman did not hesistate to interrupt successful spin to take a new ball. His team had such high all-round talents that Bradman had at least six men he could call on to bowl in most matches.

Significantly, Bradman's side was the best disciplined and unified of all Australian touring outfits, perhaps because most of the members were ex-servicemen. From reading the players' reminiscences and newspaper accounts of all three tours, there appear to have been fewer claims of misdemeanours concerning the 1948 team than for any other Australian touring party. One player was alleged to have absented himself from the side because of a lady but it didn't stop him from playing a vital role in the Tests. Above all, as Ray Robinson so wisely stressed, no other captain had Bradman's advantage of knowing he could go into a game and score more than anyone else.

Bradman was knighted in 1949 for his services to cricket — the only Australian cricketer so honoured. In 1981 he was made a Companion of the Order of Australia, which ranks six places above a knighthood. His first-class career ended in March 1949 at Adelaide when he was persuaded to play for South Australia versus Victoria for Arthur Richardson's testimonial game. His last public appearance with the bat was at the age of fifty-four in March 1963. Playing for Prime Minister Sir Robert Menzies' Eleven against the M.C.C. he chipped a ball from Brian Statham on to his stumps with his score on 4. Ahead lay a distinguished career as an Australian selector, administrator (twice chairman of the Board of Control), writer, speechmaker, and company director.

A testimonial match for Bradman at the M.C.G. in 1948–49 raised £9,432, the highest amount collected for an Australian in the history of benefit matches. Teams captained by Bradman and Hassett played the first tie in Australian first-class cricket, with Hassett's Eleven scoring 406 and 430, Bradman's Eleven 434 and 9 for 402. A feature of the match was McCool's dropped catch in the outfield when Bradman was 97. Benefit matches were omitted from the Australian domestic programme after the 1956–57 match for O'Reilly and McCabe in Sydney. They have been replaced by a provident fund scheme which is more lucrative for the players. State associations and the Australian Board credit players with set match fees after a qualifying number of games have been played. Players are paid the provident fund money due to them two years after retirement.

Bush cricket can hardly be better demonstrated than by this scene outside the pub at Mataranka in the Northern Territory in 1972. The Stuart Highway is on the left as teams from Katherine and Matarinka struggle for supremacy.
— Bruce Howard.

Betty Wilson, generally regarded as the best woman cricketer Australia has produced, in a fine example of her copybook bowling action. She took 7 for 7 in a Test and scored the first century ever for Australia in a Test against England. — Jack Pollard Collection.

Gil Langley, the outstanding Test wicket-keeper, in his robes as Speaker of the South Australian parliament. — Adelaide News

Richie Benaud in his years as Australia's cricket captain was a hard-worker in the practice nets, arriving early and staying late. Probably only George Giffen has surpassed his allround feats. — Ern McQuillan.

In Western Australia soon after the second World War a group of energetic young officials voted long-serving officials out of office and began a concerted move to win admission to the Sheffield Shield competition. This resulted in Western Australia's being admitted on a restricted basis for the 1947–48 competition. Keith Carmody, the brilliant services opener and noted strategist, was engaged as State coach and captained Western Australia in their initial Shield matches. For inclusion in the Shield competition, Western Australia had to pay expenses of teams from other States travelling to Perth. Some States, New South Wales among them, did not always bill Western Australia for this, but paying the fares for interstate teams cost the Western Australian Cricket Association more than £15,000 before 1956–57 when the Board ruled that each State should pay its own fares to Perth.

In New South Wales arguments had begun over whether Miller or Morris should captain the State following O'Reilly's retirement. While the discussion raged, Carmody left New South Wales and brought off a surprising coup by leading Western Australia to win the Shield in their first season. They played only four matches compared with seven by the other States and their points were adjusted on a percentage basis. Some of Western Australia's rivals had star players missing because of the Tests against India but their victory was still an astounding feat. At the end of their first day in the Shield competition the Western Australian side was 5 for 375, with Carmody 166 not out. Next day he took his score to 198 and Western Australia reached 444. They then bundled South Australia out for 109 and won in three days by an innings and 124 runs. Carmody, who had been shot down and taken prisoner during a daylight R.A.A.F. raid on German E-Boats over the North Sea, made 428 runs at 61.14 in Western Australia's four games and led his team with tremendous enthusiasm and cunning.

Hassett took over the Australian captaincy from Bradman for the 1949–50 tour of South Africa. Sid Barnes, who at the time formed the world's top opening pair with Morris, said he could not afford to go for a £450 out-of-pocket allowance and withdrew. In a colourful career Barnes specialised in harassing the Board through incidents such as vaulting the M.C.G. turnstiles when an attendant refused him admission, using a toy bat during Bradman's testimonial match in Melbourne, and once taking brushes, combs, hairsprays, and clothes brushes on for team-mates when he acted as New South Wales twelfth man. Selectors further weakened the team for South Africa by omitting Miller, then the world's outstanding all-rounder, but they quickly remedied this blunder by flying Miller to join the team when Bill Johnston was hurt in a car accident.

Hassett's team were unbeaten in South Africa, winning fourteen of their twenty-one games, and four of the five Tests. This was South Africa's sixth rubber against Australia without a win. Transvaal had a great chance to beat Australia before the Tests when they were set only 69 in the fourth innings, but they collapsed for 53. Miller had 5 for 40 in Australia's big first Test win — by an innings and 85 runs — demonstrating how foolish it had been originally to leave him at home. After also winning the second Test, Australia had to score 336 in the third Test on a pitch responsive to spin. The team achieved the task with what *Wisden* called 'that calculated certainty which seems an inherent part of these relentless yet intensely human cricketers'. Harvey, who averaged 132 in the Tests, made 151 not out as Australia scored the necessary runs for the loss of only 5 wickets.

Hassett brought off two magnificent tactical coups in his reign as Australian captain, the first of them in this third Test at Durban. South Africa had begun with 311 to which Australia replied with 75, her lowest-ever Test total against South Africa. The Australians found Tayfield's off-spin almost unplayable on a damp pitch and he took 7 for 23 off 8.4 overs. When South Africa batted a second time Hassett contrived to keep them in without conceding too many runs while the pitch dried out. Dudley Nourse failed to enforce the follow-on and kept batting through the second innings for a paltry total of 99. Harvey achieved the amazing feat of batting for 5 hours 30 minutes without a mistake. Tayfield, so dangerous in the first innings, had figures of 2 for 144 in the second. The Australians made thirty first-class centuries on this tour, Harvey and Morris both making eight.

Bill Watt, curator at Melbourne cricket ground for a decade, adjusts the stumps for an Aust-India Test match.
— *Melbourne Cricket Ground Museum.*

The legendary Ken ("Slasher") Mackay shakes hands with the Queen during a break in play in the Second Test at Lord's in 1961. Widely known for his eccentricity, he was a valuable cricketer in the triumphant Benaud teams.
— *Sport & General, London.*

The 1953 Australian team (L to R): Back, R.R. Lindwall, A.K. Davidson, D.T.N. Ring, J.C. Hill, G.R. Langley; Centre, G.B. Hole, R.G. Archer, W.A. Johnston, K.R. Miller, R. Benaud, D. Tallon; Front: I.D. Craig, J.J. de Courcy, A.L. Hassett, G.A. Davies (manager), A.R. Morris, R.N. Harvey, C.C. McDonald.
— Melbourne Herald.

Neil Harvey in his halcyon years as a Test batsman. He ranks among Australia's greatest left-handers, with 21,699 first-class runs to his credit.
— Ern McQuillan.

Richie Benaud's famous catch that dismissed Colin Cowdrey for 23 in the Second Test at Lord's in 1956 off "Slasher" Mackay.
— Sport & General, London.

The much criticised pitch at Manchester in 1956 as groundsmen prepare it for Australia's first innings. Jim Laker took 19 wickets on this strip, which from the start helped his off-spin.
— Sport & General, London.

Western Australian left-hander Laurie Sawle played this cut right in the middle of the bat and placed it where he believed the shot was safe — but Peter Philpott dived full-length to take a marvellous catch metres wide of the slips. New South Wales 'keeper Doug Ford said he could not believe it.
— Sydney Morning Herald.

The key to a famous victory — Richie Benaud bowls England captain Peter May around his legs for a duck in the Fourth Test at Manchester in 1961. Benaud pitched the ball in rough created by Freddie Trueman and finished with 6 for 70.
— Sport & General, London.

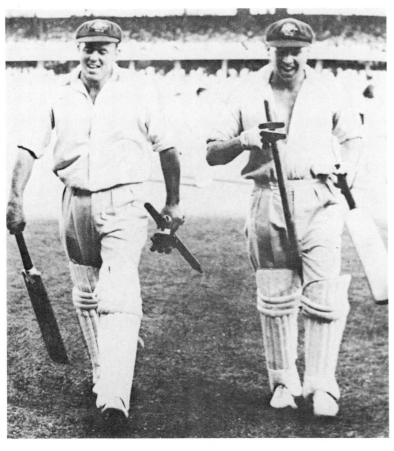

Tailenders Bill Johnston and Doug Ring leave the field after their match-winning last wicket stand of 38 against the West Indies at Melbourne in 1952. They are both clutching stumps they grabbed as souvenirs of Australia's remarkable win.
— Melbourne Herald.

Norman O'Neill gets well down the crease to play a handsome drive. He was a batsman of impeccable footwork who hit the ball tremendously hard, but suffered many nervous starts.
— Melbourne Herald.

While the first team was in South Africa, Bill Brown took an Australian second team to New Zealand, where he had veterans such as Phil Ridings, Doug Ring, and Don Tallon to help him guide a group of aspiring youngsters which included a burly left-hander, Alan Davidson. At Wairarapa, Davidson took 10 for 29 and then scored 157 not out in an all-round performance unmatched since the days of George Giffen. The Australians won three of their five first-class matches and several minor games. In the unofficial Test versus New Zealand, Tallon played a curious innings of 116 in 3 hours, mixing dour defence with big hitting that produced seven sixes and eight fours. New Zealand held out to save the game, having lost 9 for 76 in the final innings when time ran out.

Jack Iverson, the mystery spinner who tucked the middle finger of his bowling hand behind the ball, toured New Zealand in Brown's team and was immediately thrown into the 1950–51 Tests when Freddie Brown's thirteenth England team reached Australia. Davidson had to wait until 1953 in England to make his debut. The first Test was an epic match played mostly on a traditional Woolloongabba sticky wicket, and here Hassett pulled off his second tactical master-stroke. Australia batted first on a hard pitch and made 228. England was caught on a sticky wicket on the third day when play was delayed until 1 p.m. With England 160 behind, Brown declared to get Australia in on the sticky but Australia batted for only 79 minutes before Hassett declared at 7 for 32, leaving England 192 to win. Eight further wickets fell before stumps. In less than 5 hours play 22 wickets had fallen for 102 runs. Hutton scored a remarkable 62 not out in England's 122 on the final morning, giving Australia a 70-run win in an extraordinary match.

Splendid bowling by Iverson, Lindwall, and Johnston gave Australia a 28-run win in the second Test. Miller's 145 not out in the third Test proved the match-winner. In the fourth Test the Australian team increased their lead to four to nil when Arthur Morris made 206, ending a long run of failures, and Jim Burke scored 101 not out in his Test debut. Hutton batted right through England's first innings for 156. With the Ashes decided, Freddie Brown's team pulled off a shock win — their first since 1938 — in the fifth Test. This was almost entirely the result of a memorable innings for 156 not out by Reg Simpson and ended Australia's record succession of twenty-five matches without defeat. Simpson made 64 of a last-wicket stand of 74 with Tattersall.

In 1951 Molly Hide captained the second Australian women's cricket team to visit England. All Australian women paid their own fares and the English teams entertained them, paid their expenses, and met the costs of staging the matches. Betty Wilson was the star of the Australian team, scoring 175 runs in three Tests, taking 16 wickets, and creating a tenth-wicket partnership record of 39 with Mavis Jones. The Australians won one Test, lost one, and drew the third.

John Goddard led the second West Indian team to Australia in 1950–51 after a triumphant tour of England, where notable performances by Worrell, Walcott, and Weekes and the spinners Ramadhin and Valentine enabled them to defeat England three to one. As Australia had recently beaten South Africa and England, the series was described as a contest for world supremacy. In the event, Australia had little difficulty in asserting supremacy after the first Test — a tense, even struggle in which Goddard relied almost entirely on his spinners. Ramadhin bowled 64 overs in the match, taking 1 for 75 and 5 for 90; Valentine bowled 65.7 overs, taking 5 for 99 and 1 for 117. Australia won the match by only 3 wickets.

In the 500th game of Test cricket, this was how the first tie occurred: With Australia needing one to win, Lindsay Kline swings Wes Hall away to leg, left, and then there was jubilation among the West Indian fieldsman as Joe Solomon hit the stumps with his throw to run out Australia's Ian Meckiff. Brisbane, December 14, 1960.
— Courier-Mail, Brisbane.

Richie Benaud catches England opener Peter Richardson off his own bowling in the Brisbane Test in 1958-59. This was Benaud's first match as Australian captain. He lost only four of the 27 Tests in which he was captain.
— Melbourne Herald.

West Indian captain Frank Worrell — he was later knighted — gives the trophy that bears his name a polish as he hands it to Australia's Richie Benaud in Melbourne after the happy 1960-61 rubber. — Melbourne Herald.

Alan Davidson at Lord's during his last tour in 1961 goes out to the practice nets with tour newcomer Graham McKenzie. — Sport & General, London.

The incomparable "Slasher" Mackay, as Australian as a gum tree. He once got lost inside the Lord's pavilion and could not find his way to the wicket. The Guardian said he was like the common cold — there was no cure for either. — Ern McQuillan.

Thereafter the pace-bowling of Lindwall, Miller, and Johnston was a little too much for the West Indies batting stars, though Worrell managed a score of 108 in the fourth Test. Australia's sole loss, in the third Test at Adelaide, was caused by the failure of all batsmen to handle a rain-affected pitch. The Australians were out for 82, their lowest total against the West Indies, who won by 6 wickets and always gave the impression of having a better knowledge of how to bat in the wet conditions. The persistent failure of the West Indian batting on hard, fast pitches against a liberal dose of bouncers enabled Lindwall to take 21 wickets in the series and Miller 20, with Australia winning four to one.

The South African team which toured Australia in 1952–53 was virtually written off before they left home. However, the combination of Jack Cheetham's firm, assured leadership with gutsy batting and breathtaking fielding produced a fine series with two wins each and a draw. Batsmen on both sides struggled for runs, Russell Endean and Harvey excepted. Hugh Tayfield, nicknamed 'Toey' because of his habit of stubbing a toe into the ground before bowling, was the best bowler on either side and he removed key batsmen in both the Tests won by South Africa. South Africa won their first-ever Test against Australia at Melbourne, where Endean batted 450 minutes for 162 not out in the second Test, and Tayfield took one of cricket's most freakish catches. A full-blooded drive from Morris bounced off Cheetham at silly point and flew towards mid-off. Following on down the pitch, Tayfield turned and took the ball inches from the turf. Later Endean reached over the fence to catch Miller when a six appeared certain.

Needing a victory to share the series, South Africa won the fifth Test in Melbourne despite an Australian first innings total of 520. Ian Craig — at seventeen years 239 days the youngest Australian to play in a Test — made 100 runs in this match with 53 and 47. An entertaining rubber ended when Hassett bowled and conceded three fours in five balls.

Up to this point the resilience of Australian cricket had covered up persistent losses of talented players to the Lancashire League and to English counties. But now as veteran members of the Test side aged, the loss of players like Cec Pepper, Bill Alley, John McMahon, George Tribe, Jock Livingston, Bruce Dooland, Fred Freer, Jack Walsh, Vic Jackson, Keith Dollery, Colin McCool, Des Fitzmaurice, Jack Pettiford, Ken Grieves, and Harry Lambert to England started to show both in interstate and Test performances. The overseas success of these players in turn encouraged other Australians — including promising youngsters —

to try their luck in the English and Scottish Leagues. For players who missed a Test place, it became fashionable to go to England, and what had been a trickle just after the first World War now became a regular, talent-sapping flow.

Lindsay Hassett made his fourth tour of England in 1953 as captain of the twenty-first Australian team. Only seven members of the great 1948 side remained and the replacements proved ineffectual. Spinners Richie Benaud and Jack Hill struggled to take wickets when Tribe, Walsh, and Dooland were taking them by the hatful for their English counties. Ian Craig, Graeme Hole, and Jim de Courcy looked impressive enough in the nets but could not make good scores in matches at a time when expatriates made centuries almost daily. Miller and Johnston were injury-prone. Lindwall was still a great bowler but England had in Fred Trueman a bowler who matched his pace.

Australia failed to prevent a classic match-saving fifth-wicket stand by Trevor Bailey and Willie Watson in the second Test. With the match apparently won after the dismissal of Hutton, Kenyon, Graveney, and Compton for 73 runs, Australia could not separate Bailey and Watson for 3 hours and 8 minutes, although England had no hope of scoring the 342 needed to win. The match was drawn as were all the first four Tests. At The Oval Len Hutton, the first professional to captain England this century, led his team to victory by 8 wickets, so regaining the Ashes which Australia had held for a record eighteen years 362 days. Of the thirty-five matches they played, Hassett's side won sixteen, drew eighteen, and lost only one — the one that counted. The Australians grumbled about the legality of Lock's action throughout the last two Tests but to their credit made no public complaint when he took 5 for 45 in Australia's second innings in the fifth Test. Alec Bedser, who dismissed Arthur Morris for the eighteenth time in twenty Tests, broke Maurice Tate's record for an England-Australia series by taking 39 wickets.

During the 1953 tour of England the Australians made their first-ever visit to Holland. The first match between Australia and Holland took place on 16 July 1953, when Australia batted first and scored 279, largely through a stand by Morris (70) and McDonald (66). Holland batted for 3 hours to compile 122 in reply.

Hutton's feat in regaining the Ashes automatically gave him the captaincy of the England team for the 1954–55 Australian tour. He started badly in the first Test at the 'Gabba by putting Australia in to bat, the first England captain to do this since Johnny Douglas in 1911–12. Australia turned Hutton's decision into a massive misjudgment by scoring 8 for 601. The Northants speedster Frank Tyson, who had been carefully developed by Freddie Brown, took 1 for 160 in this innings. England made 190 and 257 and lost by an innings and 154 runs to an Australian side packed with new faces. In the second Test Tyson was knocked unconscious by a Lindwall bouncer and carried from the field. He recovered to bowl England to an exhilarating victory. Set to score 224 to win, Australia made 184 as Tyson took 6 for 85, hitting the stumps four times with deliveries of palpitating pace.

At Melbourne nine days later Shakespeare buff Tyson repeated his performance in the third Test and set up a win for England, this time by 128 runs. His 7 for 27 in Australia's second innings of 111 contained some of the fastest bowling seen at the M.C.G. To this day, Richie Benaud maintains that he has never seen anyone bowl faster than Tyson did in taking 6 for 16 in fifty-one balls to finish the match. Tyson had bowled off a 70-yard run at the start of the tour but shortened his approach when he gained this spectacular success. He put immense strain on his powerful frame with a long final stride and it was obvious that he had traded a long career for a season of glory. Plagued by injuries until his retirement in 1960, he seldom reached the same pace again.

West Indian wicket-keeper Gerry Alexander appeals to the umpire after a bail had been dislodged during Wally Grout's innings in the 1960-61 series between Australia and the West Indies. The umpires could not determine how the bail fell and ruled Grout not out.
— Melbourne Herald.

West Indian captain Frank Worrell bowling to Australia's Lindsay Kline at Adelaide in 1960-61, with all 10 fieldsmen close in to the bat. Kline and "Slasher" Mackay held out for just over an hour to save the match. — Adelaide News.

England won the Ashes in Australia for the first time since the bodyline tour in 1932–33 by winning the fourth Test at Adelaide to go to a three-to-one lead. There was controversy in the drawn fifth Test when Trevor Bailey deliberately allowed a ball from Lindwall to hit the stumps and give Lindwall his hundredth Test wicket against England. Peter Burge, Willie Watson, Len Maddocks, and Les Favell all made their debuts for Australia in this series but without making any immediate impact. Favell had got into the Australian team after leaving his native New South Wales to play for South Australia. He had a thrilling hook shot, an ability to cut hard, and his eagerness to score quickly won him many admirers.

Australia's first tour of the West Indies in 1954–55 produced records galore and some amazing batting. Australians made twelve of the twenty-one centuries compiled in the five Tests. Clive Walcott, a failure in Australia three summers earlier, took the individual honours with five Test centuries. Twice in a series where bowlers were consistently battered out of the attack Walcott made a century in each innings. The West Indies used ten bowlers in the first Test, which produced innings of 133 from Harvey and 147 from Miller, and an Australian win by 9 wickets. McDonald (110), Morris (111), and Harvey (133) made centuries in the drawn second Test. Australia won the third Test by 8 wickets when subtle off-spinner Ian Johnson gave his finest Test performance in taking 7 for 44 in the West Indies' second innings. The fourth Test was a drawn run feast. Australia made 668 thanks to Miller's 137, a dazzling 98 by Archer, and 118 from Lindwall. The West Indies replied with 510, with Atkinson (219) and Depeiza (122) setting a world record of 348 for the seventh wicket after six wickets fell cheaply.

The stand between Atkinson and Depeiza involved what the late Ray Robinson rated as the worst bowling change in Test history. Miller had found a nasty spot and taken two quick wickets by making the ball climb unpredictably, and with the West Indies at 6 for 146 was warming to his task.

For some unaccountable reason, Ian Johnson took Miller off. Miller had plenty to say about this in an uncharacteristic dressing-room clash with Johnson. Not for the first time this pair from the same club, South Melbourne, almost came to blows. The players were clearly on Miller's side but stepped in when fisticuffs threatened.

Australia made her highest total in international cricket in the fifth Test. Harvey headed a list of five century-makers with 204, an innings that confirmed him as the world's No. 1 left-hander. Australia lost 2 for 7 before McDonald (127), Miller (109), Archer (128), Benaud (121), and Harvey took the score to 8 declared for 758. Steady bowling disposed of the West Indies for 357 and 319, giving Australia victory by an innings and 82 runs and a three-to-nil win in the series. In this tour several of the players who had kept Australia on top after the second World War gave the last display of their quality, though Miller took a record 7 for 12 for New South Wales versus South Australia at Sydney in 1955–56.

The 1956 Australian tour of England was marked by the degeneration of big cricket to a stage where results were dictated by groundsmen. Australia, whose hopes depended almost solely on pace-bowling, was forced to bat on dustbowl pitches ideal for the spin of Laker and Lock. The Australian batting deteriorated as fast as the side's morale, and towards the end of the tour the lack of footwork and intestinal fortitude produced inept displays that shamed the nation's proud past. Johnson lacked support from some senior players who were irked by his appointment as captain. His youngsters were no match for their England counterparts Peter May, David Sheppard, and Colin Cowdrey. England, captained for the first time by May, clinched the series when Laker took 19 for 90 in the Manchester Test, a record haul in any first-class match, and the only instance of 10 wickets in a Test innings. Laker also took 10 for 88 for Surrey against Australia, whose own spinners, Johnson and Benaud, were too slow through the air to match the hostility of the great England pair.

There was a memorable incident in the Leeds Test when May was out to a full toss from Johnson when he had reached 101 after adding 187 with Cyril Washbrook. May banged the ball down from around his shoulders and Lindwall took the catch in front of his toe-caps at backward square leg. Neither May nor Washbrook could see if it was a fair catch. 'I could not tell if it was a catch, but I believe him if he says he caught it,' said May, who immediately walked from the field when Lindwall signalled he had caught it.

On their way home Johnson's team broke fresh ground when they made the first official visit by an Australian team to Pakistan and India. In the first match between the countries, Pakistan won an astounding victory by 9 wickets on the mat at Karachi. The two sides combined to score only 95 runs on the first day when Australia was out for 80. Fazal Mahmood took 6 for 34 and 7 for 80. Australia won two of the tree Tests with India, thanks mainly to the spin of Benaud who took 23 wickets in the three games. John Rutherford, first Western Australian to play for Australia, appeared in the Bombay Test. Rutherford will be remembered as the Australian who could not find his way on to the field after leaving the Lord's dressing-room with 'Slasher' Mackay to open Australia's innings against the M.C.C. They wandered up and down corridors and finally vaulted the fence 30 yards from the players' gate, 5 minutes after the scheduled start of play.

Cherubic Adelaide keeper Gil Langley was among those who retired after the three-county tour by Johnson's side. He was not one of Australia's most polished keepers, with his shirttail flapping and excess weight spilling over his waistband, but nobody has matched his record of reliability. He had ninety-eight victims in twenty-six Tests. With him into retirement went his captain Ian Johnson, at his best a subtle off-spinner with skill in flight, drift, and changes of pace that few could match. Johnson made 1000 Test runs and took 109 Test wickets. In 1957 he beat forty-five applicants to become secretary of the Melbourne Cricket club, a role he handled tactfully until Dr John Lill took over in 1983.

Cricket was first televised in Australia in 1956–57 when part of the centenary match between Victoria and New South Wales at St Kilda was shown to viewers. The Melbourne Cricket Ground could not be used because of the Olympic Games. The match provided the first-ever Sheffield Shield tie. Victoria scored 244 and 197, New South Wales 281 and 160. A fledgling left-arm pace bowler named Ian Meckiff deprived New South Wales of victory. The Board of Control fined Keith Miller £100 and Ray Lindwall £50 for serialising books on the 1956 England tour before it had ended. No explanation was given for the discrepancy in the fines.

Congregational lay preacher Ian Craig, Australia's youngest captain, led a team to South Africa in 1957–58. He was a balding twenty-two, and had to rebuild the side after the departure of all the immediate post-war heroes except Harvey. Newcomers excelled themselves as Australia won the rubber three to nil. Wally Grout, the taciturn Queenslander whom team-mates called 'The Griz',

set a world record by holding six catches in the first Test, his first as our new keeper. Left-arm spinner Lindsay Kline, who let the ball go after a kangaroo-style hop, ended the second Test with a hat-trick. Meckiff took 11 wickets in four Tests without his action being questioned. The fast-improving Benaud scored two Test centuries and took 106 wickets on the tour, including 30 in the Tests.

The following summer the team was just blossoming when Craig was forced to drop out because of hepatitis. The Board caused widespread surprise by naming Benaud as captain instead of the more experienced Harvey. Benaud was lavish in his praise for Craig's rebuilding efforts. After he had recovered Craig opened successfully for New South Wales but marriage and his work as manager of a pharmaceutical chain ended chances of a return to Test cricket. He finished a career that had been so potentially rich by playing district cricket for Mosman. This left the stage to Benaud, who over the next four years lifted big cricket from the doldrums and lost only four of his twenty-seven matches as captain, revitalising Test matches wherever Australia played. The unlucky Harvey was at his side, unflagging in his support.

Brian Booth, who also represented Australia at hockey, shows the well-balanced stance he used in 29 Tests for Australia, a model cricketer renowned for his fair play.
— Ern McQuillan.

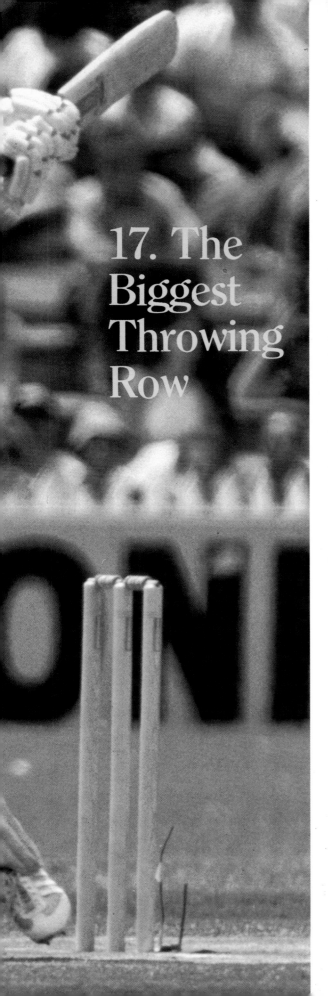

17. The Biggest Throwing Row

Richie Benaud's reign as Australian captain produced exciting cricket. He drew thrilling performances from Alan Davidson, Wally Grout, Neil Harvey, Norman O'Neill, and saw the long hours of practice pay off with a sharpening of his own skills. Benaud's candour and unfailing honesty with reporters put cricket itself under the closest scrutiny. The game stood the test well. Amid the resultant publicity, large crowds returned and this in turn stimulated the efforts of the Australian team. Cricket flourished, but not without major problems.

Benaud's team initially included Ian Meckiff, who played his way from district matches with South Melbourne, to eight seasons with Victoria, and tours of New Zealand in 1956–57, South Africa in 1957–58, and India and Pakistan in 1959–60. All this happened before he was first called for throwing by umpire Jack Kierse from square leg during a Victoria-South Australia Shield match at Adelaide in January 1963. English journalists had branded Meckiff a chucker back in 1958–59 when he took 6 for 38 for Benaud's side against England at Melbourne. Umpire Bill Priem no-balled Meckiff for throwing against Queensland at Brisbane in March 1963. Both in Adelaide and Brisbane Meckiff was allowed to continue after he had been called. In Adelaide he took 8 wickets in the match without being called again, and in Brisbane he bowled 38 overs in the match.

Meckiff bowled with his left arm, which had a permanent bend in it, and let the ball go in a blur of elbow and shoulder that was difficult to follow with the naked eye. Criticism of his action ebbed and flowed according to his success. The faster he bowled the more hot-headed his critics became. Between December 1957 and December 1963 he took 45 wickets at 31.62 in eighteen Tests but the strain of those six years took a heavy toll on his family life and caused his health to collapse. The throwing controversy was understood by very few Australian officials and showed some of them to be completely insensitive to the rights of individual players.

Greg Chappell pulls a ball to the boundary against England. He ranks second only to Bradman among Australian Test batsmen a magnificent shot-maker all around the stumps.
— Patrick Eagar.

Ian Meckiff's second no-ball in his last over in Tests. The manner of his dismissal from international cricket gave the impression he had been sacrificed for the sake of restoring peace in a game that had become almost hysterical about chuckers.
— Sydney Morning Herald.

A magic-eye sequence of Meckiff's action taken when he took 6 for 38 in Sydney against England, a coup that touched off the allegations that he was a chucker. The umpire appears more intent on where Meckiff's feet land than on his arm action.
— Jack Pollard Collection.

At the peak of the throwing row South Australia had two fast bowlers of highly suspect actions, **Alan Hitchcox and Peter Trethewey, whom club** cricketers labelled 'Pitchcox and Trethrowey'. When England's Tom Graveney faced them in Adelaide, he looked about the field after ducking a fiery ball and said, 'Who's winning this bluidy darts game?' Meckiff's team-mates in the 1958–59 series against England included Keith Slater, the Western Australian off-spinner who had been called for throwing in a match against Victoria in 1957, and occasional off-spinner Jimmy Burke, a notorious chucker. Fortunately, neither of these players had a major role in the Australian attack. When Meckiff was hurt he was replaced by Gordon Rorke, the blond giant New South Wales pace bowler. Rorke had a unique action that enabled him to slide a long way up the pitch with his entire bodyweight balanced on the outside edge of his front foot. Some were inclined to agree with English writer Brian Chapman who described Rorke as 'a honey of a chucker', but he was never called for throwing.

By the end of the rubber in 1958–59 against Peter May's team, which Australia won four to nil, the arguments about chuckers had become almost hysterical. Colin McDonald's outstanding batting in scoring 170 in the fourth Test followed by 133 in the fifth Test was almost forgotten. Indeed the Australians were so superior that they might easily have made it five to nil had Benaud accepted the challenge of scoring 150 in 110 minutes in the drawn third Test. Experts attributed Australia's success to Benaud's aggressive captaincy, Davidson's penetrative left-arm pace bowling — he took 3 wickets in 1 over in the first Test — and the all-round soundness of the team's batting, but in the Press box Englishmen claimed Australia's surfeit of chuckers swung the series.

This series, the first to be fully covered in Australia on TV, produced the slowest 50 runs in all Test cricket from Trevor Bailey, who in the first Test at Brisbane took 357 minutes to reach 50 and scored 68 at a rate of less than nine runs an hour. Bailey scored off only 40 of the 425 balls he received. More than 1,200,000 people saw England's 20 matches in a tour which saw Lindwall go past Grimmett's record of 216 Test wickets.

Park matches played on concrete pitches have been the training ground for thousands of Australian youngsters. Here is a typical scene in a Sydney park.
— Helmut Gritscher.

The Norman O'Neill sweep shot, missing from Australia's match at Bombay in 1964, when he had to drop out with stomach pains, leaving Australia to play a man short and lose half an hour from time.
— Ern McQuillan.

Australia's 1962-63 team that faced England were a happy lot, strong all round and splendidly led (L to R): Back, P.J.P. Burge, W.M. Lawry, G.D. McKenzie; Centre, B.C. Booth, B.K. Shepherd, N.C. O'Neill, B.N. Jarman, Front, R.B. Simpson, A.K. Davidson, R. Benaud (captain), R.N. Harvey, K.D. Mackay.
— Melbourne Herald.

*Bobby Simpson whose return to Tests after a ten-year absence ranks as the most astonishing comeback in Australian cricket. Here he moves off behind a smart cover drive.
— Australian Cricket newspaper.*

Long-necked Victorian Ian Redpath hammers a ball past mid-off in an Australia-West Indies Test. He was a batsman of rare tenacity and spirit despite poor running between wickets. — Australian Cricket newspaper.

Bobby Simpson went to field in the slips by accident when his captain, Keith Miller, ran out of positions for his side. He stayed to become one of the all-time great slip catchers as he shows in holding this snick from Ted Dexter in the 1962-63 series.
— *Melbourne Herald.*

Australian opener Bill Lawry raises his bat in acknowledgement of the crowd's applause after reaching his century in the Fourth Test at Old Trafford in 1961, for Lawry's technique flowered that summer.
— *Ken Kelly.*

The high calibre of Benaud's team was confirmed on a difficult tour in 1959–60, when they beat Pakistan on the mat in Dacca and on grass at Lahore, and drew the other Test on the mat at Karachi. Davidson had matured into a match-winner, swinging the ball disconcertingly across both right and left-handed batsmen, scoring valuable late-order runs with his powerful thumping, and diving yards to bring in catches. Team-mates called him 'The Claw'. Norman O'Neill supported Harvey with powerful stroke-play, Burke and McDonald were a crafty, defiant opening pair, and Grout a cheerful, agile keeper. Benaud bowled his leg-breaks, top-spinners, and occasional flippers better under his own captaincy than he did for other captains. And that likeable Queensland eccentric 'Slasher' Mackay assumed an important place in the team with his high-bouncing medium-pace cutters and stubborn batting.

From Pakistan the side embarked on a five-Test series in India and emerged from another really trying tour as two-to-one winners. Crowd demonstrations were frequent and after Australia won the first Test spectators jostled the umpires and threw bottles. Benaud took 29 wickets in the series, in which Harvey, O'Neill, and Favell scored centuries. Lindwall played the last of his sixty-one Tests at Karachi, taking his total of Test wickets to 228, a record at that time. The 6-feet 5-inch Rorke and South Australian batsman Gavin Stevens had to be invalided home during the tour. Both lost almost 2 stone in weight and neither figured prominently in first-class cricket again.

The furore over throwers led to a London conference of all the cricket nations in 1960. By then Englishmen D.B. Pearson, G.A.R. Lock, K.J. Aldridge, H.J. Rhodes, E.M. Bryant and D.W. White, South Africans C.N. McCarthy and G.M. Griffin, West Indian C. Stayers, and Australian Jack McLaughlin had all recently been called in a world-wide reaction against chuckers. Australian delegates at the conference were Bill Dowling, former president of the Australian Board and Bradman. Dowling said he had been appalled at the way the media had whipped up the campaign against Meckiff: 'It is contrary to every principle of fair play that sportsmen should be condemned out of hand without ever appearing in a country'. Bradman called the throwing affair the most difficult problem ever to be dealt with in cricket.

The conference agreed on a combination of the Australian and English drafts in defining a throw this way:

The ball shall be deemed to have been thrown if, in the opinion of either umpire, the bowling arm having been bent at the elbow (whether the wrist be backward of the elbow or not), is suddenly straightened immediately prior to the instant of delivery. The bowler shall, nevertheless, be free to use the wrist in the delivery action.

The definition was hailed as a brave attempt, but inadequate for legal purposes. Critics said it only complicated further the job of umpires. Meanwhile Meckiff had been working hard at the nets to change his action, throwing his front arm up more in the delivery stride. He was chosen for two of the five Tests against the West Indies in Australia in 1960–61, a series that has been hailed as one of the best of all time. He was in the Australian team that played the celebrated first-ever Test tie at the 'Gabba and was the batsman run out off the second-last ball to finish the match. Australia needed 6 runs to win off the last eight-ball over. Australia lost her last 4 wickets for 6 runs. During the match Davidson became the first player to score 100 runs (44 and 80) and take 10 wickets (5 for 135 and 6 for 87) in a Test match.

Bill Lawry raced pigeons as a hobby in between opening the batting for Australia and working as a plumber. Despite the sad manner of his dismissal from big cricket, he will be remembered for many gutsy innings.
— Ern McQuillan.

Stackpole struggles with Red Cross men trying to take him from the field for attention after he was hit by a ball at Port-of-Spain during Australia's tour. He completed the match after being patched up.
— Ron McKenzie, Sydney Daily Mirror.

Keith Stackpole was a Melbourne hero, an opening batsman who loved to hit the ball hard and invariably kept the score moving. Here he takes pleasure in cutting a short ball backward of point.
— Melbourne Herald.

*Dennis Lillee in his
delivery stride, body high
up above the ground, eyes
on the target, front arm
well up, fingers of his
bowling hand aligned as
required, his
concentration intense.
— Martin King.*

*Lillee a moment after he
let the ball go continues
on down the pitch,
bowling arm swinging
right across his body in a
full follow through, every
move still well controlled.
— Jack Pollard
Collection.*

This page, a typical Lillee appeal, with the index fingers of both hands raised as he pressures the umpire.
— Martin King.

England fast bowler John Snow and captain Ray Illingworth argue with famous Australian umpire Lou Rowan after he warned Snow for excessive use of the bouncer in the Seventh Test at Sydney in 1970-71. Greg Chappell is listening to the exchange. — Sydney Morning Herald.

The flooring of Terry Jenner that triggered the nasty demonstration against the England team in 1970-71 at Sydney. Jenner writhes in pain as England captain Illingworth rushes to assist him. — Melbourne Herald.

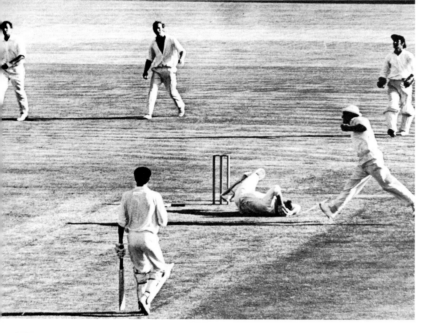

The Brisbane tie set the stage for a magnificent series. Australia went one-up with a 7 wickets win at Melbourne, where Frank Misson replaced Meckiff and Davidson took a further 8 wickets. Joe Solomon was out when his cap dislodged a bail as he played a defensive shot. The West Indies levelled at one-all in Sydney when Sobers made a magnificent 168, Gerry Alexander a stubborn 108, and Davidson picked up another 8 wickets. At Adelaide, in the fourth Test, Kline and Mackay earned Australia a draw by defying the West Indian bowlers in a 100-minute tenth-wicket stand. Gibbs took a hat-trick in this match in which Kanhai made 117 and 115, including a six off the first ball of a day's play. The second day in the deciding fifth Test at Melbourne attracted 90,800 spectators, a world record for one day's cricket. Australia won another thriller by 2 wickets, and the West Indies were given a ticker-tape farewell by the people of Melbourne after the most entertaining rubber of modern times. Davidson took 33 wickets in the four Tests in which he played. Norm O'Neill was the sole Australian century-maker with his 181 in the epic first Test.

Benaud's team had barely recovered from the tension of this series when they began play in another enthralling rubber in 1961 against England. The series hinged on the fourth Test at Manchester, with the teams level at a win apiece. When England appeared likely to score the 256 needed to win in the final innings, Benaud — who had been forced to relinquish the captaincy to Harvey for the second Test at Lord's — switched to round the wicket and aimed at the bowlers' footmarks. He dismissed Dexter, bowled Peter May around his legs for a duck, and finished with 6 for 71. England was out for 201. A magnificent last-wicket stand of 98 by Davidson and McKenzie had given Australia this chance. Davidson's 77 not out — which included two huge off-drives for 6, and 20 off an over from David Allen — ranks as one of the best of all rescue innings for Australia.

Inspired perhaps by Davidson's hitting, Tom Nilsson hit nine sixes from successive balls in a Brisbane minor game to provide a rousing start for the 1961–62 Australian season. Nilsson hit all eight deliveries of 1 over for 6 and did it again off the first ball of the next over. The research that Nilsson's feat touched off uncovered the fact that the fastest recorded century in Australian cricket came from the bat of Laurie Quinlan at Cairns in 1910, when Quinlan made 100 in 18 minutes with hits of 2,6,2,4,1,1,6,2,3,6,4,4,3,6,2,6,6,4,1,4,4,2, 4,6,4,6,1. The fastest Australian first-class century remained D.R.A. Gehrs' 119 in 50 minutes for South Australia versus Western Australia in 1912-14 until David Hookes beat this with 100 in

43 minutes for South Australia against Victoria in 1982-83. Bradman had an untimed 102 in three overs at Blackheath against Lithgow, which he believed took less than 18 minutes.

a side managed by the Duke of Norfolk and captained by 'Lord Ted' Dexter. It was a thoroughly disappointing series between evenly matched sides unwilling to take risks. Each team won a Test, the rest were drawn. Sydney schoolteacher Brian Booth proved a delightful stroke-player, scoring runs freely throughout, including 112 in the first Test, 103 in the second, and 77 in the fourth Test. Dexter scored 481 runs in the rubber but failed to get a century, proving a magnificent player when in his stride.

The world record Test match crowd of 90,800, packed into the Melbourne Cricket Ground in 1961 for the Fifth Australia v. West Indies Test.

Bob Massie in the delivery stride that produced remarkable swing at Lord's. He was unable to recapture the magic which gave him 16 wickets, but also enabled him to beat the bat so often England's finest players were left bewildered and confused. — Daily Mail, London.

Far Left (Bottom): A rare photograph of the Australian Board of Control whose meetings are held in camera. The Board controls all overseas tours by Australian teams, however lowly their status, and even sides like the Emus need Board approval for tours. — Australian Cricket Board.

*Douglas Francis Walters,
sometimes known as
"Freddie" for reasons
obscure, plays one of his
favourite leg-side pulls
against England in
Sydney. He was the first
player for whom fans
erected a banner on The
Hill in Sydney.
— Jack Pollard collection.*

*Duggie Walters, one of
the most popular of all
Australian cricketers
takes evasive action
against a bouncer from
West Indian Wayne
Daniels.
— Martin King.*

Walters at Headingley bravely faces England's Phillipe Henri Edmonds to prevent a hat-trick. Walters put bat to ball and the England fieldsman retreated. Edmonds subsequently lost his England team place to Derek Underwood, but what a difference this ball may have made had Duggie missed it.
— Sport & General, London.

the rest of the match. Benaud simply said he accepted the umpire's decision, just as he had done when Meckiff was not called for throwing. To many cricket buffs the manner of Meckiff's dismissal from big cricket was unfairly handled, and there remained the feeling that he had been sacrificed to end the biggest of all throwing controversies.

South Africa shared that rubber one-Test-all, with Simpson in the last four Tests proving to be a dour, unsmiling leader, lacking Benaud's warmth. Benaud played the last three Tests under Simpson's captaincy, taking his total of Test dismissals to a record of 248 at 27.03. He was a crafty captain, prepared to gamble on his instincts, but among his contemporaries the feeling persisted that he was blessed with more than his share of luck. England and Derbyshire pace bowler Harold Rhodes, a convicted chucker, summed it up: 'If you put your head in a bucket of slops, Benordy, you'd come up with a mouthful of diamonds.'

Simpson had played his first Test cricket while representing Western Australia, but by the time he took over the Australian captaincy Tony Lock had been imported from the Surrey county club in a move which *Wisden* said shifted the balance of power in Australian cricket. For cocksure, belligerent Lock was the ideal man to show the Westerners how to win. He had been no-balled for throwing in three different matches but now put the word around that he had changed his action and dropped the faster ball that had caused all the trouble. He was never called in Australia in a colourful eight-season stint as Western Australia's captain. He led Western Australia to win the Shield in 1967–68 and the foundation he laid in his coaching for Perth district clubs produced players who later won five Shield competitions in ten years.

Benaud captained Australia in one more Test, the first against South Africa at Brisbane in 1963–64. When Australia took the field after lunch on the second day, Eddie Barlow had made a fine 114 and Benaud had taken 5 for 68 in South Africa's first innings of 346. McKenzie bowled the first over and Benaud threw Meckiff the ball for the second over, with the wind behind him. At square leg umpire Col Egar thought Meckiff's first ball was suspect but remained silent. He then called Meckiff for throwing four of the twelve balls in his over. Everyone knew that this was the end of Meckiff's career but many of the spectators who hooted Egar were shocked that Benaud did not try Meckiff at the other end so that umpire Lou Rowan could pass judgment on him. Instead Benaud gave Meckiff just the one over, knowing that he would be a bowler short for

In the summer of 1963–64 Peter Burge, playing against New South Wales, made the highest first-class score by a Queenslander, a superb 283, studded with fierce drives and savage pulls and hooks. He went back to England for his third visit in 1964 in the team captained by Bob Simpson. In the third Test Burge was at the crease when Australia lost her seventh wicket for only 187. He then helped add a further 202 runs, taking his own score to 160 in a match-winning display of powerful strokes. This was Australia's only victory in the series — by 7 wickets. At Manchester in the fourth Test Simpson made his maiden Test century in his fifty-second Test innings and went on to 311, the highest score for Australia since Bradman's 334 in 1930. His stand of 201 with Lawry set a new opening partnership record against England. Australia declared at 8 for 656. England replied with 611 during which off-spinner Tom Veivers bowled a record 571 balls, including 51 overs unchanged.

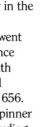

Left:
Australian pace bowler Alan Hurst jumps for joy in 1975 as he hits John Snow on the pad and appeals for leg-before-wicket. Umpire Dickie Bird moved his arm but denied the appeal.
— Australian Cricket newspaper.

Right:
The controversial 'run-out' incident at Brisbane in 1970-71. Keith Stackpole, clearly short of the crease after the wicket has been broken, was given not out and went from 18 to score 207.
— Courier Mail, Brisbane.

Below:
Apart from the tied Test at Brisbane, two Sheffield Shield games have produced ties: Victoria v. New South Wales at Melbourne in 1956 and South Australia v. Queensland at Adelaide in 1977, end of which is shown here. Queensland began the final over needing four runs, but three batsmen were run out. Last man out was Colin Cooke, shown failing to make the crease off the seventh ball.
— Adelaide Advertiser.

For Australians this rubber was notable for the match broadcasts of Alan McGilvray, who was then at the peak of his powers. Ever since the synthetic broadcasts of the 1930s when commentators in a Sydney studio tapped pencils on tables to simulate bat hitting ball and described matches from coded cables, cricket commentaries had won a vast audience in Australia. McGilvray, son of a Scottish shoemaker, represented all that was enjoyable in those broadcasts — fair, knowledgeable, and a gentleman.

On the way home from England the twenty-fourth Australian team, led by Simpson, played three Tests against India, sharing the series with a draw and a win each. McKenzie was the match winner for Australia in the first Test at Madras with 6 for 58 and 4 for 33. Australia played a man short in the second Test at Bombay when O'Neill was stricken with stomach pains soon after the start. India won by 2 wickets a half-hour from time. Two days were lost through rain in the drawn third Test. This was followed by a drawn Test against Pakistan at Karachi, where Simpson had innings of 153 and 115, in a prelude to Pakistan's first tour in the following Australian summer. The Pakistanis played only one Test in Australia, sharing the honours with a strong Australian side at Melbourne. Hanif Mohammad scored 104 and 93 for Pakistan and kept wicket throughout.

For the leading Australian players, the tour that followed in the West Indies produced the highest incidence of chucking they had known. The players were upset that Charlie Griffith, who opened the bowling for the West Indies with Wes Hall, was not called whenever he bowled his faster ball. The West Indies won two to one a rubber that yielded some dazzling batting in their first success in a series against Australia. Richie Benaud had no hesitation in calling Griffith a chucker from the press box and produced photographs to prove it. The day after the tour ended Norm O'Neill published an article in a London newspaper labelling Griffith a chucker. Finally, in May 1966 during the West Indies match against Lancashire at Manchester, Griffith was called for throwing by umpire Arthur Fagg.

Between 1963–64 and 1967–68 Bob Simpson led Australia twenty-nine times, but in a period which brought dramatic shifts in the world's playing strength he found wins hard to achieve. The West Indies teams had overcome a tendency to collapse under pressure, mixing good sense with their proved batting brilliance in a way that made them formidable opponents. Pakistan and India had surmounted the problems of the 1947 partition of British India with praiseworthy speed

and were building their strength in almost every Test. South Africa's programme of importing gifted coaches had finally produced a Test team without weaknesses.

Simpson, having missed the Brisbane Test against Mike Smith's 1965–66 England team because of a broken wrist and the Sydney Test because of chickenpox, took over from his deputy Brian Booth for the Adelaide Test. In a memorable display of stamina, he refused to let a severe gastric upset interrupt his innings and went without meals in a 547-minute stay that yielded 225 runs, and a first-wicket stand of 244 with Lawry (119) on the way. Each side won a Test in that series, which was notable for Bob Cowper's score of 307 in 727 minutes at Melbourne, the first triple Test century by an Australian in Australia. It was the fourth-longest innings in all first-class cricket and included only twenty fours. Lawry made three centuries in the rubber.

Transvaal became the first non-Test South African team to beat Australia in 1966–67. Simpson's team — the seventh side to tour South Africa — fared no better in the Tests, losing one to three to a fine South African team captained by Peter van der Merwe. After sixty-four years and twenty-two attempts South Africa had their first victory at home against Australia by winning the first Test at Johannesburg. Lindsay equalled the world wicket-keeping record by dismissing six Australians in their first innings and then batted for 274 minutes to score 182, which included five sixes. Australia's keeper Brian Taber, who had never attended a Test before, made eight dismissals in his debut for Australia.

Top Left: Crafty off-spinner Ashley ("Rowdy") Mallett in action for South Australia against New South Wales. Brian Taber is the batsman backing-up, Tom Brooks the umpire.
— Australian Cricketer.
Bottom Left:
The masterly South African right-hander Barry Richards hammers a ball through the covers. He scored 356 for South Australia v. Western Australia at Perth in 1970-71 when experts were beginning to doubt that 300 runs in a day was any longer possible.
— Eric Beecher, Australian Cricketer.

Australians in England in 1972 about to record a commercial (L toR): Rod Marsh, Graeme Watson, Ross Edwards and Paul Sheahan.
— Jack Pollard Collection.

*Dennis Lillee bowling to the ultimate slips field against New Zealand in Auckland in 1977. Rodney Marsh is the 'keeper and the nine fieldsmen in slips are (L to R): G.S. Chappell, G.J. Gilmour, K.D. Walters, K.J. O'Keefe, I.C. Davis, G.J. Cosier, A. Turner, M.H.N. Walker. Batsman Ewan Chatfield avoided dismissal.
— New Zealand Herald.*

*Alan Knott swings a ball away to the leg boundary during his innings of 38 for England against Australia at Edgbaston in 1975, watched by 'keeper Rod Marsh and Gary Gilmour.
— Ken Kelly.*

Bill Lawry took over the Australian captaincy from Simpson after the second Test against India in 1967–68. Simpson had become the third Australian to score 4000 Test runs. Australia won all four Tests in the series. Playing under Lawry in what was intended to be his last Test, Simpson held his ninety-ninth Test catch in the fourth Test at Sydney and produced his best bowling figures, 5 for 59. India was handicapped by a hamstring injury to their captain the Nawab of Pataudi, jun., who could not play until the second Test. Western Australia won the Sheffield Shield in that season, with Ian Brayshaw distinguishing himself by taking all 10 wickets for 44 runs in an innings against Victoria.

Lawry took the twenty-fifth Australian team to England in 1968 for a lack-lustre tour in which each team won one Test. Lawry showed a marked inability to handle his spinners Ashley Mallett and John Gleeson, who, like Iverson, bowled with a finger tucked behind the ball. The Australians were very disappointing and won only five of their seventeen matches against English county teams and lost to Yorkshire and Glamorgan. A spirited youngster named Ian Chappell was the most impressive of the ten newcomers to the Australian team. England was no better and only managed to share the series by winning the fifth Test with 5 minutes to spare after Australia had been caught on a pitch affected by a freak storm.

Dennis Lillee's copybook action, front arm well up, body side-on, fingers aligned on the required grip, eyes on the target, as he lets one go against England.
— Australian Cricket newspaper.

The man who captained England in the remarkable Centenary Test at Melbourne, Tony Greig. While play proceeded, most of the best players in this match had contracts to join Kerry Packer's rebels in their bags.
— Melbourne Herald.

Ashley Mallett taking one of his many brilliant catches in the gully position during the Third England v. Australia Test at Melbourne in 1974-75.
— Melbourne Herald.

Somehow Australia shrugged off this shoddy effort and the following summer (1968–69) contributed a marvellous performance against the fourth West Indies touring team. This was a sparkling series, brimful of notable batting, bowling, and fielding. Clive Lloyd, Ian Chappell, Bill Lawry, Doug Walters, Basil Butcher, Garfield Sobers, and Ian Redpath scored centuries. Walters became the first to score a double century (242) and a century (103) in the same Test when Australia finished the rubber three to one with a win by 382 runs in the fifth Test, a meritorious display against a team widely regarded as the best in the world. That season in a Queensland country game H. Morley set a world record by scoring 62 off an over, hitting nine sixes and two fours (there were four no-balls).

Australia's outstanding victory over the talented West Indian side was quickly followed by a miserable effort on tour in India and South Africa in 1969–70. Australia won the Indian series three to one and suffered a humiliating four-to-one drubbing in South Africa. The team returned home amid accusations of poor sportsmanship and dissension among themselves. Lawry as captain bore the brunt of these charges following a plate-throwing incident on a railway station and an on-the-field clash with a photographer in India, and his vulgar hand signs to spectators in South Africa. After four Tests had been played in the series against England that immediately followed (1970–71) he was sacked, the first Australian captain to be dropped during a Test rubber.

Lawry's sacking was only one of many sensations during the tour by England under Ray Illingworth. At Brisbane Stackpole, having been clearly run out at 18, went on to 207. At Perth in that city's first Test, Greg Chappell scored a century (108) in his Test debut. The third Test, abandoned after the toss had been made without a ball being bowled, caused controversy over whether it counted in the players' records. By the time of the fourth Test in Sydney (won by England) England's liberal use of the bouncer was irking spectators and Australian batsmen. Then Lawry stunned a Melbourne crowd by declaring when Rod Marsh, 92 not out, was set to become the first Australian keeper to make a Test century. The teams went to Sydney for an unprecedented seventh Test with Ian Chappell captain for the first time and Australia needing to win to save the Ashes. After Snow had felled Jenner with a bouncer crowd demonstrations led Illingworth to take England from the field. Umpire Rowan told them to return or forfeit the match. Needing 222 to win, Australia collapsed for 160, thus losing a tense, at times spiteful, series nil to two.

From the 1972 Australian tour of England Ian Chappell set about rebuilding the team that had flopped so badly in Lawry's last nine matches as captain (five losses, four draws). Starting virtually from scratch, with little knowledge of the players he had to lead, he developed a team that played stirring cricket. They lost only five of thirty matches and won fifteen while he was captain. He sometimes fell below the high standards of good behaviour for which cricket is renowned but his players revered him. He was a man's man, tough, bluntly spoken, and pugnaciously defiant in a crisis.

Australia's revival began in England in 1972. Bob Massie took 16 wickets for 137 runs in his first appearance in Test cricket with 8 for 84 and 8 for 53. Only two years before he had failed to earn a contract in a trial with Northants Second Eleven. Massie was never again the same striking force but Dennis Lillee made rapid advances. Lillee — with 5 for 58 and 5 for 123 in the fifth Test — was largely responsible for Australia's sharing the rubber two-all and took 31 wickets in the five Tests, a record for an Australian in England. This tour marked the beginning of his great partnership with keeper Rodney Marsh, whose record twenty-three victims in the Tests included ten catches off Lillee. Chappell's intelligent use of the spinners Mallett and Gleeson was in marked contrast to the way in which they had been bowled by Simpson and Lawry.

The successes continued in Australia in 1972–73 with a three-to-nil whitewash of Pakistan. This series was notable for the unhappy debut of John Watkins (who found it hard to land one of his leg-spinners on the pitch) and the dramatic arrival of the burly wrong-foot swing bowler, Max Walker. Walker took 5 wickets for 3 runs off his last thirty balls to give Australia an astounding victory when Pakistan needed only 159 to win the third Test. Walker's 6 for 15 won him a place in the Australian team to the West Indies where he again performed wonders after Lillee had broken down with stress fractures in the back. Walker's 26 wickets in five Tests was a plucky effort for a man on his first tour and paved the way to Australia's two-to-nil win in the rubber.

Jeff Thomson, on the right, tries to struggle up, while Alan Turner remains unconscious on the ground following their collision in the First Test against Pakistan in December, 1976. Thomson missed the rest of the series because of a dislocated collarbone. — Adelaide Advertiser.

Graham Yallop takes a brilliant catch to dismiss Rod Marsh in a Victoria-Western Australian Shield match. Wicket-keeper Richie Robinson is jubilant.
— Melbourne Herald.

Greg Chappell acknowledging the applause of spectators after scoring a century in the Fifth Test at the Oval in 1972. His brother Ian, shown at the other end, also made a century in this innings.
— Patrick Eagar.

The Australian Board of Control for International Cricket changed its name to the Australian Cricket Board in 1973 at about the same time as the first streakers appeared on Australian grounds. Banners applauding favoured players began to decorate the stands, many of them showing the public's remarkable affection for the boy from a Dungog dairy farm, Doug Walters. From the time he made 155 in his Test debut in 1965–66 against England and followed it with 115 in his next Test he had been the idol of spectators. His admirers multiplied when he accepted without complaint two years' compulsory Army service at a crucial time in his career.

New Zealand played her first Test in Australia at Melbourne in 1973–74 when a team captained by Bevan Congdon was defeated by an innings and 25 runs. Stackpole delighted his army of Melbourne fans with a punishing 122. John Parker made New Zealand's first Test century against Australia with 108 in the drawn second Test. Australia took the series two to nil when Marsh scored 132 to set up another win by an innings. Queensland schoolteacher Geoff Dymock made an impressive Test debut with 6 wickets, including one off his second ball. Australia went to New Zealand for a short tour at the end of that summer and at Christchurch against all the odds New Zealand won the second Test by 5 wickets, her first win over Australia. This victory was all the more surprising because of Australia's feast of runs in the drawn first Test at Wellington, where Greg Chappell made 380 runs with scores of 247 not out and 133. Australia made amends by winning the third Test by 297 runs, with Walters contributing 104 not out in the first innings and Ian Redpath 159 not out in the second innings.

England's 1974–75 Australian tour under Mike Denness belonged to Lillee and Thomson, who gave the visiting batsmen a fearful time. Australia was leading four to nil in the six-Test series when England's captain found form at last, scored 188, and saved some face by helping to win the sixth Test. Lillee and Thomson between them took 13 wickets in the first Test, 11 wickets in the second, 12 in the third, 10 in the fourth, and 11 in the fifth, during which Thomson tore fibres in his shoulder while playing tennis. Without his partner, Lillee took only 1 wicket in the final Test. Walters played the innings of the rubber in scoring 103 not out between tea and stumps at Perth, reaching his century with a six off the last ball of the day. Mallett regained the Ashes for Australia after almost four years when he took his hundredth Test wicket in the fourth Test.

One-day international matches which had been part of English cricket since 1963, achieved a new peak of popularity with the first World Cup in England in 1975. Australia reached the final by beating Pakistan and England, but lost by 17 runs to the West Indies when five batsmen were run out. In the only one of the four Tests played after the World Cup that produced a result, Australia won by an innings at Birmingham, where Lillee and Thomson took 14 wickets between them. The third Test at Leeds was abandoned after vandals multilated the pitch with knives and oil. McCosker was then 95 not out and within sight of his first Test century. He got it in the fourth Test with an innings of 127.

Greg Chappell took over from his brother Ian as Australian captain for the 1975–76 Tests against West Indies. The Chappell brothers contributed five centuries to Australia's handsome five-to-one win. Lillee and Thomson gave the West Indians a severe battering as well as consistently taking their wickets. The West Indies managed only one opening stand of more than 50 runs in the six Tests. Marsh's twenty-six dismissals in the series equalled the world record by J.H.B. Waite.

Australia followed with a drawn series one-all against Pakistan in 1976–77 and a one-to-nil win in New Zealand during the same summer.

Behind the scenes, months of preparations had been going on for the staging in Melbourne of a match to celebrate a hundred years of Test cricket. The idea was to bring together for one lavishly promoted match all the English and Australian Test players still living and to put them all in the Hilton Hotel for one glorious week of reminiscing. People were sceptical at first but ex-Test bowler Hans Ebeling, whose brainchild it was, and a special committee, overcame all problems. On 12 March 1977 Australian cricket's masterpiece, the Centenary Test, began.

*The 1965 Australian team to the West Indies in a happy mood before they faced a persistent barrage of bumpers (L to R): Back, S.C. Trimble, P.J. Allan, G.D. McKenzie, B.K. Shepherd, N.J.N. Hawke, L.C. Mayne, R.M. Cowper, D.J. Sincock, G.T. Thomas, P.I. Philpott; Front, B.N. Jarman, W.M. Lawry, R.B. Simpson (captain), R.J. Parish (manager), B.C. Booth, N.C. O'Neill, A.T.W. Grout.
— Australian Cricket Board.*

18. Jumpsuits and Thongs

The Centenary Test was a promotional triumph and rivalled the tied Test at Brisbane in 1960–61 as the most publicised cricket match ever played in Australia. Invitations were sent to the 264 surviving participants in England-Australia Tests and all bar twenty-six who were too old or infirm to travel gathered in Melbourne. It was a reunion that produced touching moments for many cricketers who believed they had been forgotten. Australia's Jack Ryder, eighty-seven, was the oldest ex-Test player present. He led the parade of old cricketers on to the Melbourne Cricket Ground, where Test matches had begun a hundred years before.

The match lived up to all expectations, and by an astounding coincidence produced precisely the same result as the match in 1877 — victory for Australia by 45 runs. After two days both teams had completed their first innings and Australia was 3 for 104 in the third innings. There were doubts that the match would last beyond the third day and discussions were held about the possibility of an exhibition match to fill in the time until the Queen's scheduled arrival on the fifth day. However, these arrangements were forestalled when players on both sides produced a series of heroic performances that took the match into a memorable fifth day during which the Queen shared the tension of a vast crowd.

South African-born Tony Greig, 6-feet 8-inch son of an English Squadron-Leader, won the toss for England. Sent in to bat, Australia was bundled out for 138. Greg Chappell tried to rescue the innings but when he reached 40 became Derek Underwood's 250th Test victim. McCosker had his jaw smashed by a ball that deflected on to his stumps. Lillee and Walker, with the crowd roaring at every delivery, gave a wonderful display of swing and pace to have England out for 95 on the second day. Marsh's four catches in that innings took him past Grout's Australian record of 187 Test dismissals.

Left: Dennis Lillee with his highly controversial aluminium cricket bat, which he used when batting in a big match in Perth. The umpires agreed with English players' objections and Lillee had to exchange it for a wooden bat.
— The West Australian.

Far left: Jeff Thomson, at his peak one of the most hostile bowlers Australia has produced, leaves the ground as he reaches the crease to deliver another thunderbolt.
— Jack Pollard Collection.

The third day produced excellent Australian batting against some equally skilful bowling from England. David Hookes sent the crowd wild by hitting Greig for five successive fours in a blazing score of 56 in his Test debut, and Marsh finished only 5 runs away from the first century against England by an Australian keeper. Next day after Marsh had lost Lillee, McCosker came out to bat with his heavily swollen broken jaw bandaged. Some critics considered that he was taking a foolish risk, but the 54 runs added by McCosker and Marsh in an unbroken ninth-wicket stand proved decisive. Greg Chappell declared at 9 for 419, giving England 463 to score in 11 hours. Marsh was not out on 110.

England seemed to have a strong chance at 2 for 191 at the end of the fourth day, with Randall 87 not out. The fifth day offered a gradual increase in excitement as Amiss and Randall added 166 for the third wicket. When Amiss was out for 64, Randall had reached his maiden Test century and was scoring freely from flowing drives and cuts and audacious hooks. Fidgety but smiling, Randall let spectators know that he was enjoying himself. When Lillee floored him with a vicious bouncer, he sprang up immediately, rubbing his head and grinning broadly.

Randall was given out caught behind on 161, but Marsh drew a sustained ovation when he recalled him. He made only 13 more. Greig made 41 and Knott a bold 42 but when Lillee trapped Knott l.b.w. at 5.12 p.m. Australia had won. England's 417 was the highest fourth-innings total made by either country since Tests began. Within a few weeks the national joy in winning this match before a unique audience of great players faded when it was discovered that many of Australia's heroes had had contracts to join the break-away World Series Cricket in their bags when they played in Melbourne.

The plans to stage international cricket matches in opposition to those organised by established administrations had been made months before the Centenary Test. Media magnate Kerry Packer had been assisted by former Australian captains Richie Benaud and Ian Chappell and by England's reigning captain Tony Greig in working out contracts that were offered to the world's best players. Packer bought the exclusive rights to the services of sixty-six cricketers from the leading cricket-playing nations because he had been denied the right to televise traditional cricket. The players said that they joined him because for years their claims for better pay had been disregarded. The Australian Cricket Board said that they paid players as much as they could afford.

Far Left: New Zealand policemen grapple with a spectator during the 1982 one-day match against Australia at Auckland; A policeman loses his cap in a scuffle with a spectator at Manuka Oval, Canberra; Greg Chappell chasing a streaker across the M.C.G. in 1979.
— Melbourne Herald.

Derek Randall was frequently hit during his memorable 174 in the Centenary Test at Melbourne. Here he takes refuge close to the stumps as another ball sails over his head.
— Melbourne Herald.

Ian Chappell in the jumpsuit (with Ray Illingworth) that lost him so many fans.
— Sport & General, London.

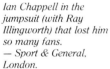

Frank Packer and his sons, Clyde, left, and Kerry at Gleneagles, Scotland, in 1959. Eighteen years later Kerry showed all his father's well-known tenacity in launching international matches in opposition to traditional matches.
— Daily Mail, London.

Big Max Walker, the Tasmanian-born swing bowler they called "Tangles", in a typically defiant mood as he reaches the delivery stride — with the wrong foot forward if you follow the coaching manuals.
— Martin King.

*Lanky Tony Greig hammers a straight drive towards the fence for the Rest of the World in their Sydney match against New South Wales. Brian Taber is the 'keeper, Alan Turner is the fieldsman.
— Jack Pollard Collection.*

The struggle between W.S.C. and cricket's establishment that followed was bitter and protracted. W.S.C. was denied use of major grounds. Most W.S.C. players were banned from playing district or county cricket and even from using practice facilities. Greig was sacked as England's captain. When the International Cricket Conference banned all W.S.C. players from Tests for two years from their last appearance for W.S.C. Packer took the I.C.C. to court. England's High Court ruled in Packer's favour after a hearing that lasted thirty-one days and cost the I.C.C. more than $A300,000 in court costs. The essence of a judgment that took 5 hours 30 minutes to deliver was that the I.C.C. and county bans were a restraint of trade. The verdict meant that English counties had to re-engage Packer players whom they had dismissed.

The W.S.C. rebels — twenty-eight of them Australians — considered that all their grievances had been demonstrated at the Centenary Test, which drew 24,873 spectators and $262,086 in gate money. The players reckoned they were underpaid at $2277 for appearing in such an extravaganza, and argued that the match proved how right they were in suggesting that big cricket needed professional promotion. Many of them would have been shocked to learn how small the return from TV rights to the match was.

When news of the Packer rebellion was revealed, the twenty-eighth Australian team, led by Greg Chappell, were at Eastbourne on the south coast of England. The manager, Len Maddocks, had an impossible job trying to lift the form of a dispirited side once it became known that thirteen of the seventeen players had signed to join W.S.C. The Australians won only five of their twenty two matches and only once on the tour scored more than 400 — against the inferior Notts attack. Only Greg Chappell scored 1000 runs and only Max

One of Australia's major hopes in the Centenary Test was Garry Cosier. In a situation ideal for his big-hitting, he failed lamentably, when a few big hits would have sufficed.
— Melbourne Herald.

A typical incident on the 1977 tour of England, with Rick McCosker, dropping a catch off Boycott at Trent Bridge. Boycott then 13, went on to a century.
— Ken Kelly.

Walker took 50 wickets. England, astutely led by Brearley, won the series three to nil.

Packer was forced to stage his W.S.C. matches initially at football grounds on prefabricated pitches. He introduced coloured uniforms for his players; play at night under floodlights with a white ball; and a rule preventing fieldsmen from retreating to the outfield until 15 overs had been bowled. He found for cricket a new audience who cheered boisterously, heckled the players, and decorated the grounds with banners and flags. Rock bands provided entertainment during breaks.

But playing in outlying suburbs on grounds unsuited to cricket was so restrictive that established cricket appeared certain to overcome the challenge to its authority. Here Packer pulled off a master-stroke by arranging for the Sydney Cricket Ground Trust to erect six 250-foot light towers that transformed the ground. On 28 November 1978, after a year of bitter feuding with the Australian authorities, Packer staged the first match under lights on the S.C.G. It was an incredible evening watched by a crowd estimated at 58,000. Packer had lost about $4 million on the first year of W.S.C. but with floodlit games at the S.C.G. to boost takings lost far less in the second year. Public and media support for his matches was growing when the announcement

came that the A.C.B. had negotiated a settlement with W.S.C.

Packer won what he had always wanted in the settlement — the right to televise big matches. His players were all paid the sums he had guaranteed them — $30,000-a-year in most cases — and returned to matches run by the establishment. To their credit, neither side indulged in recriminations and the settlement was achieved peacefully. The A.C.B. and the State cricket associations, which had suffered grievous losses in the two years of W.S.C. were quickly restored to a healthy financial condition. The A.C.B. responded to the players' revolt by dramatically improving match payments and the provident funds for players with long service.

The advent of the rebel W.S.C. outfit forced the establishment to coax Bobby Simpson out of retirement. His novice Test team played an enjoyable series against Bishen Bedi's Indian lineup. Simpson is shown completing a run after dropping his bat.
— Daily Mirror, Sydney.

The brash advertising that characterised World Series Cricket was typified in these enormous posters displayed among cranes and workmen attending to the hideous new light pillars.
— Sydney Daily Telegraph

*Ian Chappell swings the
ball away towards the leg
boundary during a World
Series Cricket match
between Australia and
The Rest. Tony Greig is
the close-in fieldsman,
Allan Knott the 'keeper.
— Martin King.*

Mosman-born former baseball star Allan Border flicks a ball to leg during a limited over match between Australia and the West Indies. He has repeatedly rescued Australia's fortunes under varying conditions all around the world.
— Martin King.

Rodney Hogg, spurned by Victorian selectors had to go to South Australia to earn his chance in big cricket. The Packer rebellion gave him his chance for fame.
— Melbourne Herald.

When the Packer players first began staging matches in opposition to established cricket in 1977–78, the A.C.B. persuaded Bob Simpson to return to first-class cricket at the age of forty-one to captain a completely new Australian team. Simpson's come-back after a ten-year absence ranks as the most amazing in Australian cricket, for he went on to play in ten more Tests. He made 82 and 57 against Bishen Bedi's popular Indian team in the first Test after his return and led Australia to a 16-run victory despite the presence in the team of six players new to Tests. In the next Test he made 176 and took his hundredth Test catch. Altogether twelve Australians made their debut that summer but Simpson still contrived a three-to-one win in the rubber.

Simpson's raw youngsters on tour in the West Indies in 1977–78 succumbed to a barrage of bouncers and lost the first two Tests within three days. Then a dispute between the West Indies Board of Control and their W.S.C. players culminated with the resignation of Clive Lloyd as captain and the withdrawal of W.S.C. players from the Test team. This produced evenly contested matches in which the West Indies were also forced to introduce new youngsters. Trailing one to three in the series after collapsing for 96 in the last innings of the fourth Test, Australia was denied an almost certain win in the fifth Test when spectators rioted. Attempts to coax umpire Ralph Gosein to continue amid a hail of bricks on the scheduled last day failed, and the match was declared a draw.

Back in Australia Simpson asked the A.C.B. for a guarantee that he would be chosen for the first Test against England in 1978–79. The A.C.B. declined to make this guarantee and Simpson retired permanently. The A.C.B. appointed Graham Yallop as Australia's captain. Despite the spectacular success of fast bowler Rodney Hogg, who took a record 41 wickets in Tests that summer against England and Pakistan, Australia lacked character under Yallop. After Australia had lost six of the seven Tests he captained, Yallop was replaced by Kim Hughes, one of the few outstanding players W.S.C. had failed to secure. Brearley's England side had beaten Australia five to one. Hughes, the first Western Australian to captain Australia, took over for the second Test against Pakistan, who had had a resounding triumph over Australia when Sarfraz took 7 for 1 in thirty-three balls in the first Test. Australia won its first match under Hughes but not before two unseemly events had marred play.

Alan Hurst ran out tail-ender Sikander Bakht at the bowler's end without giving him the customary warning for backing up too far. When Australia batted, Sarfraz got even by appealing for 'handled the ball' when Andrew Hilditch picked up the ball and passed it to Sarfraz. Umpire Tony Crafter had no alternative but to allow the appeal. Hilditch who at the time was spoken of as a future Australian captain, has not appeared in Tests since his six Tests in India in 1979-80.

The vulnerability of the Australian team without the W.S.C. stars was clearly demonstrated on the tour of India in 1979. Australia played eleven matches without a win, losing three and leaving eight drawn. Hilditch, Wood, Yardley, Sleep, Higgs, and Hogg all failed to live up to expectations. Tireless Dymock alone among the bowlers, and only Hughes, Border, and Yallop among the batsmen, showed the form required of players in an Australian team. Kapil Dev's 28 wickets helped India clinch the rubber two to nil.

*Bob Willis' bouncer flies over the head of a jumping John Dyson in the First Test at Perth in 1982-83.
— Vivian Jenkins, PBL Marketing.*

Kepler Wessels, who returned to South Africa after the 1985-86 season, claiming the ACB's pay was too low.

Meanwhile W.S.C. played sixteen so-called international matches, six in Australia in 1977–78, four in Australia in 1978–79, as well as one in New Zealand, and five in the West Indies. None of these matches is now recognised as first-class and the performances by the players do not count in the assessment of their first-class averages. This is unfortunate for Marsh, who had fifty-four dismissals in the sixteen matches, for Lillee, who took 79 wickets at 23.91 in the international games, and for batsmen like Greg Chappell whose 1578 runs at 58.44, top score 246 not out, cannot be included in their career figures.

The standard of cricket in W.S.C. matches was extremely high, with the players striving determinedly for big prize money. The players earned their money the hard way when they went on tour in the West Indies. Rioting spectators forced the second four-day international match at Bridgetown, Barbados, to be abandoned as a draw, and the fourth four-day international at Georgetown, Guyana, to be shortened to three days after the abandonment of the first day's play. The Bourda ground at Georgetown was strewn with bottles and debris and the players were beseiged in their dressing-room for more than 2 hours while bottles and pieces of timber crashed into walls and doors.

Cricket lovers approached the first season after the settlement between the A.C.B. and W.S.C. with trepidation, but players who had been ostracised for two summers were welcomed back. Hard-pressed association treasurers began to smile again as big crowds packed into the main venues to watch Mike Brearley's England team and Clive Lloyd's West Indians. Australia, with the W.S.C. players dominating events, outplayed England in all three Tests. None of the English batsmen made more than 200 runs and only two bowlers, Underwood and Botham, took 10 wickets. Ian Chappell returned to Tests after four years to play under his brother's captaincy. Dennis Lillee upset even his staunchest fans in Perth when he tried to bat with an aluminium bat. The West Indies proved an entirely different proposition, supporting brilliant batting with a four-man pace attack (from Holding, Roberts, Garner, and Croft) that won a bouncer-laden three-match series by two Tests to nil.

One of the surprising features of World Series Cricket was the success of promotion of national loyalties. This man waving an Australian flag typifies the warm-hearted, not all that serious attitude Packer matches achieved.
— Ken Piesse, Australian Cricketer.

Geoff ("Henry") Lawson invariably leaps high like this in his delivery stride, flicking his front foot to the right. He has proved a match-winner for Australia in the absence through injury of Lillee and Alderman, an oustanding strike bowler.
— Patrick Eagar Collection.

Graeme Wood pulls a ball to the square leg boundary. His gifts for timing and strokeplay have thrilled Australian fans.
— Martin King.

Bruce Laird played for the World Series Cricket promoters with great pluck and plenty of skill. Since then centuries have eluded him, although he still scores well.
— Sydney Daily Mirror.

The outstanding player World Series Cricket failed to sign was Kim Hughes, shown here just making his ground in a match against England in Sydney.
— Sydney Morning Herald.

Ray Bright shows some confusion as he is dismissed by the big bird, Joel Garner, leg-before-wicket in a World Series match.
— Australian Cricket newspaper.

The successful West Indies' bouncer-prone attack unfortunately set the pattern that was followed by other nations. Slow bowlers virtually disappeared from the game and at all levels Australian cricket was studded with fast bowlers who pitched the ball short of a length and tried to make it bounce up into the batsman's rib-cage. Over-rates fell dramatically because of the long approach runs and tempers frayed as batsmen ducked to avoid the short-pitched deliveries. Helmets, chest pads, thigh pads, and pads to protect forearms became as common as coloured clothing. Tasmania, which had entered the Sheffield Shield competition on a restricted basis in 1977–78, struggled hard for wins but still appealed to mainland experts because their team usually included spinners.

From the time cricket began in Australia, umpires had painstakingly followed the laws of cricket laid down at Lord's. Local laws were tried occasionally but generally discarded after one season. Interpretation of the laws had been left to an outstanding list of men whose umpiring for more than a century has matched the best overseas standards. Bob Crockett, a meticulous, stony-faced man set a record which still exists when he umpired 32 Tests. George Hele, who umpired the difficult bodyline tests, was the son of Andrew and the father of Ray Hele, who brought a record three generations to first-class umpiring. Over the years the strain on umpires has increased because of wider newspaper exposure of their decisions and the television replays. But there remains a strong conviction among old Test players that Australian umpires could have helped the game enormously had they moved to prevent persistent bouncers before this practice became so widely accepted.

Greg Chappell took Australia to Pakistan in 1980 for their first visit in fifteen years. The Australians were critical of the doctored pitches and some claimed they were the victims of cheating by opponents who appealed continuously. Of the three Tests, only the first at Karachi produced a result. The tiny (5 feet 6 inch) left-arm spin bowler Iqbal Qasim bowled Pakistan to victory by taking 7 for 49 in Australia's second innings of 140. Pakistani spinners dominated the series, with Iqbal Qasim as leading wicket-taker (16 wickets at 39.38) and Tauseef Ahmed (12 at 29.66) combining effectively. Lillee bowled long spells on ultra-slow pitches without success and took only 3 wickets in the series.

One of the great catches: former soccer goalie John Dyson leaps high to hold a brilliant outfield catch in the Sydney Test against the West Indies in 1981-82.
— Melbourne Herald.

Terry Alderman winces in pain from his shattered shoulder as team-mate Allan Border comforts him and police lead away a bare-chested man. This incident in the Perth Test between England and Australia in 1982-83 led to tighter security at all Australian grounds.
— West Australian, Perth.

Kimberly John Hughes, the curly-haired Western Australian right-handed batsman who appears to be curbing his erratic habits. Few batsmen have matched his power when in full flight but he has only recently learned to graft when runs are hard to score.
— *Martin King.*

Big-hearted Lennie Pascoe, the Yugoslav-born Sydney pace bowler, lets one go in his halcyon days. Leg injuries have hampered his efforts to regain peak form.
— Martin King.

Three years after the magnificent Centenary Test at Melbourne the M.C.C. staged a match in London to commemorate the first Test in England a hundred years before. This 1980 match was attended by all the surviving England and Australian Test players fit to travel and had all the nostalgia and lavish presentation of the Melbourne venture but was ruined by rain. The match was held at Lord's which provided greater spectator space than was offered by the more historically correct Kennington Oval. Graeme Wood and Kim Hughes produced some spectacular hitting in Australia's first innings of 5 for 385 declared and Hughes repeated the dose in the second innings of 4 for 189 declared. Lillee (4 for 43) and Pascoe (5 for 59) bowled England out for 205 but too much time had been lost to prevent a draw.

An unhappy feature of Australian cricket as it entered the 1980s was the sloppy off-the-field dress of the players and their bad behaviour on the field. Since the days of Ian Chappell, who once turned up for a function in a purple jumpsuit, standards had deteriorated. Thongs and shorts were fashionable and watching the motley array of players lined up for meetings with the Press one could not help but compare them with the neatly attired teams of the early post-Second World War years. On the field 'sledging' was

common and when the offenders were disciplined their fines were ludicrously small.

During his last season in first-class cricket Ian Chappell was suspended twice for abusing an umpire — in Hobart and in Adelaide. At Sydney in the match between South Australia and New South Wales 'sledging' reached a new low point. Chappell at one stage removed a stump and placed it wide on the offside where he alleged New South Wales bowlers like Walters were pitching most deliveries. The umpires ordered him to restore the stump to its proper place. It was later denied by Pascoe but other players said they clearly heard unkind references made to his Yugoslav ancestry.

The following summer India and New Zealand toured Australia and the player's behaviour aroused more discussion than their batting or bowling skills. India under the captaincy of 'Sunny' Gavaskar did a splendid job to share the three-Test series one-all against a full-stength Australian team, but Gavaskar's attempted 'walk-off' in Melbourne attracted all the headlines. Gavaskar was so angry at being given out l.b.w. that he tried to take his opening partner Chauhan with him when he walked off. The Indian manager S.K. Durrani prevented further idiocy by waving Chauhan back to the crease.

Upset by the umpire's decision that brought his dismissal, Indian cricket captain Sunil Gavaskar gave Chetan Chauhan a push to get him to leave the Melbourne ground in protest. The Indian manager waved Chauhan back into the middle. — Melbourne Herald.

Allan Border makes his ground just in time in the First Test against England in 1982-83. The value of grounding the bat properly is evident. — West Australian, Perth.

Rodney Marsh loses his helmet when struck in the face by a West Indian bouncer at Adelaide in the 1981-82 season. — Melbourne Herald.

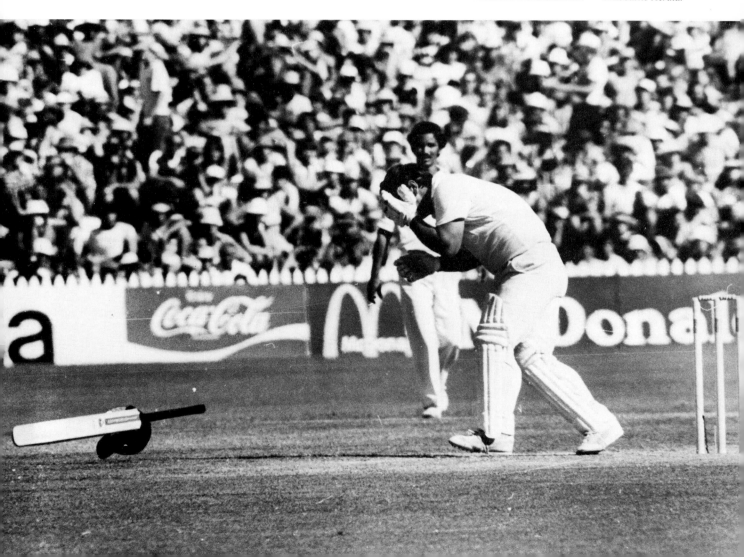

The legendary confrontation in Perth between Pakistan's volatile captain Javed Miandad and Australia's Dennis Lillee, with umpire Tony Crafter bravely stepping between the contestants.
— Vivian Jenkins, PBL Marketing.

The sad end to spectators' invasion of the field at Perth in 1982 during the England-Australia Test, with Terry Alderman being carried from the ground with a dislocated collarbone. Cuffed over the head by a spectator, Alderman gave chase and hit the turf hard as he tried to down the culprit with a Rugby-type tackle. — Vivian Jenkins, PBL Marketing.

The catch that made Geoff Miller a cricket celebrity and ended an epic last wicket bid to win by Australia. The ball bounced off Tavare, Miller spinning round to end Australia's innings three runs short of victory in the Fourth Test at Melbourne, 1982-83.
– Patrick Eagar.

Trevor Chappell, a very useful allround cricketer, misses with an attempted cut. He retired from first-class cricket in 1985-86, ending the Chappell brotherhood's outstanding reign.

Down two Tests to nil, New Zealand suffered an appalling piece of bad luck when the last Australian pair, Walters and Higgs, were batting. The New Zealanders started to leave the field after Higgs edged a ball to their wicket-keeper but the umpire called them back and explained that he had no-balled Lance Cairns, a fairly gentle medium-pace bowler, for excessive use of the bouncer against Higgs. Walters, who was on 77, took his score to 107, adding 42 runs in 69 valuable minutes to take the Australian score to 321. Set to score 193 in 145 minutes, New Zealand reached 2 for 95, but their effort fizzled out when they lost 3 wickets in quick succession. New Zealand finished on 6 for 128 so the runs and time lost when Australia's last-wicket stand unexpectedly resumed proved decisive.

One-day matches in Melbourne in 1980–81 attracted crowds of 52,990, 31,882, 30,590, and 23,601; the numbers in Sydney were 29,171, 28,555, and 27,662, whereas the best audience for a single day at the Tests was 28,671 for the first day of the Australia versus New Zealand match in Melbourne. This trend towards bigger one-day attendances continued in 1981–82 when a world-record 78,142 watched the one-day match between Australia and the West Indies in Melbourne. A week later 52,053, a record attendance for night cricket, saw the West Indies play Australia at Sydney. All these records were surpassed however, in January 1983 when a world-record one-day crowd of 84,153 paid $250,000 to see Australia (5 for 217) beat England (5 for 213).

The biggest sensation in the history of limited-over cricket was watched by 52,990 at the M.C.G. in February 1981, when Greg Chappell instructed his brother Trevor to bowl the last ball of the match underarm, with New Zealand needing 6 to tie and 7 to win. Rodney Marsh was heard shouting, 'Oh, no, skip', when Chappell informed the umpire at the bowler's end of his intention. This incident caused international argument. Australian Cricket Board delegates from some States were so incensed at the poor sportsmanship of the underarm ball that Greg Chappell's Australian captaincy was at risk for a time.

The underarm ball dribbled along the pitch into Australia's cricket history. Next day the laws of one-day matches were altered to prevent a recurrence of such an incident, but that did not stop New Zealand Prime Minister Robert Muldoon from commenting that it was appropriate for the Australians to play in yellow uniforms. Batsman Brian McKechnie, who blocked the underarm ball without attempting to score, said, 'I couldn't believe they would stoop so low'. To former Test cricketers the underarm ball was the predictable climax to a decade of shameful behaviour.

Greg Chappell upset the purists even further by the manner in which he discarded the Australian captaincy and then sought reappointment. He was unavailable for the 1981 Australian tour of England, where Kim Hughes took over the job again for a dramatic rubber. Australia could easily have led three to nil but once Ian Botham gave up the cares of captaincy to concentrate on batting and bowling he virtually beat Australia single-handed. His century at Leeds saved the Ashes for England in just 2 hours. In that time he hit a six and twenty-seven fours, rescuing England from a likely innings defeat, and setting up a miraculous win, with a classic 149 not out. Even then the Australian team had to score only 130 to win but they collapsed for 111. Botham repeated his performance in the fourth Test, taking 5 for 1 with his last twenty-eight balls to have Australia all out for 121, 30 runs short of the required 151. He won his third consecutive man-of-the-match award in the fifth Test by scoring 118 not out, including thirteen fours and six sixes. England won by 103 runs to clinch the series three to one.

West Australian medium-pacer Mick Malone in action during Australia's match at Arundel Castle in April, 1977. This match began a tour ruined from the outset by the WSC defections.
— Ken Kelly.

Queensland's best-ever effort — the six international representatives in 1982-83 (L to R); Back, Jeff Thomson, Carl Rackeman, Kepler Wessels; Front, Greg Ritchie, Allan Border and Greg Chappell.
— Courier Mail, Brisbane.

David Hookes, who provided more thrills for spectators than any other player during the 1982-83 England-Australia rubber. Here he plays a ball off the back foot through the covers.
— Martin King.

Rodney Marsh, who in 1983 appeared certain to set records for Test appearances and wicket-keeping dismissals that may never be broken. His durability in a demanding job is one of the marvels of world cricket.
— Vivian Jenkins, PBL Marketing.

Ian Botham fails with an attempt to run out Jeff Thomson during the Fourth Test at Melbourne in 1982-83. England won this match to take the series to a deciding Fifth Test in Sydney.
— Melbourne Herald.

Ian Gould jubilantly leaps into the arms of David Gower after catching Greg Chappell for two off the bowling of Norman Cowans in the Fourth Test at Melbourne in 1982-83.
— Melbourne Herald.

Before Botham unleashed his amazing display of powerful hitting in the third Test, England was quoted at 500 to 1 by bookmakers at the Leeds ground. Later Lillee and Marsh confessed that they thought these odds so appealing in a two-team contest that they backed England. A.C.B. chairman Phil Ridings commented that he was certain the Lillee and Marsh bets had not affected their whole-hearted performances for Australia, but added that all future Australian teams would be instructed not to bet on their matches.

With millions watching the matches in Australia every summer, money from sponsors and television advertisers poured into the game. Test matches and one-day international games held the nation spellbound, but the great nursery of Australian first-class cricket, the Sheffield Shield competition, was almost completely neglected. Most States lost money in presenting their Shield games and there was urgent debate among administrators about taking Shield games away from the main capital city grounds and staging them on less expensive country or suburban ovals. Most critics remained puzzled at the refusal of Packer's Channel 9 network to give the Shield the promotion it allowed Tests and the 'pyjama games'.

Lillee, seldom out of the headlines for long since he came into big cricket in 1969–70, filled the front pages again at Perth in 1981–82 in an infamous clash with Javed Miandad. In the early sessions of play uncomplimentary remarks could be heard from both sides. When Miandad ran down the pitch to complete his thirtieth run, Lillee stood directly in his path and so Miandad pushed him off balance with his bat. Miandad grounded his bat and turned to find Lillee moving towards him with his fists up. Miandad shaped to swing the bat at Lillee and at that point umpire Tony Crafter moved between them, preventing what appeared certain to be a nasty physical clash. The Australian team sat in judgment that night and decided to fine Lillee $200. The A.C.B. later altered this to a two-match (both one-day fixtures) suspension. Australia won the Perth Test and the next Test in Brisbane to clinch the rubber, leaving Pakistan to gain some solace from winning the third Test by an innings and 82 runs, the biggest win in their history.

The West Indies outplayed Australia for most of the three Tests that summer and overshadowed Pakistan as crowd-pleasers. More than 355,000 people watched the three West Indies-Australia Tests, compared with a total of 90,000 spectators for the matches with Pakistan. The West Indies had one bad day in the rubber and paid heavily for it when their batting failed on the final day of the first Test at Melbourne. One-up after this surprise result, Australia held on grimly for a draw in the second Test at Sydney. They had their chances on the last day of the third Test at Adelaide but superb batting by Gomes, Richards, and Lloyd, and some lusty hitting by Roberts and Garner gave them a convincing win which meant sharing the series.

Lillee set a new Test record by taking 10 wickets in the Melbourne Test against the West Indies. His 7 for 83 in the first innings was his best Test analysis and he followed it with 3 for 44 in the second innings. This took his total of Test victims past West Indian Lance Gibbs' previous world record of 309. By the end of the 1982–83 Australian season Lillee had lifted his total of Test victims to 332 at 23.35 each and his first-class figures to 779 wickets at 22.62.

Greg Chappell, having resumed the Australian captaincy took the team to New Zealand at the end of the 1981–82 season. There he scored a major personal triumph by silencing New Zealand critics of his sportsmanship in the under-arm delivery incident. More than 43,000 people attended Eden Park, Auckland, for the Australians' first match — the biggest-ever crowd in New Zealand for a cricket match — and they all left impressed with the elegance and surety of Chappell's stroke-play. There was laughter as a spectator rolled a lawn bowls ball on to the field to remind Chappell of his misdemeanour in Melbourne, but none of the forecast unpleasantness occurred. The series ended with a win apiece and a draw, Chappell playing the notable innings of the rubber with 176 in the third Test.

Greg Chappell christened Melbourne Cricket Ground's new computer scoreboard with a duck against England in 1982-83. Similar boards are expected to provide big revenue for most major Australian grounds. — Melbourne Herald.

The most successful wicket-keeper Australia has produced, old "Iron Gloves", otherwise Rodney Marsh, leaps sideways for a typical catch during the 1982-83 rubber against England. — West Australian, Perth.

*Steve Smith belts a lofted four off New Zealand's Ewan Chatfield on his way to an impressive 117 in the limited over final at Melbourne in 1982-83. **He jeopardised his future by joining the South African 'rebels' in 1985-86.** — Sun-News Pictorial, Melbourne.*

The frenetic pace of big cricket continued in 1982 and 1983, with Australians playing against as many as four nations in a year, but heavy television promotion ensured that public interest seldom flagged. The 1982–83 Australian summer attracted more than $4 million for international matches and more than a million spectators, figures that did not include ground members. England, the traditional enemy, was beaten three to one in a captivating rubber. Australia was only one hit away from victory in the fourth Test at Melbourne after a brave last-wicket stand by Thomson and Border. Thomson edged a ball to slips where it hit Tavare on the shoulder. Geoff Miller moved behind Tavare and caught the ball as it ricocheted over Tavare's head, and England had won their only Test of the summer by 3 runs. Australia's pace bowlers, allowed to bowl a liberal ration of bouncers, tipped the scales between two moderate sides.

Pressure on umpires increased throughout the summer. Replays of close decisions disclosed several glaring mistakes, none worse than the disallowed run-out appeal against John Dyson before he had scored in the fifth Test. Dyson went on to make 79. Verbal abuse of rival players continued with only a few minor fines for the culprits. The New Zealander Glenn Turner, one of the few batsmen to score a hundred first-class centuries, said that playing in Australia was like spending time in the Vietnam war zone. Turner was the man who said that just having to use the same dressing-room as Ian Chappell was an ordeal.

On the Sydney Hill larrikinism increased to such an extent that parents were afraid to take their children there, preferring seats in the more

Overleaf: Vivian Jenkins marvellous shot of a big moment in Australia's cricket history — the first night cricket match at V.F.L. Park, Melbourne, taken just on sunset with the big lights just starting to illuminate the ground. — P.B.L. Marketing.

Australian fast bowler Geoff Lawson lunges forward after delivering a ball against England at Adelaide in the 1982-83 season, when he proved Australia's No. 1 strike bowler. — Melbourne Herald.

expensive Brewongle stand, a most impressive addition to a most famous ground. At Melbourne a giant electronic scoreboard provided instant replays that enabled players to see just how they had gone wrong as they left the field. At Perth beer-swilling yahoos rushed the field and one of their number struck Terry Alderman on the head. Instinctively, Alderman gave chase and downed the man in a badly executed Rugby tackle that broke Alderman's collarbone and for a time threatened his career.

A tumultuous season that brought to Australian cricket prosperity undreamt of a hundred years ago ended with New South Wales regaining the Sheffield Shield after 16 years in the first ever Shield final. This gave New South Wales their thirty-seventh win since the competition began in 1892–93, compared with twenty-four wins by Victoria, twelve by South Australia, and eight by Western Australia. Queensland and Tasmania (which only joined the Shield competition as a full member in 1982–83) had yet to win the trophy. The New South Wales team was sprinkled with highly talented youngsters like Steve Smith, Greg Matthews, Dirk Welham, Michael Whitney, and Murray Bennett. Their counterparts in other States included Greg Ritchie, Robbie Kerr and Brett Henschell (Queensland), Michael Taylor and Dean Jones (Victoria), David Boon and Stuart Saunders (Tasmania), Wayne Phillips (South Australia), Ken MacLeay and Tom Hogan (Western Australia).

Dirk Wellham led a team of these outstanding youngsters to Zimbabwe early in 1983, a tour on which their gentlemanly conduct shone as brightly as their growing skills. Greg Chappell captained Australia's senior team to Sri-Lanka around the same time, Australia comfortably winning an historic first ever Test between the two nations. Financial inducements for young cricketers were high but the manner in which Australia's district club system kept producing such gifted youngsters remained a tribute to the organisers who over the years have fashioned the Australian system. Even today when you talk to the men who offer themselves without pay to countless committee meetings it is refreshing to learn how determined they are that no talented lads will be overlooked. This applies just as much to kids in the bush and the players who appear every week on concrete wickets such as Sydney's Moore Park and Centenial Park competitions as it does to grade players in big centres. There is no need for Australian cricket to worry about occasional setbacks such as failing to make the 1983 World Cup finals in England.

19. 'When Gimmickry Reigned Supreme'

Greg Matthews' infectious enthusiasm for big cricket is dramatically conveyed in this shot of him celebrating taking a wicket.
— *Sunday Times, Perth.*

When the Australian Cricket Board negotiated the settlement with Kerry Packer's cricketers in May 1979 the anger most cricket-lovers felt towards the rebels lingered on. Old-timers believed that the P.B.L. players had betrayed the game and spoke of them as traitors. Despite the efforts of thoughtful cricketers like Mike Brearley, who urged the acceptance of Packer and his players into the body of cricket, that anger still smouldered five years after the settlement.

This was partly the fault of the players who refused to show their gratitude for higher pay by behaving more acceptably on and off the field. When Dennis Lillee was found guilty of using abusive language towards spectators in the Western Australia versus South Australia match at Adelaide in February 1983, his suspended fine of $600 appeared hopelessly inadequate. Indeed the leniency of the Players' Tribunal towards its fellows made a mockery of that body.

The other cause of continuing public disquiet over the settlement with Packer was the failure of his company, P.B.L. Marketing, to promote the traditional stronghold of the Australian game, the Sheffield Shield. P.B.L. was a profit-making company and claimed that the Sheffield Shield was simply not a money-making competition. This insistence on profits at all costs, coupled with the unashamed lack of taste in marketing cricket on television, made many keen observers wonder what was in the settlement contract that prevented the A.C.B. from moving in and asking for changes.

The P.B.L. film that promoted the 1982–83 series between England in Australia, in the words of *Wisden*'s editor John Woodcock, 'caricatured in a gratuitously offensive and quite erroneous way, the English view of Australia's chances'. The Englishmen were clearly annoyed at this attempt to market cricket like a soap powder but the A.C.B. seemed powerless, or unwilling, to make changes.

A.C.B. treasurer Ray Steele was, with Bob Parish — long-serving member, and former president, of the A.C.B. — the chief negotiator in the settlement with Packer. Steele upset the 1979 English team in Melbourne by a speech of welcome in which he said that only minor concessions had been made to Packer. Geoffrey Boycott, in his book *Opening Up*, summarised the English attitude in these words:

> If Steele calls giving Kerry Packer exclusive television rights for 10 years a minor concession I wonder what the hell we were supposed to be arguing about for two years? If it was minor why did world cricket become involved in £200,000 worth of litigation?

Steele promised a bonanza, said Boycott, but at the end of the tour the seventeen English county clubs received only about £30,000 to share between them. Each county's share, £1,765, was not even enough to pay a season's salary for one player.

The best thing about the Packer settlement appeared to be that it had restored the flow of cash from the A.C.B. to the State associations, which in turn were able to distribute funds once again to the district clubs. By the mid-1980s the annual cost of running a district club was at least $20,000, and treasurers around Australia breathed more easily as the cheques came in. The A.C.B. initiated a 'Kanga Cricket' coaching programme in 8,000 Australian primary schools, and funded competitions and tours for the under-sixteen and under-nineteen age groups. The A.C.B. boasted that it had more than 10,000 qualified coaches throughout Australia, and spoke of players like Craig McDermott, Wayne Phillips, Greg Ritchie, Greg Matthews, David Gilbert, Robbie Kerr, and Steve Waugh who were products of the State teenage competitions and the Esso scholarships to England. Those who believed that coaches could restore Australia to the top of world cricket foresaw a rosy future, but plenty of sceptics — Bill O'Reilly among them — claimed that the coaching emphasis was misplaced.

The insistence of Channel 9 cameramen on highlighting controversial events placed intense pressure on umpires, who saw their mistakes repeated from a variety of angles in dozens of replays. This became even more intolerable with the erection in Sydney and Melbourne of electronic scoreboards, whose operators were allowed to replay umpires' mistakes for the benefit of spectators. No less an authority than Sir Donald Bradman suggested that the time had probably come for match umpires to have the help of a third official, off the field, who could convey the evidence of television replays to the men in the middle.

P.B.L. Marketing's claim that Sheffield Shield cricket was not a marketable operation was puzzling in the light of exciting Shield events. In 1981–82 South Australia, having scored only 6 points from their first four matches, won the Shield for the first time since 1975–76 with a thrilling final game. In 1982–83, when a final was played for the first time, New South Wales won the Shield despite an outright defeat by Tasmania, which was playing as a full member of the competition for the first time. There were emotional scenes galore as McCosker, in his last first-class match, led New South Wales to victory. In the following season, 1983–84, Queensland appeared likely to win their first-ever Shield competition when they led by 68 runs on the fourth morning. They were then bundled out for 154 by Western Australia, set 223 for victory. With Thomson in full flight, Western Australia were 5 for 138 before a riveting stand by veterans Laird and Marsh took them to victory and their ninth Shield.

Queensland's disappointment, strangely enough, could be blamed partly on the high number of no-balls bowled by their pace men, Harry Frei, Jeff Thomson, and Craig McDermott. Thomson alone bowled 29 no-balls. Geoff Marsh rescued Western Australia's first innings by batting for 4 hours to score 107 before he was bowled by what his partner, Rodney Marsh, insisted was a no-ball from Thomson. Marsh remonstrated so forcibly with the umpire for again not calling Thomson that he was

Ray Steele, one of the men who negotiated Australian cricket's most important contract, the contents of which remains secret. — The Age, Melbourne.

Right: Western Australian Tim Zoehrer, who in the 1985-86 season took over as Australia's Test wicket-keeper and proved a competent batsman, as this pull shot for four demonstrates. — Sunday Times, Perth.

Far left: The M.C.G.
during the third Test
between Australia and
the West Indies in 1975
showing the crowd which
paid a record $129,775.
Left: The captains of the
1985 World Cup teams in
Australia (L to R); David
Gower (England), Javed
Miandad (Pakistan), Clive
Lloyd (West Indies), Allan
Border (Australia), Sunil
Gavaskar (India), Geoff
Howarth (New Zealand)
and Duleep Mendis
(Sri Lanka).
Above right: India's
captain Kapil Dev just
fails with a dive to catch
Australia's David Gilbert
in the 1986 Test in Sydney.
Above left: Gilbert holds a
brilliant catch off his own
bowling in the 1986 Test
against India in Sydney.
— News Limited.

reported for 'showing dissent by throwing the bat'. The Players' Tribunal confirmed its weakness by simply announcing that Marsh had received a severe reprimand.

Marsh had announced his retirement from Test cricket a few weeks earlier at the fifth Test against Pakistan in Sydney, the Test which also marked the retirement of his team-mates Gregory Stephen Chappell and Dennis Keith Lillee. For more than thirteen-and-a-half seasons this trio had provided Australian cricket fans with a hatful of records and some spectacular entertainment. At the close of the second day's play Chappell announced that this would be his last Test. Later the same evening Lillee said that this would be his last test as well. At the end of the match Marsh followed their example but said that he would finish the season with Western Australia.

Lillee — who, like Chappell, had begun his Test career in 1970–71 — had played in seventy Tests and had taken 355 Test wickets, more than any bowler in the game's history and 30 more than Bob Willis, next best with 325. Chappell, in his final innings for Australia, scored 182 in 526 minutes and hit seventeen fours. During this innings he surpassed Don Bradman's aggregate of 6,996 runs and became Australia's highest Test run-getter.

Chappell had played in eighty-eight Tests, and captained Australia in forty-eight of those for twenty-one wins, fourteen draws, and thirteen losses, a record which established him as one of Australia's finest captains. He took over the captaincy from his brother Ian and probably ranks behind only Ian, Richie Benaud, and Bradman among our Test leaders. He stood, all style and elegance, like a cricket god, dismissing the ball from his presence. Don Bradman said, after Greg had extended the Australian Test record to 7,110 runs: 'His runs were made with aesthetic and imperious quality few others can emulate'.

Chappell's on-driving reached a standard that has been matched by few and surpassed by none. Turning the ball off his toes through mid-wicket, he was a model of footwork and timing. His off-driving was often brilliant, and he could cut excitingly in front and behind point. His running between wickets was superb, as was his farming of the strike according to the needs of a match. An analysis of his Test innings shows that he was out caught eighty-three times, clean bowled twenty times, leg-before-wicket sixteen times, run out five times, caught and bowled four times, and stumped only four times. In 151 Test innings, he was undefeated nineteen times. His highest Test score was 247 not out against New Zealand. He finished with a Test

Jubilant New South Wales players after the State's 39th Sheffield Shield win in the 1985-86 final at the S.C.G. It was NSW's second successive victory over Queensland who, like Tasmania, have yet to win the Shield.
— PBL Marketing.

average of 53.86 (compared with Bradman's 99.94), having hit thirty-one fifties and twenty-four centuries.

Chappell took his 121st catch in his last test, thus surpassing Colin Cowdrey's Test record of 120. Many of those catches were in the slips off Lillee's bowling. The catching record alone does not reveal the all-round excellence of Chappell's fielding: he had a superb throwing arm and could field with equal brilliance in any position on the field. His bowling, like his batting and fielding, was full of astuteness and planning. He could swing the ball either way, he varied his pace shrewdly, and he seldom gave hitters anything loose. He finished with 47 Test wickets at 40.70, with his best figures 5 for 61 against Pakistan at Sydney in 1972–73. His figures in all first-class cricket were more impressive — he took 290 at 29.76 and five times had 5 or more wickets in an innings. These figures do not include his remarkable achievements in the two years of World Series Cricket.

Greg was Australia's leading batsman during the two years of W.S.C. He scored 1,578 runs in fifteen matches, at an average of 58.44, on some very rough tracks and against some extremely quick bowlers. When he declared the Australian innings closed at 6 for 538 at V.F.L. Park he was 246 not out — 1 run short of his best score in big cricket. Palsy, caused by a virus in his ear, paralysed his right eyelid for a time, but he recovered and was able to join the W.S.C. tour of West Indies, in which he scored 90 at Bridgetown, 150 at Port of Spain, 113 at Georgetown, and 104 and 85 in Antigua — an astounding achievement considering the conditions and the best scoring sequence of his career. It is a feat that should be remembered when Chappell's seven ducks in the 1981–82 Australian season are mentioned.

The Chappell brothers had been at the centre of the Packer rebellion and there is little doubt that W.S.C. would have worked much less successfully without their support. The late Ray Robinson disclosed in his book *On Top Down Under* that Greg Chappell was the last Australian to sign with Packer. Greg was dismayed during the 1977 tour of England when the news broke that the W.S.C. had been set up. The revelation during the thrilling Centenary Test in Melbourne that many of his players had W.S.C. contracts in their bags undoubtedly harmed his public image. It was in this match that Greg earned applause for calling Derek Randall back after he had been given out on 161. Randall had not heard Marsh shout that it was not a catch.

'WSC was foreign to all I had known about cricket,' Greg Chappell told Robinson. 'I

understand how people were shocked because that's how I felt at first. For people to whom cricket was almost a religion we were heretics.' Robinson said that two factors had swayed Greg — the standover attitude of the A.C.B. and the need to justify the time he gave to cricket in securing his future. Pressures brought about by long absences on tour had caused his brother Ian's marriage to fail and cricket commitments had been responsible for rough patches in his own marriage to the former Judy Donaldson.

I have always felt that Greg Chappell's reputation suffered unfairly because of the larrikin antics of his brother Ian. Close scrutiny of Greg's behaviour in the first-class arena reveals only one incident for which he could be criticised — the notorious underarm ball affair. This came at the end of a hot, exhausting day in Melbourne in which he had, in his own words 'played his guts out'. Ian's record was altogether different, studded with suspensions, clashes with officials, bad language, and rude hand-signals.

Marsh's contribution was probably more remarkable than that of either Lillee or Chappell, as he lacked their natural talent. When he made his Test debut in the 1970–71 season old-timers scoffed at his display and called him 'Iron Gloves'. Through sheer hard work and determination he held the job for ninety-six Tests and made a world record 355 dismissals, ninety-five of them off Lillee's bowling. His pugnacious left-hand batting made him the first Australian wicket-keeper to score a Test century and gave him a career total of 3,633 Test runs at 26.51. No other batsman could bring a crowd to its feet as Marsh did when he swatted a ball out of the park.

Marsh had to keep to some of the deadliest pace bowlers in the history of cricket and there were only twelve stumpings in his Test record. He took Jeff Thomson, Dennis Lillee, Len Pascoe, Max Walker, and Carl Rackemann at their fastest but, apart from his two years with World Series Cricket, played all his Tests consecutively. The first time he missed a game through injury was in Melbourne, in the 1983–84 season against the West Indies. Throughout his long career he shrugged off regular knee trouble and thrilled spectators with his headlong dives to pull in catches that flew from the edges. He stamped himself as a remarkably acrobatic cricketer and one of the game's greatest crowd-pleasers.

Predictably, London newspapers were far less charitable than their Australian counterparts over the retirement of the great trio. *The Observer* said they had shown a meanness of spirit, a poverty of sportsmanship, and a surfeit of spite that the game had done well to withstand: 'Had their attitudes prospered among their Test opponents, there is no telling what example cricket would now be setting'. The critics who had praised Freddie Trueman's posturing and invective as colourful stuff judged these qualities in Lillee to be meanness of spirit.

Most critics agreed that Australia would take some time to recover from the loss of three such great players as Chappell, Lillee, and Marsh. And so it proved to be. For the one-day series immediately following their departure, Australia

One of the most controversial dismissals in recent Test cricket, with Australia's Wayne Phillips given out, caught by England's captain David Gower. Phillips hit the ball hard into the calf muscle of Allan Lamb and the ball lobbed up in the air for Gower to take the catch. Umpire Constant had no hesitation in ruling that the ball had not hit the turf.
— Ken Kelly.

Above: Towering Western Australian left-arm pace bowler Bruce Reid, who consolidated his place in the Australian team with some fine displays in the 1985-86 season.
— Sunday Times, Perth.

Right: A fine study of Mark Waugh, one of the gifted Sydney family, batting for New South Wales against Victoria in 1985-86.
— News Limited.

tried a number of young players — for example, David Boon, Greg Ritchie, and Simon O'Donnell — who were obviously going to need time to develop into top-class Test cricketers.

The West Indies' eighteen-match tour of Australia in 1983-84 did not include a single first-class match — a typical example of P.B.L. Marketing's approach to programming. There was considerable bitterness among the West Indian players after they had won the first of the finals and tied the second against Australia. The West Indians believed that this should have secured the World Series Cup for them, and that a third match was unnecessary. They ultimately played, and won, the third match in Melbourne with only four specialist batsmen in their side. Captain Clive Lloyd did not attend the presentation and Vivian Richards accepted the Cup and the winning cheque without grace.

The trouble stemmed from conflicting views on the tour conditions after the tie in the second final. The West Indian manager, Wes Hall, said that in the event of a tied series, the team with most wins in the preliminary matches should be declared the winners. The West Indies had by far the best record in the preliminary matches against Pakistan and Australia. After a long, six-Test tour the West Indies did not take kindly to being deprived of a rest, and only reluctantly appeared in Melbourne. Justice was done when the West Indies won by 26 runs but P.B.L. and the A.C.B. had another one-day coup when a world-record crowd for limited-overs cricket, 86,133, turned out.

Despite the record crowd critics of one-day cricket continued their attacks, blaming the failure of young Australians to make the jump from their State teams to the Australian side on the bad habits they learnt in one-day matches. Bill O'Reilly, the great leg-spin bowler and a respected critic for more than forty years, was particularly vehement in his condemnation of programmers who provided such a surfeit of one-day matches. He showed his contempt for them by staying away. Even on the days of large attendances the members' stands, where the old-timers congregate, were seldom even half-full.

Australian cricket had changed under P.B.L. Marketing, and many of the changes were regretted by lovers of the game. The cacophony of pop music at the luncheon and tea breaks irritated members who could barely make themselves heard when they tried to discuss events. Sydney Cricket Ground, with its grotesque light stands, electronic scoreboard, and new stands, had become an architectural obscenity.

Above: Greg Dyer batting for New South Wales in the tense 1985-86 Sheffield Shield final against Queensland. Ray Phillips, Queensland's 'keeper, is a model of concentration, as is Kepler Wessels in slips. — News Limited.

On the field there were worrying signs that the West Indies' obsession with pace bowling, much of it vicious and directed at the batsman's body, was also changing the tactics of big cricket. Helmets, once an oddity, had become an absolute necessity in the face of a West Indian attack that included up to five fast bowlers. When they were held up by dour stands from tail-end batsmen, the West Indians had no hesitation in bowling at a batsman's head and rib-cage. Much though one admired the athleticism of the West Indian fieldsmen and the brilliance of their bowling and fielding as they went round Australia in 1983–84 — winning ten of their World Series Cup matches, losing two, and tying one — it was difficult to condone bowlers of the pace of Michael Holding, Malcolm Marshall, Wayne

Daniel, Winston Davies, and Eldine Baptiste, bowling three bouncers an over. They were good enough to be able to do without the injured Joel Garner in all bar the finals, but they did nothing for the spirit of cricket.

The Laws of Cricket clearly set down that 'the relative skill of the striker' should be taken into account by umpires faced with deciding if bouncers are frequent enough to amount to intimidatory bowling. The failure of Australian umpires to call bowlers like Marshall when they bowled bouncers at Australian tail-enders suggests that the umpires rated our batsmen far more highly than their averages indicated.

Not only is the regular delivery of three bouncers

an over contrary to the sportsmanship which has made cricket famous, but it also produces dull cricket. Fast bowlers taking approach runs that start out near the sight screens cannot possibly achieve crowd-pleasing over-rates. Richie Benaud, a shining light in a period of abysmal cricket commentary, was quite right to condemn the West Indians when they produced only 15 overs an hour. It was a pity that Clive Lloyd and Wes Hall did not take notice of this criticism and lift their team's over-rate.

Hopes that the disappearance of Ian Chappell, Dennis Lillee, and, to a lesser extent, Rodney Marsh, from the first-class arena might bring a return to disciplined on-the-field behaviour during big matches were soon dashed. Signalling the

Above: The notorious aluminium bat incident in Perth during England's 1983-84 Australian tour. Lillee hurled the bat away in disgust when the umpires agreed with fieldsmen's objections, leaving the offending bat on the turf until his captain Greg Chappell persuaded him to resume with a normal bat. — News Limited.

An historic moment as the lights go on for the first time at the Melbourne Cricket Ground during the 1984-85 V.C.A. Centenary celebrations.
— News Limited.

Peter Clifford, one of the heroes of New South Wales' 1984-85 Sheffield Shield win. His last wicket partnership with Dave Gilbert won a wonderful final, sadly neglected by Channel 9 cameras.
— News Limited.

direction of the dressing-room to dismissed batsmen, petulance when appeals were rejected, and open abuse of umpires continued. The mystery of why players fighting for places in the Australian team should indulge in such childish behaviour was matched only by the refusal of many of them to get fully fit. Quite a few of the youngsters who were considered possible Test material had bulging waistlines and fielded carelessly, a sloppiness they compounded by appearing untidily dressed in public. The 1984 *Wisden* summed it up as follows:

> Fired by chauvinism, and the exaggerated gestures of some of the Australian players, as well as the frantic nature of much of the cricket, the atmosphere seemed at times more like that of the Colosseum than a cricket ground. There were days when gimmickry reigned supreme, a development which not only the most conservative watchers viewed with some anxiety.

20. A Game Without Loyalty

The Packer revolt emphatically demonstrated to the Australian Cricket Board the need to improve the welfare of Australia's leading players. From the time of the 1979 settlement, the Board worked with new-found zeal to improve conditions for Test players. It is ironic that some critics considered the Board made too many concessions. The efforts to free players from the money worries which had been at the hub of the Packer rebellion culminated in 1984 when the Board introduced a system of two-year contracts for players. These contracts provided substantial new benefits for seventeen players nominated by the national selectors.

The Board must have believed that it could thus proceed with a programme in which the Australian team played full-time from September 1984 until April 1986 without any further bickering over players' rewards. For it was inherent in signing the contracts that the players should show the Board loyalty and concentrate on lifting their performances. The way had been cleared for the Australian team to bring in better results. Before the 1984–85 season was over the Board's hopes had again been frustrated by another players' revolt.

Kim Hughes was appointed captain and Allan Border vice-captain at the start of the season. In September and October the Australians toured India to celebrate the fiftieth anniversary of the Ranji Trophy. The Australian team showed they meant business when they assembled in Canberra for six days' rigorous physical training before they began the tour. Fitted out with uniforms designed by the Australian Wool Board's couturiers, and

Left: Wayne Phillips, South Australian left-handed batsman and wicket-keeper, who became the fourteenth Australian to score a century in his first Test match when he hit an impressive 159 against Pakistan at Perth in 1983-84.

accompanied by a doctor to protect them against everything from finger sprains to tummy wogs, the team won four of their six matches in India and had draws in the other two — all were one-day affairs.

With confidence boosted, the team began the 1984–85 series against the West Indies at Perth in fine style. Early in the match the West Indies were 5 for 104, but dropped catches enabled them to go on to an easy win. Australia gave another poor performance in the second Test at Brisbane, but the West Indies' convincing win was completely overshadowed by Kim Hughes' dramatic announcement at the end of play that he had resigned the Australian captaincy. At a packed media conference Hughes started to read the following statement:

> The Australian captaincy is something that I've held very dear to me. However, playing the game with total enjoyment has always been of the utmost importance. The constant speculation, criticism and innuendo by former players and sections of the media over the past four or five years have finally taken their toll. It is in the interest of the team, Australian cricket, and myself that I have informed the A.C.B. of my decision to stand down as Australian captain.

Hughes broke down and left the conference in tears. The final part of his statement was read for him by team manager Bob Merriman. Even Hughes' strongest critics were saddened by his decision to give up the biggest role in Australian sport in such a way. Many hoped that, once free of the worries of captaincy, he would return to the form which a season or two earlier had made him one of the world's best batsmen. But as the season advanced his efforts showed him to be a pathetic replica of the batsman who had delighted spectators from Perth to Lord's and made some of post-war cricket's biggest hits.

Hughes was given every chance to regain his form but the trauma of resigning the captaincy, and the pain he must have felt at comments such as Alan McGilvray's that he was 'a boy who had not grown up', affected him badly. The A.C.B. stressed that Hughes had served Australian cricket loyally throughout his career and as captain in twenty-eight matches, in which he led Australia to four wins, eleven draws, and thirteen losses. When the selectors picked the team for England at the end of 1984–85, there was widespread conviction that Hughes would benefit from a rest. His form simply did not justify his inclusion.

Allan Border took over the Australian captaincy for the hundredth Test on Adelaide Oval, a joyous

Far Left: David Boon at the start of his career as an opening batsman, plays a typically powerful drive against New Zealand. — Sunday Times, Perth.
Left: Allan Border shows his elation as he reaches his century in the fourth Test at Old Trafford in 1985. — Patrick Eagar.

Above: Kim Hughes leaves the 1984 Brisbane press conference in tears after announcing his retirement as Australia's captain, leaving team manager Bob Merriman to finish reading his statement.
— Jack Pollard Collection.

Far Right: Queenslander Robbie Kerr, a splendid stroke player when in form who has found a Test berth hard to win.
— Courier-Mail, Brisbane.

Right: Kepler Wessels is run out as he just fails to beat a smart return from David Gower in the second Test at Lords in 1985.
– Patrick Eagar.

occasion to which the South Australian Cricket Association invited former Test captains from all the cricket nations. The captains, most of them looking extremely trim for their mature age, paraded around Adelaide Oval in vintage cars, Don Bradman in a wide-brimmed hat to protect him from the sun, Bishen Bedi in a colourful turban.

From the start, Border showed himself a captain of much greater character than Hughes, a cricketer who blamed failures on himself rather than on others. He began, amid the Centenary celebrations in Adelaide, with a loss which gave the West Indies the series, but held them to a draw in the fourth Test in Melbourne, ending their run of eleven successive Test wins. In the fifth Test in Sydney, Australia won by an innings and 55 runs, with the West Indies showing signs of panic against the spin of Bob Holland and Murray Bennett. This was a fine achievement by the Australians. It was the West Indies' first defeat in twenty-eight Tests and their first loss by an innings since 1968–69 when the team led by Bill Lawry had defeated a team captained by Gary Sobers by an innings and 30 runs, after Lawry and Ian Chapell had added 298 for the second wicket in Australia's 510.

Mixed with the elation over a celebrated Australian win there was regret that Clive Lloyd's great career had ended with a defeat. In a career of 110 Tests, seventy-four as captain, Lloyd had seen the West Indies develop from a side prone to collapse under pressure to a calm, craftsmanlike outfit. He was a captain of rare tactical acumen, showing the way with magnificent fielding and catching, hitting powerfully with a very heavy bat, coaxing the best from his bowlers.

Above: Prime Minister Bob Hawke has his glasses shattered as he misses an attempt to hook a short ball from a Press team bowler in Canberra. Below: The Press XI fieldsmen administer first aid as they try to ensure that Hawke's sight was not affected.
— *News Limited.*

At their best the West Indies under Lloyd reached a standard that could be challenged by few Australian teams, and Border's side did well to hold them to a three-to-one win. Of past Australian teams, only four had the balance and all-round skills that would have made them a match for the West Indies: the side which toured England in 1884 under Billy Murdoch; the 1905 team to England led by Joe Darling; the 1921 team captained by Warwick Armstrong; and Bradman's unbeaten 1948 side. In 102 years of Test cricket the record suggested that no other Australian team would have come near them.

The West Indian team led by Lloyd were seldom subjected to top-class spin and on their 1984–85 displays at Sydney they would have been sorely troubled by O'Reilly and Grimmett working in tandem. The West Indies played quality medium-pace and fast bowling with consummate ease, and their fielding was of the highest calibre. The one niggling criticism that could be made of them was their sustained use of bouncers through bowlers using long approach-runs. Yet, good as this team

were, they did not attract capacity houses to the Tests; in fact, they drove people away with their tedious over-rates. The editor of *Wisden* chastised Malcolm Marshall for bowling bouncers at Pat Pocock in England. The same criticism could have been directed at all the West Indies pace men in Australia.

With Lawson and newcomer Craig McDermott also bowling off unnecessarily long approaches, a series that should have been thrilling had long, yawnful periods. Australia averaged only 79.2 overs per day, the West Indies 74.4. As a result the A.C.B. decided to alter future tour conditions to guarantee a minimum number of overs in a day, a move which had the support of all the cricket nations but which came too late to influence Lloyd's captaincy.

Sri Lanka toured Australia for an international series for the first time in 1984–85. They competed with Australia and the West Indies for the World Series Cup, and after Christmas they appeared in the World Championship Cup in Melbourne. They

Paul Hogan bowling in a charity match at Sydney's Drummoyne Oval. One of the umpires is Barry Humphries. Batsman at the bowler's end is Bruce Francis, manager of the 1985-86 rebel tour to South Africa.
— Jack Pollard Collection.

failed to extend the West Indies but their win over Australia proved them to be a rising force in world cricket, although in need of a match-winning bowler. Duleep Mendis, Sidath Wettimuny, and Ravindran Ratnayeke were players of world class, as was later underlined by Sri Lanka's Test win over a full-strength England team in Colombo.

Melbourne had suffered months of acrimony as trade union action threatened to prevent the installation of the lights for the World Championship matches at the M.C.G. All this was forgotten on 17 February 1985 when the lights were switched on at sundown for the first World Cup match outside England. A crowd of 82,494 attended this historic event between traditional rivals England and Australia. The lights had cost $4 million and proved considerably less offensive than the horrors in Sydney. When the lights came on Australia was chasing England's 8 for 214. To the delight of a noisy crowd, Australian youngsters Robbie Kerr, 87 not out, and Dean Jones, 78 not out, produced a swashbuckling stand, sparkling with fine shots and brilliant running, which carried

Two fine shots of gifted Queensland batsman Greg Ritchie: Left, Ritchie punches a short ball past mid-off; Above, he moves well down the pitch to drive. Few batsmen time the ball as well as Ritchie. — Martin King.

Australia to 3 for 215 and a 7-wicket win.

After this great start Australia lost to Pakistan by 62 runs and to India by 8 wickets, and missed getting a place in the semifinals. The West Indies, hot favourites, lost to Pakistan in the semifinal at the M.C.G. India qualified for the other spot in the final by defeating New Zealand in Sydney. India were a big surprise, having been defeated by England at home on the eve of their departure for

Australia. They repeated their 1983 World Cup victory in England by taking the final with accomplished cricket, a fitting reward for Sunil Gavaskar, who was captaining India for the last time. Ravi Shastri, a superb all-rounder, received a car for winning the Player of the Series Award.

New South Wales won the Sheffield Shield for the second time in three years in a final that was a great pleasure to watch after the eminently forgettable cricket of the two one-day competitions. Ignored yet again by the Channel 9 organisation (P.B.L. Marketing's TV compatriot), the Shield produced one of the finest cricket matches in Australian history, with a struggle that grew more intense during each of the four days.

Queensland, as leaders of the competition, appeared set for a final in Brisbane — a venue that would have favoured them in their quest for their first Shield win. But in the last round New South Wales, aided by a Dave Gilbert hat-trick, beat Victoria by 25 runs. South Australia then surprisingly defeated Queensland in Adelaide, and set the stage for a Sydney final.

Border won the toss but when his promising openers Andrew Courtice and Robbie Kerr went through the gate to start Queensland's innings they must have regretted his luck with the toss. For the demolition contractor chose that moment to send the roof of the old Sheridan stand toppling into a pile of rubble and dust. The openers were unable to recover their poise and both were out with the score at 19. Imran Khan and Gilbert bowled tenaciously for New South Wales but Border's 64, Glenn Trimble's 38, Trevor Hohns' 103, and a waspish 58 from Ray Phillips enabled Queensland to reach 374.

New South Wales replied with 318 in a fine example of gutsy team batting, with each player fighting hard. Steve Smith top scored with 76 but Steve Waugh's 71 was more impressive. Queensland collapsed to the bowling of Imran and Bennett in the second innings, in which Imran added 5 for 34 to his first innings' haul of 4 for 66. This set New South Wales 218 to score for victory, but at 3 for 64, with a day to play, it was anybody's match. All through that memorable last day the tension mounted. Telecom received more than 100,000 calls for the score and the voices of radio newsmen quavered in excitement as they relayed the scores to the news bulletins. Wickets fell at 76, 100, 140, 173, 175, and the ninth at 209, leaving last man Dave Gilbert with anchorman Peter Clifford to score the 21 runs needed to win.

Jeff Thomson and Carl Rackemann bowled their hearts out. Clifford fended one off with his head and took another on the body. Gilbert called him down for a conference and said: 'Don't stuff it up by getting out — I've waited all season for this'. Gilbert had batted in twelve matches for 96 runs at 48.00, with thirteen not outs. Now he scraped together 4 more, with Clifford defiant at the other end. With the scores level, Queensland could still have earned a tie by taking a wicket, but Gilbert gave New South Wales the Shield for the thirty-

Above: Cricket buff Chris Harte, left, places a wreath on the grave of Australian Test star Jack Ferris during the rebels 1985-86 South African tour. Ferris, who took 813 first-class wickets at 17.33, died in Durban in 1900. — Chris Harte.

eighth time by putting Rackemann away for 4. Rackemann came off in tears but the impression that he was a cream-puff bowler who folded under pressure had gone forever. Even on the last day of this epic game of cricket, Kerry Packer's cameras were missing; but it didn't matter to the New South Wales players as the champagne corks popped. Clifford had made 83 not out and had as many bruises to show for his efforts.

In March 1985 Australia sent a team to Sharjah, in the United Arab Emirates for a four-nation tournament on the Sharjah Cricket Ground, which had been built by the Arab businessman and cricket-lover Abdul Rahman Bukhatir. All four matches were sold out. Australia won its first match against England with a last-ball single, while India accounted for Pakistan in the other match. In the final, India had little trouble passing the Australian score of 139, thus maintaining its position as the world's number-one nation at one-day cricket.

The following month news was leaked that a number of players who were contracted to the A.C.B. intended to join a rebel tour of South Africa in the summer of 1985-86. The Board realised

immediately that it was powerless to take action against the non-contracted players – Terry Alderman, Trevor Hohns, Rod McCurdy, Steve Rixon, Greg Shipperd, and Michael Taylor — who planned to join the South African tour. But the Board resolved quickly that it would take legal action against any contracted player who sought to breach his contract by going to South Africa, and against any party who was guilty of inducing players to break their contracts.

The Australian team originally chosen to tour England was: Allan Border, Andrew Hilditch, Murray Bennett, Wayne Phillips, Dirk Wellham, Graeme Wood, Terry Alderman, Rod McCurdy, Steve Rixon, Greg Matthews, Robert Holland, Greg Ritchie, Kepler Wessels, Geoff Lawson, David Boon, Craig McDermott, and Simon O'Donnell. But once the signatories of contracts for the South Africa tour became known this team was never assembled and the script for the next few weeks was vintage Gilbert and Sullivan.

Australian Cricket Board chairman Fred Bennett initially denied knowledge of the South African tour. In Johannesburg South African Cricket Union secretary Joe Parmensky and consultant Dr Ali Bacher, a former Test captain, also denied there would be a tour. 'It is not the first time rumours of a tour have surfaced, but they are not true,' said Dr Bacher. The intention had been to wait until the Australian team was in England and then to leak news of the tour, but dressing-

Above: A section of the colourful S.C.G. crowd during one of the 1985-86 limited over matches, universally known now as 'pyjama games'.
— Martin King.

Left: Greg Matthews dates his success from the time he started to 'hustle', and became a non-stop, all-action cricketer whether batting, bowling or encouraging team-mates like this.
— Martin King.

Opposite Page: Dirk Wellham, tactically the best captain in Australia in 1985-86 but unable to make the most of chances to clinch a permanent Test spot. In form, he is a fine strokemaker.
— PBL Marketing.

room gossip around Australia's major cricket grounds anticipated this plan. Confirmation came when the wife of one of the signed players talked about the South African tour.

Prime Min ster Bob Hawke, whose spectacles had been smashed when an attempted hook shot deflected on to his face when he was playing in a charity match, did not fare any better in trying to dissuade yet another lot of rebel players from touring South Africa. His Minister for Sport, John Brown, called on the A.C.B. to take punitive action against any player who went to South Africa. Bruce Francis, the former Australian opening batsman who had acted as liaison officer for the South African Cricket Union, described Brown's statement as 'the most obnoxious request ever put by an Australian government to a sports organisation'.

All over Australia cricket writers were telephoning virtually every player who could hold a bat to check who was in the team for South Africa. They quickly confirmed the names of all the players who had signed for the tour. Meanwhile public opinion polls were being taken on the morality of touring a country where policemen regularly beat up blacks, where even schoolchildren were imprisoned without being charged, and where segregation of whites and blacks was the way of life.

Surprisingly, the polls showed that most Australians supported the South African tourists.

The chief executive of the Australian Cricket Board announced that all players who toured England would have to sign a statutory declaration guaranteeing that they would not tour South Africa. Media magnate Kerry Packer gave the Board some help by persuading the three best players signed for South Africa — Graeme Wood, Dirk Wellham, and Wayne Phillips — to change their minds. The terms of Packer's deal with these players remained secret but Wellham later emerged as advertising manager of Packer's P.B.L. company in Sydney. It was a smart business move, for Packer had invested a lot of money on television coverage of the English tour. Murray Bennett voluntarily joined Wood, Wellham, and Phillips by extricating himself from contracts with the S.A.C.U.

Part of Packer's deal with the players was that he would pay legal fees if they were sued for breach of contract. Bob Hawke also offered support: 'If the players have signed contracts with the South Africans, the Australian Government will be ready to assist them should there be any legal action against them for breaking such contracts'. This was fair enough, but Hawke went too far when he threatened to ensure that players who went to South Africa would be under close taxation scrutiny. Most

Above: Greg Dyer brilliantly stumps Robbie Kerr in the 1985-86 Sheffield Shield final in Sydney. Kerr moved out of his crease momentarily, missed with an attempted drive, and Dyer had the bails off before he grounded his bat.
— Sydney Morning Herald.

Left: Wayne Phillips' favourite cut behind point. Phillips' outspoken criticism of selectors for omitting him from the Australian tour of India in 1986 brought him a heavy fine.
— Sunday Times, Perth

newspapers had by then fixed the payment to each rebel who toured South Africa at $300,000 for two tours.

Until the very moment of the Australian team's departure for England on 30 April there was intense speculation over who would sign the statutory declarations. Finally Terry Alderman, Rod McCurdy, and Steve Rixon decided not to sign, and withdrew from the English tour. The A.C.B. promptly replaced them with Ray Phillips, John Maguire, and Carl Rackemann, only to find that Rackemann and Maguire were going to South Africa. At the last minute, by which time few cricket fans were really sure who was left in the team for England, Dave Gilbert and Jeff Thomson were brought in. There was no confusion in the mind of Kim Hughes, however. He grabbed an invitation to captain the rebels in South Africa, saying that he was sick of being messed about by the A.C.B. and that loyalty meant nothing in Australian cricket.

In addition to persuading Wood, Wellham, and Phillips to abandon the South Africa tour, the Packer organisation further protected its interests by signing five promising youngsters to three-year contracts at $45,000-a-year. This money, a bonus on whatever they earned from appearances in representative teams, was a means of successfully retaining Steve Waugh, Peter Clifford, Robbie Kerr, Dean Jones, and Mike Veletta for establishment cricket. The first year's money was paid so quickly that Clifford was showing off his new car before the Australians left for England.

On 2 May 1985 the A.C.B. began action in the Melbourne Supreme Court against South African tourists John Dyson, Rodney Hogg, Tom Hogan, John Maguire, Carl Rackemann, Steve Smith, and Graham Yallop, for breach of contract, and against Bruce Francis for his actions on behalf of the South African Cricket Union. When Hughes joined the rebels, a further action was initiated against him. The matter was set down for hearing on 15 August, but before then the S.A.C.U. requested a 'without prejudice' conference.

After weeks of negotiation the A.C.B. agreed on a settlement, an action which appeared to be an admission of defeat, but which was wise in view of the huge financial risks involved. The A.C.B., if it had proceeded, would have been liable for more than $300,000 in legal costs, an outlay that still would not have guaranteed success in the courts. In return for $120,000 towards their legal costs to that time and for the release of the eight contracted players to tour South Africa, the A.C.B. received a promise from the S.A.C.U. that no further raids would be made on contracted players and

This Sydney Morning Herald cartoon by Tandberg cleverly summed up the stance taken by critics of the Australians' lucrative appearance in South Africa in 1985-86. — Sydney Morning Herald.

recognition that the A.C.B. contracts with players were legally enforceable.

Following the settlement Peter Faulkner (Tasmania) and Mike Haysman (South Australia) joined the South African rebels, bringing the tour party to sixteen, with Francis as manager. The A.C.B. promptly terminated its contracts with the eight contracted rebels and resolved that players touring South Africa would be ineligible for payment from provident funds — a condition that cost Hughes and Yallop a huge amount of money. All the players who toured South Africa were also banned from representing Australia for three years, and from representing their State for two years, a move which effectively ended the Shield and Test careers of several veterans.

Given the trauma that had preceded the tour, Allan Border did a fine job in England in 1985. As well as batting superbly, he held his team together against a poor England side until the last few weeks. It was a curious series, marred by foul weather which limited the opportunities of some players. After an outstanding display at Lord's, where he helped Australia level the series at one-all, Bob Holland lost his wrong'un but everybody was delighted to see a leg-spinner back in Tests. There was nothing pleasurable, however, in watching Andrew Hilditch continually fall into Botham's trap by hooking straight into the hands of fieldsmen at deep square leg.

At the beginning of the series England appeared

to have a popgun attack. Some hard-heads claimed this was the worst opening attack in memory, with Botham bowling a high percentage of poor deliveries. But from the time Richard Ellison came into the English side, the entire attack sharpened and finally proved too much for the inexperienced Australian team. Lawson's inability to break through the early English batting as he had done in Tests since his début in 1982 lessened Australia's chances, with Holland reduced to the role of a stock bowler and McDermott losing his early fire. Nobody suggested that Australia would have done better with the help of any of the South African rebels.

Allan Border was disappointed at how poorly Australia played under pressure. 'We don't appear to be able to fight our way out when we are in trouble,' he said. This was painfully clear in the series against New Zealand which followed in Australia. Richard Hadlee's feat of taking 33 wickets in three Tests gave New Zealand her first-ever series win over Australia. With Australia's bowlers operating from wide out on both sides of the stumps, Hadlee got in close to the stumps as he let the ball go in a copybook demonstration of 'wicket-to-wicket' bowling. Those who criticised the A.C.B. for its insistence that coaching would cure all Australia's problems could not resist pouring scorn on Australia's rising young Test players for their puerile efforts against workmanlike opponents.

There was no improvement in the three Tests that followed against India. Allan Border saved Australia from defeat but even he could not bring about victory: Australia was fortunate to emerge with a drawn series. One critic pointed out that, coming after India's recent defeat by Sri Lanka, this dismal showing meant that Australia should be ranked as the worst of the world's cricket nations. India failed to take the series only because they allowed Border to control the strike through most of the final innings of the third Test in Sydney. Border did this in such masterly fashion that India missed the chance of their first series win in Australia, though they were clearly the better team.

During the three Tests against New Zealand and the three against India, Border repeatedly despaired at the dismal performances of his bowlers. There was, however, no need for him to mourn over the efforts of one of cricket's beguiling characters, Gregory Richard John Matthews. After two moderate tours with the Australian team in the West Indies and England, Matthews suddenly blossomed into a national hero in 1985-86. Off the

Above: Rebel tourists Terry Alderman and Carl Rackemann chatting with Graeme Pollock and Dr. Ali Bacher at one of the many functions staged in the Australians' honour. The tour was completed without demonstrations or public interest.
— Chris Harte.

field he wore the clothes of a punk rocker — tight-ankled pants, belts with heavy metal studs — and the story went that on his first trip away with the New South Wales team he had asked manager Allan Crompton to look after the jewel he wore in his ear lobe while he went in to bat.

His team-mates in big cricket took a while to get over Matthews' outlandish appearance but within a couple of seasons they had come to appreciate his great talents as a hyperactive middle-order left-handed batsman, right-armed off-break bowler, and superfine fieldsman. 'He's a fighter,' Border told one newspaper. 'He never gives up and he never allows anyone on the team to give up. We've been critical of him in the past because he was trying to be a showman without producing the goods. But he's a natural enthusiast and nothing negative ever crosses his mind.'

Matthews' success at this time came as a surprise. His recent form in England had only been good enough to win him selection in one of the six Tests: he had scored just 21 runs in his two innings and failed to take a wicket with his 9 overs. But the experience of a close look at the game's great

players left him confident in his own ability on his return home. He modified his ponytail haircut and, after two blazing centuries for New South Wales, won a Test berth in Brisbane against New Zealand. With Australia in trouble, he stayed with Border in a memorable stand, lobbing the ball over the fence for 6 to reach his first Test century. He spontaneously went into a dance of joyous celebration, punching the air and racing halfway to the grandstands in jubilation, throwing kisses to the crowd, and drawing a big 'M' for 'mamma' with his glove (for the benefit of his mother, Neita Matthews, who was watching it all on television in Sydney's West Ryde). In six straight Tests G.R.J. Matthews made two centuries and a 59, took 8 wickets, and became the, most popular cricketer in Australia after Allan Border.

Spectators considered him an extraordinary extrovert, teenagers idolised him, but the truth was that Matthews had toned down his behaviour. He said:

I never strum my guitar any more, and I don't do as many dances on the field. It disappointed me because I found things like that relaxing. But

I don't do things for Brownie points. My thing on this earth is to play the best I can and if I think something can help me, I shall continue to do it. To give people pleasure is an honour. It's something to be cherished.

While Matthews was becoming a national figure in the Tests and one-day matches against India and New Zealand, the rebel tour of South Africa had lost all public interest. Long before Kim Hughes' team completed their itinerary the major Australian

newspapers had recalled reporters covering the tour. None of the widely forecast demonstrations against the Australians had eventuated. Crowds were down, the cricket was desultory stuff, and even the disclosure towards the end of the tour that the South Africa Government was to fund the bulk of the payment to the Australians aroused little public comment in Australia.

The Cape Town newspaper *Business Day* said the two main sponsors, the National Panasonic television company and the *Yellow Pages* telephone directory, would pay only 10 per cent of their final sponsorship bills. The remaining 90 per cent of the money would be made up by hefty rebates from the South African Government. The total cost of the

Australian rebels' two seasons in South Africa was estimated to be $5 million.

This news only confirmed what most Australians had already suspected: the $300,000-per-player deals offered to the rebels could not possibly have been paid by the South African Cricket Union from tour receipts and had to be funded by the South African Government in some way. The rebels had chosen to play for big money in South Africa, in spite of apartheid's presence throughout South African life. Most public opinion polls supported their right to make that choice.

Carl Rackemann, in an article in the English *Wisden Cricket Monthly*, openly admitted that he had joined the rebels solely for the money he would receive. 'The South African Cricket Union, through these "rebel" tours, is trying to save the sport in that country from dying and to give cricket-lovers in South Africa, whatever their colour, a chance to see their national team playing at an international level,' Rackemann wrote. 'Like us, they are only interested in cricket, not politics.'

Cricketers or political pawns, according to your point of view, the Australians lost a lack-lustre series by collapsing for only 61 runs in the final innings of their third international, giving South Africa the series one-nil. Mick Taylor and Steve Smith were the batting successes of the tour, and Carl Rackemann and Steve Rixon confirmed their reputations as world-class cricketers. Kim Hughes' first-ball ducks in both innings of the final international showed how correct Australia's selectors had been in leaving him out of the 1985 England tour. Like a punch-drunk fighter vainly trying to relive the good years, Hughes in 1986 had all the earmarks of a washed-up international player.

In Allan Border's first year as captain, Australia had suffered series losses to the West Indies, England, and New Zealand. Border's status as a left-handed batsman of the highest order had grown, but doubts over his leadership remained. The captaincy still carries more prestige than any job in Australian sport, but in a country where winning is everything it also brings more savage condemnation of failure.

Meanwhile the Australian Cricket Board had been receiving its customary share of flak. The Board's efforts to command loyalty from leading players had been marked by failure ever since the players' revolt in 1912. Lucrative contracts for Test players, and all the efforts of the Board's lawyers, had failed to win the Board more respect.

Left: Allan Border accepts David Gower's congratulations as he reaches one of the eight centuries he made on Australia's 1985 English tour.
— News Limited.

Professionalism, far from solving the Board's problems, had increased them.

Eighty years of Board administration had left Australia with a better Test record than any other cricket nation could claim and it had produced many of cricket's greatest players. But even the unprecedented success of the 1986 one-day games — a triumph for the Board's marketing policies — could not compensate for Test match losses, lucrative though the one-day gates have been.

Australia lost a series at home for the first time to New Zealand in 1985-86, mainly because of the magnificent bowling of Richard Hadlee, who at 34 agreed he was past his best. Hadlee said he had reduced his pace, but tried to bowl medium pace 'from wicket-to-wicket', moving in as close as possible at the moment of delivery to the stumps at the bowling end. By bowling in line with the stumps at the bowling end, he believed he gave himself far more chance of success with lbw appeals. And so it proved.

By contrast Australia's bowlers were wayward in length, astray in width, and gave away far too many no-balls. New Zealand won the series on merit after Australia had luckily scraped through with a draw in the second Test. A short time later in New Zealand the Kiwis underlined their newly-acquired top nation status with another splendid display at home, Martin Crowe's batting lifting the New Zealand performance to the highest class, Jerome Coney leading his side with skill and batting superbly.

For Australia, the problems of replacing great players like Greg Chappell, Dennis Lillee and Rodney Marsh overnight were not improved by Allan Border's reluctance to handle the captaincy with the resolution shown by a long list of predecessors. Border's threats to resign the most prestigious job in Australian sport may have been designed to make his team lift their game, but they did nothing for the traditions of Australian captaincy. And they certainly distracted from his great achievements with the bat.

The major gain for Australia was the arrival of Greg Matthews as a bona fide Test player and one who could attract large numbers of people through the turnstiles. His hustling demeanour on the field, whether batting, bowling or fielding, won him an enormous following, which, his candid, forthright interviews enhanced. Matthews was by far the most unusual cricketer Australia had produced in a period of frequent Australian losses, but he also represented a big hope for the future. Australia's problem was to find eleven players ready to try their hearts out as Matthews always does.

One of the phenomenons of Australian cricket in the 1980s is the eagerness of young fans to spend hours producing a wide variety of signs. No wonder English critics have compared scenes like this to a bullring.
— Melbourne Herald.